THE TERROR OF GOD

To my parents
Sakineh Shafizadeh-Kermani
and Djavad Kermani

THE TERROR OF GOD

Attar, Job and the Metaphysical Revolt

NAVID KERMANI

TRANSLATED BY WIELAND HOBAN

polity

First published in German as *Der Schrecken Gottes* © Verlag C.H. Beck oHG, München 2005

The translation of this work was funded by Geisteswissenschaften International – Translation Funding for Humanities and Social Sciences from Germany, a joint initiative of the Fritz Thyssen Foundation, the German Federal Foreign Office, the collecting society VG WORT and the Börsenverein des Deutschen Buchhandels (German Publishers & Booksellers Association).

Polity Press
65 Bridge Street
Cambridge CB2 1UR, UK

Polity Press
350 Main Street
Malden, MA 02148, USA

ISBN-13: 978–0–7456–4526–1
ISBN-13: 978–0–7456–4527–8 (pb)

A catalogue record for this book is available from the British Library.

Typeset in 11 on 12 pt JaghbUni Regular
by Servis Filmsetting Ltd, Stockport, Cheshire
Printed and bound in Great Britain by MPG Books Group Limited, Bodmin, Cornwall

For further information on Polity, visit our website: www.politybooks.com

CONTENTS

ACKNOWLEDGEMENTS

The occasion to venture a book on *The Book of Suffering* was my invitation to the Wissenschaftskolleg [Institute for Advanced Study] in Berlin in 2000. In the three years of my fellowship, but also afterwards, the Wissenschaftskolleg helped me in more ways than I can count. Above all there was the library, where the service is ominously close to perfection. I was able to invite the scholars and writers Jan Assman (Heidelberg), Almut S. Bruckstein (Berlin), István Eörsi (Budapest), Michael Friedrich (Hamburg), Karl-Josef Kuschel (Tübingen), Susanne Lanwerd (Berlin), Martin Mosebach (Frankfurt), Angelika Neuwirth (Berlin), Friedrich Niewöhner (Wolfenbüttel) and Wilhelm Schmidt-Biggemann (Berlin) to a study weekend on the subject of my book that was both intensive and satisfying, and which provided me with countless suggestions. In general, I learned an infinite amount from my conversations and correspondence with the fellows and permanent fellows, guests and employees at the Wissenschaftskolleg. The project 'Jewish and Muslim Hermeneutics as Cultural Critique', which I was able to initiate there together with Almut S. Bruckstein in conjunction with the study group 'Modernity and Islam', had – as will scarcely surprise the reader – the most lasting effects on this book. In this context I would especially like to thank Georges Khalil, the manager of the study group, but also the Thyssen Foundation, whose sponsorship made the project possible.

Almut S. Bruckstein, Monika Gronke (Cologne), Alois M. Haas (Zurich), Karl-Josef Kuschel, Isabel Schayani (Cologne) and Stefan Wild (Bonn) read through the manuscript at various stages and substantially improved it with their comments and corrections. Naturally I bear the sole responsibility for those errors that have remained.

Manutschehr Amirpur (Winterscheid) went through the translations with me and saved me from a number of my errors. Ulrich Holbein (Allmuthshausen) and Jürgen Reinecke (Cologne) helped me to find a language that would do justice both to Attar's verses and the purpose of this book as far as possible. I also thank Ulrich Holbein for a number of valuable observations and finds from early Middle Eastern studies and critical theory.

Djamshid Razban (Berlin) was my teacher in classical Persian poetry. He introduced me to Attar's work, and passed on the wonder and enthusiasm that I hope will also take hold of the readers of my book.

I discussed God and the suffering in the world with my eldest brother Khalil already as a child. My own attitude to life developed in constant admiration for his ethos, though often in opposition to his views. He also accompanied my engagement with Attar, often questioning it, and always enriching it. Together with everything else, it is also to him that I owe many of the memories of Aunt Lobat, Mr Engineer Kermani and the other relatives from my parents' generation. Having been born thirteen years before me, his memory extends further back than mine. No doubt my relatives remember some episodes differently; for the images from my childhood, among other things, I cannot always draw the line between reality and imagination. All I can say in my defence is that I have tried to portray Aunt Lobat, Mr Engineer Kermani and the other relatives as they presented themselves to me. And whoever shares the good fortune of having known them knows that they were undoubtedly being themselves.

Like all my previous books, I also wrote this one alongside my wife, Katajun Amirpur-Kermani. She read more than one version of the manuscript, encouraging me when I needed it and not being satisfied when the book needed it. After so many years, her contribution to this book can no longer be measured in individual improvements; it is the life we share.

I thank Karl Schlamminger (Munich) for the calligraphies and for the gift of friendship I have received from him and his wife Nasrin.

I have often asked myself what the secret of my publisher Wolfgang Beck's success might be. I think I found the answer during my work on *The Terror of God*: a humanity that spreads to every level of the publishing house. I am grateful to him and his wife Marokh for the ideal home they provide for my academic books (and often enough for myself and my family).

Like my previous two books for C. H. Beck, this one was also copy-edited by Ulrich Nolte. To put it as briefly and painlessly as his restrained, modest character might just about bear: there can be no better reader. Impossible. Nor can anything bad come of a manuscript that has passed through his hands. This, at least, gives me hope for my own book.

Navid Kermani
Cologne, May 2005

NOTES ON TRANSLITERATION AND CITATION

Transliteration and pronunciation of Persian and Arabic words

In the interests of readability, and to keep the number of diacritics to a minimum, I have restricted the use of academic transliterations in the main text to Arabic and Persian terms and titles. All Arabic and Persian names (as well as Hebrew terms) have been written in simplified transliterations, assuming that Western spellings have not become established in any case. Not so in the notes and the bibliography: here I have used the system below, which follows the guidelines of the German Oriental Society (DMG) for the transcription of the Arabic and Persian language, for all titles and proper names:

ʾ	strong glottal enunciation of initial vowels, as in German *be-achten*
aw	(only in Arabic) diphthong similar to *au* in German *Augen*
ʿ	voiced fricative sounding like *a* forced up from the throat; produced by tightening the pharynx (in Persian, like ʾ)
ā, ī, ū	long vowels in Arabic. Persian vowels are kept short; the *ā* in Persian is a dark *a* similar to the Swedish *å*
č	(only in Persian) *ch*, as in 'child'
ḏ	(only in Arabic) like the voiced *th* in English, as in 'that'
ḍ	(only in Arabic) emphatic, dark *d* formed at the upper palate
ġ	palatal *r*, like the French *r* (in Persian, softer, like a hinted-at, voiced guttural *r*)
ǧ	soft *g*, as in 'German'
ḥ	like English *h*, but pronounced as an audible consonant, also

	at the end of a syllable. Exception: the Persian *h* at the end of words, which is simply an extension of the vowel
ḫ	like *ch* in 'loch'
ou	(only in Persian) diphthong similar to the *o* in 'hello'
q	dark, guttural *k* (in Persian, like *ġ*)
s	unvoiced *s*, as in 'bus'
š	unvoiced *sh*, as in 'show'
ṣ	emphatic, dark *s* formed at the upper palate (in Persian, like *s*)
s̱	(only in Persian) like *s*
ṭ	emphatic, dark *t* formed at the upper palate (in Persian, like *t*)
ṯ	(only in Arabic) sharp *th*, as in 'thing'
w	like *w* in 'wonder' (in Persian, like German *w*, as in *Wilhelm*)
ż	(only in Persian) like *tz*
ẕ	(only in Persian) like *tz*
ž	(only in Persian) like French *j*, as in *Jacques*

I have deviated from the rules of the DMG in writing the Persian *-e* ending as *eh* in order to emphasize it; it should be pronounced like the first part of the diphthong in 'clear'. In Persian words, *u* and *i* are transcribed without lengthening marks.

Persian terms, names and titles are transcribed in Persian fashion (e.g. Soruš instead of Surūš, Ḥoseyn instead of Ḥusayn). The name of an author is transcribed in Persian fashion if he wrote all or most of his texts in Persian. This means that Muḥammad al-Ġazalī's name is written with the Arabic article, while that of his brother Aḥmad is written in the Persian manner without an article; but there is simply no way of distinguishing between Persian and Arabic names that does not involve some peculiarity.

Quotations

Page numbers for passages from Attar's *Moṣibatnāmeh* are given in the main text, while all others are located in the notes. In the case of *Moṣibatnāmeh* I have also added the chapter and section number to facilitate finding them later on in other editions (2/0 = chapter 2, frame story; 2/7 = chapter 2, story 7; 0 = introduction; E = epilogue). None of Attar's other works can be similarly divided into chapters and sections; I have therefore only used the page numbers of the current editions available in Iran.

Because al-Ġazālī's *Iḥyā' 'ulūm ad-dīn* exists in countless editions, with reprints constantly appearing and no universally recognized edition, I have augmented volume and page numbers with the headings of chapters and sections to facilitate finding the passages.

Orthography and capitalization of quoted translations have generally been adapted to the rest of the text.

The new edition of *Encyclopaedia Islamica* is referred to in the notes with the abbreviation *EI2*, and *Encyclopaedia Iranica* with *EIran*.

THE CALLIGRAPHIES

The calligraphies represent six of the ninety-nine attributes or most beautiful names of God (*al-asmā' al-ḥusnā*) connected to the subject of the book. Here the number ninety-nine has a primarily symbolic meaning, indicating infinity; in fact, there are far more names circulating in the Islamic world. In the Islamic view of God, they are assigned to the One God according to his nature and actions. God is ever-living, all-knowing, all-powerful, all-hearing, all-seeing, all-merciful, and none of these qualities are comparable to those of humans. Most of God's names or attributes have positive connotations for humans; but frequently there are also more confusing names.

On the cover, inside front and back covers and the title page stands the name *al-Qahhār*, 'the Subduer'
Page 1: *aḍ-Ḍārr* – the Afflictor, the Harmer
Page 35: *al-Ḫāfiḍ* – the Humiliator
Page 79: *al-Makkār* – the Cunning (not one of the official names of God; in Islamic mysticism, however, one of God's attributes is *makr*, 'cunning')
Page 115: *al-Šabbār* – the Compeller, or He Who Seals Fate
Page 171: *al-Muqtadir* – the Dominant

The calligraphies are written in Kufi, one of the oldest forms of the Arabic script. Originally common on monuments, it was also used for the Koran after the inception of Islam. It is an emphatically static script that largely eschews round shapes or arabesques and is characterized by long, steep lines and a strict geometrical order. Only in later times did the Kufi script become more ornamental.

The calligraphies designed for this book by Karl Schlamminger follow the Kufi script as used on bricks for mosques or minarets. Hence the Persian name for this script is *ḫatt-e bannā*, 'the builder's script'. It results from the placing of the bricks, and can only be read in the shade of the protruding stones. In later periods, this unity of building and writing was further emphasized with coloured, glazed bricks. In this reduced form, the stylistic means of the Kufi script are purely vertical and horizontal lines, as well as the dots for letters and diacritics. The Kufi building script is based on strict geometrical units determined by the individual brick. The interstices or empty units are no less important than the bricks themselves.

Karl Schlamminger was born in 1935 in Kempten (Bavaria). After studying at the Academy of Visual Arts in Munich he taught in Istanbul and Tehran. Since 1979 he has lived in Munich as a freelance sculptor. In 2000 he designed and built large calligraphic walls at the Ismaili Centre in Lisbon.

There is nothing more whole
than a broken heart.
Rabbi Nachman of Bratzlav

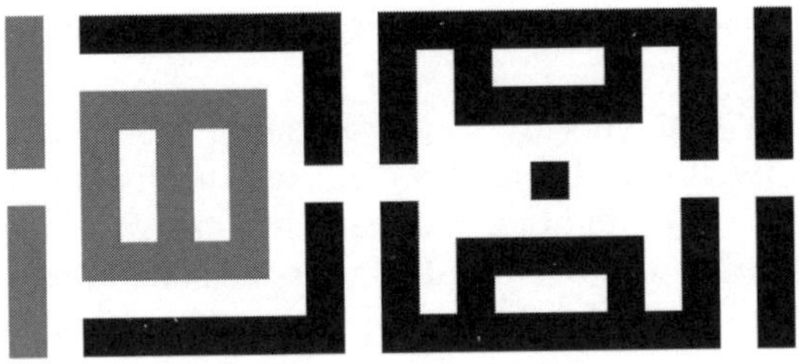

— 1 —

JOB'S QUESTION

For there are none like them in this land

I should probably explain why I am beginning a book about an epic poem from the twelfth or thirteenth century with recollections of my aunt. Life has not yet brought me any hardship that would justify anger towards the creation; the reasons I have constantly despaired at life since puberty are not worth mentioning. For my age, I have travelled a great deal and read a reasonable amount. Whatever I encountered was sufficient for me to discard the assumption that life could have any justifiable purpose. But my relationship with God is not close enough for me to reproach Him for His work, to have the right to reproach Him justly. I have managed to preserve the religiousness of my childhood, but its significance is largely pragmatic; I do not draw any intellectual conclusions from it. It does not exist in opposition to the suffering of others that I see all around me; it does not even attempt to do so, yet still helps me through everyday life like a fairy, whispering in my ear that my path is following some trail. I am willing to believe this voice for the simple reason that it prevents me from standing still. The faith of my aunt and the other people of whom I will speak, the ones of whom the poet Faridoddin Attar speaks, has a different consistency: their faith pervades their entire being. One can criticize this philosophically, one can look down on it or reject it for oneself. But if I ask myself the simple, fundamental question of what ultimately distinguishes one person from another, they hold a privileged place – for in the end, on the last day or before the final judgement, it is only goodness that counts, nothing else. I see that the religious people among my fellow humans – by which I mean primarily those relatives from the generations of my parents and grandparents – are good people, good in the emphatic sense: they are as loving as they are charitable, they neither lie nor deceive others. Perhaps one cannot discuss everything with them, but one can always depend on their affection; they pardon even the greatest affronts, and are always the first to forgive. They are tolerant in the true sense, in that they treat what is foreign to them with a friendly distance without needing to understand, let alone like it.

Naturally other people can also be good. But the religious people of the kind I am referring to, and whom Attar refers to, most certainly are. Goodness is intrinsic to their being. One's sense of security becomes particularly keen when travelling, and I have noticed that I trust someone instinctively and without second thoughts if I recognize that most noble form of piety in them. Obviously I am not speaking of the bigots or literalists, the nitpickers and religious bookkeepers, but rather those 'who believe and do good', as the Koran expresses it succinctly in one of its recurring formulations – believe *and* do good. The people I mean do not have to be simple in character, but their faith is simple. They observe the rituals that are passed on to them strictly, without asking why; they follow the values that revelation hands to them quietly and consistently; and they even praise God for their existence when it torments them. By their words, and even more by their example, they constantly admonish others to have a charitable faith (they are not so concerned about which faith that happens to be; it is more faithlessness per se that perpetually troubles them). They admonish, no more; but, to our occasional displeasure, also no less. That is the religiousness which made its mark on me as a child, and as clearly as I may perceive the disastrous offshoots of religion today, especially Islam, I never forget those people who, to this day, have set an example of virtue for me – for example my grandfather, who put up with the mocking whispers of his young, impertinent daughters when leading the extended family's prayers before them. In his memoirs he begins by proudly recounting the anecdote of how our great-grandfather, a highly respected theologian, spoke out in defence of the Bahais in Isfahan when other mullahs unleashed the mob on them; it must have been at the start of the last century. As a member of the upper classes, my grandfather was a staunch democrat, and as a representative of the Isfahan notables, he travelled to Tehran – no brief journey in those days – solely in order to tell the baffled opposition leader Mossadegh that he approved of his battle against the monarchy. He was not liberal in the sense we understand it, however, but rather a conservative man of orthodox severity who always had praise for God on his lips and set high moral standards for himself and others. If he, who had himself studied at a theological school in Isfahan, scorned the small-mindedness of street preachers and state theologians alike, it was not in the spirit of the Western Enlightenment and the Universal Declaration of Human Rights, but rather in the name of the greatest spirit of all, the Almighty.

Then there is Mr Kermani the engineer, my Aunt Eshrat's husband, who taught us both backgammon and prayer, a legendary chainsmoker who liked to squeeze his massive body into the kind of clothes Gamal Abdel Nasser used to wear, those light brown or light blue cotton suits where the jacket is a shirt at the same time. Mr Engineer – I did not even forget to use the title *Āqā-ye Mohandes*, 'Mr Engineer', when talking to myself – *Āqā-ye Mohandes* Kermani was a truly imposing figure, the tallest and fattest of all my relatives, with a giant, round bald head and a gold front tooth in a mouth that often smiled. As far back as I can remember, he supplied the houses of all our relatives and acquaintances, even those who lived in Europe and the USA, with a self-designed brown poster bearing the words 'Remember God' in three languages – English, Arabic and Persian.[1] My parents still have it hanging in their hall.

Mr Engineer was religious, but never small-minded. I was too young to recognize his full greatness, but my oldest brother reported how Mr Engineer once took him aside during the holidays in Tehran and pointed to his trouser fly. At the time my brother was on the brink of puberty, which is accompanied in Islam by the obligation to perform ritual prayer.

'Now listen', he said to my brother, 'soon you'll notice something very special and very nice happening to your body. Your penis will sometimes become big and firm, and maybe you'll wake up one morning with a stain at the front of your pyjamas, or notice that it's fun to play with your penis. Then something white might squirt out of it, a liquid that looks like milk. That's nothing to worry about; it's a wonderful thing. It's one of God's greatest gifts to us. You mustn't be ashamed or scared. You're allowed to enjoy it.'

For all his rejoicing over God's goodness, Mr Engineer Kermani did not forget to tell my brother about his imminent obligation to ritual prayer. Regarding sexuality as godly did not make him a freethinker; he saw it as one more reason to thank God. For Mr Engineer, loving God meant loving the creation. For him, serving God meant serving God's creatures. My brother also told me about a beggar's wedding Mr Engineer had organized. The beggar had asked him for alms on the street, and instead Mr Engineer found employment and later a wife for him, and even paid the dowry. The other beggars and poor people could also count on him, and he founded a home for the orphans of Isfahan that is still the largest and best organized in the city. Time and again we saw him collecting money for his orphans at family parties and big celebrations in Isfahan, and whenever someone died, instead of laying the usual flower arrangement on their grave, he placed a large panel there calling for donations to the home. After a while no one even thought about bringing flowers to funerals any more, and everyone simply gave money to the orphanage from the start. The older relatives, including my parents, insist that God granted them every wish that was reinforced with a donation to Mr Engineer's orphans. Mr Engineer lived with God day in, day out. It was through him that I began to understand how God can be 'closer to man than his jugular vein', as stated in Surah 50:16. When my brother was a little older, Mr Engineer confessed to him that he had sometimes got an erection during prayer, such was his ecstasy at speaking with God, and that, conversely, he often had the feeling when sleeping with our aunt that he was very close to God and serving him. No, Mr Mohandes Kermani was not typical in his faith, nor was he a typical Muslim. The believers described by Attar are also atypical, both for their time and for Islam as a whole. That is why I am writing about them: because they were special. There are enough stereotypes already, especially Islamic ones.

One or two floors lower down in the same apartment, opposite the Soviet embassy in the middle of downtown Tehran, which has long stopped being the area where the rich have their homes, lived his friend Mehdi Bazargan. He had been a long-time resistance fighter against the shah, briefly prime minister directly after the revolution, and then a long-time resistance fighter against the Islamic Republic; he was a no less profoundly religious person, and his resolute peacefulness even touched his opponents. I have written about him elsewhere.[2] And naturally, again in Isfahan, there is also my Aunt Lobat, whom I already loved dearly as a child because she told 'the most beautiful of all tales' – I am tempted to use the formulation *aḥsanu l-qaṣaṣi*, which the Koran applies to itself in Surah 12:4 – but also because her warm-heartedness knew no bounds, least of all towards us children. I never heard her utter a loud or unfriendly word, hardly ever a complaint, even though she suffered from terrible arthrosis and all manner of other ailments during her last ten or twenty years, and was often plagued with such pains that all she could do was cower in a corner, at most letting out a muted groan. She used to say that God always leaves a space somewhere for us to thank him.

I cannot say that her forbearance was an absolute model for me, but I respected Aunt Lobat from the bottom of my youthful heart. Everyone found it amazing how closely she resembled her mother, my paternal grandmother, who died when I was four or five. The gratitude Aunt

Lobat must have learned from her cannot be reduced to modesty; it rather presupposes the ability to receive. Whenever my mother tried to save money, my grandmother would reprimand her in a way that I will often mention in this book. 'Don't give God bad habits', she would say. 'If He sees that you're content with less, He'll give you less.'

My three brothers still enthuse today about a car journey from Germany to Iran some forty years ago. For a whole week, the three sons sat next to my grandmother on the back seat of the Mercedes and argued amongst themselves, played, were bored, made a noise, screamed and generally drove my parents mad. It was only my grandmother who remained calm, her smiling, forgiving equanimity not faltering for a second. I can still see that smile, and remember clearly how shocked and uncomprehending I was on the day I saw grandmother no longer smiling. It was when my father and I visited her for the last time at Aunt Heshmat's house, the day before we flew back to Germany. Although no one had told me, it was clear that she would not be there for the next holidays – *Māmānǧunǧun*, as Grandma was called a little long-windedly, but very beautifully in children's Persian, with a double diminutive. *Māmān* means 'Mummy', and can be made more affectionate by adding a single *ǧun*; this suffix is not simply an empty syllable like 'y' or 'ie', however, but means 'soul' – resulting in 'Mummy-soul'. The doubling of *ǧun* indicates the grandmother. With a view of the courtyard, Mummy-soul-soul lay in the little room next to the front door, which was normally used by Mr Afrahi, the husband of my resolutely pious Aunt Heshmat, to entertain his friends with backgammon, opium, vodka and poetry. How much I could write just about those two! For example about the water that Aunt Heshmat secretly poured into the vodka bottles to lighten her husband's sins a little – or, rather, the mischievous smile on her face when she told us about it. And then the tremendous Mr Afrahi, who only came up to his wife's shoulder: he caressed the senses with his vices, and wooed God with his poetry. But Aunt Heshmat and Mr Afrahi – that would make for a different book, as much as they also suffered. It would be a book about the art of living amidst desperation. The present book begins where that art ends.

One of my earliest memories, I think, relates to my grandmother, though it could just as easily have been Aunt Lobat. She was visiting us in Germany and looking after me. I must have been two or three years old at most. When my mother returned home from town, she found me lying on one of those gigantic Persian quilts made of printed calico that are large enough for two dozen relatives to squat on at supper – right in the middle of a mountain of barberries[3] or some other ingredient that my grandmother or aunt had taken over the task of cleaning, cutting or stoning. The entire living room must have been full of these barberries, or whatever it was (maybe rice, or – worst of all – *ālbālu*, Persian sour cherries), for I was splashing about in the reserves like foam in the bathtub. My grandmother or aunt was sitting peacefully next to me on the quilt, her legs wrapped in it, smiled benevolently at my dumbfounded mother and simply said: 'Oh, it's just a bit of fun', or, as she probably said in Persian, *āḫeh touri ke našod* – 'It's not so bad, I'll clean up afterwards!' This is how they acted towards me and all children, my grandmother and my Aunt Lobat, and my grandfather and Mr Engineer Kermani were not much different. It was more than a general tenderness of perception that opened their hearts wide enough to harbour all Adam's children. Their attitude stemmed – not exclusively, but significantly – from their faith; I recognized that instinctively at the time, and am still certain of it today in spite of all reflection.

The concept of brotherly love is rightly associated with Christianity, but people in the West, even specialists who work with texts, do not realize how profoundly the concept of compassion determines the daily actions of many Muslims. It is the religious element of compassion that makes things in life and faith softer, more flexible, more permeable than their respective words would suggest. And yet compassion also comes from the word: it is the most common motif in the Koran, as mystics have always emphasized, and accompanies the dogmas and laws as their opposite. In the cases of the people to whom I am referring, at least, goodness came from piety. Because I grew up in an Iranian household, they happened to be Muslims (every religious community draws sustenance from them), and because the poetry I will be considering was written by a Persian poet, they fit in with these reflections all the better (though one can probably find Attar's motifs in all European and Eastern literary cultures). As a child I thought Aunt Lobat, my grandfather and Mr Engineer Kermani were especially nice people; today they seem like saints to me, like figures from the verse epics and hagiographies of Faridoddin Attar, ever showing us anew the virtue of mildness and magnanimity.

They had probably not always been as deeply infused with faith as they were when I knew them; but I did not experience them in younger years. I do not know why they became as they were: no doubt the trials and the pain of personal failure weighed on their shoulders, as on those of all saints. I can imagine it in Aunt Lobat's case; one of her sons had killed himself as a teenager, and her youngest daughter's husband suddenly died of a virus on a business trip in Asia. Mr Engineer Kermani's two daughters had died as children. He blamed himself for the illnesses of both: for the blood disease of the first, because he was distantly related to my aunt, and for the spastic disorder of the second, because once, when she was a small child, he had thrown her so high while playing that her head had struck the ceiling. My brother said that Mr Engineer only became a chainsmoker after that, and that the headaches which had tormented him almost daily, as well as the insomnia – which I also remember, because in Tehran he always paced up and down the hall at night – had started around the same time. He never showed a trace of all this during the daytime. On the contrary: how often we saw his gold crowns in that laughing mouth, and, of all our adult male relatives, it was he who paid the most attention to us children. It is not the saints who are dying out, but the generation of people who were already old when I was still a child; and the subsequent generation is not yet old enough for that benevolent wisdom of the aged – or I am too old to recognize it in them.

One does not have to be pious to be good; but the people I am speaking of were also good because they were pious. One could not claim the reverse – that they believed in God out of goodness. From the outside, and probably even for themselves, faith could only be profitable: it equipped them with confidence, provided them with hope and gave them strength, and its rituals offered a rich aesthetic experience several times every day. For them, practising religion was more than simply carrying out duties; it also involved pleasure, as the ecstasy in their faces sometimes revealed. As the early Sufi teacher Abu Sulayman ad-Darani (d. 830) already stated: 'He who truly knows God does not leave his prayer after two prostrations, before he has tasted their sweetness.'[4] This faith did not undo their suffering, but God helped them to bear it by enabling them to view it as a test, or as a fleeting, even necessary stage on the way to the promised life beyond. I rarely met people facing death, but I did learn that it was easier for the pious to find a way of dealing with it. Aunt Lobat held onto her prayers like her last remaining thread. When she groaned loudly from the pain, she not only reassured us with a smile, she also at the same time faced the pain with defiance. Aunt Lobat had grown old with the maxim: 'If God loves one of His servants, He tests him with a stroke of fate. When the servant is struck by it, he remains patient.'[5] She kept her end of the bargain for God's promise to the sick and the infirm: 'If I strike a servant with pain, and he remains patient and does not lament about Me to those who find him, I will exchange his flesh for a better flesh, and his blood for a better blood.'[6] She never complained; if she did let out a sigh of pain, she thanked God in the next breath for the mercy He granted her and all her loved ones.

Yet give thou good tidings unto the patient
who, when they are visited by an affliction,
say, 'Surely we belong to God, and to Him we return';
upon those rest blessings and mercy
from their Lord, and those – they are the truly guided. (Surah 2:155f.)[7]

She never said so, for she was too modest, but her faith gave her the conviction that one who suffers will be richly rewarded. God is too noble to punish a sinner twice (and my aunt would never have claimed to be without sin). If someone is punished with suffering in this world, their wrongs have already been atoned for in the next. God even forgives one sin for the scratch from a thorn. And more than that: if someone becomes ill, the angel scribes note down better deeds than the person could ever have performed while healthy.[8] God himself says 'I am ashamed' (*istaḥyaytu*) to weigh up the good and bad works of the suffering on the scales at the end of days.[9] Once, when the wife of the mystic Fath al-Mausili (d. 835) slipped and broke a bone, she laughed. People asked her whether she did not feel any pain, and she answered: 'The joy at the reward that will be granted to the suffering has erased the bitterness of pain from my heart.'[10] Sartre said that one should not ask whether God exists, but whether one needs him. Aunt Lobat did need him – at the end, with every breath.

The mention of thy Lord's mercy
unto His servant Zachariah;
when he called upon his Lord secretly
saying, 'O my Lord, behold
the bones within me are feeble
and my head is all aflame with hoariness.
And in calling on Thee, my Lord,
I have never been hitherto unprosperous.' (Surah 19:1–4)

Five or six years ago, Aunt Lobat suffered a stroke. She had already found walking difficult, and both sitting and lying down caused her pain, but that never stopped her from laughing. She had such a mischievous grin: whenever her daughter Badri, her son Massoud or her sister Ghodsi expressed overly loud sympathy for her, she cast a roguish look at me, as if to say that I shouldn't pay any attention to their talk, and that she still told the best stories. 'How is your illness?' we asked her (using the formal address, as is customary with aunts of her generation in Iran). *Engāri ke hič* – 'As if nothing had happened', she replied. And she was always praying, praising God in every second she was not communicating with others. She was – I must resort to a hagiography in order to convey how she handled her arthrosis, her constant pains, her spreading paralysis – she was like someone from the following story, which could easily have been penned by Attar. In this case it was Martin Buber who wrote it down:

> When Rabbi Shmelke and his brother visited the maggid of Mezritch, they asked him about the following. 'Our sages said certain words which leave us no peace because we do not understand them. They are that men should praise and thank God for suffering just as much as for well-being, and receive it with the same joy. Will you tell us how we are to understand this, rabbi?' The maggid replied: 'Go to the House of Study. There you will find Zusya smoking his pipe. He will give you the explanation.' They went to the House of Study and put their question to Rabbi Zusya. He laughed. 'You certainly have come to the right man! Better go to someone else rather than to me, for I have never experienced suffering.' But the two knew that, from the day he was born to this day, Rabbi Zusya's life had been a web of need and anguish. Then they knew what it was: to accept suffering with love.[11]

But then she suffered that stroke. When we arrived in Isfahan some time later, Massoud and Badri had already had the smallest of the three rooms leading onto the courtyard converted into a sickroom. The walls were freshly painted, and the floor, which had previously been covered by an old Persian rug on grey felt, now had white tiles. They had also obtained a proper sickbed, with wheels and an adjustable backrest. Aside from that and the metal chairs, the room was empty. I assume this was for reasons of hygiene, but I felt that all the memories had been removed along with the furniture. In the house of Mr Madani and Aunt Lobat, the clinically white room seemed as foreign as if it had been installed by some quack. The house behind the Shah Mosque was characterized by shades of brown, grey and dark red, and everything seemed to be clean, but at the same time a little run down and murky, because the layers of long family life had settled on the carpets, furniture and curtains, and my aunt even insisted on cleaning the large rooms herself (or at least helping to do so) when she could hardly move (she would sit on the floor, pushing herself through the apartment with the cloth). Now there was a room where all those layers had been eaten away, a room disinfected for imminent death, and my angrily gasping aunt, the storyteller, had been rolled into the middle of it.

Massoud had warned me that her whole body was sore from a rash, and evidently itched terribly; she had to be constantly massaged, rubbed with oil or simply scratched. Although they gave her morphine, she whimpered pitifully all day long, or let out such screams that even the neighbours' hair must have stood on end, or immediately fainted from the pain. One reads in novels how people can age half a lifetime from one day to the next. That was the case here: a year ago, I had said goodbye to a pain-ridden but cheerful woman of seventy or seventy-five years, and now I had returned to a skin-covered skeleton whose age one could no longer even guess. The only parts of her body she could move were her hands, and all she could utter was an incomprehensible jumble of syllables. Her hair, which had always been tied up and hidden under a headscarf when visitors came, was now spread out snow-white in all directions, the tangle extending over her entire pillow and down to her chest. She was so emaciated that her face, once round and chubby, now revealed all the arches and furrows of the skull. This made her eyes seem all the larger, and they stared at me from their deep sockets when I entered the room.

> I am nothing but skin and bones; I have escaped by only the skin of my teeth.
> Have pity on me, my friends, have pity, for the hand of God has struck me. (Job 19: 20–21)[12]

I will never forget her gaze: it showed more than simply suffering; it showed rage and simultaneously deep childlike fear, in strained contemplation, clueless, helpless and at once ashamed. Yes, she was embarrassed – not simply for having been cast into such a state, but also for being seen by everyone, and for all the inconvenience, effort and expense she caused them. Massoud had told me beforehand that her mind was clear so that I wouldn't be shocked; but I would have seen it immediately from her gaze in any case.

There was no need for me to hide the tears in my eyes, because she knew what was going on. She also cried. She observed exactly what was happening to her, what she was enduring, and that we were watching; she reflected upon it, as the concentration in her gaze indicated, but the means to react to it, at least to comment on it, had been taken away from her. She didn't want to accept it – anything, but not that. And so she kept making new attempts to speak, yet was unable to move the tongue to form the words that were on her lips. She stammered something, looked at our questioning faces, realized that she had once again failed to make herself understood, and in the same moment her chin twitched upwards to turn her head away from us bitterly. I found this harder to bear than her cries of pain: this head, twitching upwards and then turning away, the gesture of throwing away it hinted at – or, rather, the attempt to throw it away, this miserable life that was no longer worth the effort. But it didn't work, not even that; it stuck to her, this life, and she couldn't simply shake it off. 'Normally one says to a person whose condition is hopeless: "Give up, lie down and die!"', writes Sadeq Hedayat (d. 1951) in his story *Zendeh be-gur*. 'But what happens if death doesn't want you, if it turns its back on you, if it simply doesn't come to you, doesn't want to come to you?' She was forced to hold out before our eyes.

And yet, as unpleasant as it was for her, this woman of strong faith and endless patience, to be displayed to us so wretchedly – it was even worse for her when we left her, even if it was only to go to the toilet; for she was unable to judge whether that person would come back or not. She evidently only understood fragments of what we yelled at her, and even then she often seemed not to believe us; she thought that Badri or Massoud were just being kind when they told her that her granddaughter, brother or nephew would come back in a moment. As soon as she noticed that we were about to leave the room, she begged in panic like a little child that doesn't want to stay at home alone, because she always thought that we would return to Germany and she would never see us again. If there was ever someone whose faith and spiritual constitution had made them strong enough to endure pain and misfortune, it was she; but this simply went beyond her powers – even hers. She had never expected it to be so bad; no one had told her that. It wasn't written in any book – not even God's book, in which she had read every day. It dragged on for almost a year, a year of itching, pain and pus: an ordeal. 'The Lord said to Satan, "Very well, then, he is in your hands"' (Job 2:6), and Satan soon struck Job with vicious sores from head to toe: '"My body is clothed with worms and scabs, my skin is broken and festering"' (7:5).

Certainly Job is not someone from our everyday lives. Nonetheless, one does not have to look to history or remote areas shaken by crisis and catastrophe to find him. A trip to the hospice is enough. One need not even go to those patients suffering pain; all nurses say that shame is equally capable of eating a person away. I met a man there who weighed only 46 kg, sitting on the bedpan and shitting a light brown liquid. It was smeared on the bed and his clothes. The male nurse put on gloves and carefully washed the whimpering man's bottom and genitals with a sponge. Job himself could not have looked at me with more distress. What was far worse for my grandfather than the pain was that, at the end, he lost control of his bladder. People in Europe cannot imagine what it meant in Iran two or three decades ago to be the head of a family, how much dignity it both presupposed and conveyed. And now, thirteen years old, I saw *Bābānğunğun* wet himself in front of everyone, and I was there when my aunt Jaleh changed his underwear. And yet he had asked only two things of God, as my brother had sometimes overheard: to die before his children – a wish he was denied when his youngest son drove into a tree in a state of exhaustion – and to die before he had to depend on the help of others. And now God had spelled out his helplessness to him, the proud family man, like a pedantic, intransigent teacher. Aunt Lobat was also tormented by shame at her own weakness; I could see that very clearly. Not even Job, sitting naked on the ashes and scratching himself with a piece of broken glass, the once universally praised Job, could bear being made a laughing stock by God: '"My breath is offensive to my wife; I am loathsome to my own brothers. Even the little boys scorn me; when I appear, they ridicule me. All my intimate friends detest me; those I love have turned against me"' (19:17–19).

At least Job could still lament; my aunt was denied even this every time she tried to articulate at least one sentence. '"Oh, that I had someone to hear me!"' (31:35). Everyone in my family, the old ones too, agreed that she had gone through the most dreadful process of dying that any of us had ever witnessed or even heard of – and her of all people, the most pious, the most righteous of us all. That is exactly what Job experiences: not only suffering, to which Christianity gave a decisive response in the form of the cross, but also its injustice, the God-willed injustice to which even the cross provides no answer. No man deserved it less than he did: '"There is no one on earth like him; he is blameless and upright, a man who fears God and shuns evil"' (1:8), says God before leaving Job to Satan. It is precisely because Job is righteous that he must suffer. And just as Job says to God, '"Tell me what charges You have against me"' (10:2), my aunt's penetrating gaze seemed to contain the question: why had God abandoned her to evil – her of all people? '"Is there any wickedness on my lips? Can my mouth not discern malice?"' (6:30). In any other situation, that could have been a selfish question. Here it was the question about meaning, Job's central question: how can the suffering and injustice in the world be reconciled with the image of God that was taught to us?

Goodness, omnipotence, cognizability

We learn that God is good, that He loves humans and is merciful to them. What sets monotheism apart from other, earlier religions is that the one God is kindly disposed towards humans – unlike the many gods of polytheism that were evil or malicious, unreliable or fickle. We consider God's love constitutive of monotheism. We also learn that God is just. We do not always notice the tension between these two statements. Someone who loves is not always just; he forgives without measure. Someone who is just cannot pardon everything. Some remember that these religions also involve God's wrath and violence, even vengefulness. Someone who loves grows angry late on, but all the more fiercely. Being just means destroying what is destructive; if anything, it is those violent, frightening aspects often retouched by contemporary exegetes in order not to upset us that would most readily allow them to preserve the image of the just and loving God, as they could be used to explain tribulation as a punishment, as a test, or also as an expression of disappointment at man's disloyalty. The third-century Christian philosopher and theologian Lactantius already realized this when he turned against the 'favourable and popular cant' that God is only a 'gentle, tranquil, propitious and kindly preserver'. For Lactantius, anger is a divine emotion that is part and parcel of His love, His rule and His responsibility for the creation. A God who is not angered by evil and malice cannot be a loving God. 'God is moved by kindness; therefore, He is also moved to anger.'[13]

It is not impossible, then, to reconcile the attributes of love and a righteousness whose effects are not always mild. But the monotheistic view of God involves not only love and righteousness, or, to summarize the ethical attributes we ascribe to God in a single word: goodness. One axiom also seems to be the omnipotence of God – and that there are ways to recognize His wisdom. Comprehensibility is not necessarily considered part of God's nature, but is nonetheless a feature of His message, His worldly acts, His very existence: God speaks to us, and we can comprehend His revelation; God acts, and we can recognize a meaning in it – we can believe the statement 'God saw all that He had made, and it was very good' (Genesis 1:31). This elementary expectation of the monotheistic view of God is expressed in the concept of cognizability. The Koran renews the biblical command 'Taste and see that the Lord is good' (Psalm 34:9) in appealing constantly to humans finally to recognize the signs of God, which are self-evident – visible, audible, smellable, palpable, accessible to the mind and understandable to the heart. Unlike the book of Genesis, the Koran declares not only the origin of the creation good, but also the world as it can be experienced at all times, in all places and by all people if they only open their eyes. The creation is not only praised, as in Psalm 104, in its beauty and order; no, in the Koran its absolute harmony is also manifest as a verifiable, and hence not seriously disputable reality. For the Koran, the idea that the world could turn out to be discrepant or disturbed upon closer inspection is a misguided one.

> Thou seest not in the creation
> of the All-merciful any imperfection.

> Return thy gaze; seest thou any fissure?
> Then return thy gaze again, and again,
> and thy gaze comes back to thee dazzled, aweary. (Surah 67:3–4)

The standard set by the Creator for His work could not be higher: there is to be not even the trace of a flaw, and humans need only use their senses and their mind to recognize God in His wisdom. All other attributes ascribed to the Creator, including reason and aesthetic categories such as beauty, splendour and sublimity, can be assigned to this triad of goodness, omnipotence and cognizability. Strictly speaking, the question of theodicy arises only where the view of God unifies these three attributes – that is, only in monotheism. Job believed in God's goodness, he did not dare question His omnipotence, and thought he could recognize the wisdom of divine action, as it seemed that the righteous were rewarded and the unbelievers punished. When disaster struck him, he was determined to find out why.

Job's example runs through the history of the three monotheistic religions. Time and again, believers – laypersons, theologians, philosophers, poets, and also prophets – have questioned their image of God in the light of a reality full of hardship. Certainly the main branches of all three religions have turned a blind eye to the contradiction, relativized suffering and, above all – without any further consideration of God's omnipotence – pointed to those scriptural passages that give humans the sole responsibility for evil, as they sin of their own free will or are seduced by Satan, from the Fall of Man in Genesis to Surah 4:79:

> Whatever good visits thee, it is of God;
> whatever evil visits thee is of thyself.

The logical objection that God, in His omnipotence, could easily have spared humans their suffering by creating them without a predisposition towards evil, is opposed by verses in both the Bible and the Koran that present suffering as God-willed, whether as a test –

> We try you with evil and good for a testing (Surah 21:35)

– or for educational purposes:

> We tried them with good things and evil,
> that haply they should return. (Surah 7:168)

The Bible develops the same idea at many points, for example Deuteronomy 8:5, Revelation 3:19 and Proverbs 3:11–12, and refers to the last of these in the following passage from Hebrews 12:6–11:

'. . . because the Lord disciplines those He loves, and He punishes everyone he accepts as a son.' Endure hardship as discipline; God is treating you as sons. For what son is not disciplined by his Father? If you are not disciplined (and everyone undergoes discipline), then you are illegitimate children and not true sons. Moreover, we have all had human fathers who disciplined us and we respected them for it. How much more should we submit to the Father of our spirits and live! Our fathers disciplined us for a little while as they thought best; but God disciplines us for our good, that we may share in His holiness. No discipline seems pleasant at the time, but painful. Later on, however, it produces a harvest of righteousness and peace for those who have been trained by it.

In all three Abrahamic religions, attempts to justify God start from this interpretation of suffering: what humans perceive as evil is not actually evil, but follows a higher wisdom. The monotheism of the Bible and the Koran leaves no room for an absolutely evil power that is completely independent of God; and biblical and ancient Judaism hardly made evil an object of theological reflection. The first rabbinical doctrines that address the problem of suffering at all are in the Mishna, the body of Jewish religious laws written in the third century. There, however, suffering is viewed as the punishment for sins, and hence virtually the proof of God's justness as described in many passages in the Hebrew Bible, for example in 1 Samuel 12:15:

But if you do not obey the Lord, and if you rebel against His commands, His hand will be against you, as it was against your fathers.

The Mishna almost completely ignores the imperfection of reality, instead painting the picture of a world that was undoubtedly better than the present one. The Halakhic or Tannaitic midrashim, which follow the Bible verse by verse, at least acknowledge suffering as a potential problem, but demand that one endures it humbly. Anyone who doubts God's justness is harshly condemned. It was only in the fifth and sixth centuries, with the Babylonian Talmud, that interpretations of suffering began to diverge considerably and an increasing number of Jewish authors took the liberty of questioning the necessity of misfortune, and even the justness of the Creator.[14] The dominant view, admittedly, held that suffering was God's way of fulfilling the just intention of His creation. Some Kabbalistic texts even refer to evil specifically as one of the potencies that lie within God, and through which He affects the material world.[15]

It is scarcely a coincidence that the Koran uses the Jewish prophet as an example to illustrate that God's justice also prevails where humans do not see it. This Koranic tale follows a pattern already preformed before the advent of Islam in Jewish and Eastern Christian literature: a pious protagonist – a hermit in the Christian legend, and Rabbi Akiba (d. c.135) in the midrash – experiences three successive, obvious injustices that transpire at the end of the story as God's mercy.[16] In the Koranic version, Moses asks a 'servant of God' blessed with graciousness and wisdom if he can follow him in order to become acquainted with the correct path. The servant lays down one condition, namely that Moses must not ask for explanations when he does not understand something. Moses promises and they set out. Three times, however, Moses breaks his word: when the servant makes a ship capsize, when he strikes an innocent boy dead, and when he saves the citizens of a town from the collapse of a wall, even though they had previously shown miserliness towards a group of hungry people. Three times Moses cannot keep his thoughts to himself, and asks the servant for the reasons for his actions. The servant speaks:

> 'This is the parting between me and thee.
> Now I will tell thee the interpretation
> of that thou couldst not bear patiently.
> As for the ship, it belonged to certain poor men,
> who toiled upon the sea;
> and I desired to damage it,
> for behind them there was a king
> who was seizing every ship by brutal force.
> As for the lad, his parents
> were believers; and we were afraid
> he would impose on them insolence and unbelief;
> so we desired that their Lord
> should give to them in exchange one better than he
> in purity, and nearer in tenderness.
> As for the wall, it belonged
> to two orphan lads in the city,
> and under it was a treasure belonging to them.
> Their father was a righteous man; and the Lord
> desired that they should come of age
> and then bring forth their treasure
> as a mercy from the Lord. I did not
> do it of my own bidding.
> This is the interpretation of that
> thou couldst not bear patiently.' (Surah 18:66–82)

The Koran reduces the folk legend to its archetypal core: to show that there is a difference between what humans see and the meaning that God bestows upon events. The thesis of the best of all worlds, which, with Leibniz (d. 1716), occupied not only European Christian philosophy, but also Arab-Islamic thought from the early twelfth century intensely until well into the nineteenth, is precisely the attempt to explain the hidden wisdom of God. It was first formulated by Muhammad al-Ghazali (d. 1111): 'There can be nothing more beautiful, more complete and more perfect than that which is.'[17] The great theologian, mystic and critic of philosophy makes the imperfect a precondition for perfection: only the imperfect can enable justice to show preference for the perfect; only hell can demonstrate the merit of heaven. Without the creation of the imperfect, the perfect remains unrecognized. It is part of the greatest order that something less ordered occasionally happens, argues Leibniz, using an example from aesthetics against the notion of a world in which everything is equally good: 'A little acid, sharpness or bitterness is often more pleasing than sugar; shadows enhance colours; and even a dissonance in the right place gives relief to harmony.'[18] An almost identical argument had been developed earlier by the Andalusian philosopher Averroës (Ibn Rushd, d. 1198), who says that God creates evil in order to do good.

> In this way His creation of evil would be quite just. To illustrate: fire has been made because of its necessity for the existence of things, and without it they could not have existed at all. It also destroys things by its very nature. But if you think of the destruction and evil which it causes, and compare it to the advantages which we derive out of it, you will find that its existence is better than non-existence, that is, good.[19]

There is little difference between this and the arguments of many Christian scholastics to explain evil in the world, except that they place greater emphasis on human sin. God allows evil, and is thus its indirect cause, but He is following a good purpose – primarily that of punishment. Thomas Aquinas goes so far as to elevate the moral experience of evil to the proof of God's existence, as the ethical option this opens up could only be directed at God: 'If evil exists, God exists. For, there would be no evil if the order of good were taken away, since its privation is evil. But this order would not exist if there were no God.'[20] Even more bizarre, from today's perspective, is a treatise by Jalaluddin as-Suyuti (d. 1505), in which the theologian lists all known earthquakes in history, rejects physical explanations and attempts to prove that every single one of these was 'a God-willed misfortune (*sū' al-qāḍā'*)' and thus 'for believers a mercy, a blessing and a reprimand, and for unbelievers a warning, a sign of wrath and a punishment for evil.'[21]

Someone who lives in the best of all worlds has no interest in changing it. Once injustice and suffering have been declared necessary, it is only a small step to concealment of reality, whitewashing and power-serving apologetics of all kinds, as have developed whenever theologians worked in the interest of maintaining the status quo. Where the self-identity religion stood in opposition to prevailing circumstances without actively seeking to change them, it could still respond to people's sense of injustice by referring to the expiatory power of suffering and the offsetting of debt in the afterlife – or conversely with the promise of later punishment, as in Calvin's drastic response to the question of why godless people fare so well: 'Because the Lord is fattening them like pigs for the slaughtering day.'[22] In Judaism and Shia Islam especially, the state of waiting for justice was heightened through a chiliastic twist: not man, but God himself will establish a final kingdom of justice on earth. The impulse for this need not be apologetic; it can stem from the despair that constituted an early psychological component in Judaism and Shia Islam, but also in Christianity, in the latter above all as a promise for the hereafter: 'For here we do not have an enduring city, but we are looking for the city that is to come' (Hebrews 13:14). Schiller takes up this promise in the most prominent of contexts, in his 'Ode to Joy':

> Endure courageously, millions!
> Endure for the better world!
> Yonder, above the starry canopy
> A great God will reward you.

The denial of God

As great as this promise was, not everyone was content to be put off by it. There was – and is – naturally also a very different answer, already formulated surprisingly vehemently in the Arab-Persian Middle Ages (or however else one wishes to term the period),[23] to questions of suffering, injustice and evil: to dispute the existence of God. Stendhal (d. 1900) encapsulated this most violent solution to the theodicy problem with a witticism for which even Nietzsche (d. 1900) envied him:[24] 'God's only excuse is that He doesn't exist.' While it is usually only the conclusion, not its explanation, that is quoted, the death of God proclaimed by Nietzsche stems precisely from the suffering of mankind. What did He die of? 'God has died of his pity for man.'[25] Elsewhere, in *Daybreak*, Nietzsche justifies his atheism with the view that he cannot simultaneously acknowledge both the omnipotence and the cognizability of God:

> A God who is all-knowing and all-powerful and who does not even make sure that his creatures understand his intention – could that be a god of goodness? Who allows countless doubts and dubieties to persist for thousands of years, as though the salvation of mankind were unaffected by them, and who on the other hand holds out the prospect of frightful consequences if any mistake is made as to the nature of the truth? Would He not be a cruel god if He possessed the truth and could behold mankind miserably tormenting itself over the truth? – But perhaps He is a god of goodness notwithstanding – and merely *could* not express himself more clearly! Did He perhaps lack the intelligence to do so? Or the eloquence? So much the worse! For then He was perhaps also in error as to that which he calls His 'truth', and is himself not so very far from being the 'poor deluded devil'![26]

Senseless, unjust hardship, and hence the impossibility of conceiving of a God who is simultaneously good and almighty, runs through centuries of world literature as the true reason for unbelief, or, rather: the inability to believe, the loss of belief – as the 'rock of atheism', as Georg Büchner (d. 1837) called pain.[27] The other monotheistic traditions have also produced a multitude of scholars, theologians and poets who could no longer believe in God because suffering had become too powerful. The prophet Ezekiel reports that many Jews lost their faith through the catastrophe of the destruction of the temple, and writes of twenty-five of them: 'With their backs towards the temple of the Lord and their faces towards the east, they were bowing down to the sun in the east' (Ezekiel 8:16). The prophet Malachi also knows of those people who became heretics because of the world's injustice: 'You have said, "It is futile to serve God. What did we gain by carrying out his requirements and going about like mourners before the Lord Almighty? But now we call the arrogant blessed. Certainly the evildoers prosper, and even those who challenge God escape"' (Malachi 3:14–15). In the Jewish tradition, the most prominent figure to fall away from faith because he could not justify God in the face of suffering was the first-century personality Elisha ben Abuya. He found no answer to the suffering of innocents, and so he became an *acher*, 'a completely different person', an unbeliever. Some say he witnessed the death of a boy in an accident that occurred while carrying out a biblical commandment. Others hold that, when he saw a pig dragging the tongue of the martyred Rabbi Chutzpit the Interpreter through the dirt, he called out: 'The mouth that pronounced pearls of wisdom is now licking the dust.' Then Elisha went forth and sinned.[28] Ibn ar-Rawandi (tenth century), the most famous atheist in Islamic intellectual history, similarly justifies his unbelief with the injustice of the world: 'How many of the wisest among the wise leave in misery, and how many of the most foolish among the foolish receive their daily bread! That is what brings confusion into our thoughts and turns the great religious scholar into a heretic.'[29]

Atheism only seemingly offers an answer to the question of God's responsibility for injustice, however; the atheist Ernst Bloch recognized this more acutely than any theologian. For him, denying God's existence and leaving it at that was too easy a solution. In Bloch's view, a completely areligious atheism implicitly denies that the world can be changed: the present state cannot be everything. For Bloch, resistance in itself had a religious element because it presupposes the utopia of a different world from the existing one. One does not find hope everywhere one finds religion, admittedly; but he placed the inversion of this proposition in italics in his book *Atheism in Christianity*: '*Where there is hope, there is also religion.*'[30] Marxism, he argues, deals with the same core questions as religion: whether there are no alternatives to the existing world, or rather a better one. Vulgar atheism, he continues, does not even ask itself the question of salvation, because it fundamentally disbelieves the possibility of a substantially different world. Bloch's understanding of Marxism has nothing to do with such positivism, whereas it at least shares the question with Christianity. From the vulgar atheist perspective, Bloch writes, the problem of theodicy seems like an apologetics without *causa sui*; in the absence of an enthroned deity, the questions and reproaches of Job and his whole rebellion seem redundant, a waste of effort. 'Can that really be so?' asks Bloch: 'Does the Book of Job, with all its bitter questioning, possess no more truth for easy-going atheists than the historical or the psychological? [. . .] An unfeeling universe remains; one still so badly adjusted to human finality. And if we can no longer react to this with accusation, we can and do react with searching questions, and with massive negative amazement.'[31]

Hardship as proof of God's existence

The abolition of God may succeed in the philosophical seminar, satisfy in everyday life or give occasion for dramatic proclamations of self-assertion; as a means of fending off the presumptuous demands of life, however, it fulfils its purpose only if one is still able to maintain one's comfortable stoicism in situations of extreme need. Part of the presumption is that it demands to be understood, just as the disturbing aspect of death is not that we cannot know what it brings, but rather that it forces us to *want* to know it. The needs of reason are both inescapable and unrealizable, as Kant (d. 1804) famously taught; following on from that, one could invert theodicy – which absolves God of responsibility for misfortune – into the statement that nothing supports God's existence more than misfortune, because this is what evokes the question of the cause in the first place. One need not think of genocide, slavery, tyranny or great natural disasters to find the question inescapable. Any life is enough – the experience of sickness, old age, the destruction we see before our eyes, unbearable physical and emotional pain, or the loss of our closest loved ones. Perhaps Aunt Lobat could even come to terms with not finding any consolation. But she couldn't stop asking why this was happening to her – and, for her, that meant why God was doing it to her. The question loomed in her eyes, which were now enormous, to the very last day. Heinrich Heine (d. 1856), mortally ill, also asked Job's question: 'Why must the righteous man suffer so much on earth? That is the question I grapple with day and night on my martyr's bed.'[32] Heine described the shock of my aunt, the terror of God, when he discarded agnosticism in his 'mattress grave': 'Human misery is too great. One *must* believe.'[33]

Heine had always suffered from illness. During his studies in the 1820s he had severe headaches, in 1832 his first symptoms of paralysis appeared, and from 1844 his body entered a rapid decline. 'Confined to his bed, all his limbs paralyzed and suffering from the most agonizing convulsions, which often last 3 times 24 hours',[34] Heine endured more torment in the remaining twelve years of his life 'than the Spanish inquisition could ever have devised'.[35] It was a 'living death', without his lips, feet, jaws or bowels functioning; he could 'neither chew nor crap', condemned to a 'non-life' as someone who loved life 'with such fervent passion!'[36] Day in, day out, Heine was huddled, turned slightly to one side, under a thin white blanket, his once well-fed body now terribly thin, the skin stretched over the bones, his legs twisted from spasms into a position only a cripple could endure as a permanent state. Four wounds had been burned into the back of his neck; these were kept open artificially so that they could be sprinkled with grey opium powder. He could move his upper body and arms, but was deaf in his left ear and blind in his left eye. To look at someone, he would pull the lame lid of his right eye up with his left hand, showing a wanly glowing, dark eyeball. This quickly tired him, and then his hand would sink back onto his chest and darkness would envelop him once more. Yet the days were still better than the nights: 'Mad with pain, my poor head is thrown back and forth in those terrible nights, while the bells on the old cap ring with unmerciful gaiety.'[37]

Heine's ordeal must have been similar to that of my aunt, but went on for longer. Another, in my view decisive, difference: Heine could, albeit with great effort, speak, take notes and write some of the most moving poems in the history of world literature; this made him one of the most precise witnesses of the experience on which this book is based, the experience of my Aunt Lobat and the fools and saints presented by Attar. The Friday sermon and the catechism are meaningless in the face of this hardship, which makes the question of God no small matter. 'Great, sublime and ghastly thoughts have come over me', wrote Heine to his publisher on 1 June 1850, 'but they were thoughts, flashes of light, not the phosphorous fumes of pious piss.'[38] Heine saw himself returning to 'the base level of God's creatures', where he once again 'paid tribute to the omnipotence of a supreme being that presides over the fate of this world, and should henceforth also guide my own earthly matters.'[39] He explained his return to the God of the Hebrew Bible – often with the most lugubrious sarcasm – with the neediness his ordeal had imposed on him. 'I lie in great pain and have begun to pray again, which is always a bad sign.'[40] Just under two years before his death, in the winter of 1854, he noted:

> In this condition it is a true boon for me that there is someone in heaven to whom I can always whimper the litany of my woes, especially after midnight, when Mathilde lays herself to rest, of which she often has great need. I am not alone in such hours – thank God! – and I can pray and bawl as much as I want without embarrassment, and I can pour out my heart completely before the Almighty, and confide things in him that we would normally keep even from our own wives.[41]

Before he can even refute it in the manner of Büchner, religion is brought forth by pain, being 'the sigh of the oppressed creature, the sentiment of a heartless world' – as a further atheist, Karl Marx, said before the statement that has been taken out of context for the last century, namely the one concerning opium. '*Religious* misery is, at one and the same time, the expression of real suffering and a *protest* against real misery.'[42] Marx defined misery in social terms, and was convinced that the revolution could do away with it; if one defines misery in existential terms and loses all hope of being able to alleviate it, be it only because death and suffering seem inexorable, the critique of religion changes into a description thereof. 'Heaven was invented for those whom the earth no longer has anything to offer', formulated Heine on his deathbed: 'Hail to this invention!'[43] Even one who denies God seeks explanations for being, and thus also for death; to claim that both being and death lack any meaning is itself an explanation, and ascribes meaning to life even in its negation. This meaning, however, is nothing other than the empty space taken up by God in theology, and by nothingness in mysticism. Perhaps atheism can explain being, but certainly not death; this was clear to the joker who read the graffiti 'God is dead. Nietzsche' and sprayed underneath it: 'Nietzsche is dead. God.'

I genuinely think that my aunt would have been relieved on some evenings if God – and no one else could have convinced her, who had believed in Him for her whole life – had revealed to her that He did not exist. But the situation was precisely the opposite: the longer she suffered, the more her consciousness was reduced to her relationship with the Creator. She was not silent, after all. When she didn't happen to be watching us, speaking to us with her eyes or making another one of her fruitless attempts to force her mouth into speech, when she had returned into herself without sleeping, without lying motionless with exhaustion or screaming in pain, she mumbled something; and the one thing I understood was that it was directed at God. I understood this because every four, five or ten seconds, amid the stream of stammered vowels, I heard the word 'God' gasping for air – or, more precisely, the honorific of God, *ey ḫodā* or *ḫodāyā*. At the end her life, to the extent that she still controlled it, was a single address to God. Not expressions of gratitude, that much is certain. One may be able to ignore death, but not pain. Perhaps only Büchner's 'crack in the creation', produced by the 'slightest twitch of pain, and be it only in an atom',[44] can hint that the world is a creation, and hence not everything. Heine learned from the blessed Professor Hegel that he was a 'two-legged God',[45] but the pain in his spine convinced him that the Hegelians were 'villains'.[46] Even 'Greek antiquity, as beautiful and lively as it is, is no longer enough for me now that I myself am no longer beautiful or lively.'[47]

> Thank God that I have a God again, for now I can allow myself various invective blasphemies when assailed by an excess of pain; the atheist does not have that luxury.[48]

That it is precisely suffering and injustice which bind humans to God leads Heine to a third way of dealing with hardship: by neither justifying nor denying God, but rather accusing Him; denying not his omnipotence or comprehensibility, but rather his goodness with all its components – justice, love and compassion. 'I lie hunched together, in pain day and night, and even if I do believe in a God, I do not always believe in a good God.'[49] Someone who recognizes, defends, or even insults the Creator in His terror, wilfulness and aloofness does not have to abandon Him; but he refuses to absolve God of the responsibility that stems from His omnipotence. So someone who accuses God may love Him, but seems to have lost faith in being loved. That brings me to Faridoddin Attar. His response to Job's question is a 'book of suffering'.

Attar's life and legends

Hardly anything is known about the life of Attar.[50] Neither his teachers nor his friends are known, nor even the people he dealt with. His everyday life is as much of a secret as his exact dates of birth and death, his social status or his standing among the mystics of the period. There are no sources to tell us whether he had a wife and children, what his full name was, what his parents were called, or in which of the Sufi chains of initiation, if any, he stood. Among the classics of Persian literature there is no one whose life is as much of a mystery as that of Faridoddin Attar. The scholars who in recent decades investigated the poet's biography – alongside the Middle East scholar Hellmut Ritter, these were the Iranian literary scholars Hoseynchan Fourughi, Badi'ozzaman Foruzanfar, Sa'id Nafisi, Mohammad Reza Shafi'i-Kadkani and Abdolhasan Zarin-Kub – gradually found out that existing reports of Attar's life are false, improbable or at the very least dubious.[51] Even in the case of Sana'i (d. c. 1131), who lived a century earlier and was the first significant poet in the new-born Persian literary history, our knowledge is incomparably more precise. With Attar, on the other hand, all that is now certain is that a poet of this name lived around the turn of the thirteenth century in or near Nishapur, the most important town in the region of Khorasan in the north-east of modern Iran, and worked as a pharmacist or 'druggist', as his name already states and he himself occasionally confirms in his works – that is, he sold medication, essences and fragrances, and certainly also treated the sick himself.

For all the reservations they had about surviving reports, the aforementioned researchers were able to compile a number of clues suggesting that Attar was born around 1145 – towards the end of the Sanjar dynasty – in Nishapur or the nearby village of Kadkan. His father, whose name some sources report as Esma'il, supposedly already worked as a druggist and associated with Sufis. Taking into account the many epithets used for Attar in the various chronicles, it seems most probable that his full name was Mohammad ebn-e Ebrahim ebn-e Eshaq-e Attar-e Kadkani. That he died during the Mongol invasion of Iran in 1221, as reported in the chronicles and older sources, cannot be verified; nor, however, is there any proof to the contrary. The fact that this would have made his life over seventy years long is supported by the references to him in contemporary sources as an old man, and by his own hints that he wrote his central works at an advanced age.[52]

There are no contemporary accounts to confirm this, but one can assume that Attar picked up many Sufi tales and legends from his customers, or as a child in his father's pharmacy, especially as his books or other contemporary sources make no mention whatsoever of any travels (unlike the legends, admittedly, some of which portray Attar as a globetrotter among other things). Possibly he healed people not only with herbal medicine and fragrances, but also with his stories and teachings. The education Attar received at home or from a religious scholar consisted at the time of calligraphy, mathematics, Koran study and literature. From his works one can conclude that he was already interested in mysticism early on. At one point, for example, he mentions 'that I felt drawn to the Sufis from childhood without reason, and my time and the joy of my heart belonged to their words even then.'[53] Later he associated with Sufis, read their writings and visited the mystic leader Majdoddin Kharazmi (drowned c.1209), as he notes himself.[54]

Attar was a mystical thinker, meaning that he dealt with themes and motifs from Sufism – i.e., Islamic mysticism. It is unknown whether he belonged to an official order, meditated regularly himself, embraced asceticism and participated in *sama'* – 'listening', as the Sufis called their communal ritual. But Attar admits repeatedly in his poems that he was at best an adept, certainly not a master, that he was still at the beginning of the path taken by the holy men. Attar himself emphasizes that he did not belong to the knowers of secrets, but only told of them (E9, p. 372), and expands on this by telling the story of the roadsweeper who chose the square in front of the king's castle to sweep so that everyone would call him the king's roadsweeper. Even if later Sufis and chroniclers often called him enlightened,[55] Attar himself, as far as he himself mentions it in his writings, seems to have been more an empathetic observer of Sufism than an active exponent. More poet than mystic, this distinguishes him from other mystical poets such as Jalaloddin Mowlana Rumi (d. 1273), who was himself one of the great Sufis and wrote many of his verses in a state of ecstasy. As a poet, Attar considered himself the greatest of his time,[56] but, as one in search of God, he never claimed to have been enlightened like the holy men he wrote about.

> If I listened to words myself,
> I would not be so intent on talking.
> If the path to God were open to me,
> I would not have the heart to write poetry. (E3, p. 369)[57]

During his own lifetime, Attar does not appear to have been known outside of his hometown. Only two contemporaries mention him: Oufi (d. after 1223) and Khaje Naser at-Tusi (d. 1273). Perhaps one can conclude from this that Attar led a secluded life, as his accounts of himself likewise suggest. He writes that he kept his distance from the poet colleagues he viewed disparagingly as panegyrists,[58] but even the once elitist field of mysticism was already perceived in Attar's time as something corrupted. In the eyes of many contemporary authors, its increase in popularity had been accompanied by a loss of truthfulness and seriousness – a development we would probably describe today as commercialism. In previous generations, no Sufi far or wide would have dared to place himself next to one of the great sheikhs of mysticism – someone like Abu Sa'id Fazlollah ebn Abi l-Kheyr (d. 1049) in Nishapur. A hundred years later, however, in Attar's day, complaints that self-appointed holy men were opening Dervish monasteries on every corner and attracting paying customers had grown into a veritable topos in Sufi literature. Attar himself made no secret of his contempt for the religious life of his time, and wrote that every nobody who came along was acting like a mystic now, and hence the habit worn by the Sufis had lost all meaning as a form of identification.[59]

Perhaps Attar also – like Ruknoddin Akkaf (d. 1155), who practised mysticism in the guise of a legal scholar, or Abbas-e Tusi (d. 1153), who only appeared as a preacher and a Koran interpreter – consciously kept his distance from the Sufi scene, concentrating all the more intently on saving the great legacy from oblivion with his *Lives of the Saints* and verse epics.[60] That could explain why Attar was hardly mentioned for a long time after his death, except by Mowlana Rumi and his order.[61] In the fifteenth century, towards the end of the Timurid dynasty, it seems that Attar's poems – by whatever strokes of luck – finally became known in larger circles practically overnight. Attar, the collector of legends, now himself became the subject of legends, such as those written by the poet Jami (d. 1492) or the chroniclers Dowlatshah (d. late fifteenth century) and Ahmad Razi (d. early seventeenth century). Some of them can be found in the inscription in the mausoleum erected in Nishapur by the politician and thinker Mir Ali Shir Nawa'i (d. 1501) some two hundred and fifty years after Attar's death.

Individual embellishments certainly seem realistic, for example in the description of how the very young Attar already picked up the tales, both invented and ones actually experienced, he heard the customers tell at his father's pharmacy. Other stories serve the purpose of idealization, such as the claim that he lived longer than any other great poet before him, and wrote 114 works (that is, exactly as many as there are Surahs in the Koran). In summer he supposedly sat in the fire and in winter in the snow, and was occasionally seen up on the domes and trees of the town, which even the birds would have found difficult to scale. He already warned his disciples of Genghis Khan (d. 1227) before anyone suspected a Mongol invasion. Subsequently Attar – like the twelfth imam of the Shia – disappeared. The Haydari order stylized Attar into an early member, while the Shiites, who were being persecuted at the time, claimed him as one of their own. People imagined all sorts of encounters, possible and impossible alike, with the great Sufis of his time. It is said that he learned from the Sufi sheikhs of his time, such as Najmoddin Kobra (d. c.1220) or Sa'doddin Hammuya (d. 1252), and that those who came later were chosen by him: late in life, Dowlatshah recounts in his dictionary of poets, Attar met the young Mowlana Rumi when the latter's family stopped off in Nishapur on their pilgrimage to Mecca. The aged poet immediately recognized the child's disposition. 'Your son will kindle a fire in the lovesick of the earth', Attar revealed to the baffled father, before giving the son a copy of his *Asrārnāmeh, The Book of Secrets*.[62] Rumi later described himself as a planet orbiting the sun of Attar. He said that Attar had progressed through seven cities of love, but he, Rumi, was still at the entrance to the first alley. In his *Masnavi*, he varied many of Attar's stories and positioned himself as his immediate successor.[63]

Like his encounter with Rumi, the account of Attar's mystical vocation is also one of the legends surrounding him. The poet may have invented it himself. Dowlatshah recounts that Attar, 'already like a venerable teacher', was sitting in his pharmacy full of fragrant essences and precious medicines – merely looking at them gave the passers-by 'shining eyes and perfumed noses' – when one day a 'madman' (*divāneh*) entered, presumably a crazed wandering Dervish, louse-ridden, with long straggly hair and a matted beard. Such characters would have been all over the place at the time, as many mystics' handbooks lament, and it must have been difficult to tell apart the true Sufis, who had renounced all possessions, from the simple beggars who masqueraded as Sufis in the hope of receiving pious offerings. Attar will not have greeted his visitor with great enthusiasm, at any rate, especially as the Dervish neither moved nor uttered a word for some time, simply staring at the shelves with wide eyes before bursting into tears. Attar feared the man would drive away his customers and told him to leave.

'Easily done, my good sir', answered the old man. 'My baggage is light, for it consists only of the rags I wear. But you, what will you do with these sacks full of precious objects when the time has come for you to go? How will you take it all with you? I can disappear from the bazaar of this transient world quickly and effortlessly, but you should think about what to do with your goods and how to carry them.'

Attar was unimpressed by the old man's words. In the hope that the uninvited guest would leave his pharmacy, he asked him: 'And? What do you have to do to leave this bazaar?'

'This', spoke the fool, lay down on the floor of the pharmacy, took his rags as a pillow, and was dead.[64]

Thereupon Attar allegedly closed his pharmacy, devoting himself to asceticism and Sufi meditation under the leadership of the famous holy man Ruknoddin Akkaf. Dowlatshah writes that Attar spent thirteen years at the shrine of Imam Reza (Ali ar-Rida', murdered 818) in Mashhad, and also visited Reyy, Jufa, Damascus, Egypt, Mecca, India and Turkestan, before returning to Nishapur to write his major works. On his travels he is said to have met the most important Sufis of his time, whose experiences, stories and memories he collected over a space of thirty-nine years for his *Tażkerat ol-ouliyā'*, the most famous collection of saints' legends in Persian literary history.

Attar's death also has a story associated with it. It places the poet once and for all in the line of Sufi martyrs he wrote about, such as al-Hallaj (executed 922). Dowlatshah and others report that Attar was 110 years old when Genghis Khan's Mongols attacked Nishapur. Just when an enemy soldier was about to kill the poet, a different Mongol appeared and took pity on the venerable old man. He offered his comrade a thousand dirham to release Attar. The soldier was just about to accept the offer when Attar – 'joyous in the expectation that the bird of his blessed soul would finally leave the cage of his body' – advised him to wait a little, perhaps until someone made him a better offer. After a while another Mongol came along. The soldier asked him what he would give him for the old man.

'A sack of straw', answered the other Mongol.

Attar laughed and said: 'Accept the offer. A sack of straw – that's exactly what I'm worth.'

The first Mongol, angry that he had been deprived of a thousand dirham, drew his sword and beheaded the poet.[65]

These are legends, as stated above; they tell us more about the poet's reception than about the actual man. Perhaps Attar has been retrospectively stylized into a Sufi holy man not only out of admiration but also to restrict the heretical potential of his work; for saints and fools are allowed to utter what would be sacrilege for ordinary people, as Attar himself already knew when he placed the most flagrant blasphemies in the mouths of the venerable and the insane. As so often in literary history, literary provocation establishes itself through its canonization, which simultaneously restricts it.

The works

Of the 114 works Attar is alleged to have written, only the *Lives of the Saints* (his only prose work), *The Book of Selection* (*Moḫtārnāmeh*, a collection of quatrains from the last phase of his life) and the poems he lists as his works in the foreword to *The Book of Selection* are likely to be authentic: alongside the early *Divān* with ghazals,[66] these are the six verse epics or masnavis, two of which – *The Book of Jewels* (*Ǧawāhernāmeh*) and the *Explanation of the Heart* (*Šarḥ ol-qalb*) – he claimed to have burned. This leaves *The Book of Secrets* (*Asrārnāmeh*), *The Conference of the Birds* (*Manṭeq oṭ-ṭeyr*), *The Book of Suffering* (*Moṣibatnāmeh*) and *The Book of God* (*Elāhināmeh*).[67] The last is referred to in *The Book of Selection* as *The Book of Khosrow*, but Mohammed Reza Shafi'i-Kadkani showed some years ago that this can hardly be the adventure novel of that name, which Western scholars view as one of Attar's early, still purely literary works.[68]

The verse epics owe their generic name to the specific rhyming form: the classical form of the Persian poem, the ghazal, is characterized by the unchanging end rhyme and the quatrain (*robā'i*) with the pattern AABA. In the masnavi, on the other hand, it is always the two halves of a line that rhyme with each other, while the end rhyme changes. Attar probably wrote the masnavis only relatively late in life, after the Divan and the *Lives of the Saints* – presumably not before his fiftieth birthday. Like his shorter poems, his epics describe the misery of being in all its shadings – metaphysical, existential and social – and speak of the human yearning to break free from oneself in order to attain fulfilment in God. But God is to be found only in one's own soul, as his protagonists recognize – if at all – and only after long, painful journeys.

The Book of Secrets is the shortest, and probably also the earliest of Attar's masnavis: it dispenses with a frame story, so that, as in Jalaloddin Rumi's *Masnavi*, different themes are treated without any recognizable connection, often in didactic fashion. In *The Book of God*, a king tells his six sons each to name their greatest wish in life so that he can fulfil it. The sons do not hold back: the first asks for the fairy princess; the second for the gift of sorcery; the third for Jamshid's magic cup, in order to glimpse the secrets of the world in it; the fourth for the water of life; the fifth for the ring of Solomon; and the sixth for the art of alchemy. Instead of keeping his promise, however, the father then conducts a dialogue with each son to explain the baseness and worthlessness of his wish.

The Conference of the Birds takes up the motif of the 'bird treatise' (*risālat aṭ-ṭayr*), which four of the most renowned thinkers in Islamic intellectual history explored in their writings: Avicenna (Ibn Sina, died 1037), the brothers Muhammad and Ahmad Ghazali (d. 1123), and finally Shehaboddin Sohrawadi (executed 1191). A flock of birds sets out to find their mythical kind Simorġ. After thirty of them have only narrowly managed to pass through the seven valleys of searching, love, insight, needlessness,[69] unity, confusion and unbecoming, they realize that Simorġ is none other than they themselves: *si* (thirty) *morġ* (birds). A further journey of the soul, but that of a single traveller through the cosmos, is described in *The Book of Suffering*, which may have been Attar's penultimate masnavi, but more probably his last; at 7,539 lines, it is also his longest. It forms the central focus of my book.

Attar is one of the greatest poets of the Persian language. Nonetheless, his popularity – both in Iran itself and in the West (Goethe, for example, touched on him only briefly in his *West-Eastern Divan*) – does not match that of Ferdowsi (d. 1020), Omar Khayyam (d. c.1132), Rumi, Saadi (d. 1292) or Hafiz (d. 1389); occasionally he is even omitted from the line of seven Persian poet-princes in favour of Jami (d. 1492) (aside from the aforementioned, the line also includes Nezami, d. 1209, and Anwari, d. c.1190, though not the agnostic Omar Khayyam). One possible reason for this is that the composition of his poetry is too artful, too complex to be effective in the town squares and teahouses, while at the same time, many of his stories and figures may seem too coarse, too folk-like and too sarcastic to be at the forefront of the high spiritual literature cultivated at courts in former times and in middle-class households today. Attar's poetry, on the other hand, is far less stilted than that of most Persian poets but, rather, unadorned, clear and immediate. The pain it expresses is not spiritually filtered as in Rumi, far less metaphysically elevated than in Saadi, and not sublimated into pleasure as in Omar Khayyam – where Hafiz turns the earthly into the mystical, Attar strips mysticism down to its leaden, earthly foundation in order to scream his longing to the heavens.

In the modern context, Attar initially seems very antiquated. For Iranian intellectuals and men of letters during and after the constitutional revolution of 1905–6, at a time of new beginnings and enthusiasm for all things new, his invocation of suffering, ascetic tendencies, demonstrative inwardness and contempt for the world were scarcely relevant. It was only in the 1940s that scholars began to edit his works, to untangle the legends about Attar's life, and to relieve him of the works that had wrongly been attributed to him and had substantially contributed to his outdated reputation as a poet of inwardness – though this has not prevented some authors, even very recently, from criticizing Attar for poems he did not actually write.[70] Around the same time as the Iranians Nafisi and Foruzanfar, Hellmut Ritter discovered Attar as a world poet in his monumental study; nonetheless, the poet's reputation did not spread to a larger Iranian audience. In his homeland, Attar remained a case for specialists on the one hand and fairytale-tellers on the other. He kept his position on the pedestal of the classical poets, but some literary figures of the Pahlavi era considered his poems in particular too plain, even clumsy – if they were believed worthy of study at all, then only from a historical perspective. In the late 1960s, Mehdi Hamidi derided Attar as a 'man of many words and few thoughts' and the 'forerunner of the first degenerations of Persian poetry'.[71] The literary critic spoke of the 'highly despicable worldview' in Attar's epics.[72] The backlash caused by Hamidi's attack, however, gained Attar renewed attention. Literary critics gradually began to recognize precisely the immediacy of Attar's poetry as a valuable quality, to highlight the multifaceted nature of his epics, and to praise his narrative skill all the more resolutely.[73]

As many are reluctant to afford him too large a role, however, it is only the *Lives of the Saints*, *The Book of God* and, above all, *The Conference of the Birds* that form part of the literary canon in Iran today. The last work has also gained a certain fame in the West.[74] After reading it, Martin Buber called Attar 'the boldest of poets',[75] and Borges even placed Simorġ above the eagle in the *Divine Comedy*.[76] *The Conference of the Birds* also became known to a wider audience through several adaptations for theatre, beginning with Peter Brook's legendary production in the 1970s and directed most recently by Andrea Breth at the Berlin Schaubühne. In addition, Western esotericism has long since discovered Attar's tale for itself and thrown it into its pan-religious stew.

Though one could deem *The Book of Suffering* Attar's most substantial work for more reasons than simply its length, it is not nearly as well known as *The Conference of the Birds* – not even in Iran.[77] This may be due to its mood; *The Book of Suffering* is by far Attar's most grim and forbidding text, and probably one of the darkest works in the whole of world literature. Even those Iranian scholars and literary figures who praised Attar viewed him as an exponent of Iranian love mysticism and the creator of Simorġ. Only Hellmut Ritter gave *The Book of Suffering* its full due, as evidenced by his allusion to it in the title of his monumental study on Attar. An examination of Ritter's *Ocean of the Soul* is the prerequisite for all further research on Attar – it has long since been translated into Persian – but also extends beyond Attar as a key to Islamic intellectual life.[78] Something peculiar has happened with Ritter's excellent book, however, which would already be sufficient on its own to justify Middle East scholarship in the West: the expert world seems almost paralysed with awe. The well-deserved recognition for his bulky work was so great, so unanimous, that in a certain sense its success was turned on its head. After Ritter, scarcely any Middle East scholar dared to look closely at Attar – a truly lethal effect.[79]

Ritter did not trivialize Attar, make light of him or reduce him to pretty bird figures and clever dramaturgical ideas; he did not idealize him as a mystic of love and argue away his pain esoterically, as is still the rule to this day – not least in Iran. Ritter admired Attar in all his harshness, his boundless despair, and also in his bitter criticism of social conditions. One reason for Ritter's affinity was probably also the fact that his own situation during his immersion in Attar's poetry – large parts of the monograph were written in Turkish exile during the Nazi era – was of a similarly apocalyptic bitterness to those described by Attar. By treating all of Attar's verse epics as a single text, however, Ritter almost completely levelled out the difference between the individual works. The fact that the late work *The Book of Suffering* conveys a far more pessimistic interpretation of the world, and appears to condemn social conditions far more emphatically if taken on its own than if one compares it to the earlier works, for example, is inevitably passed over in *The Ocean of the Soul*. Because I have chosen to concentrate on a single work by Attar and a small number of motifs in that work, my representation is more partial, but in some aspects perhaps more focused than would be the case with a treatment of his entire output. And, as *The Book of Suffering* appears to be Attar's late work, one can certainly take it as a summing-up of his work and his lifelong occupation with Islamic mysticism. It is more consistently informed, down to the most subtle dramaturgical ramifications, by the theory and practice of Sufism than his other works; at the same time, Attar poetically sublated the inner experience of the mystic into an experience of being that goes beyond Sufism. This is precisely what makes Ritter's assessment of Attar's work as world literature of the highest order an accurate one.

Hellmut Ritter presented Attar in the context of Islamic intellectual history. What he did not concern himself with is that Attar is located not only between Sana'i and Rumi, but also between Sophocles (d. c.404 BC) and Schopenhauer (d. 1860), and that he is related not only to Abu A'la al-Ma'arri (d. 1058) and Omar Khayyam, but also to

Büchner and Beckett. As unmistakable as the specific Sufi connotations and possibilities of allegorical interpretation in his verses may be, they simultaneously develop – often already in the direct sense of the words – existential, metaphysical or social meanings that can be understood both historically and universally. It would be a mistake to assume that, because Attar's unjust ruler at once stands for God, he did not also have the unjust ruler in mind.

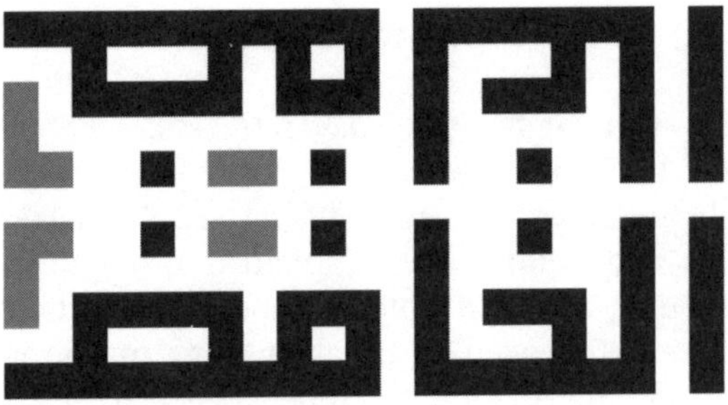

— 2 —

THE BOOK OF SUFFERING

The frame story

Referring to the ritual of the forty-day retreat (*čeleh*), which is still a part of Islamic mysticism today, *The Book of Suffering* recounts a journey through the cosmos in forty stages. Each chapter poetically represents a state within immersion explained at length in theoretical treatises of the Sufis, and is devoted to specific moods, perceptions, images and views experienced by the meditating mystic in the course of his inner journey. In Sufism the number forty stands for endurance, patience and submission in suffering until fulfilment approaches; one could also think of the children of Israel's forty-day trek through the desert, the forty days Moses spent on Mount Sinai, or the forty-day period of fasting in Christianity. The retreat usually takes place in a tiny room in which the Sufi, instructed by his *pir*, spends forty days solely meditating, reading the Koran and repeating a prayer phrase several thousand times. The teacher often reduces the novice's food during the *čeleh* or makes him adopt an uncomfortable position – spending hours or days on tiptoe, for example, or placing his head on his knees. The student reports the manifold illuminations, visions and insights ideally experienced during meditation in the course of the forty days to the *pir*, who interprets them and gives him new instructions.

In *The Book of Suffering*, consciousness, which progresses into unimagined, often threatening and occasionally exhilarating spheres, is personified in the shape of the 'wanderer of thought' (*sālek-e fekrat*), a disciple of one such *pir*. Possibly the traditional account of the spiritual journey undertaken by the famous mystic Bayezid Bestami (d. 874), which he himself retells in his *Lives of the Saints*, inspired Attar to add a frame story. Here Bayezid travels through the cosmos with his thoughts and ideas during a retreat, which he spends partly on tiptoe and partly with his head on his knees, like the Prophet on his heavenly journey to Jerusalem.[1]

According to custom, the book begins with extensive praise for the Creator, emphasizing in particular his omnipotence and greatness; in certain surprising turns of phrase, however, it already refers to the wilfulness at whose mercy angels and humans find themselves:

> A hundred thousand years of obedience
> Are rewarded with the bridle of his curse. (0, p. 3)

After a long section describing the Prophet's outstanding qualities, Attar speaks first of the virtues of the first four caliphs, then the two Shiite imams Hassan (murdered c. 669) and Hossein (fallen 680). The reason for his unfailing consideration for Shiite sensibilities, despite being firmly on Sunni ground, is indirectly given in the following chapter; for it is entirely devoted to the dangers of *ta'ṣṣob*, religious dogmatism or fanaticism, a subject to which he will angrily return many times later on. The preliminaries are completed by a meticulously detailed discussion of mystical states, a vehement advocacy of justice and the meaning of poetry, and finally a short polemic – foreshadowing Pascal's (d. 1662) *Pensées* – against philosophy and its presumptuous attempt to understand religion purely rationally, place reason above revealed knowledge, turn its back on sensual experience and ignore the insight of the heart.[2] As we shall see, there are further lines of thought connecting Attar and Pascal. Attar opens the main text with the admission that his book may scare off readers: that what he says in it sounds forbidden and twisted, 'bent as a bow' (0, p. 55). We are told, however, that in the 'tongue of that state', in mystical-poetic speech, those things that are lies in normal speech become true.

The narrative begins with the adverse situation of the wanderer. Out of favour with himself and the world, he waits in vain for a glimmer of hope. He is full of anger at his fellow human beings, and even more at himself. He trusts no teacher or master. He is prepared to join neither the Zoroastrians nor the Dervishes. Destitute, friendless, without wife or family, he considers himself more worthless than a stone. He can no more distinguish between good and evil than between being and nothingness, the whole and the parts, the straight and the crooked or the body and the soul. No longer is he prepared to adopt any supposition, any faith – not even doubt. His heart blind, his feelings numb, his eyes tightly closed, he no longer wants to feel anything, and suffers from being neither something nor nothing. He knows no happiness – neither that of the Muslim nor that of the heretic. Wherever he looks, he sees only misery, lies and deception. Not only is there no real Islam – no, there is not even enough will for true unbelief in the society that presents itself to the wanderer: no advice from anyone, no secret revealed, no path to discover, and if there were one it would consist only of ditches. The divine law – the Sharia – is restricted to accusations, philosophy and useless mental acrobatics, while hundreds of thousands of people are needy in a world full of misery and ever new wars, with no one trusting anyone else and each the wolf of the other.

> The one goes astray like a pig,
> The other uses tricks like a fox.
> The one does it like the elephant, with force,
> The other runs about like a crawling thing.
> The one a dog in nature and deeds,
> The other oh-so-clever like the mouse.
> The one walks into a trap – for a grain,
> The other cooks in the fire, yet remains raw.
> The one robs corpses like a vulture,
> The other croaks mournfully like a raven.
> The one's sadness changes into rage,
> The other's misdeed into the evil glance.
> The one a judge, pregnant with power,
> The other a policeman, dull as menstrual blood.
> The one a lion, inflates himself to roar,
> The other a wolf, bites yapping into the flesh.
> The one a crocodile, devours his prey unchewed,
> The other a tiger, tears everything to pieces.
> The one wants to swim – but gasps as a fish out of water,
> The other wants to fly – but limps through the air as a partridge.
> (0, p. 60)

And thus it continues: the poet speaks of people's miserliness and greed, of their coldness and hot-headedness. He complains of blindness, folly, falseness and envy. People torment one another – and why? Merely to distract from their own depravity. Even teachers and scholars tell nothing but lies, for they are equally at a loss. Life is a cheap spectacle, and human manners are hypocritical, feigned and laughable. The one feels splendid with his pompous boasts, unaware that the others are gawking at him like a chicken in a cage. The Sufis are like cows: all they think about is stuffing themselves – and yet their turbans make them look like pheasants! The great men are not great, the heroes have no guts, each astray on a different path – the faithful of the different religions, the philosophers, the nihilists, to say nothing of the blabbermouths. There is no one who does not ape someone else. Religious narrow-mindedness was declared the norm, hair-splitting was elevated to theology, and slyness was presented as logic. In short: things are not looking good. And the wanderer is in the midst of it all, swimming in this bubbling ocean called 'world' like all other humans, no better, cleverer or nobler than they, simply aware of a single fact: his irredeemable helplessness. It is also on their account that I mentioned Pascal:

> I know not who put me into the world, nor what the world is, nor what I myself am. I am in terrible ignorance of everything. I know not what my body is, nor my senses, nor my soul, nor even that part of me which thinks what I say, which reflects on all and on itself, and knows itself no more than the rest. I see those frightful spaces of the universe which surround me, and I find myself tied to one corner of this vast expanse, without knowing why I am put in this place rather than in another, nor why the short time which is given to me to live is assigned to me at this point rather than at another of the whole eternity which was before me or which shall come after me. I see nothing but infinites on all sides, which surround me as an atom, and as a shadow which endures only for an instant and returns no more. All I know is that I must soon die, but what I know least is this very death which I cannot escape.[3]

In Pascal's writing – partly conditioned by the fragmented structure of his *Pensées* – metaphysical disconsolacy repeatedly shines through, often only to be cloaked by Christian hope in the next paragraph. As Nietzsche recognized, Pascal was one of the first who 'sensed a piece of immorality in the *deus absconditus*', and only spoke so confidently of faith because he did not want to admit this feeling to himself – 'and thus, like one who is afraid, he talked as loudly as he could.'[4] With Attar, on the other hand, for all his piety, the consistent pessimism with which he views all being seems – at first glance – repeatedly to approach the metaphysically motivated atheist Arthur Schopenhauer, who saw the world as similarly depraved when he declared it the 'playground of tortured and anguish-ridden beings that endure only by eating one another. Therefore, every beast of prey is the living grave of thousands of others, and its self-maintenance is a chain of torturing deaths. Then in this world the capacity to feel pain increases with knowledge, and therefore reaches its highest degree in man, a degree that is the higher, the more intelligent the man.'[5] Attar shares with Schopenhauer the comprehensive, ever newly outraged character of his tirades, their shrill, unreserved, dogged and also witty nature. Yes, witty. Just like Schopenhauer, Attar noticeably enjoys spitting in the face of life, the enemy: once he has started, he cannot stop – here the spit, there a blow, and another and another, and take this kick too! By the end, every thought of redemption has been dispelled; and yet the story has hardly even begun.

It begins when the wanderer is visited by a *pir*, a Sufi master, 'one travelling at rest', as Attar calls him, who illuminates the earth like a sun, yet is himself shocked by his confusion. As is customary in the religious practices of Sufism, the *pir* in *The Book of Suffering* also emphasizes that no one should embark on an inward journey without the guidance of a leader. The wanderer learns that his suffering is what called – one is almost inclined to say spawned – his *pir*.

What need have you for medicine if you have no pain?
  What use is a command if you are not a slave?
As long as you do not burn with pain,
  The fire cannot illuminate you.
Let suffering be your elixir, go and find it,
  Surrender your soul in the hope of soul. (0, p. 63)

Finally the 'wanderer of thought' sets out to find salvation, hope or at least solace.

The wanderer, love his being, persistent his efforts,
  Burned with longing.
He shed the skin of this longing, this frenzy,
  He plunged naked into the sea,
Renounced all praise and lament,
  Took the path that has no end. (0, p. 64)

The wanderer sees a hundred thousand paths leading in all directions, a hundred thousand oceans of blood, stray worlds, a bulging cosmos in his breast. He passes a hundred thousand paradises and hells. No matter how often he knocks, no door opens. He grows lost and sinks to the ground; his body dies off. He wants to fly and cannot, he roams around, screams, runs, and exhausts himself. He stands still yet does not want to stay, and, when he goes on, he wants to retreat with every pore. Finally he loses his mind, and with it all knowledge. He speaks to pain, he caresses it, he submits to it. Pain becomes his belief and his unbelief. He gathers his remaining strength, rouses himself one last time, but still he cannot get any further. Once again he sees the world in blood and confusion, as a place of lamentation, not effort. There he grows quiet, gives up his will and finally sees his fetters removed. He stands up and reaches – 'exhausted to death like an ant' (1/0, p. 66) – the first stage of his journey.

There he finds the archangel Gabriel. The wanderer praises him before complaining that he is helpless, cast into the world without head or foot; he asks Gabriel if he knows of a cure for the pain. Gabriel, however, tells the wanderer that he is in a far worse state, and that he should not even approach him, for he cannot tell anyone of the terror (*heybat*) he faces, the terror of the one whose name he dare not utter.

'No one could bear to hear what I endure with every breath.'

Gabriel sends the wanderer away without an answer: 'Go now, our own pain is enough for us!' (1/0, p. 67).

At the end of the first chapter the wanderer returns to the *pir*, who briefly interprets his experiences and teaches the wanderer the peculiarities and merits of the one he has just visited. Gabriel, the wanderer learns, had to go a long way, had to wait seventy thousand years before he could even dare to address God – so how could the wanderer have the gall simply to speak of God as if there were nothing to it?

As in this chapter, the wanderer returns at the end of each subsequent one to the *pir*, who teaches him what his experiences mean and places the words he hears on his travels in their theological context. The function of the master can be understood first of all in a very practical sense, as *The Book of Suffering* retraces the course of a mystic's forty-day retreat in poetic images. For the meditator, a companion and guide is considered indispensable – even if he appears only as a vision, a dream, not a real person. At the same time, the figure of the *pir* in *The Book of Suffering* precisely confirms Gershom Scholem's observation that 'all mysticism has two fundamental, contradictory or complementary aspects: the one conservative, the other revolutionary.'[6] The mystic's quest takes place within a particular tradition and affirms its authority; at the same time, he transforms the meaning of that tradition in which his life is rooted: 'Recognition of the unaltered validity of the traditional authority is the price which these mystics pay for transforming the meanings of the texts in their exegesis.'[7]

Through his upbringing and training, the mystic is defined in a completely natural and unquestioned way by traditional views and symbols, and feels an affiliation with them; nonetheless, the Sufis, the Kabbalists, the Yogis – and also the Catholic mystics of the Middle Ages – were aware that mystic experience by its nature transgresses the canon of religious tenets, that it can even turn against this canon and replace it with a new one based on fresh, previously unimagined insights. This is one of the reasons why, in almost all mystical doctrines, the view developed that the searcher – as far as he may have progressed on the mystical path – nonetheless always requires a spiritual leader, a guru or *pir*. Aside from guidance and psychological support during the threshold experience of the mystical retreat, the *pir* represents religious authority in its traditional state: 'He moulds the mystic's interpretation of his experience, guiding it into channels that are acceptable to established authority.'[8]

It is primarily due to the instructions of the *pir* that a text such as *The Book of Suffering*, which blatantly contradicts the traditional understanding of Islam and the Koranic image of God in countless passages, was hardly ever perceived as heretical – in contrast to other Sufi texts, for example by al-Hallaj or Shehaboddin Sohrawardi. The boundary overstepped by al-Hallaj or Sohrawardi in their religious experience can be precisely defined in Scholem's terms: they not only reinterpreted religious authority, but also claimed the founding of a new authority, or even placed themselves above all authority as a law of their own. 'I am the truthful one', as al-Hallaj declared,[9] or 'I am greater', as Bayezid Bestami proclaimed upon hearing the prayer call *Allāhu akbar*, 'God is great'.[10] Attar, on the other hand, as revolutionary as his verses may seem, always clings to the principle of subordination, which balances out the rebellious aspect in keeping with traditional teachings.

The wanderer moves on to the angel Israfel, who kills humans with one blow of his trumpet and resurrects them with a second, and asks to be either resurrected or killed. But Israfel says that he himself awaits his fate with trembling, that he stands still with his trumpet at his lips and mourns every soul that he wipes out with his trumpet blow. He sends the wanderer away to continue his mourning undisturbed.

The remaining angels also turn the wanderer away. Michael, who holds the keys to the treasuries of the creation, uses meteorological phenomena to illustrate his distress: lightning is the convulsion of his pain-filled heart, the wind his sighing, and rain and snow are the angel's tears. Azra'il, the angel of death, whom the wanderer begs to take his life so that his heart can be revived, is in an even worse state. 'If you knew my pain, you would not ask such of me', answered the angel.

For a hundred thousand years I have pulled, day and night,
  The souls from their bodies, one after another.
For every soul I tear down,
  A wound in my own flesh opens up.
I have taken away so many that my heart
  Has emptied drop by drop, until nothing was left.
Who has been made to endure what I have endured?
  Many hundred worlds of blood guilt rest on my shoulders.
If you learned but one of my hundred fears
  You would immediately crumble into dust. (4/0, p. 88)

The wanderer, Azra'il mocks, should move on and continue his whining: 'You are not a man of the way.'

The angels that carry God's throne are no better off. On their shoulders they bear the overpowering burden, while beneath their feet lies the void. They should groan with effort, and their whole bodies should tremble with fear of no longer being able to carry the load. 'But', called out one of God's throne-bearers from his uncomfortable position, 'my standing is so insecure that if a single fibre of my body moved, I would fall into the depths' (5/0, p. 96).

The wanderer now leaves the angels and moves on to the throne, the sky of fixed stars, the heavenly table and the reed pen, but no one can help the wanderer; each figure he encounters is even more lost on a seemingly never-ending ladder of misfortune. Even paradise complains, as if it were the righteous who had gained admission to it! In truth, paradise – in its own view – is a vale of tears inhabited by simpletons. Its appearance is deceptive: 'You see the beauty of the candle, but what you don't see is the candle burning up in solitude' (10/0, p. 132).

And so it goes on and on: hell is weary of forever tormenting and burning humans, when it is itself consumed by fear that its fire will one day go out; the shining stars are revealed as glowing coals; and the sky wears the blue colour of sadness by day and hides in the black water by night. The sky is bloody like the dawn from all its searching; its robe is of black tar, its head is spinning, and it has no idea what to do. The sun is yellow with suffering and lovesickness. The moon, its face completely pockmarked from anguish and tears, thinks that the whole world ridicules it because it is so thin. Fire, which constantly carries ashes on its head; the wind, which strays about futilely in all the world's nooks and crannies; the water, which consists of nothing but tears and yearns for fire; the earth, which complains about the mould from all the dead unloaded into it; the mountain, which is ashamed to have a heart of stone and wants to run away but has its feet bound; the sea, which sweats with shame and suffers the greatest thirst of all; the Kaaba, which wears the black robe of mourning; the plants, which wilt every summer, so soon after they have finally blossomed in spring, and whose hope of enduring is thus dashed every summer; the different animals, Satan, spirits, humans – all of these respond to the wanderer's wretched, yet hopeful request with a heart-rending elegy on their own misery. Attar develops a cosmology of pain, as comprehensive as it is radical, in which all worldly and transcendent phenomena – much as in the Hebrew Bible or the Koran – are signs; not signs of God, however, signs of his compassion, but rather signs of despair, signs of God's abstinence and the painful nullity of the world's course, which permits being only amid fragmentation: 'Who gave us the sponge to wipe away the entire horizon?' asks Nietzsche:

> What were we doing when we unchained this earth from its sun? Where is it moving to now? Where are we moving to? Away from all suns? Are we not continually falling? And backwards, sidewards, forwards, in all directions? Is there still an up and a down? Aren't we straying as though through an infinite nothing? Isn't empty space breathing at us? Hasn't it got colder? Isn't night and more night coming again and again?[11]

Attar thus inverts the Koranic creation story in particular, in which God creates all life on earth, natural phenomena, and indeed history, human emotions and sensual pleasures so that they will testify to their creator: he preserves the sign character of creation, but the meaning he sees in these signs is negative.

In three darknesses, a seed without heart or religion,
  Pressed mud, dipped in brackish water,
He was struck this way and that like a ball in a game,
  So that he would learn confusion from the start.
Grown in blood, over nine months,
  His sustenance was the blood of the womb.
What happened to him there – better not to ask.
  I spoke to you of his body, his soul – better not to ask.
He tumbled headlong from his mother's lap,
  Only to land in blood again.
As his beginning was already in sewage,
  Do not bother to hope for purity.
A plaything, he grew fond of the blows from here and from there,
  Meaning: confusion became his nature.
Nine months he spent in his own blood,
  Meaning: devouring blood is the start of everything.
Thrown headlong into the world, drenched in blood,
  Meaning: it begins with separation, with reversal.
In tears, he then searched for the milk with his lips,
  Meaning: weep, for you belong to the species of mammals.
Clawed into the bosom, he saw nothing but blackness,
  Meaning: now live, bitterly and darkly.
As a child he ran, never lingered,
  Meaning: far from children is the peace of the soul.
In his youth he pined, so foreign did he feel,
  Meaning: youth is nothing but a wayward path.
Soon his mind became skewed from age,
  Meaning: expect no felicity from the foolish old man.
At a loss, he finally sank into his grave,
  Meaning: no trace of a pure soul did he ever find. (0, pp. 57f.)

The wanderer drags himself to the prophets, to Adam, Noah, Abraham, Moses, David and Jesus, but only Mohammed is able to give him a hint: he should look within himself, not in the world. The wanderer now travels through his self and reaches – via the stages of sensory perception, imagination, reason and emotion – his soul, which informs him that he has traversed the cosmos in vain, only to reach the shore of its ocean at last.

'What you have sought is within you', speaks the soul, and instructs the wanderer to sink into its ocean.

'O soul, if you were everything, why did you let me wander so far first?' asks the wanderer, and the soul replies:

'So that you would recognize my worth. Your search', the soul continues, 'was a search for yourself.'

The tale ends with the wanderer sinking into the ocean of his own soul. Up to this point the journey was to God, the poet tells us at the end; now begins the journey in God.

This is the frame story of Attar's great verse epic. Clearly it takes up the notion of *šafā'a*, the 'intercession' of the prophets, in particular Mohammed. According to one *hadith* [reported statement or deed of Mohammed], the souls seek out the prophets in heaven on the Day of Judgement and ask them to intercede on their behalf with the Lord so that he will not damn them. The structure of the *hadith* is similar to that of *The Book of Suffering*: each section begins with the supplicants praising the respective prophet. The prophets disappoint them with the response that they themselves are in need and fear the wrath of the Lord. Only upon asking Mohammed do the believers find help: he intercedes for them with the Lord, and the Lord accepts the intercession.[12]

The *hadith* on intercession would have been only one of many literary sources Attar used for his poetic journey through the cosmos, however: the soul flying through heaven and hell – foreshadowed in the didactic poem 'On Nature' by Parmenides (c.500 BC), the 'True Stories' of Lucian of Samosata (d. late second century AD) and the myths of the soul in Plato's (d. 347 BC) *Phaedo* – is one of the most important and fascinating topoi in the literatures of the Orient. Merkabah mysticism, which developed among the Jews of Palestine between the third and fifth centuries, describes the ascent of the soul, which leaves earth and travels through the different spheres before reaching its home in God's light-world.[13] In Islamic tradition, the topos of the heavenly journey continues with Mohammed's Koranic nocturnal voyage (*mi'rāğ*), which is described in the anonymous *The Book of Ascension* (*Kitāb al-Mi'rāğ*) together with its folkloristic additions.[14] Aside from Bayezid's aforementioned vision, we should also mention al-Ma'arri's finally translated journey to the beyond from the 'Epistle on Forgiveness', Avicenna's philosophical treatise 'Salaman and Absal' and his story 'Hayy ibn Yaqzan',[15] which returns in Hebrew in the work of Abraham ibn Ezra (d. 1167) as 'Hayy ben Meqis', and Ibn Arabi's (d. 1240) *The Book of the Night Journey* (*Kitāb al-isrā'*), as well as *The Conference of the Birds* in its different variations. European literature takes up the notion of a cosmic journey of the soul with Dante's (d. 1321) *Divine Comedy*. It later appears in Milton's (d. 1674) *Paradise Lost*, in Johann Amos Comenius's (d. 1670) *Labyrinth of the World and the Paradise of the Heart* from the seventeenth century, in Henry Fielding's (d. 1754) *Journey from This World to the Next*, in Goethe's *Faust II*, or also in Thomas Mann's description of Joseph's ascension to heaven or Gerhart Hauptmann's *The Great Dream*. The fairytale in Georg Büchner's *Woyzeck* about the poor child with no father or mother almost reads like a miniature version of Attar's *The Book of Suffering*:

> And seeing there was nobody left on earth, he wanted to go up to heaven, and the moon gave him such a friendly look, and when in the end he came to the moon he found, it was a lump of rotten wood, so he went to the sun, and when he came to the sun, it was a withered sunflower, and when he came to the stars, they were tiny golden insects stuck there as though by a butcher-bird on a blackthorn, and when he wanted to come back to earth again, the earth was an upturned cooking pot, and he was all alone, so he sat down and cried, and he's sitting there still, all on his own.[16]

The paths taken by this topos, which has thus also been very fruitful for European literature, have meanwhile been at least partly revealed; nonetheless, some Romance scholars have reacted sceptically to research on the Arab origins of Dante's *Divine Comedy* – sceptically, and often enough even with the blatant wilful ignorance of those who refuse to believe what they do not want to be true. In the key text for Europe's attainment of identity, Arab-Islamic culture could not appear as more than a footnote – let alone a central element. It is likely that Dante not only knew the Islamic *The Book of Ascension*, which was translated into Old Spanish by the Jewish doctor Abraham al-Faquim (d. 1284), then from this version into Latin and French by Bonaventura de Siena (with the title *Libre della scala*), but in fact used it as a model when he wrote *The Divine Comedy* (which did not prevent him from assigning Mohammed a place in hell). Another source he may have drawn on is the aforementioned Hebrew version of Avicenna's 'Hayy ibn Yaqzan'.[17] But the question of whether Dante had translations of these, and, if so, which ones, is not the decisive one. Reception processes between cultures cannot be limited to the reading of texts. Even if none of the translations circulating at the time had ever reached him,

Dante and his contemporaries were influenced by Arab culture, in which themes and ideas of heavenly journeys were widespread.

Even though Dante is unlikely ever to have heard of Attar, then, the many similarities between his *Divine Comedy* and *The Book of Suffering*, or also al-Ma'ari's 'Epistle', are not coincidental, as all three refer to the same literary topos and partly even the same sources. Just as Attar reinterpreted the heavenly journey in Sufi terms, Dante reworked the Islamic original into a Christian version, even its minor details. In its Eastern elements, Dante's work is more than a simple adaptation; *The Divine Comedy* can almost be read as a reaction to those elements of Arab culture whose influence Dante considered especially dangerous: the heresy of Averroism and the poetry of overly self-centred love. In many parts, Dante's heavenly journey reads like a veritable anti-*mi'rāǧ* intended to demonstrate the erroneous nature of Islam and the superiority of the Christian faith. Thus Dante's *Divine Comedy*, perhaps more than any other text, exemplifies both the absorption of Arab-influenced culture in Europe and the reaction against it.[18] It is precisely the comparison with *The Divine Comedy*, however, that makes the immense range of themes in *The Book of Suffering*, the refinement of its poetic structure, Attar's radical negation of all existing earthly things and theological promises, and his humanistic breadth all the more surprisingly apparent. After one has discovered his precursor, Dante seems veritably sanctimonious.

The entwined motivic chains that run through Attar's poetry are manifold. Many would deserve an examination of their own, for *The Book of Suffering* not only develops a cosmology of pain but is itself a cosmos of themes, intellectual positions and ideas. It not only laments the terror of God but at once also praises His infinity, splendour and greatness – just as *The Book of Suffering* in general places completely different, partly conflicting motifs alongside one another. It would be wrong to combine them in a synthesis: the statements are true in their respective poetic contexts; this too shows that Attar is a poet at heart, not a theorist. It is precisely this inner disparity within a uniform, closed outer form that is one of the fundamental characteristics of Attar's three great epics, and it results not least from the alternation between the ongoing frame story and the individual tales.

Weaving differently coloured threads into a main narrative is a fundamental strategy in Eastern literature, and its origin remains apparent when it returns in European literature – in *Don Quixote*, *The Divine Comedy*, *The Decameron* and also the Alice books of Lewis Carroll (d. 1898). 'One can create a peculiar effect by using stories contained within other stories, almost a sense of infinity, with a vertiginous quality', said Jorge Luis Borges in a lecture on *The Arabian Nights*, in which he went on to list Western authors who had 'imitated' the Arab principle.[19] This is also evident in the narratives of the Koran. In particular a number of longer Surahs – the Joseph Surah, as well as the Surah 'The Poet' – leave their story for several verses, take the preceding tale to a different, usually didactic level or change to some other, seemingly unrelated motif, branch off, and shortly afterwards glide back into the main thread of the recitation. One can observe this narrative principle even more clearly in the Jewish midrashim, where every passage interpreted is surrounded by numerous stories. This phenomenon is thus widespread in Middle Eastern culture as a whole, beyond the boundaries of the literary realm.

In Persian prose, the form of the frame story established itself through *Kalila and Dimna*, the translation of *Pančatantra*, the Indian mirror for princes – also in the *Sendbădnāmeh*, the tale of the wise teacher of princes Sinbad, in the *Mārzbădnāmeh*, the story of the seven viziers or masters and, finally, albeit quite statically in formal terms, in the *Arabian Nights*. This poetic structure was brought to fruition by Attar. In his three great verse epics, the frame story consists of an ongoing, dynamically developing narrative that is far more than the ring holding together a colourful bouquet of stories. Each individual tale refers to the point in the frame story at which it is told, varying, commenting on or even contradicting its motif. As the inserts always correspond to the frame story, but also often consist of tiny episodes, sometimes a mere three or four lines long, which Attar takes the liberty of sprinkling in unexpected places, his approach in these compositions is both strictly formal and dynamic. This results in complex, seemingly organically developed narrative webs in which every cell is woven together with the next – and yet can still breathe for itself. Different or openly conflicting interpretations of a single motif are nothing unusual here. The piety and praise of God in certain passages do not dilute the effect of the many lamentations and accusations, and vice versa.

In concentrating on the rebellious aspect of *The Book of Suffering*, I am inevitably guilty of a certain one-sidedness. On the other hand, I feel that Attar's text itself strongly justifies this emphasis; for, despite some brighter moments and didactic passages, it is ultimately dominated by blackness. What Scholem termed the conservative aspect of mysticism, which almost always accompanies the revolutionary, is – in contrast to Attar's other epics – presented in an almost careless fashion here. Take the answers given by the *pir*: they almost always seem bland and half-hearted, especially considering the highly dramatic descriptions of misfortune to which they react. Hardly any of the *pir*'s metaphors or turns of phrase are striking enough to remain in the memory. While his God-pleasing, preaching tone may serve to make the horrors which Attar uses to question God's reason and justice seem more bearable, his interjections are simultaneously too brief and generalized to cover up the theological insubordination of the complaints. Attar is concerned not with the guide's answers, but with the wanderer's ever-new questions, which are perhaps always triggered by the *pir*'s answers precisely because those answers prove so inadequate. Attar places the full emphasis of his poetic imagination on the wanderer's confusion and the harrowing views that confront him in the course of his journey. His spiritual journey is a trip on a ghost train: there are straight stretches that let him catch his breath, but behind every corner lurks some new misfortune. I am not, therefore, pursuing some secondary aspect in seeking to highlight the extreme desperation in *The Book of Suffering*, that state in which humans turn against their creator. The reader should not be deceived by the seemingly reconciliatory ending: Attar's fundamental concern is the pain of existence, which makes nothingness seem so tempting. His book is indeed a 'book of suffering', as its title states. In its narrative, the God who is 'closer to man than his jugular vein' is distant. He exists, but He is distant. At best.

The shift to the utopian

Upon reading the final chapter, one may gain the initial impression that the negativity of the preceding account has happily disappeared, the suffering has been justified, and the poet's reputation of piety has been restored; one may feel relief because the wanderer ultimately finds his own soul. At the very least, it is surprising to read the fortieth chapter; one can hardly reconcile it with the other thirty-nine. The poet seems to have turned everything he said before on its head (or its feet, if viewed from the orthodox perspective) with one fell swoop. At the same time, however, this resolution seems strangely forced; the language itself takes on a hymnal tone that seems too shrill for the happy end of a sad story, the telos to which the other thirty-nine chapters have been leading. Rather, when reading it for the first time, one cannot help but feel that Attar ended his work in this conciliatory fashion for transparent reasons – in order to conceal its provocation. This impression is deceptive, however.

As soon as one reads on, it becomes clear that the fortieth chapter does not erase the despair of the previous thirty-nine, and that the ostensibly hopeful ending does not light the darkness of the world. With this, the suspicion of apologia also disappears. The book contains a long epilogue in which the poet, still interrupted by other stories, speaks about himself and his work. As was the custom among poets at the time, he begins by praising himself and notes that he does not write for the general public, least of all in this book. The praise of a few astute readers means more to him than the approval of the masses. To illustrate his point, Attar relates an anecdote about Plato in which the philosopher bursts into tears upon hearing that a certain man has praised him.

'Why are you not happy?' asks the confused messenger, and Plato answers that unfortunately, this praise has come from a fool.

'If I only knew how I had pleased him, I would turn away from it' (E3, p. 369).

Attar continues that it would have been better for him not to say the things he has said in the book; for it is impossible to express them in words – already with Attar, one is to remain silent about what one cannot put into words, and thus the poet views his entire work as a wasted effort:

> Oh woe, oh woe! Every single thing I wrote meant nothing,
> My eye blind, all paths entangled. (E3, p. 369)

There follow tales and sayings in verbose praise of silence: to speak wisely, Attar quotes one pious man, demands great wisdom; but, for a wise man to be silent, his wisdom would have to be immeasurable. Plato reached the highest level of perfection when he replied to Alexander's (d. 323 BC) request for advice with silence, and Aristotle (d. 322 BC), when asked what innocent person deserved to be imprisoned, responded: the one imprisoned by teeth – namely the tongue. Up to that point, the final section had remained within the boundaries of convention; the fortieth chapter is convincing. But then, all of a sudden, comes this outburst from the poet. He writes – no, he practically screams – that he is unable to contain himself because love has made him drunk, consumed by longing and miserable. Perhaps God wanted his soul to be calm so that he could finally remain silent for ever – but he cannot, for Attar is not among God's initiates, the saints, the knowers of secrets (those who can hope, like the 'wanderer of thought', to reach the fortieth stage of immersion). He simply cannot keep quiet, the poet tells us, for the pain squeezes the verses out of his fingers. And so Attar, to the bafflement of the reader, now turns his back on the praise of silence he presented a moment earlier:

> Henceforth I shall speak without reservation.
> The grave will give me ample opportunity for silence. (E10, p. 372)

Then Attar speaks of his imminent death, and asks the reader to visit his grave and cry for him:

> There I speak to you with an ecstatic tongue,
> There you must go deaf to hear the voice of the mute.
> Will you feel my thirst when I lie buried?
> Give me water, just one drop from the purest tear.
> Oh, if only I had never been born, oh woe! And were nameless!
> And had never been drawn into this tumult here!
> Whoever had to face what lies before me
> Would surely weep blood, even with a hundred hearts.
> All souls together, the most rebellious from a hundred worlds:
> Before the grave they must all despair and lay down their weapons.
> (E10, p. 373)

The final stories are characterized by this mood: no prospect of salvation, no hope of mercy. Thus Attar does not revise the end of the frame story at all – but the epilogue shifts it to the utopian level. There could be fulfilment, redemption, happiness, or whatever one wishes to call it (Attar does not name it); *The Book of Suffering* still clings to this possibility. One could sink into the ocean of the soul – it does exist – and yet the poet will never reach its shores; nor will any ordinary person in this life, let alone in death. So where will he end? The space between life and death is precisely the same size as in the great aesthetic projects of modernity: the fiction of Kafka (d. 1924) and Pessoa (d. 1935) and the philosophy of Adorno and Benjamin (d. 1940). Max Horkheimer formulates a specifically modern idea of aesthetics that is very apparent in *The Book of Suffering*: 'Without thinking of truth, and hence what it guarantees, there can be no knowledge of its opposite – human forlornness.'[20] The stories of Sadeq Hedayat, to name a modern Iranian author, also contain the figure I mean, which constantly recurs in twentieth-century writing: holding on to the fundamental possibility of redemption, but only as a lacuna – as the 'other' of the present state. The long trek across the expanses of the soul undertaken by Hedayat in *The Blind Owl* has something of the mystic's forty-day inward journey, which, as in Attar, turns out to be a horrific trip. And yet both utter the 'dream of another world in which things are different',[21] as Adorno fundamentally claims of the poem as such. Where he insists on that minimum promise of happiness 'that does not sell out to any consolation',[22] Hedayat equally refuses to give up the utopian in art, writing in a programmatic essay: 'But as complete as the catastrophe may be, there still remains a small opening, and it is not clear whether hope is still left inside it, or has rather disappeared forever.'[23]

Hedayat insists that an other could exist, but offers neither the comfort that it truly exists nor any information about its possible nature. At the same time, however, he knows that art would disappear without the hope of an other. There is no more hope than this in *The Book of Suffering*. Attar does not consign redemption to the hereafter; on the contrary, he expects even worse torment in death. He merely states that we can find ourselves within ourselves; there we would be in equilibrium with ourselves and find peace of mind. What 'finding ourselves' means remains a mystery, however, as Attar describes only the journey *to* the soul, not the journey *within* the soul. The *hadith* of intercession referred to in the fame story is reinterpreted at the decisive point; for Attar lets Mohammed bring not a solution, but simply the instruction to look within oneself rather than in the world. Attar thus remains adamant about the fundamental possibility of redemption, but refrains completely from hinting at how this bliss might look or feel, or of what it might consist. But this is not all that remains uncertain; for, at the end of the book, he clearly rules out the possibility that he and all ordinary people might experience the joy of self-discovery – no differently to the way he did at the beginning.

Everything is one, but I do not know it.
If there is a way – I have not found it.
The longer man walks, the more distant his goal becomes,
He is lost, and grows more so by the hour.
The path must be taken beyond eternity,
And mankind must wade through blood. (0, p. 9)

The shift to the utopian that concludes the mystic's inward journey occurs precisely through this twofold paradox: holding on to the idea of reconciliation, but a) not naming it for its own sake and b) practically excluding its fulfilment in real history by reserving it for the saints. The almost unpleasantly garish, or at least hardly comforting, lightening in the fortieth chapter can perhaps be better understood in its peculiarity, but also its modernity, in the light of Adorno's reflections on Gustav Mahler (d. 1911). The affirmatory finales of Mahler's desolate, pain-ridden symphonies make a similarly alien, inappropriate impression to the resolution of *The Book of Suffering*. Like Attar in *The Book of Suffering*, Mahler was 'a poor yea-sayer', as Adorno observed. 'His vainly jubilant movements unmask jubilation, his subjective incapacity for the happy end denounces itself.'[24] Reconciliation itself has not been abandoned, but the hope of attaining it has; this marks the shift to modernity, the contrast to Beethoven. Yes, there is a door, and who knows what lies behind it; but 'we all remain outside like the knocker at the door', as Attar writes elsewhere, in *The Book of Secrets*[25] – already six hundred years after Mohammed, but only eight hundred years before Kafka, as Ulrich Holbein, appropriately modifying the perspective, points out.[26] *The Book of Suffering* is by no means the only work in which the opening sought by Attar remains closed in real terms. Though *The Conference of the Birds* spreads more optimism on the whole, it reaches the same sobering conclusion:

Life has been no use to me.
   Vain all my work and words.
No one helps me, nowhere a friend.
   Life wasted, not one success.
When I still could, I knew not what for,
   And once I knew, I no longer could,
Now I know of no other way,
   Know only helplessness and misery.[27]

Thus the epilogue of *The Conference of the Birds* continues, with stories and statements from Attar himself, no less bitterly than in *The Book of Suffering*:

I know not to whom I belong,
   Where I am, or who.
Sick in my body, without luck, with empty hands,
   Without possessions, without peace, without heart,
I spent a life in my liver's blood,
   A life that had no use.
All action was punishment for me.
   Now my soul longs to escape.
My heart has slipped through my fingers, my faith is lost.
   Left with neither my exterior nor what lies within it.
I am neither heretic nor Muslim.
   Stand confused between the two.
Neither heretic nor Muslim, whatever shall I do?
   Lost, beset, whatever shall I do?[28]

And the earliest of Attar's three epics, *The Book of God*, ends equally gloomily:

I have nothing in this world but fear of death,
   Am the interpreter of my own pain.
No well-being have I seen in my life,
   Have known much harm, but little use.
My life could only bring me joy
   If I were finally allowed to end it.[29]

Attar then tells the following story: a poor vagabond begs a shop-owner for alms. The shop-owner turns out to be a sadist: 'I won't give you anything until you wound yourself. If you do that, you can ask me for money.'

At this, the beggar shows his naked body and speaks: 'Look at this! If you can find a single unharmed spot on my body, then show me so that I can strike a wound; for I know no part of it, from head to toe, that does not have a hundred wounds! So go ahead and cough up.'[30]

'I am', Attar continues, 'like that beggar; there is no part of my body without a hundred wounds.'

The idea of fulfilment, then, is melted down to the smallest possible residue not only in *The Book of Suffering*, but also in the epilogues (if not earlier) of his other epics. There has to be something else – for consciousness, as Adorno writes, 'could not even despair over the grey, did it not harbour the notion of a different colour, whose dispersed traces are not absent in the negative whole.'[31] The people in Attar's world have a notion of bliss; they know where it would be, namely in God, which means in ourselves. But they do not find happiness – they simply keep rebounding off the rocks of fate, or, to take an image from *The Book of Suffering*, are like the thread that will not go through the needle's eye. The eye is there, it would be a perfect fit – but the thread simply refuses to go in; it slides off, it frays, and the more impetuously the thread assails the eye, the more rapidly it falls apart (0, p. 10).

A princess spills a sack of millet and tells her suitor to pick up each individual grain with a needle. From that point, the poor man spends the rest of his life crawling along the ground, without managing to stick his needle into a single grain (12/6, p. 152).

God exists; but he cannot be found. A man meets a madman lying in blood and dust, confused and distraught.

'You miserable fool, what are you doing here all day and night?'

'I search for God day and night.'

'I am also in search of God.'

'Then do as I have done: sit down in a pool of blood for fifty years. Drink it, the blood, and when you have drunk it, pass me the cup so that I can drink too, until the sea – or if not the sea, then at least our actions – dwindle away.'

> You will never unravel the knot,
> No sense in life or in death.
> I only know that because I turn, turn, turn so much
> That I know nothing, know nothing, know nothing and nothing. (11/2, p. 150)

Someone who goes on a pilgrimage wanders halfway across the world to the Kaaba – simply to walk around in circles once he is there (12/4, p. 151). Household remedies are no more effective as a cure for confusion: a farmer ties a pumpkin to his leg for fear of getting lost in his sleep. A joker comes along, pilfers the pumpkin and ties it to his own leg. The farmer then wakes up, and does not know whether he is himself or the other (23/4).

Foam here, foam there, and you? Merely a bubble.
Not enough dignity for you? Do you think one can have any more?
At the end you're told: 'Go', without an idea
Of what was, what is, and what will be.
At the start you don't know what was there before.
When it stops, you don't know what lies ahead.
I am between this one and that, neither that one nor this one,
With no idea of body or soul, neither the one nor the other.
A heretic by nature, my faith weak,
My urges triumphant, my desires strong, my heart fragile.
Whatever shall I do? Whatever shall I do? I have searched for so long.
I was already confused, now I am in love too.
I stand helpless in time, yearning without hope,
Jealous even of an ant's wings.
Not knowing where this comes from, where it is going, or what it is.
Poor is my mind, my soul overflowing with love.
Have known nothing since the time I began knowing,
And even if I knew everything, I would still know nothing.
My knowledge is nothing but ignorance itself,
And my ignorance nothing but confusion,
My mad straying has numbed me,
And my numbness has become death. (17/6, p. 186)

Even animals are not exempt from the 'truth', which Schopenhauer sums up in a nutshell: 'we ought to be wretched, and are so.'[32] Since falling in love with Solomon, the restless woodpecker has been striking the trees with his beak day and night, regardless of whether the wood is soft or hard. For Solomon has promised to hear him if he brings him a wood that is neither dry nor moist, and neither straight nor bent. Like the woodpecker, the people also go in search of a non-existent wood.

Stop looking for this wood,
Give up the search.
There will never be any such wood,
So content yourself with its name. (12/5, p. 152)

There is no sense in life. What remains is that last 'gossamer thread of consolation' which Nietzsche later discovered in Schopenhauer, who had stated that 'the meaning of the whole of history is understanding its own meaninglessness'.[33]

'What makes people unhappy is looking for the reason', says a fool merrily: 'I, on the other hand, am happier in the world of unreason. I have been brought here on the path of unreason, and have been granted happiness through my insanity. Whoever falls into the unreason of the truthful will forever partake in the joy of the absolute' (8/2, p. 119).

Blessed are the resigned, the insane: a fool smashes all the windows of a glass shop in Baghdad with relish, enjoying the racket. People come and confront him with the damage he has caused the owner.

'It was just fun to hear all the smashing and rattling', answers the fool: 'And I did it because it was fun. The harm or use of an action no longer means anything to me' (8/4, p. 120).

Happiness suddenly appears where all hope is lost: a murderer is sentenced to death. On the way to his execution he is in the best of spirits.

'How can you be so cheerful when you are about to die?'

'If fate has left me such a short time to live, it would be foolish to spend it in sadness' (16/4, p. 177).

And even if the heavens fall to earth
  Be sure to remain cheerful. (8/3, p. 120)

A fool is known as 'Beautiful' (*ḫoš*) because his only response to whatever he sees and experiences is 'Beautiful, beautiful'. Even when his house collapses, killing his wife and children, he says, 'Beautiful, beautiful', because he saw everything preordained by God (8/3, pp. 119f.).

But such equanimity, which is more familiar from the work of Omar Khayyam, can only be attained by the mad. The rest cannot stop asking questions:

Whatever you are looking for, you will never find it,
  Much less ever stop searching. (12/4, p. 151)

Attar compares himself to a dog that finds a moon-shaped piece of cake and simultaneously discovers the cake-shaped moon. The dog discards the cake and tries to catch the moon. Having failed at this it runs back, but the cake is already gone, so it chases the moon again and ends up with nothing, wandering back and forth between the vanished cake and the unattainable moon (12/9, p. 154). In a different episode, Attar imagines us as beings suspended head-down over a cistern like the fallen angels Harut and Marut. It is terribly hot, and they are so thirsty that they are sure they will die of yearning for a drop of water. But they do not die. The water flows, fresh and clear, a finger's breadth below their outstretched tongues. They cannot stretch their tongues out any further, nor does the water rise even a centimetre. If their thirst had a value of 1, the poet tells us, the sight, sound and smell of the nearby water would increase it one hundred thousandfold (5/3, pp. 97f.).

A document of its time

The notion that the possibility of a different world exists in order for us to despair at existence is a recurring motif in the twentieth century, and also appears in the work of Hedayat, who wrote about Kafka's stories: 'Their movement has the goal of ultimate defeat, and it is frightful how they torture hope – not by condemning hope but, on the contrary, because they cannot condemn hope.'[34] This idea is substantiated in analytically and morally exemplary fashion in Adorno's philosophy, which absorbs the dark regions of the twentieth century like no other and rejects all shades of positive historical dialectic. There is no need to invoke superlatives of historical catastrophe to underpin the suspicion that Attar's apocalyptic terror and refusal to acknowledge any sense in life were also based on real events. One need only look at his time: *The Book of Suffering* must have been written before the Mongol invasion of Persia. The omens of their rampage, which would sweep away centuries-old kingdoms, depopulate entire cities and probably also cost the aged poet his life, would already have been visible – especially in the north-eastern province of Khorasan, whose most important city at the time was Attar's home. It may have been that news of the approaching troops (historians today estimate between 150,000 and 200,000 riders, each with several horses)[35] had reached Nishapur, or simply that Attar's environment, its social, intellectual and political structures, was already in the state of dissolution that enables such a rapid and comprehensive defeat in the first place. Muslim historians, at any rate, interpreted the Mongol invasion not as one disaster among many, but as a punishment from God for a society that had become decadent and sinful – of a magnitude which the world, according to the great historiographer Ibn al-Athir (d. 1233), 'has not seen witnessed since its creation and will not witness again, except perhaps for the destruction of Gog and Magog.'[36] Those historians would certainly have found much to support their diagnosis of the time in Attar's descriptions.

Though *The Book of Suffering* is a Sufi work in which even an anecdote about a roadsweeper is to be taken as an allegory of mystical experience, that anecdote is at once about a roadsweeper, a ruler, an obstinate legal scholar or a simple mother – people like those who lived in Attar's time. This is one difference between Attar's verses and those of Rumi: the poet Attar, who expressly laments his own down-to-earthness, does not operate in the vacuum of the pure spirit; in his verse epics one feels the sharp air of earthly conditions, of social and religious reality. Attar's depictions of poverty or the wilfulness of officials, his anger at the simple-mindedness of theologians, his advocacy of religious tolerance and his mockery of rich men and rulers – they are simultaneously concrete and allegorical. Attar wittily attacks the ministers and bureaucrats, naturally also the brutal tax-collectors, but above all the rulers: 'I know of no other Islamic writings in which social criticism of the rulers is expressed with such severity', observed Hellmut Ritter.[37] Whenever rulers appear in *The Book of Suffering*, they are moody, jealous, violent and unjust. They live off the blood of the poor, and the ministries stink of blood. Here it is fitting that the Persian word for authorities or government, *divān*, is perfectly suited to puns with *divāneh* ('mad'). This results in everyday sighs of exasperation that are completely unmystical, but timelessly true:

When I think of the authorities,
  I lose my mind. (13/2, p. 172)

With their hasty execution orders, pointless campaigns and wilful decisions, Attar's rulers constitute a threat to all decent people. They steal their money and claim it is theirs: an old man finds a coin on the street, already black and worthless from age and wear, and wants to give it to the neediest person. He looks everywhere, then finally requests an audience with the king and gives him the coin. The king grows angry: 'Do I need a coin like that?'

'You must be the most needy of all people', answers the old man, 'for there is not a single mosque or market without someone demanding money for you. There is not a pore in your body that does not desire something. You beg at every door – and why? Simply so that you can play the king for a while' (7/7, p. 115).

Attar was proud of never having prostituted himself as a court poet, unlike most of his poet colleagues in the region – but also unlike his precursor and probable model Sana'i, whose Divan contains many songs in praise of princes and religious dignitaries. Attar even criticized the great Ferdowsi because he had accepted money from Sultan Mahmoud of Ghazna for his *Book of Kings* (*Šāhnāmeh*) (E1, p. 367).[38] A ruler has food served to Bohlul, the most famous holy fool in Islamic culture. He throws it to the dogs.

'No one has ever done that!' say the people around him, angered by Bohlul's insolence: 'Don't you know what shah you are dealing with?'

'Shut up!' reprimands Bohlul: 'If the dogs hear where their food has come from, no amount of beating will make them touch it' (7/5, p. 114).

On another occasion, Bohlul – taking an inconspicuous leap of two hundred years back in time – goes to Haroun ar-Rashid (d. 809) and sits down unabashedly on his throne. Immediately the guards pounce on him and beat him bloody.

'I only sat here for a moment and I was already beaten bloody', Bohlul calls out to the caliph: 'You, who have sat on this throne your whole life, will have every bone in your body broken' (7/10, p. 117).

Attar grew up among the Seljuqs, whose rule had become distanced both from the old Arab tribal system with its many leaders and from early Islamic theocracy, in which the four 'righteous caliphs' (*al-ḫulafā' ar-rāšidūn*) also acted as theological governors. In the twelfth century, the caliphate in Baghdad maintained the religious character of its rule over the Muslim community only as a formality; the real power had long since been transferred to secular authorities, which often no longer even pretended to justify their actions theologically. Hence the doctrine of rule developed in his mirror for princes (*Siyāsatnāma*) by the famous Seljuq vizier Nezamolmok (murdered 1092) mentions peace, justice and welfare a great deal, but hardly ever touches on the caliphate or the religious ramifications of political office. Instead, the vizier refers in passing to the divine intervention that enables an aspirant to defeat his rival.[39] By posing as guardians of the Sunna, the Seljuqs appeared with a theological mission, but its ultimate aim was in fact to defend the secularity of power against the theocratic demands of the Ismailite Shia. In the latter period of their rule, which Attar experienced, the Seljuqs were in any case occupied more with infighting than with spiritual demands; in the end, their power crumbled, and local princes, bandits or warlords were free to oppress the ordinary people. It is hardly surprising, then, that many believers viewed their rulers with reservation, if not express hostility. Attar normally voices criticism without naming the ruler in question, or he falls back on historical figures such as Alexander the Great, Haroun ar-Rashid or Mahmoud of Ghazna. Occasionally, however – and more often in *The Book of Suffering* than his other epics – he does name the last great Seljuq ruler of Iran, Sultan Sanjar ebn-e Malekshah (d. 1157). An ascetic inveighs against him:

You ransack the houses, even rummage through the cellars,
  Simply to gild your horses' bridle.
You spill the blood of so many, and for what?
  For feasts, and God-forbidden ones to boot.
You rob even the poorest of their wheat,
  The greediest of all beggars – that is who you are. (7/6, p. 115)

In *The Book of Suffering*, the great Sufi Ruknoddin Akkaf even declares it a duty to pay the poor tax to the sultan, as none of his goods belong to him: 'Everything you own belongs to those from whom you stole it' (7/7, p. 115). Apart from the four 'righteous caliphs', only the pre-Islamic Sassanid kings led by Anushirvan are shown in a positive light; Sultan Mahmoud's epithets vary. One also finds a more congenial counter-figure to the later sultans in Attar's depiction of the early Seljuq Grand Vizier, Nezalmolmolk. As a political philosopher, he was interested in more than simply power and wealth. One should probably also read Attar's occasional admonishments to be tolerant towards Shiites, and not to force them to convert to Sunni Islam, against the background of anti-Shiite propaganda (0, pp. 38ff.).[40] Although he disagreed with their convictions, Attar again takes up a mediating position: in the foreword, he not only praises the virtues of the Prophet and the four first, in Sunni opinion, 'righteous' caliphs, but also pays tribute to the Shiite imams Hassan and Hossein.

A citizen of Kufa (a Shiite) is asked which Islamic confession he belongs to and which rites he practises.

'Does one ask such things, you horrible fellow?' (0, p. 41).

As is the case in this tiny story, Attar rails against inquisition, coercion and religious dogmatism (*ta'aṣṣob*) throughout the book. Instead of welcoming the diverse forms of faith, this mentality will accept only one form of belief – its own. I assume Attar had the violent confrontations between Hanafites and Shafiites in mind, which escalated repeatedly in Nishapur during the second half of the twelfth century and resulted in the destruction of many of the city's mosques and places of learning. In the foreword, Attar spends an entire chapter directly addressing *ta'aṣṣob*. Alluding to the *hadith* of the seventy-three confessions[41] into which Mohammed's community will supposedly be divided, he states in the opening passage:

> Without you, seven hundred confessions would be at peace,
> Because of you, the seventy-two are already at war.
> There are countless religions, paths and peoples.
> Your lifetime is too short to count them all.
> Even if you do not befriend every one,
> Refrain from drawing your sword against them.
> You are just one, try to understand their perspective,
> So that each can live in harmony with the other. (0, pp. 37f.)

One can generally say that religious dignitaries, with their hypocrisy and stubborn religious mindset, are not well-loved figures in *The Book of Suffering*: Sana'i sees a lavatory attendant and a muezzin doing their jobs.

'There is no difference between the two', Attar makes his predecessor say. 'The one is as unknowing as the other, and both work for their daily bread. But no', Sana'i corrects himself in the next moment: 'the lavatory attendant is probably better than the man from the mosque after all; at least he does real work and is an honourable man, whereas this hypocrite simply dazzles people with the veneer of his office' (25/5, p. 240).

Attar does not like the mullahs. He demands that they keep away from the royal courts and live in poverty, with the common people. They must give up their bigotry and stop preaching narrow-mindedness. Instead of limiting religion to laws, they should set an example of compassion and love.

You have castles like those of kings,
  You live like Khosrow, not in the poverty of Ali.
You have prettier robes than the ladies,
  Ride on horses like those in Qarun's stable.
Your faces are darkened and grim,
  Your characters and ways are devilish in nature.
Bound to Pharaonic customs,
  The mourning rites of those who worship the flames.
Your qualities are worthy of King Shaddad,
  Megalomania, greed, and lust for popularity.
All these are your attributes, and there are still worse,
  Only one is alien to you: the faith of Mohammed.
You are captives to custom, dignity and office, by day or by night,
  There is only one thing you lack: the faith of Mohammed. (38/7, p. 343)

This hardly reads like a text written nine hundred years ago – let alone by an Iranian. 'Attar's tolerance', noted the recently departed Tehran literary scholar Abdolhasan Zarin-Kub, 'testifies to a breadth of thought that surpasses his own century, but also ours – who can dispute that today?'[42] The stories with which Zarin-Kub accused his own time, his own state, are spread evenly throughout all of Attar's epics. They also make two things clear, however: firstly, his defence of those who followed different faiths should not be mistaken for a modern ideal of religious tolerance, not even the religious universalism of some other mystics. Unbelievers remained unbelievers for Attar; he did not think they should be punished on earth, but considered their salvation possible – if at all – only through divine mercy (which was already in short supply for Muslims). Secondly, Attar depicts an Islamic culture in which tolerance towards those with different beliefs was certainly not one of the more highly regarded qualities. The following episode from

The Conference of the Birds underpins both of these qualifications (that Attar's concept of tolerance is neither modern nor characteristic of the society in which he lived). The mystic Abu Bakr Muhammad al-Wasiti (d. after 932) passes a Jewish graveyard.

'These Jews are excused, but one mustn't say that too loudly around here.'

Someone hears Wasiti's words and drags him to the *qadi* (religious judge) in outrage. Confronted by him, the sheikh answers: 'You may not judge these depraved people excused, but God does.'[43]

'Depraved', but nonetheless 'excused' – this is as far removed from today's standards of well-meaning as it is from the religious zealotry of those (and other) times. Attar would probably also have had a thing or two to say about the rule of the legal scholars: for him, religion and state – he makes this even clearer in *The Book of Suffering* than in his other epics – do not belong together: 'The royal courts are not the place to issue fatwas' (23/14, p. 228).

'Do two swords fit in one sheath?' a fool asks the Vizier Nezalmolmolk. 'You have dominion over this world, you do not need religion. But if you do want it, then do not make the world your possession. To have both together is unwise; beware of that' (9/6, p. 130).

Ethos and religious maxims

To whom should believers listen if not to theologians? Tradition, certainly – and themselves. For a poet of the twelfth and thirteenth century, it is quite remarkable – perhaps even unique – how decisively Attar emphasizes the responsibility of the individual to experience the reality of the Creator independently, and to follow His commandments in accordance with one's own volition, not blindly. This too makes Attar, whom many twentieth-century Iranian intellectuals considered antiquated, the herald of an enlightenment whose standards are not met by the present intellectual and social climate in many areas – especially the highest echelons. Imitation (*taqlid*), is almost as repulsive to Attar as dogmatism (*ta'aṣṣob*). The children of asses are simply not destined to follow the path of Sharia, he says; if they take it nonetheless, one knows that they are blindly following their mothers. Because religious laws are not part of human nature, one cannot relieve people of the choice to follow or reject them through coercion.

Whoever takes the path merely to follow others
May act as great as a mountain, but is lighter than straw. (0, p. 38)

Far from wanting to dilute the commandments and rituals of Islam, Attar, like other mystics, nonetheless makes no secret of his distance from the external forms of religion. A Hindu sees a Muslim caravan setting off on a pilgrimage, and is told that God has a house. Drunk with joy and hope, he immediately follows suit and walks to Mecca. Having finally reached the Kaaba, he asks where God is. When the pilgrims make it clear to him that God naturally does not live in the house, he loses his temper and curses the Muslims for causing him to undertake the gruelling journey: 'What good is the house to me without its owner?' (19/4, p. 198).

The law is part of faith, but without faith the law means nothing. It is important because people need it. The law does not apply to those with no need for it: prophets, saints and madmen. Moses is allowed to shatter the tablets of the law because he is one who loves (27/4, p. 255). Asked which way to face during prayer, Majnun answers: 'The Kaaba, if you are a tile; God, if you love; and the face of Layla for Majnun' (19/6, pp. 198f.).

Attar often uses his stories to express ethical principles. They remind the reader to be modest, magnanimous, and not bound to material possessions. When Alexander reaches China, the emperor serves him a dish of jewels and pearls.

'No one can eat this!' exclaims Alexander in outrage.

'Do you Greeks not eat jewels?' asks the emperor, seemingly amazed.

'Oh, I eat only two slices of bread a day', his guest boasts: 'that is all I need.'

'But were those two slices of bread nowhere to be found in the whole of Greece, such that you had to go forth and conquer so many countries, cities and people?'

Ashamed at these words, Alexander declares that he has had enough of his conquests and departs within the hour (24/3, p. 115).

If I am not mistaken, the model to which Attar refers most often is Jesus – for example, when he tells of a journey undertaken by Jesus and a companion. Jesus has three pieces of bread with him. He eats one of them, gives one to his companion, and the third is left over. When Jesus stops to drink from a lake, his companion secretly eats the third piece of bread. Jesus comes back and asks him what has happened to the bread.

'I know nothing', answers his companion.

They continue the journey and reach the sea, which they cross by walking on the water. 'By the God who has worked this miracle, tell me the truth about the bread', Jesus says to his companion.

'I truly know nothing', says his companion.

They continue their journey and discover a gazelle, which Jesus kills merely by calling it, so that they can feed on its flesh; then Jesus breathes new life into the bones and the gazelle leaps away. Once again Jesus asks his companion about the bread, and once again he swears he knows nothing about it. They set off again and come to three mounds of earth. Jesus turns them into gold and says: 'One heap is mine, the other one is yours, and the third belongs to the one who secretly ate the bread.'

'I did it!' his companion immediately exclaims.

Having thus exposed the liar, Jesus continues his journey alone without paying any further attention to the three heaps of gold. Then two other people come along, see the gold and start quarrelling with Jesus's former companion. Finally they agree to share the gold. As they are hungry, one of them is sent out to buy bread in town. He goes out, eats his fill, then poisons the bread he is supposed to bring back. The two others agree to kill the third and divide up his share of the gold. When he comes back, they kill him, only to die shortly afterwards from the poisoned bread. Jesus returns and sees the three corpses. Then he changes the gold back into earth lest it kill even more people (15/1, pp. 169ff.).

Compared to the sensuality of a poet such as Omar Khayyam, Attar's maxims, with their complete renunciation of worldly goods, seem from a different, earlier world. His ethics are a different matter, full as they are of compassion, love, generosity and tolerance in the aforementioned pre-modern, yet perhaps true sense: Attar and his holy men do not consider those of other faiths right (in which case leniency would hardly be notable), but on many occasions they demand that one should even accept what is wrong. Probably because the God portrayed by Attar cannot be relied on, many of his verses are moving through a stance that strikes the modern reader sometimes as enlightened and sometimes as existentialist: he constantly emphasizes the responsibility of the individual, and the psychology of the creative process is discussed more than in any other classical Persian work. He has – as in *The Conference of the Birds* – a whole chapter against fanaticism, and dozens of passages advocating compassion, clemency, charity and such ostensibly new-fangled phenomena as religious pluralism, which is not simply accepted, but even praised as highly valuable. At one point, Attar even states dialectically that unbelief is a necessary and hence justified prerequisite for the recognition of faith (40/2, p. 358). Such positions and the overall individuality of writing, perception and convictions seem like harbingers of modernity. For them to have found their way so explicitly and repeatedly into a text of the twelfth or early thirteenth century, however, points to the spread and Sufi adoption of the same humanism that had already developed among the Buyids in Baghdad – but a humanism that Attar considered at risk, otherwise he would hardly have advocated it so angrily.[44] The Mongol invasion provided the final confirmation of Attar's fears. At the same time, he lived in the period when Europe was beginning to absorb ideas from the Middle East in all areas and discover the human being as a subject. And so in the West too, the twelfth century – as has become ever clearer since Charles Homer Haskin's 1927 book *The Renaissance of the Twelfth Century* – takes on a special significance as a time characterized by the disruption of religious worldviews and the transition to more rational structures of consciousness (contrary to the traditional view that this process began only in fourteenth-century Italy). The humanism Attar feared for continued its development in a different culture.[45]

The last days

The despair espoused more radically in *The Book of Suffering* than in any other of Attar's works, or indeed in any work in the mystical literature of Persia (one perhaps finds similar levels of desolation in the work of Omar Khayyam, who stands outside mysticism; but he holds on to the happiness of sensual pleasure, which, while it does not make the world better, at least makes it more bearable) – this rigorous negation – is not explained by the historical situation of the aged Attar, but it certainly makes it easier to understand. Though we know little about Attar's life, the books of chroniclers and historiographers do give a fairly precise idea of the horror and confusion that the world he inhabited held in store.[46] The order of the once splendid Seljuq dynasty in Baghdad had collapsed. In Khorasan, Seljuqs and Khoresmians were taking over each other's cities and losing them again, and Turkmen nomadic tribes exploited the weakness of the dynasties to ransack villages and towns; the Ghaznavids were fighting for survival in the east, while Muslims were battling crusaders in the western parts of the Islamic world. Amid the ruins of Seljuq rule, every prince, every governor, every warlord, every commander and every landowner – as is still widespread today in the northern and eastern regions of historical Khorasan – created his own little dictatorship, in which the powerful were not subject to prohibitions or morals and the poor were given no protection from the soldiers, who took what they wanted: possessions, women and children. Khorasan was fair game for plunderers, and whoever could not afford an army was raided. The most beautiful women were taken by the troops of Caliph Abu l-Abbas Ahmad an-Nasir li-Din Allah (d. 1225) to his harem in Baghdad; this descendant of the Prophet liked to show off his new-found theological authority, and attempted to restore the unity of religious and political authority. The cities of Marv and Nishapur were pillaged time and again, Samarkand fought the Turkish Khorezmians, and the eastern Ghaznavid territory was plagued to its centre by battles and firestorms. It was an agitated, bloody time in which robbery, whoring and drunkenness spread as widely as mysticism, asceticism and inwardness. Ala'oddin Mohammad Khorezmshah (d. 1220) boasted of his love for Sufism, and had Majdoddin Kharazmi, the great Sufi of the period, whom Attar had also visited, drowned in the River Oxus (now Amudarja) on a whim. Jurisprudence in Khorasan was dominated by individual clans or extended families, meaning that theological authority was due less to education and morals than to lineage and good connections. Criticism of rulers and clerics was responded to with the accusation of unbelief, and protest, in so far as there was any, was sharply suppressed. At least, adds Abdolhasan Zarin-Kub, who provides a vivid description of the situation in Attar's Khorasan, at least conditions were better in some ways than those eight hundred years later – in the great literary scholar's own time, that is – as political-religious rule had not yet taken complete control over education, research, literature and creativity in general.[47]

All too often, interpretations of Attar's poetry pass over the fact that the hell he saw on earth was not simply a metaphor for an inner state, but rather an immediate reality. If Attar was born around 1145, he had already become acquainted with the utmost brutality as a child. In 1153 Nishapur was attacked by the Ghuzz, Turkmen nomads, who had risen up against Sanjar, the Seljuq sultan; he had been exploiting them via his tax-collectors to finance his military campaigns.[48] Through the sultan's recklessness, the local rebellion grew into nationwide retribution. When he fell into the hands of the Ghuzz on a journey and his frightened or corrupt soldiers no longer had a commander, the settlements of Khorasan fell to the Turkmens without a fight. The people in Nishapur fled the city or at least buried their valuables. The shops were closed, the bazaars deserted. When the Ghuzz finally took over the city, they pillaged all houses – abandoned and inhabited ones alike. Men were tortured until they revealed where they had hidden their belongings, women were raped, girls and boys abused. To steal the women's bracelets and necklaces, they cut off their arms and heads if they were in a hurry. Children fled, wandering around without parents, and women sought refuge with their infants. Whoever was suspected of hiding their belongings would be beaten, and sometimes the Ghuzz also beat those with nothing simply to intimidate the others. The Ghuzz dug new holes every day on their search for the inhabitants' buried valuables, and whoever dared to resist the raiders met an agonizing end in the fires that burned somewhere or other every night. Because food was no longer being delivered to the city from the surrounding villages, the population was starving. The madrasahs were closed; like everyone else, the scholars and their students were also in hiding. The city's mufti and greatest scholar, Mohammad ebn-e Yahya, issued a fatwa calling for resistance; the Ghuzz arrested him and stuffed his mouth with soft earth until he died of the torture.

There is no indication that the house of Attar's parents, who lived either in Nishapur or in the nearby village of Shadyakh, was plundered. We know that Shadyakh was spared, for the sultan's soldiers had withdrawn there. Many people had fled there from Nishapur. Death and poverty, hunger, disease and panic were also rampant in Shadyakh, however. So, whichever part of town Attar inhabited as a child, he grew up in a world of death, cruelty and hardship – especially if it is true that his father had already worked as a druggist and treated the sick.

Even after the Ghuzz had left Nishapur, peace took a long time to return. Sanjar was able to escape from the Ghuzz and regain his throne in Marv in 1156, after three years of captivity, but died only a year later as a result of his ordeal; evidently the Ghuzz had found it entertaining to torment the sultan. Hardly any of the buildings – the Ghuzz had destroyed twenty-five madrasahs and twelve libraries, to say nothing of private houses – were reconstructed. Even worse, many of the mosques and teaching centres in Nishapur that had remained standing were razed later in the course of the violent confrontations between the Shafiite and Hanafite theological schools that broke out after the Ghuzz withdrew. Following Sanjar's death, the whole of Khorasan suffered under the quarrels and fighting between the members of his family and the officers of his army. In 1158 the druggists' bazaar went up in flames, and with it perhaps the pharmacy of Attar's father. Hunger and poverty held the city hostage. In 1161 the Sanjars set up their headquarters in Shadyakh. A large part of Nishapur's population followed them, leaving the city centre, including the citadel, to deteriorate completely; it was now no more than a home for sheep, snakes and wild animals. After Nishapur had already been ravaged by one earthquake in 1145, several thousand people were killed by another in 1209. Several nearby villages were wiped off the map, supposedly without a single survivor.[49]

As a pharmacist and doctor, Attar dealt with hardship his whole life. The suffering of his book's title surrounded him in everyday reality.

Not only is his work populated by madmen, eccentrics and freaks – so also must have been the society in which he lived. According to contemporary accounts, the madness of his time drove a conspicuous number of people to insanity. They roamed through the land as vagabonds or stayed in the villages and towns, living off the charity of their neighbours.[50] At one point in *The Book of Suffering* Attar refers explicitly to the Ghuzz invasion of Nishapur: the entire city, including the authorities, has fled from the nomads. A single fool is left. He climbs a high tower, ties his robe to a stick, waves it as a flag and calls out: 'O folly, it is for a day such as this that I possess you! On such a day, when fear has stolen the hearts of all people, a man lost of heart is king of the whole land!' (11/2, p. 143).

When Attar wrote *The Book of Suffering*, Nishapur had probably already fallen into the hands of the Khorezmians, who took the city from the Seljuqs again in 1187 after doing so in 1142. Their ruler was the tyrannical Sultan Ala'oddin Mohammad Khorezmshah. Nonetheless, Nishapur returned to life, and throngs of merchants passed through the city again. In the bazaars, however, the stories about the Mongols quoted in contemporary accounts were probably already circulating. Even before they invaded Khorasan, those Iranians who had dealt with them – primarily merchants – spoke of their ignorance and brutality. In Nishapur, young people joined forces to form a sort of militia, hoping to be better prepared for the new intruders than they had been when the Ghuzz attacked half a century earlier. And, indeed, they initially repelled the Mongols when they finally invaded Nishapur, killing a son-in-law and close confidant of Genghis Khan. His cavalry had not encountered such resistance on any of their previous campaigns. When the Mongols took the city after all, presumably on 10 April 1221, they ravaged it for two weeks until nothing was left but rubble. Except for the four hundred craftsmen and artists who were taken to the Khan's court as slaves, scarcely anyone in the city escaped death. Attar's manuscripts must already have reached other cities, or some of those fleeing took them with them; nothing was preserved in Nishapur itself. As one chronicler writes, all the Mongols left behind was smoking ruins, whose deathly silence was occasionally broken by the barking of a dog, the crowing of a cock or the howling of wolves. Perhaps Attar anticipated the scene that presented itself to the chronicler; or perhaps he had simply been thinking of the Ghuzz attack on his childhood Nishapur or one of the other raids his city had endured, or else he meant one of the other cities in Khorasan whose destruction he had learned of – he would not, at any rate, have required much imagination to tell, in *The Book of Suffering*, the story of the fool who arrived at a 'once strong, but now largely destroyed city' that had 'already been eaten up by salt from head to toe in the naked sun'.

Wherever his gaze wandered, every wall, every door,
Everything had been turned on its head, a wild mess.

The fool looked in amazement on the 'signs of wrath', unable to avert his eyes, stayed there beyond midday, then sat down. He was still staring incredulously when someone came by and asked him: 'Why are you sitting here rooted to the spot, wandering fool, so confused and stooped? Why are you gaping?'

'I am astonished, for when this city still stood, radiant and full of people, where was I, that I did not know of it? And now that I am here, where are all the people? Where was I then, where are they now? When I was not here they were, and when I appeared they had vanished. I cannot understand that, and so I am astonished. Who knows what this circle means, and if there is anything that remains untouched by it? I have wandered so far without finding anything, which made me lose heart and lose my mind. No one can escape confusion. No one learns the meaning of this coming and going' (16/9, p. 180).

In German history, the time in which Attar wrote his poems could probably be compared most readily to the Thirty Years' War, which claimed two-thirds of the population in Thuringia, the Palatinate, Pomerania and Württemberg. And it is no coincidence that this period of capitalistically organized violence, when military entrepreneurs such as Albrecht von Wallenstein (d. 1634), Ernst zu Mansfeld (d. 1629) or Gottfried Heinrich zu Pappenheim (d. 1632) unleashed their troops like swarms of locusts upon villages to strip them bare, these most violent three decades of pre-modern German history, brought forth Andreas Gryphius (d. 1664), the German poet of sorrow who is closest to Attar: 'I weep day and night / I sit amid a thousand tribulations.'[51] Except for their church spires, the destroyed cities mourned by Gryphius could just as easily have been located in Khorasan.

We are now completely / nay, more than completely devastated!
The horde of insolent peoples / the wild trumpets
The sword, bloated with blood / the thundering cannon
Has consumed all sweat / and effort / and supplies.
The towers are but embers / the church overturned.
The town hall sits in terror / the strong struck down /
Our maidens defiled / and wherever we turn
There is fire / pestilence / and death / piercing the heart and the spirit.
Our trenches and roads / are ever full of fresh flowing blood.
For three times six years / our rivers

Brimming over with corpses / have oozed slowly forwards.
Yet I have not spoken of something worse than death /
Grimmer than the plague, / the blazes and the hunger /
That the treasures of so many souls / have also been plundered.[52]

No other German poet showed such hopeless piety, and no one described the earthly world, which he saw desecrated by human violence and malice, as the scene of mankind's godlessness with such devout provocation as Gryphius. His works – eulogies, memorial sonnets and funeral odes – are a powerful testimony to the loss of humanity, sometimes brutally invoking visions of horror, sometimes feebly whispering and driven to madness by suffering, and, as with Attar, the lament sometimes turns into accusation: 'Alas! He covers his face! Destroys me in my greatest need.'[53] When Gryphius describes the plague of Glogau in his 'Thränen- und Danck-Lied' [Song of Tears and Thanks] from 1657, he portrays God not as the father of peace, but as the enemy of Job known also to Attar: 'Lord, alas! Can You act so terribly, / Transform Yourself into such cruelty?' And yet the people whom God has chosen as the targets of his vengeance are 'nothing but dust and steam' anyway, as Gryphius says in the same poem;[54] 'Foam here, foam there, and you are but a bubble', wrote Attar (17/6, p. 186). For both poets, transience is not a philosophical problem, but an everyday experience in a world where human lives are swallowed like water. As Gryphius puts it: 'Now flowers, tomorrow excrement'.[55] Attar tells of Sheikh Abu Sa'id Fazlollah ebn Abi l-Kheyr, who stops in front of a latrine and gazes at it long and closely.

'What are you doing?' someone asks him.

'The excrement is speaking to me. It says: I too was once a gift from God' (17/2, p. 182).

And what are we humans? A house of grim anguish
A ball of false happiness / a ghost light of our times.
A scene of bitter fear / full of sharp sorrow /
A snow that soon melts and burnt-down candles.
This life flies past like idle talk and jests.
Those who shed the robe of the frail body before us
Their names long since written in the dead-book of great mortality
Have vanished from our hearts and minds.
As a vain dream is easily forgotten
And as a river races through / when no force can stop it:
So too must our names / praise / honour and fame disappear /
What draws breath today / must flee with the air /
What comes after us / will drag us into the grave.
What am I saying? We vanish like smoke in a strong wind.[56]

It is evidently in times of apocalyptic decline, the collapse of an intellectual and social framework, that one finds not only rampant decadence and escapism but also the production of such poetic works as *The Book of Suffering*. Perhaps this is why it corresponds to certain perceptions of the twentieth century.

'Tis the world's work to be born, only to die,
  To appear from here and vanish from there.
'Tis the world's work never to end.
  To ache for all eternity, never to heal.
'Tis the world's work to exceed our powers,
  so that we never heal, however much we scream. (23/11, p. 226)

Longing for nothingness

The Book of Suffering is a little-known, but frightening and disturbing piece of world literature. It speaks to us not only in its hopeless blackness, but also in its deeply black humour – for example when Attar tells the story of a fool who must have known Beckett's statement that we are born astride of a grave: after a funeral, he simply stays sitting by the grave and makes himself comfortable. Asked why he is not returning to the city, he replies that he does not want to take any unnecessary detours. 'Woe that I am going, alas that I came', says the fool and turns away from his interlocutor (4/3, pp. 90f.).

Elsewhere, Attar is even briefer: a rider asks the famous ascetic Ibrahim ibn Adham (d. between 776 and 790) where the closest settlement is, and is directed to the cemetery (18/5, p. 192). And, even more drastically: a wise man passes a graveyard and a dung heap, and speaks: 'Here is God's gift, and there lie those who distorted it' (17/5, p. 184).

As in Schopenhauer, insight is ultimately reduced to recognition of the world's senselessness, and is thus by necessity connected to suffering. In Attar's work, as is generally the case in Islamic mysticism, it is the prophets who suffer most, then the holy men, the wise men, the pious, and so on. In Attar, however, Mohammed's statement 'If you knew what I know, you would weep much and laugh little',[57] which is usually understood as a threat referring to the next life, is applied to the pain of being. The sharper the awareness, the more profound the hardship – a hierarchy of knowledge Schopenhauer formulated thus: 'The lower a man is in an intellectual respect, the less puzzling and mysterious existence itself is to him; on the contrary, everything, how it is and that it is, seems to him a matter of course.'[58] If, Nietzsche writes, someone were able 'to grasp and feel mankind's overall consciousness in himself, he would collapse with a curse against existence.'[59]

Someone for whom life is so painful longs only for destruction.

'I do not want anything at all from You', speaks a fool to God one night: 'What You have given me so far is enough, it is far too much. Yes – take back this life You have given me, I do not want it' (22/3, p. 216).

It is the Sophoclean lament 'Oh, if only I had never been born' that Attar declaims. It is Job's cry: 'Let the day perish on which I was born' (3:3), or Jeremiah 20:15–17:

> Cursed be the man who brought my father the news, who made him very glad, saying, 'A child is born to you – a son!' May that man be like the towns the Lord overthrew without pity. May he hear wailing in the morning, a battle cry at noon. For he did not kill me in the womb, with my mother as my grave, her womb enlarged for ever.

With his curses upon being, Attar varies a topos first encountered in texts from ancient Egypt, from the First Intermediate Period, around 2000 BC: 'The misery of life is so immeasurable: I wish that I were dead; and even the little children already say: If only I had not been brought to life.'[60] From Hesiod (c. 700 BC), Theognis (sixth century BC) and Herodotus (d. 429 BC) to Euripides (d. c. 406 BC), Socrates (d. 399 BC) and Seneca (d. AD 65), the wish never to have been born runs through Greek and Roman tragedy and philosophy. The monotheistic religions, on the other hand, declare the creation to be God's work and thus tend to place a taboo on the longing not to have been created. When the aforementioned passages from Jeremiah and Job, or Jesus's words at the Last Supper – 'It would be better for him if he had not been born' (Matthew 26:24; Mark 14:21) – called for interpretation, the curse upon existence was turned into a curse upon humans: that is, into cursing oneself. An exegetical textbook from 1646 summarizes the consensus among existing doctrinal opinions thus: 'Man curses the day of his birth because that is what creates the possibility of sin.'[61] It was not only with Shakespeare (d. 1616), Voltaire (d. 1778) and Lord Byron (d. 1824) that cursing creatures once more came to mean cursing the creation, however; it was already widespread in classical Arab and Persian literature:

> As the stars do naught but multiply suffering,
> replacing nothing without stealing it again:
> If the unborn knew how much suffering the cosmos bestows –
> they would not come towards us.[62]

It was by no means only freethinkers such as Omar Khayyam – who penned these verses – or al-Ma'arri who extolled death as preferable to life: Ibn Abi d-Dunya (d. 894) wrote a text of his own about companions of the Prophet, successors and pious old men who adopted Job's wish never to have been born, or – if they had to be in the world anyway – at least to be 'green herbs' that would be 'eaten by camels'.[63] Ibn ash-Shibl (d. 1081) even cursed 'the lust that, to our great misfortune, our parents enjoyed.'[64] In *The Book of Suffering*, Attar lets the Prophet Mohammed himself utter the wish: 'If only God had not called me into existence' (35/8, p. 318). At least since Gryphius ('All this stinks to me / and so I wish for death!')[65] the topos of cursing existence has also been present in German literature and philosophy, where Nietzsche and Schopenhauer, Heine and Hölderlin (d. 1843), Bahnsen (d. 1881) and Büchner outdid one another in denouncing existence.[66] In the twentieth century it is Cioran who most prominently laments 'the trouble with being born', as his most famous book is entitled. Sigmund Freud elevated the 'death instinct' to a human principle, and became subject to it himself with increasing age. Immediately after his oft-quoted diagnosis that Hamlet's question is 'sick', the terminally ill Freud wrote: 'There is an advertisement going around in my head that I consider the most daring and accomplished piece of American advertising: "Why live, if you can be buried for ten dollars?"'[67] There is a similar tone of hopeless mockery in the exclamation of a fool in *The Book of Suffering* who sees a man running late to a funeral: 'Why are you in such a hurry to reach the cemetery? Are you scared the soup over there will get cold?' (11/4, p. 143).

Attar's wise men also yearn for destruction: a sheikh goes with his disciples to procure an urgently needed, expensive millstone. When one of them stumbles and the stone falls to the ground and breaks, the sheikh is ecstatic. The disciples are disgruntled that they have carried the stone over several days for nothing – so why, to crown it all, is the sheikh ecstatic about such misfortune? By breaking, the sheikh answers, the stone has been saved from constantly turning in circles, saved from its confusion and from wandering about. If it had remained intact, it would have had to keep turning constantly; but now the stone has found peace.

'When I saw that the stone had found peace by breaking, my heart too became as soft as beeswax; the stone revealed the secret to me.'

Whoever has been taken over by unrest
  Will be freed; he need only break.
Whoever stays confused and restless
  Will not find relief for all eternity. (12/1, p. 149)

In a different work, these verses could be reduced to their mystical content, pointing to a Buddhist influence (redemption through dissolution in nirvana) or the longing for spiritual annihilation, the *unio mystica*. In *The Book of Suffering*, however, they also have a real, immediate sense: that of no longer wanting to live in this life. Schopenhauer thought that, on closer inspection, the natural human attachment to one's existence is blind and unreasonable. 'If we knocked on the graves and asked the dead whether they would like to rise again, they would shake their heads.'[68] In *The Book of Suffering*, a similar notion leads to desiring death not only for oneself, but for all mankind: the fool Bohlul is lying on a grave and does not want to leave. When someone tells him finally to return to the city, Bohlul explains that he is lying on the grave because the dead man is entrusting him with secrets. For the deceased has sworn not to shake off the earth until, like him, all people were lying under the earth (4/3, pp. 90f.).

The dominant reaction to life in *The Book of Suffering*, however, is not the desire to lose it, but an even more desolate insight: that there is not even peace under the earth. Even the hope of destruction is eradicated. Attar writes the following about al-Hasan al-Basri (d. 728), the early Islamic ascetic and originator of Sufism:

A man was buried in the earth,
  And Hasan al-Basri came to the pit,
Looked on the pit and the graveyard too,
  Sat down and wept for himself.
Bleak, he said, things look bleak for us,
  If the grave is our final resting-place,
And at once the passage to the other world.
  Thus we begin and end under the earth.
Why cling to this world, which torments us,
  Until we end afflicted in this grave?
But how terrible must that world be
  If its entrance already lies under the earth?
What remains to be said if this is the end?
  Woe to us, woe that this will be the beginning. (4/1, pp. 88f.)

Whoever expects justice in the hereafter, or at least considers it possible, could perhaps comfort themselves in the face of earthly suffering. 'Yes, a man who believed in destruction! It would be a help to him / there is no hope in death, it is just a single kind of rot, while life is a more complex, organized one.' Danton's famous statement about the creation has always struck me as a fitting motto for *The Book of Suffering*:

> How I curse the dictum that 'something can't become nothing'! And I *am* something, that's the misery of it! Creation's so rank and rampant that no void is left, there's a seething and swarming wherever you turn. Nothingness has killed itself, creation is its wound, we are the drops of its blood, the world the grave in which it slowly rots.[69]

Whoever denies the possibility of a life beyond can at least assume that the torment will end. Someone who believes in a hereafter while ruling out salvation, however, who is certain that life will continue after death but will be no better, and hence projects that torment into infinity – only that person lives in the worst of all possible worlds. I cannot imagine how such despondency could be surpassed. 'We are even more helpless than you in this pit, this prison', says a deceased master to his novice in a dream in *The Conference of the Birds*.[70] And that, in a nutshell, is the message of Hamlet's famous monologue: not only is non-being decidedly preferable to being ('a consummation devoutly to be wish'd'); there is not even an alternative. For Hamlet, death by no means amounts to destruction. Schopenhauer took up this insight: 'But who would go on living life as it is, if death were less terrible?'[71] One finds an extreme Christian version of this in Jean Paul's (d. 1825) 'Speech of the Dead Christ from the Top of the Universe: That There Is No God', in which he imagines that not even the saviour is saved: 'When the sorrow-laden lays himself, with galled back, into the Earth, to sleep till a fairer Morning full of Truth, full of Virtue and Joy, – he awakens in a stormy Chaos, in the everlasting Midnight, – and there comes no Morning, and no soft healing hand, and no Infinite Father!'[72] It is curious that Attar also depicts the ghastliness of dying with the figure of Jesus, who – in spite of his perfection – sweated blood from fear at the thought of death (4/10, p. 94).

Attar saved most of the stories illustrating that not even death will save us from being – and, worse, that the real torment still awaits us in the next life – for the epilogue (i.e., directly after the light ending of the frame story). Thus self-subsumption, which is not actually described there but is announced for later treatment, no longer seems like a unification, but rather pure annihilation, as the implosion of being in itself, which is desirable, but not realistic even for prophets and saints – let alone mere mortals such as Attar.

> Fozeyl, that most excellent scholar and sprinkler of tears,
>   Spoke: I envy not the prophets,
> For before them lies the grave and the resurrection
>   And a path as narrow as a razor's edge.
> And even the angels I cannot envy,

For they know nothing of love and its entanglement.
I only envy those, for all eternity,
Who are never born into this world.
If only I could return to my father's back,
And had never landed in my mother's womb.
Woe! If only my mother had never born me,
Then my unbeliever's soul would be spared death. (E/11, p. 373)

There are also other Sufis whose yearning for dissolution in God moves towards the Buddhist longing for nothingness, but none of them show the transition so explicitly as a result of psychological pain, of immediate existential hardship. Here Attar's thought once again approaches the philosophy of suffering developed by Schopenhauer, who could imagine redemption in the Buddhist sense of a self-redemption only in nirvana. But that is also exactly where both writers suddenly reveal a paradoxical optimism: while Attar chooses pain as a 'remedy' (12/7, p. 157), because this alone provides the stimulus to overcome pain in the manner dreamed of in the fortieth chapter – 'I am alive through this pain' (0/1) – Schopenhauer sees the purpose of life in the fact that it is meant to be 'spoilt [*verleidet*][73] for us'. It is 'difficult to conceive', he continues in wonder, 'how anyone could fail to recognize this, and be persuaded that life is here to be thankfully enjoyed, and that man exists in order to be happy.' Remarkably enough, his words do not even sound mocking here.

> On the contrary, that continual deception and disillusionment, as well as the general nature of life, present themselves as intended and calculated to awaken the conviction that nothing is worth our exertions, our efforts and our struggles, that all good things are empty and fleeting, that the world on all sides is bankrupt, and that life is a business that does not cover the costs, so that our will may turn away from it.[74]

The question that poses itself in *The Book of Suffering* is one of the oldest questions common to religion and literature. It is the existentialist question deemed pathological by Freud and assigned only to the third stage of fear by Paul Tillich, the question posed by Hamlet that was so central in the twentieth century: the question of life's purpose, its sense, amid the manifest senselessness of world events. The answer hinted at by Attar in parables seems modern in several respects: first of all in its unreserved negativity, in its yearning for a reconciliation that is not described, and even more precisely in its Beckettian sarcasm, its Schopenhauerian scepticism, its sober view of the world and the motivations of its inhabitants. A man is asked what the highest name of God is. 'Bread', he answers.

The questioner is appalled, but the other man explains that he experienced a famine in Nishapur. He spent forty days in the city without once hearing the call to prayer, or even finding a single mosque open. Instead, everyone was crying out for bread. 'Since then I have known that the highest name of God is "bread"' (29/6, p. 267).

A refined gentleman walks past the latrine and holds his nose.

'Stop that nonsense!' a fool calls out to him. 'Soon, very soon, they'll bring you exactly the same thing and tell you: eat! So don't hold your nose at what you will eat joyfully tomorrow.'

> People turn even God's gifts into excrement.
> And still believe they are entitled to strive for power. (17/3, p. 184)

As familiar as the assortment of themes, motifs and mentalities that unfolds in the book may seem to the modern reader, it is simultaneously foreign. Its outrage, its accusations levelled at God and the world, and its metaphysical wretchedness are formulated with a radicalism one could scarcely find in any modern text, and with good reason: God is still omnipresent. What sets *The Book of Suffering* apart most clearly from the literature of modernity is its religious furore. This is what gives the rebellion its passionate and exalted character, its excess and craziness, the righteous anger and desperate heresy. It is precisely because God is still viewed as an unlimited, an undoubted and, above all, a longed-for and vainly beloved reality that the disappointment and anger are concrete. They are directed not at the general fate of the world, but at a Creator, declared just and compassionate, who is responsible for human suffering. *The Book of Suffering* rejects the possibilities found by the Abrahamic religions to absolve God of the responsibility for evil. In the following chapter, I shall begin by summarizing these in order to understand the intellectual context and Attar's particularity.

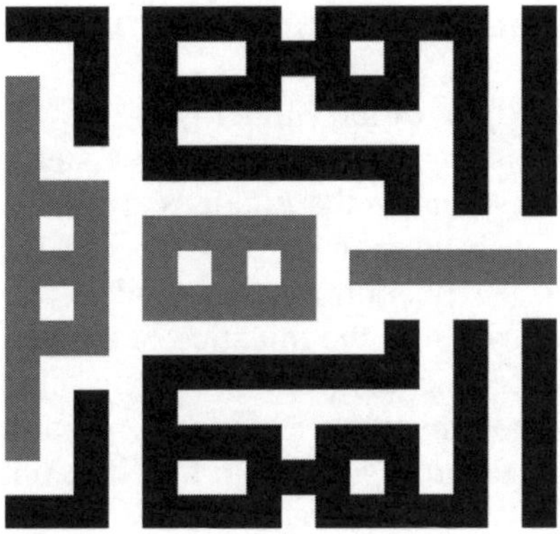

— 3 —

THE JUSTIFICATION AND TERROR OF GOD

Omnipotence versus wisdom, freedom versus providence

Long before the philosophy of the Modern Age developed the concept of 'theodicy', monotheistic religious thought registered that the state of the world did not correspond to the goodness of the one and almighty Creator. For older Jewish literature alone, David Birnbaum lists more than twenty different, partly contradicting models for justifying God,[1] and in Islam, too, inquiries into the injustice of the world and senseless human suffering were 'especially popular among scholars', as the lexicographer and Koran commentator Murtada az-Zabidi (d. 1791) noted almost retrospectively regarding a debate that has, until recently, been largely overlooked in Western literature. Only in recent years (thanks not least to Eric L. Ormsby's significant 1984 study *Theodicy in Islamic Thought*) has the cliché of the 'fatum mahometanum', which was one of the stimuli for Leibniz's theodicy,[2] begun to disappear. Az-Zabidi wrote:

> If one begins to speculate, the answer seems easy, but if one reflects upon it, it becomes a riddle whose solution has exhausted many sheikhs – their opinions diverge, the discrepancies multiply, and they separate into many different factions.[3]

Just as there is no *one* Christian or Jewish concept of evil, equally there is no *one* uniform or even slightly coherent interpretation in Islam. Not even the Bible or the Koran offer consistent answers: Oliver Leaman rightly noted that the reason why one should not consider the Bible a system of arguments is not that it lacks them, but that it contains too many,[4] and one could say the same about the Koran, which rarely presents a single, unambiguous view of a matter. Similarly, one should speak of religious interpretations of misfortune in Jewish, Muslim or Christian literature in the plural. In many cases they have developed through a process of reciprocal, inter-religious cross-fertilization, like Sufism and Kabbalah, which have in turn affected Christian mysticism: in their structures, references, concepts and images, Jewish and Islamic mysticism within the Arab-influenced cultural realm have far more in common with each other than Islamic mysticism does with Islamic philosophy. The ecstatic poems of the mystic al-Hallaj share their religion, but not their religious sentiment, with the cutting rationalism through which Attar's contemporary Averroës secured his place in the history not only of Islamic, but also of Jewish and Western philosophy. Conversely, the Arab philosophical debate shows a direct dialogue between Jewish and Muslim arguments. The examination of the problem of theodicy in the work of Sa'adiya Gaon (Sa'id al-Fayyumi, d. 942) or Maimonides (Ibn Maymun, d. 1204) develops along the lines drawn by the dialectical theology of Islam. The fact that, for Maimonides and other Arab-Jewish philosophers, Job was quite clearly a prophet points to the cultural context in which they lived and wrote, for the Koran and the Islamic traditions, unlike the Bible, list Job among the prophets. Similar concepts, even identical formulations, are also possible in cases where different lines of thought have developed independently of one another, as one can observe in the theodicies of al-Ghazali and Leibniz.

Practically every conceivable way of interpreting the injustice of the world religiously can, in its structure, be found in the three monotheistic religions. In so far as they examined the pre-modern Arab-influenced cultural realm, the immense variety of source texts would automatically rule out such popular conference or lecture titles as 'Islam and Evil' or 'Islam and Violence', as well as similar generalizations for Judaism and Christianity. Attar's work in particular illustrates vividly how chains of motifs are interwoven, parallel or temporally shifted in relation to one another, and certainly do not follow strict confessional boundaries, so that a purely intra-Islamic geometry of his thoughts and ideas is inadequate and even the adjectives 'Jewish', 'Islamic' or 'Christian' lose their fixed identities. I therefore organize the diverse teachings, images and modes of expression in which the experience of suffering is rationalized, theologized or poetically condensed not according to their religious allegiance, but according to their content. The division into theodicies that limit the omnipotence of God or insight into His wisdom, as one finds in Western intellectual history, corresponds exactly with the choice at the centre of classical Islamic theology, or more precisely the dispute between the Mu'tazilites and Ash'arites:

human free will versus predestination. Or, focused on God: justice versus omnipotence.

The unfathomable God

If religious thought in monotheism sought to insist on God's goodness without idealizing suffering as a test, promising worldly deliverance in the indefinite future or hoping for compensation for suffering in the next life, it was faced with the two possibilities named by the philosopher Hans Jonas:[5] either to give up faith in God's omnipotence or to follow Job's example and stop judging His acts by human standards: 'Surely I spoke of things I do not understand, things too wonderful for me to know' (Job 42:3). In the end Job submits to God, but not in the manner demanded by Elihu: in the two grotesquely brief, laconic closing speeches, he does not find fault with himself, but rather accepts that he cannot understand the logic of divine action: 'I am unworthy – how can I reply to You? I put my hand over my mouth' (Job 40:5).

One stops understanding God if one presupposes that He is good and just, but has to conclude that He does not use his omnipotence to prevent innocent suffering. And, behold, it was good, we are told – but what we see is not good, so it cannot be everything, otherwise what is written would be false. One has to accept that the purpose behind His actions and His creation cannot be understood by humans. The exemplary formulation of this – and for Arab-Persian intellectual history – was provided by Epicurus (d. 70):

> God either wishes to take away evils and he cannot, or he can and does not wish to, or he neither wishes to nor is able. If he wishes to and is not able, he is feeble, which does not fall in with the notion of god. If he is able to and does not wish to, he is envious, which is equally foreign to god. If he neither wishes to nor is able, he is both envious and feeble and therefore not god. If he both wishes to and is able, which alone is fitting to god, whence, therefore, are there evils, and why does he not remove them?[6]

Epicurus' question not only returns frequently in European thought, in Bayle (d. 1706),[7] Hume (d. 1776)[8] or the Marquis de Sade (d. 1814),[9] but also in Islamic literature, for example al-Ghazali:

> If a better world were possible, and God had simply not created it because He had the power, but not the will to do so, this would have been an expression of meanness that would contradict goodness, an expression of

> injustice that would contradict justice. But if He had not had the power to create a better world, this would be an inability that would contradict godliness itself.[10]

The formulation of al-Ghazali's question already suggests the positive answer he subsequently provides. The sceptic al-Ma'arri presents the paradox quite differently:

> If our Lord desires nothing but good, then the following applies to evil: either He knows about it or He does not. If He knows about it, He must either desire it or not. If He desires it, He is essentially the perpetrator. Just as one says, 'The emir cut off the thief's hand', even if he did not do it personally. But if our Lord does not desire evil, one must trust His intentions as one would not trust those of an emir on earth. For if something happens in an emir's jurisdiction that he does not want, he expresses his displeasure and orders for it to stop. But this is a knot that dogmatists have sought in vain to undo.[11]

The question of God's justice, and hence the problem of theodicy, was one of the earliest questions in dialectical theology in Islam – perhaps even the very first.[12] It was raised in connection with human free will: could one still maintain that God is just if humans were not free to avoid evil? The Mu'tazilites, the earliest school of dialectical theology in Islam, denied this, and were prepared to qualify God's omnipotence in favour of human free will in order not to compromise the concept of divine justice. But their opponents, the Ash'arites, whose orthodoxy ultimately prevailed, believed without reservation in fate, and hence in God's responsibility for all events. They had to admit, however, that it was then no longer possible to make a rational case for God's justice in each individual aspect. Justice or injustice are not intrinsic to the deeds but based entirely on God's nature; to the extent that He is just, all events on earth are also just, as God makes them occur. Hence justice is always in place, regardless of how humans perceive it: if God rewards the righteous and punishes sinners, it is just, and if He instead punishes the righteous and rewards sinners, it is equally just; if God fulfils his promise, it is no more or less just than if He does not. It is sufficient to know that God is just. The ways in which God's justice manifests itself are beyond human understanding.

Abu l-Hasan al-Ash'ari (d. 935), the founder of the school of the same name, supposedly turned away from the rationalism of the Mu'tazilites because, among other things, their aim of identifying divine wisdom in the course of the world did not satisfy him. According to an oft-cited anecdote, al-Ash'ari asked his Mu'tazilite teacher al-Jubba'i (d. 915) whether God had done the 'best possible thing' in the cases of three deceased persons: a believer who was rewarded in the next life, an unbeliever who was punished, and a child that was neither rewarded nor punished:

'What would God reply if the child said, "O Lord, would it not have been better to let me live, for then I would have had the possibility to enter paradise?"'

'God', answered al-Jubba'i', 'would tell the child: "I knew that you would have become a sinner and gone to hell if I had let you live longer."'

'But then the unbeliever', countered al-Ash'ari, would cry out in hell: "O Lord! Why did You not kill me as a child so that I would not have been able to sin, and would not have landed in hell?"'

Al-Jubba'i could not offer any answer to this that satisfied al-Ash'ari.[13]

Rejecting the Mu'tazilite theodicy, he and his successors returned to the emphasis on divine omnipotence that predominated in early Islam – and thus the restriction, or even the negation, of human free will. In doing so, however, as the influential Shiite theologian Morteza Motahhari (murdered 1979) argued, they did not absolve God from guilt, but rather the sinner, who can no longer be made responsible for his actions in the case of strict predestination.[14] In fact, al-Ash'ari expressly made God responsible for evil, as all events are ultimately His work: 'Good and evil occur through the will and the power of God. We believe in God's will and in His power – in the good and the evil, the sweet and the bitter aspects.'[15] What is notable about this statement is that there is only very meagre support for it in the Koran, which, unlike the Bible, barely connects suffering to God. On the contrary, it repeatedly emphasizes – probably in deliberate contrast to Jewish and Christian notions: 'Surely God wrong not men anything, but themselves men wrong' (10:44; see also 9:70, 41:46 and many other verses). The only topos the Ash'arites can invoke is that God 'has set a seal on the unbelievers' hearts and on their hearing, and on their eyes is a covering' (2:7), and that He 'leads astray whomsoever He will, and whomsoever He will He guides' (35:7, 16:93, 74:31). But there are, as the philosopher Averroës noted in his critique of Ash'arite philosophy, far more verses 'which apparently contradict them – the verses in which God denies injustice to himself. For instance, in Surah 39:9, He says: "He approves not disbelief in His servants". So it is clear that as He does not like disbelief even from them, He certainly cannot cause them to err.'[16] Averroës, like the Mu'tazilites and almost all Shiite theologians, opposed this radical theocentrism in Ash'arite thought, which suggests that God 'is not just at all, and that all His actions are neither just nor unjust'.[17] He thus took up an old rationalist doctrine formulated by Wasil ibn Ata (d. 748), the founder of the Mu'tazilite school:

> God, the sublime, is wise and just. It is therefore unacceptable to make any connection between Him and evil or injustice. He wants nothing from His servants except what He commands. And He would not punish them for something He Himself had desired. So it is man who produces good and bad things, belief and disbelief, obedience and sin, and who is rewarded or punished for his deeds.[18]

The Ash'arite attribution of all actions – expressly including evil or unjust ones – to God can hardly rely on the Koran for validation, and is in fact closer to statements in the Bible, for example in Amos 3:6: 'When disaster comes to a city, has not the Lord caused it?', or the traditional formula recorded by the prophet Isaiah: 'I am the Lord, and there is no other. I form the light and create darkness, I bring prosperity and create disaster; I, the Lord, do all these things' (Isaiah 45:6–7). In Christianity it was Calvin who created a new awareness of this when he rejected the scholastic notion of permitted evil: 'it is the merest trifling to substitute a bare permission for the providence of God'.[19] Luther also argued for absolute predestination, stating that everything else would limit God's sovereign will and therefore be blasphemy: 'Therefore we must go to extremes, deny free will altogether, and ascribe everything to God.'[20] The Ash'arites, and after them Luther and Calvin, believed it was impossible to resolve the contradiction between this position and faith in God's compassion and justice rationally – except that the Ash'arites, in contrast to the early Muslims, sought to explain precisely this irresolvable conflict, which limited the divine attribute of justice, dialectically and with the same rational methods as their Mu'tazilite opponents.

With a greater emphasis on human freedom of will, and as an attempt to reconcile the physical – i.e., rationally explicable necessity of all events with divinely conditioned contingency – other Arab philosophers, such as Maimonides and Avicenna and later the Christian scholastics, developed various theodicies – or, more precisely, rejections of theodicy. They drew a line between divine and human logic. The question of God's responsibility for evil was thus already answered at the outset: God's actions were subject to different laws from those of humans. That this situation included terror for humans was self-evident for the majority of Jewish-Islamic philosophers, who saw it as no reason to dispute the goodness of God. Referring to the three stoic attributes of the divine as all-powerful, all-knowing and all-responsible, which Epicurus considered irreconcilable with the evil in the world, Avicenna wrote:

> For were it not the case that this world is compounded so as to give rise to goods and ills and to promote both sound and unsound actions in its denizens, the world's order would be imperfect and incomplete.[21]

Avicenna argued for the futility of the human question as to God's justice in a special treatise on the matter, which he had been moved to write by the lament of a Muslim about the unjust distribution of material goods among Muslims and Christians. Here he referred to the endlessness of human wishes, which would have absurd consequences if they were all fulfilled.[22] Averroës, who provided the most extensive rationalization of God's actions, likewise emphasizes that God 'is not just in the same way as man is just'.[23] Maimonides, the Jew among the three great classical Arab philosophers, teaches in negative-theological terms, and with a precise knowledge of Muslim dogmatics, that God is so fundamentally different from anything we could imagine that we cannot assign any attributes to Him at all. When humans suffer, the only explanation is their failure, as free will makes them capable of evil and they must accordingly face the punishment:

> Even when a person suffers pain in consequence of a thorn having entered into his hand, although it is at once drawn out, it is a punishment that has been inflicted on him, and the least pleasure he enjoys is a reward; all this is meted out by strict justice.[24]

Maimonides does concede that not every instance of individual suffering is necessarily a direct consequence of that person's sinfulness; in a wider sense, however, one could definitely say that all suffering is caused by the finitude and fallibility of humans, and hence cannot be attributed to God, who equipped humans with freedom – including the freedom to harm themselves. So for Maimonides individual hardship exists, but injustice does not; the problem of evil is a false problem. Job's questions are thus posed incorrectly to begin with, Maimonides argues, an expression of intellectual weakness: what Job lacked was rationality, as he would otherwise have recognized, firstly, that his suffering was a necessary consequence of his material existence and, secondly, that he was incapable of understanding God's plan anyway. Once he had realized his error, everything turned out well.[25] With reference to Maimonides, the Jewish neo-Kantian Hermann Cohen renewed the refusal to judge God by human standards – which dominates the whole of Arab philosophy – for the late nineteenth century. Whoever poses the question of theodicy, he states, presupposes theism; but the kind of knowledge on which theodicy by definition rests contradicts human reason and God's sovereignty – and, in addition to that, to suppose that one knows anything about Him amounts to a negation of God. 'Therefore any trace of an interest in a subjective or in an individual ground for suffering has to be eliminated.'[26] Thus the appropriate affirmation of God's sovereignty excludes knowledge and delegates the problem of evil to ethics. 'If the meaning of physical suffering, of physical ill in the human world, has always been a question for theodicy, then one could perhaps state this meaning in a paradox: the suffering, the *passion* [*Leiden*] is for the sake of compassion [*Mitleid*].'[27]

In Christian thought, Augustine (d. 430) argued strikingly for the unfathomable nature of God, which likewise became the main path of Christian theodicies until the Modern Age. Asked what God did before he created the world, the church father responded dryly that God created hell for those who ask such impudent questions. In his later doctrine of grace, Augustine invokes St Paul to condemn the 'impudence'[28] of seeking to judge God's actions by human standards. Paul says:

> But who are you, O man, to talk back to God? Shall what is formed say to him who formed it, 'Why did You make me like this?' Does not the potter have the right to make out of the same lump of clay some pottery for noble purposes and some for common use? What if God, choosing to show his wrath and make his power known, bore with great patience the objects of his wrath – prepared for destruction? What if he did this to make the riches of his glory known to the objects of his mercy, whom he prepared in advance for glory. (Romans 9:20–24)

In European philosophy it was famously Leibniz who sought, by means of transcendental logic, not simply to justify God's goodness in the face of life's malevolence, but even to explain it rationally. 'The defence of the highest wisdom of the creator against the charge which reason brings against it for whatever is counterpurposive in the world':[29] this is Immanuel Kant's classic definition of the challenge faced by the philosophy of the Modern Age in the form of theodicy. The defence of the highest wisdom – so rationalist metaphysics too is essentially concerned with the insistence on comprehensibility. Its precursor was the rationalism of the Mu'tazilites, which was renewed by Averroës precisely with reference to evil. As God, according to Mu'tazilite doctrine, could not have done anything without wise intentions, and as all His actions served the well-being of every single human being, it was necessary to recognize this wisdom of divine action in every event, as unremarkable or unjust as it might seem – to find him out, so to speak, so that one could defend divine justice. Al-Ghazali

– although he subscribed to the Ash'arite emphasis on divine omnipotence and the contingency of all events – also believed that he could prove God's justice rationally. Through him the Mu'tazilite intention was continued, albeit in a gentler form, in Ash'arism. The charge that, despite his outstanding prestige within orthodoxy, he had followed the heretical views of the philosophers Abu Hayyan at-Tauhidi (d. 1023), Avicenna and the Brethren of Purity (Ikhwan as-Safa, tenth century) confronted him practically with the first response.[30]

It was Al-Ghazali's ambition to prove the perfection of the world and the necessary rightfulness of everything existent – that is, the wisdom of the divine plan – without limiting God's power or freedom. Leibniz faced exactly the same task, that of deciphering the divine plan in its wisdom, when he declared God's creation a harmonic system that can be decoded without any constructs of faith. Thus Hans Blumenberg, in *Matthäuspassion* [St Matthew Passion], describes theodicy as the final attempt 'to find God's ulterior motive [. . .], ultimately less to defend him, as the name "justification" pretends, than to see through him'. Leibniz's apologetic interest is directed at God on the surface, but actually at human reason, which must be capable of explaining God – so as to behave in God-like fashion, as Blumenberg notes: 'The snake had simply exaggerated a little. For seeing through someone means, strictly speaking, either being or being able to be like that person.'[31]

The super-elevation of the human capacity for knowledge marks the difference, and the specifically philosophical aspect, of Leibniz's theodicy compared to the confessional apologetics that preceded it. But herein lies also the reason for its failure – for, without a quasi-religious faith in reason, it was simply not apparent why this of all worlds, with its natural disasters, wars, scandalous injustice and daily suffering, should be so perfect and just in the first place. This is precisely the charge levelled at al-Ghazali by later theologians, even if one of those critics who dared to question the authority of the sheikh in the face of the world's miserable state – Ibrahim ibn Burhan ad-Din al-Baqa'i (d. 1480) – had to hide from the mob at times in his Damascus home. At first glance a forerunner of Voltaire, he reversed al-Ghazali's theorem: 'Something more glorious than that which is would be possible.' As rebellious as the formulation may seem, its impulse was exactly the opposite. Al-Baqa'i attacked the most respected representative of Islamic orthodoxy from, in a sense, an ultra-orthodox position (as well as attacking him for his supposed weakness in the study of *hadith* and the introduction of new ritual practices). For in fact it was not the intention of al-Biqa'i, unlike al-Mar'arri before him and Voltaire after him, to deny the Creator's justness, or even to call His existence into question. Rather, he was emphasizing the limited nature of humans. Considering actual conditions, human understanding could only view the world as imperfect; in order to prove right away that, from a human perspective, almost everything in the creation could be different – indeed, better fashioned – al-Baqa'i presents a long list of natural, but partly also fantastic examples of the world's insufficiency, hardship and injustice. As it is, the world simply cannot be the perfect manifestation of that absolute power; if it is a sign at all, as al-Ghazali and his successors insisted so vehemently, then surely a sign of what God could have done if He had only wanted – but, for whatever reasons, simply did not want to do. The obvious imperfection of the world only proves how little it reflects God's might. 'No one in their right mind could doubt', for example, that this world would have been better if God had given wisdom and goodness to all humans – not only because of physical illnesses such as lameness, blindness or leprosy, but also inner ones such as 'deviousness, brutality, hate, and the weakness that ensues in the hunt for superficially repulsive things'. If the imperfections of the world had a smell, al-Baqa'i writes bitterly, 'then the whole of being would stink, and everyone would flee from this world.'[32]

For al-Baqa'i, divine omnipotence becomes a pure article of faith that he consciously separates from the empirical realm, which contradicts it. His pessimism is cutting and undoubtedly a product of the real conditions of his time, which he describes at length; theologically, however, his concern is not with the imperfection of the world, but with the absolute superiority and sanctity of God. Some authors, however, were able to offer the same pessimism more laconically and without dialectical intentions. 'So long as you are in this world, be not surprised at the existence of sorrows. For, truly, it manifests nothing but what is in keeping with its character or its inevitable nature',[33] writes the Egyptian Sufi Ibn Ata'illah (d. 1309), robbing the readers of his *Book of Wisdom* of the illusion that things might still improve in the world.

As often as al-Ghazali's optimism was rejected, his doctrine of the best of all worlds nonetheless survived into the nineteenth century, and in a few cases even into the twentieth.[34] It was not only comforting but also combined contrasts: al-Ghazali rehabilitated rationalism and integrated Sufism into Ash'arite orthodoxy – but set strict limits for both elements, the reason of the philosophers and the spiritual insight of the mystics, through the primacy of divine providence. For al-Ghazali, too, all human explanations are provisional, for ultimately no one will ever understand the 'secret' of God's goodness anyway, and must simply believe in it:

> Never doubt that He is the most merciful of the merciful, or that His mercy takes precedence over His anger, and never doubt that whoever would pursue evil for the sake of evil and not for the sake of good is unworthy of being called merciful; for in all this lies a mystery whose divulgence the law forbids. Be content with prayer, and do not demand for it to be divulged. You have been instructed through signs and directions whether you belong to His people.[35]

The notion of the best of all worlds emerged six centuries later in Europe than in Arab-influenced cultures – and was obsolete sooner. For what is considered classical theodicy today was, in fact, scarcely current for more than a century, if one includes the three Tübingen seminarists Hegel, Hölderlin and Schelling (d. 1854) as Leibniz's successors; the three of them imagined the rebirth of a kind of thought that viewed the world in Christian terms not as fallen but rather as infused with divinity, and viewed man not as a sinner but rather as a darling of the gods. Voltaire – thirty-five years after Leibniz – already pointed out the aporetic nature of Leibniz's argument. His full satirical wit, subtlety and sharpness of thought culminate in the 'Poème sur le désastre de Lisbonne', in sympathy with the downtrodden that admits to its own perplexity and helplessness.

Voilà le nœud fatal qu'il fallait délier.	This is the fatal knot you should untie.
Guérirez-vous nos maux en osant les nier?	Our evils do you cure, when you deny?[36]

Voltaire's poem, which appeared one year after the Lisbon earthquake of 1755 and was read and discussed all over Europe (some twenty editions of the poem were printed in 1756 alone),[37] formulated an altered perception of the world that made the optimism of Leibniz's theory seem increasingly untenable. After Voltaire, Kant – likewise in a late work – rejected all efforts to define the truth of the Christian faith in the sense of a philosophical acceptance as deception. Reason's inherent need to explain cannot be fulfilled by reality, he taught apodictically. Reason, he argued, has needs whose subjectively inescapable nature does not correspond to the way in which things in themselves are given. As we know, however, the nature of things in themselves cannot be deduced with the tools of reason. Kant himself drew the logical conclusion – rarely challenged seriously after him – that all philosophical attempts at theodicy are doomed to failure – because all statements about God can only fail (hence Heine's reference to Kant's *Critique of Pure Reason* as 'the sword with which deism in Germany was executed').[38]

Without admitting it, the philosophers before Kant had argued similarly; the difference was that they had incorporated the unfathomable nature of divine actions into theodicy itself, declared as an objective purposiveness which our subjective understanding is insufficient to recognize. Leibniz compared the divine order of the world to an especially artful novel in which all confusion is resolved at the end in complete harmony. In aiming to prove that what subjectively seemed counter-purposive by no means lacked purpose in objective terms, the theodicies that came after Leibniz followed – despite claims to the contrary – the main path of monotheistic crisis theory: explaining injustice and suffering with the inexplicability of God. After all, it is no more than speculation if the protagonist of a novel makes assumptions about the author. Kant not only put an end to the sham out of philosophical consistency; his late essay on theodicy betrays a profound pessimism, indeed an undisguised despair, at the world in its present state. As with al-Baqa'i, and as so often in the history of philosophy, it is the immediate experience of life with its wars, illnesses and everyday depressions that thwarts high-flown reason. In 'The Conflict of the [philosophical and medical] Faculties', Kant fundamentally questions the intention of 'macrobiotics' to prolong human life: for Kant, a long life may very well be a 'long drudgery, and the part of it spent in sleep as an escape from this much hardship'.[39] Hence, in the text on theodicy, Kant rejects the argument advanced by Job's friends against cursing existence, namely that, 'however bad someone's lot, yet everyone would rather live than be dead', and that one therefore cannot possibly look unfavourably upon life, which would be mere 'sophistry'. The reply to this may safely 'be left to the sentence of every human being of sound mind who has lived and pondered over the value of life long enough to pass judgement, when asked, on whether he had any inclination to play the game of life once more, I do not say in the same circumstances but in any other he pleases (provided they are not of a fairy world but of this earthly world of ours).'[40]

With Kant, who stated that God eludes reason and life does not follow any positive purpose, the philosophical engagement with the question of unjust suffering returned to the restraint it had exercised in the Middle Ages. For the less than modest school of idealism, which elevated reason itself to the divine, the question was a different one; it did not even consider applying the standard of human morality to God or the world spirit. From then on, aside from the metaphysical exploits within the analytic philosophy of the twentieth century, it remained largely the domain of theology to probe reason, of all things, for comforting answers to the problem of suffering. The optimism that had inspired Leibniz, and al-Ghazali before him, had become philosophically dubious in Europe since Kant, and morally discredited by the time of Schopenhauer, if not earlier, as 'a truly *wicked* way of thinking, a bitter mockery of the nameless sufferings of mankind'.[41] The one thing for which he gives Leibniz credit is presenting Voltaire with the occasion to write his opposing text – 'in this way, of course, Leibniz's oft-repeated and lame excuse for the evil of the world, namely that it sometimes produces the good, obtained proof that for him was unexpected.'[42] Inverting Leibniz's claim, Schopenhauer calls the world 'the worst of all possible worlds', for, 'if it were a little worse, it would no longer be capable of continuing to exist.'[43]

> If, finally, we were to bring to the sight of everyone the terrible sufferings and afflictions to which his life is constantly exposed, he would be seized with horror. If we were to conduct the most hardened and callous optimist through hospitals, infirmaries, operating theatres, through prisons, torture-chambers, and slave-hovels, over battlefields and places of execution; if we were to open to him all the dark abodes of misery, where it shuns the gaze of cold curiosity, and finally were to allow him to glance into the dungeon of Ugolino where prisoners starved to death, he too would certainly see in the end what kind of a world is this *meilleur des mondes possibles*. For whence did Dante get the material for his hell, if not from this actual world of ours? And indeed he made a downright hell of it. On the other hand, when he came to the task of describing heaven and its delights, he had an insuperable difficulty before him, just because our world affords absolutely no materials for anything of the kind.[44]

What remains once all answers have been driven out is the question. The problem of evil is the decisive problem that philosophy still has to tackle, sensed the aged Schelling – and did not manage to resolve it himself. His great model of a Christian version of real-idealism that grasps the senselessly destructive, unordered force in life as the expanding principle of all being was more announced than executed in the text on freedom from 1809.[45] Three years later Schelling, who had published one celebrated major work after another between the ages of nineteen and thirty-five, fell almost completely silent as an author; at that point he still had another forty-two years to live. The central texts of his overlong late period appeared posthumously and gained little attention, just as the question of good and evil generally disappeared from the metaphysical field of view. This did not mean that evil became less important; on the contrary, the devil's greatest ruse, as foreseen by the preacher in Charles Baudelaire's short story 'The Generous Gambler', was 'to persuade you that he does not exist'.[46] Schelling's examination of the problem of evil proved to be prophetic and had far-reaching consequences for the history of philosophy. Neither Schopenhauer's *World as Will and Representation* nor Nietzsche's *Will to Power* are conceivable without Schelling's definition of evil as part of the actual principle that creates life. And the European philosophy of the twentieth century, where it proceeds seriously, can be understood as an engagement with the dark side of being, which was now perceived above all as a man-made historical disaster. The paradigm was no longer Lisbon but Auschwitz.

The qualification of divine omnipotence

Only the God envisaged by the monotheistic religions, God as a personal creator, attracts the suspicion of omnipotence. Polytheism obviously knows no such problems, and even the simplest dualism, as taught by Zarathustra (seventh century BC) or Mani (d. c.277), did not need to trouble itself with the absolute responsibility of the One, as there was a second element – Ahriman in Zoroastrianism, darkness in Manichaism – that necessarily limited its power. Beyond strict monotheism, then, evil is by no means an obstacle to understanding God; He simply cannot prevent it. Reaching this conclusion does not require speaking of God in the plural – but one does need to posit an opposing principle or substance, as shown by Platonism and neo-Platonism. Evils exist, argues Plato in *Timaeus*, as Plotinus (d. 270) did in his treatise *On Providence*; suffering exists, but God had no other choice than to permit it, as it is inherent in the matter from which God created reality. Here, in contrast to the genesis of the world in the three Abrahamic religions, God does not produce matter from nothingness; it exists independently of God and possesses His power. Without God there would be only chaos; God succeeds in forming the chaos into the best possible order. But matter remains itself, and hence does not come from God. Plotinus delegates the responsibility for evil to godless matter: 'We cannot complain about the lower in the higher; rather, we must be grateful to the higher for giving something of itself to the lower.'[47]

The Gnostic Marcion (d. 160) and the young St Augustine did not differ fundamentally from Plotinus in their justification of evil, in so far as it could not already be explained through sin, or original sin. In their interpretation, too, God is forced to permit suffering, as there is something that opposes his salvation or his creation: for Marcion, the evil creator god,[48] or, for the young Augustine, man, who sins of his own accord.[49] In his tract on free will, *De libero arbitrio*, Augustine goes so far in his apology for the one Creator – intended as a direct attack on the dualism found in Gnosticism and Manichaism – as to ascribe almost complete freedom of will to humans. In order to absolve God from responsibility for evil, humans are declared autonomous creatures. But whether it is Plotinus' matter, Marcion's demiurge or human freedom in early Augustinian thought that limits God's omnipotence, in each case God has an 'alibi', as Odo Marquard has noted.[50]

In many interpretations of Christianity, God at least comes to the aid of the sole culprits, namely humans, by extending the hand of salvation to them through Jesus Christ. This does not put the world in order, but in a world of disaster it is the best thing that can happen. Such a notion has a solid biblical foundation; neither the Hebrew Bible nor the New Testament gives many indications that God is actually omnipotent, something that most Christians today take for granted. While German Bible translations speak of the 'Almighty' [*Allmächtiger*], the original text uses the title *El Shaddai*, which some exegetes derive from the verb *sadad* (damage, destroy, do violence) and others translate in the sense of 'the sublime' or 'the high Lord'. 'The Almighty', at any rate, is not the literal meaning of *El Shaddai*. In addition, the majority of the word's uses (thirty-one out of forty-eight) appear in the Book of Job – a text that attacks God precisely in the application of His power. Job uses the epithet *El Shaddai* (6:14) for the God whom he blames for the injustice he has suffered, who does violence to men (10:3), who locks Job's feet in shackles like an executioner (13:27) and generally behaves like a tyrant (19:11, 30:21ff.). So, where God's omnipotence is implied in the Hebrew Bible, it is not usually accompanied by goodness (the same applies to Isaiah 13:6, Joel 1:15 and Ruth 1:20). God cannot simply let the kingdom of love begin; the establishment of his rule depends on whether humans want that rule, as expressed in the Jewish idea of the thirty-six righteous for whom God has to wait. The good creation extends as far as God created it; in many places, however, the natural chaos that existed before the creation repeatedly comes to the fore. 'In the beginning God created the heavens and the earth. Now the earth was formless and empty' (Genesis 1:1–2). The Hebrew phrase for 'formless and empty' is *tohu wa bohu*, and is also applied to the barrenness of the desert. The exegetes spoke of chaos as the initial state into which God projected his creation. As God's creation, from this perspective, is not yet complete; it is not chaos or evil that should surprise us but rather God's intervention, which is the origin of good.

The New Testament refers even more rarely to God's omnipotence. None of the recorded statements made by Jesus permit associations of omnipotence. On the contrary, the New Testament maintains the view that God's order will only be fully realized in heaven, while on earth the struggle continues because humans fall short of fulfilling this order. Klaus Berger reminds us that the phrase 'Your will be done' in the Lord's Prayer did not at first express primarily submission to God. By God's will, the Jesus tradition rather means the commandments which the believer resolves to preserve. It was only with the establishment of Christianity as a state religion that the notion of an omnipotent God was cemented, not least because it gave His earthly servants a welcome licence to exercise their political and clerical power. Augustine's late 'doctrine of grace', which defined Christian speculation on evil for over a millennium, spiritualizes an absolute hierarchical relationship between the omnipotent God and humans, sinners by definition, who are presented as unable to avoid evil or achieve salvation through their own efforts.[51]

The Koran leaves no doubts about God's omnipotence, and it would be interesting to investigate whether this is a result of Mohammed's revelation setting itself apart not only from polytheism but also from the Bible – or whether, on the contrary, the Koran takes up the Church's concept of omnipotence. At any rate, 'God is powerful over everything' (Surah 2:20). Hence there is little room for evil in the Koran, and where it appears in God's creation nonetheless, it is essentially understood as a dialectical aspect of the plan that God introduced with the creation of humans. The tension between God's omnipotence and the reasonable nature of His actions, which is given equal emphasis in the Koran, was interpreted in favour of omnipotence by the Ash'arites, and hence Sunni orthodoxy: then God is ultimately also responsible for man-made disaster. Where exactly there is room for disaster in God's plan of salvation is not revealed to humans, admittedly. In this reading, humans are instructed to acknowledge God's omnipotence, avoid evil and refrain from further questions, because:

> He shall not be questioned as to what He does,
> but they shall be questioned. (Surah 21:23)

Although the Koran, unlike most books of the Bible, places great emphasis on God's omnipotence, it remained a controversial issue in Islamic theology. For the Koran teaches the justness of God even more vehemently than His omnipotence: 'Surely God shall not wrong so much as the weight of an ant', one reads in Surah 4:40. So how can God want his creatures to blaspheme against Him and punish them for something that He has preordained by making the unbelievers 'deaf, dumb and blind' (2:171 and elsewhere)?

> And God encompasses the unbelievers. (Surah 2:19)

Because the Koran highlights God's omnipotence and the reasonable nature of his actions so clearly, the problem of theodicy is more urgent in Islam than in Judaism or Christianity. Very early on, Muslim theologians faced the challenge of balancing God's omnipotence with his compassion and justice. The first answers turned out in favour of justice: asked by the Umayyad caliph Abd al-Malik (d. 705) whether God eternally damns those whom He did not guide towards Islam, the ascetic al-Hasan al-Basri, one of the influential early Islamic scholars, answers that God is 'too compassionate (*arḥam*) and too just (*a'dal*) to do that to His servants'.[52]

> God the Sublime is too just to blind a man and then tell him: 'See, or I will punish you!', or to close his ears and then say to him: 'Hear, or I will punish you!', or to make him dumb and then say to him: 'Speak, or I will punish you!'[53]

In order to maintain the comprehensibility of God while absolving Him of the responsibility for evil, Hasan argues in favour of human free will and implicitly limits God's omnipotence. The founders of the Mu'tazilite school, Wasil ibn Ata and Amr ibn Ubayd (d. 761), belonged to al-Hasan al-Basri's circle in Kufa. They developed an Islamic doctrine of free will, partly as a reaction to the hypostatization of divine omnipotence in sects such as the Mujbiriyya (or Jabriyya), who advocated strict predestination. It was espoused beyond the Mu'tazilite school, however, by a broad, albeit scarcely coherent movement known as *Qadariyya*. Together, Mu'tazila and Qadariyya were known as the 'party of justice' (*Adliyya*), because their emphasis on free will was based on the aim of proving God's justice dialectically. And so they too, because they clung to the belief in goodness and justice, were forced to qualify God's omnipotence, even to dispute it factually, and instead emphasize the free choice of humans in order to explain evil. In Islam, this view persisted only in Shiite theology; in Sunni orthodoxy, as in Catholicism, a middle ground was established between human freedom and divine omnipotence where all power is assigned to God, yet nonetheless all guilt to humans. Sunni orthodoxy accepted the Ash'arite doctrine of *kasb*, whereby humans can 'acquire' (*kasaba*) the actions already preordained by God in an act of self-responsibility, while, with the Council of Trent, the Catholic Church adopted Thomas of Aquinas's distinction between God 'causing' and merely 'permitting' evil.[54]

God himself suffers

If one maintains that humans have free will, however, then God cannot do anything about evil; it would follow from this that He Himself suffers most. The world came about only through God's forgetfulness, wrote Nietzsche, taking up Luther's words; if He had thought ahead, God 'would not have created the world'.[55] Both the Bible and the Koran contain a number of verses that can be read as references to God's suffering. The wrathful God can be understood as a God who despairs at the humans He Himself created, because their ignorant and malicious natures prevent them from following the path He made so explicitly clear to them, the open, broad path of their salvation – 'the straight path' (*aṣ-ṣirāṭ al-mustaqīm*). The Koran and Islamic tradition push this drama between God and mankind even further by declaring the entire creation and its history, all pleasures, civilizations, emotions and natural phenomena – in short, literally everything that exists on earth – signs given to humans by God so that they might understand. And they go even further: God, as interpreted in many passages in the Koran and expressed in an extra-Koranic divine statement – 'I was a treasure and wanted to be recognized; therefore I created the world'[56] – really brought forth the creation only so that mankind would recognize Him: 'O son of Adam. I created you for my sake and created all things for your sake.'[57] How much it must pain such a creator that, despite all His efforts, mankind turns away from Him! Often the Koran, especially in the early Meccan Surahs, seems like the message of a lover to his ungrateful beloved: God courts, lures and flatters, He rages and damns, He dictates, is magnanimous, threatens and promises, while man covers his eyes and ears, closes himself off, and even worse – he mocks God, to whom he literally owes every hair on his head. If one takes the Koran's description of their relationship seriously, one could believe that it is not man who suffers, namely under the evil in the creation, but rather God, who must endure the ingratitude of his creatures. This is not made explicit in the Koran, however. It is the Book of Hosea that tells the story of God's relationship with humans as a tale of unhappy love that goes through all possible cruelties, even to the point of sexual abuse. And it was left to the New Testament to make God's suffering central – though suffering *for* humans, not *under* humans. The cross gave the answer to Job, wrote C. G. Jung in his book of the same name, relating the crucifixion to theodicy. In a Christian interpretation, Jesus Christ can be understood as the saviour – or, as the Hebrew *goēl* should actually be translated, as the 'advocate' or 'blood avenger' – on whom Job calls as a witness of his innocence and a liberator from violence, so that he can defend himself against the murderous god Yahweh, who breaks the law (19:25).[58]

The rabbinical tradition has given considerable space to the notion that God himself mourns and laments the state of mankind.[59] But in the early Church there also developed a belief – later rejected by Catholic orthodoxy – that God the Father suffered no less on the cross than the Son. In a very different fashion, but with undeniable Christian aspects, the idea of the suffering God flowed into the post-Kantian idealism of Hegel and Schelling. Both developed their entire philosophy from the notion that God, or the absolute, is realized throughout the world and thus suffers history. Odo Marquard sees theodicy as a decisive motive for transcendental idealism: the acquittal of God is achieved precisely through the idealistic turn from creation theology to the position of autonomy, which makes humans, in their freedom, responsible for the state of the world.[60]

The suffering God became current once more in the 1960s and 1970s as the last possibility to reconcile world events with the notion of a God who is loving and close to us: if God is good and we cannot believe that he would shut us out, there is only one explanation for suffering: He cannot do anything about it. An almighty God who permits Auschwitz was an unbearable thought for many Jewish and some Christian theologians, and left little room to justify God by pointing to the unfathomable nature of his will. God cannot possibly have wanted Auschwitz and, if He did not want it but it happened nonetheless, He cannot be almighty.

Within a very short time, the once heretical view that God himself suffers from history became almost a new orthodoxy, formulated in Catholic terms by Hans Urs von Balthasar and Walter Kasper and in Protestant terms by Karl Barth, Dietrich Bonhoeffer, Erberhard Jüngel and Jürgen Moltmann, to name its most prominent advocates in German theology. Many thus believe that the question of theodicy has been answered, for, 'if God himself suffers, then suffering can no longer be used as an objection to God',[61] as Walter Kasper writes with noticeable relief. Kasper circumvents the problem of omnipotence by stating that God suffers voluntarily, 'out of love and from His love, which is excess of being'.[62] God cannot do away with suffering any more than Kasper can, but 'is transformed from within – transformed into hope'.[63] It is probably Jürgen Moltmann who has gone furthest in this direction: he sees 'Auschwitz, like the cross of Christ, within God Himself', namely 'absorbed into the pain of the Father, the devotion of the Son and the power of the Spirit'.[64]

Moltmann explicitly invokes the rabbinical theology of God's self-abasement and its creation-theological development in the Kabbalistic *tsimtsum* doctrine, to which the Jewish philosopher Hans Jonas also refers in order to formulate a similar thought. According to this doctrine, the decision to perform the creation presupposed that God would limit Himself and contract in order to create a God-free space, in which He could create a world different from Himself. Thus God suffers Israel's suffering, he goes into exile with Israel, feels the torment of the martyrs and waits for deliverance with his people. In his famous speech on the concept of God after Auschwitz, Hans Jonas describes God as a powerless witness: 'Having given himself whole to the becoming world, God has no more to give: it is man's now to give to him.'[65] While Moltmann sees the responsibility for God as an unmanageable burden for humans and therefore states that 'God himself [. . .] must help us',[66] Jonas believes that 'it is not God who can help us, but we who must help him.'[67] In both cases, God is excused. Whether it genuinely helps humans to abandon divine omnipotence simply in order to be able to cling to God's goodness has often been questioned since then, in both Judaism and Christianity. As one example among many others, we shall take the complaint of Karl Rahner, who, before all theological and hermeneutical justifications, argues as directly as the fools in *The Book of Suffering*: 'To put it somewhat primitively: when I am trying to get out of my dirt, chaos and despair, what good does it do me to know that God – crudely put – feels just as rotten?'[68]

The terror of God

My point of departure was the triad of the monotheistic notion of God, as summarized by Hans Jonas: goodness, omnipotence, cognizability. The God presented in Attar's stories is omnipotent; He could alter the pitiful fate of humans if He desired, but He simply does not want to do so; He is not interested – in fact, He even seems to enjoy tormenting humans. As far as anyone can tell, God does the things He does deliberately. A man sees a fool crying and asks him what is the matter.

'How could I not cry when I am so hungry?'

'You may be hungry, but that's no reason to cry like that!'

'But that's why he is making me starve – so that I shed tears like a spring cloud' (21/12, p. 213).

God is certainly omnipotent; but are his actions accessible to human comprehension? What God does seems to elude all logic, or at least all positive logic. Thus one fool declares God stupid, another calls Him crazy. The second fool is sitting on the ground in winter, eating snow.

'Why are you eating snow?' someone asks him.

'My stomach is hungry.'

'But that won't fill it.'

'Tell that to God. His answer to my pleading was that I should eat snow if I'm hungry. No madman says something like that. No madman says he can fill me up without bread' (27/7, p. 251).

Perhaps God simply cannot do any better. Perhaps He has the power, but is inept or stupid. When the cattle plague breaks out, a farmer quickly sells his cows and buys donkeys. Ten days later the donkey plague breaks out. He looks up to the heavens and calls out: 'You, who know all secrets, can't you even tell the difference between a donkey and a cow?' (27/15, p. 255).

In *The Conference of the Birds*, Attar tells of a fool who runs around naked while everyone is wearing magnificent clothes.

'Lord, give me a shirt!' exclaims the fool: 'Let me be just as cheerful as the other people!'

'What are you complaining about?' answers the voice of God: 'We gave you the sun, so let it warm you.'

'Lord, how long will You still torment me? Do You really have no better garment than the sun?'

'Very well, wait ten days and I will give you a shirt.'

Ten days later the fool does indeed receive a shirt, but from a man who is himself very poor. And that is how the shirt looks: a coat of rags, patched together from a thousand shreds of cloth. The fool calls out to God: 'O knower of secrets, did You need ten days just for this patchwork? Have the decent clothes in Your treasury all been burned, that You had to sew all these rags together? Sewing a hundred thousand patches together – where did You learn Your tailor's craft?'[69]

Accusing God of incompetence or idiocy is reserved for a few isolated outbursts, however, and these all tend towards the grotesque. The people in *The Book of Suffering* may reproach God for His mistakes, but they do not really believe that He lacks power or wisdom. Attar does not follow the path shown by Ibn ar-Rawandi when he said – much like one of Attar's fools, but without any humorous intent – 'You distributed livelihoods among people as ineptly as if You were drunk. If a man divided something up like that, we'd tell him: you've gone mad, get some treatment!'[70] Ibn ar-Rawandi, who initially belonged to the Mu'tazilite school before becoming a heretic, exemplifies the boundary between belief and unbelief: the terror of God is conceivable in a state of piety, but whoever declares God insane no longer takes Him seriously – he no longer believes Him, and hence no longer believes in Him, albeit not in the same sense as an atheist.

The free-thinking tone of Ibn ar-Rawandi, who makes fun of God as someone who cannot even add three and three together, is found in Attar only in a few individual accusations. Those who mock God in *The Book of Suffering* are deadly serious. It is only funny – if at all – to the observer. God may act against all reason, but Attar's protagonists know very well that He bears the responsibility. They know what kind of God they have, for He constantly reveals Himself through His deeds – if only He were less manifest! The problem with God's wisdom is not that it is inaccessible, but that it does not serve the good of humans. The problem is God's absolute wilfulness, not the limited nature of human understanding. In the first chapter I quoted the criticisms of Attar with which Mehdi Hamidi caused a stir in the Iranian literary scene in 1969. I also view Hamidi's stylistic assessment as untenable; what is less easy to dismiss, however – and hardly considered by any of Attar's defenders – is the ideological aspect of his criticism: Attar's view of the world and especially of God is highly disturbing, to say the least. One cannot completely refute Hamidi when he notes that the God presented by Attar in his poetry is a 'terrifying monster' that

> lies roaring on its giant heavenly throne, issues impossible commands, and is equipped with a power more terrible than anything one could imagine. He is a being that shimmers behind a sea of light in the shape of a confused nightmare and seems visible in its invisibility, a being that not only unifies all the shameful qualities found among creatures, but has also developed each of them to a godly level.[71]

The image of God conveyed by *The Book of Suffering* is one that was all but foreign to Persian love mysticism, as whose early representative Attar is usually presented. *Lā ilāha illā l-'išq* – 'There is no God but love': this was the poet Fakhroddin Eraqi's (d. 1289) altered version of the Muslim creed as a mystical axiom still upheld by Sufis today.[72] The later mystics usually understand God's wrath as concealed grace – for does the Koran not state: 'He loves them, and they love Him' (Surah 5:59)? From this perspective, to use Rumi's images, Attar sees the dust but not the wind; he looks at the foam on the waves, but not at the seabed.[73] Attar would not have denied the existence of the seabed, but, firstly, he would not have been so sure that it really holds anything comforting and, secondly, he would not have had any hope of reaching such depths anyway. This connects him superficially to the disenchanted world of our own age, but even more to the ascetics of early Islam, whose fear of God is documented in countless exclamations and behaviours. Through their knowledge of God they sit on a throne, 'crowned with a crown of honour', as Abdulwahhab ash-Sha'rani (d. 1565) knew.

But above their heads hangs a sword, suspended by a single hair, and two wild beasts are loose at the gate, so that they are 'threatened with destruction' at every moment.[74]

The circumstance that the Creator lulls his most loyal worshippers into a sense of security (*istidrāǧ*), only to cast them suddenly and all the deeper into misery, was passed on to Sufism by the early mystics as a warning. Then they always spoke of *makr*, the 'cunning' of God, which became a topos of its own within Sufi literature; the appropriately named scholar Ayyub (Job) al-Qurashi from Damascus (d. 1660) even devoted an entire treatise to the subject.[75] Bayezid Bestami, probably the boldest of all Sufi holy men next to al-Hallaj, was even displeased if God granted him a miracle. When he came to the River Oxus, the two banks moved together so that he could cross without becoming wet.

'Lord, why this cunning?' exclaimed Bayezid and turned around without crossing the river: 'I have not served You for this.'[76]

The fear of God's cunning took on even more curious manifestations among the early Sufis. Sari as-Saqati (d. 865 or later), for example, supposedly looked at his nose several times a day because he was afraid that God may have coloured his face black.[77] He warned his fellow humans: 'If someone entered a garden with many trees and a bird perched on each tree, saying to him in perfect Arabic: "Peace be with you, friend of God!", and he did not fear that God's cunning was behind it, he would have fallen prey to God's cunning.'[78] The famous Shibli (d. 945) spoke especially of the malicious treatment to be expected from the Creator: 'Under every gift from God lie three acts of cunning, and under every act of obedience lie six',[79] he lamented, and warned: 'Beware of his cunning, if only with reference to his command "eat and drink!" [Surah 2:60].'[80] Ruwaym (d. 915), a further exponent of Sufism, was also worried that God might deceive humans: 'He concealed His cunning in His lenience, His deception in His graciousness, and His punishment in His merciful gifts.'[81] The Sufi theorist Abu Talib al-Makki (d. 996) wrote:

> The disastrous end will come through God's cunning, which one can neither describe nor explain, nor grasp. His cunning is endless, because His will and His decisions have no limits. Hence the well-known account: 'The Prophet and Gabriel were weeping for fear of God. Then God said to them, "Why are you weeping when I have promised you safety?" They answered, "But who is safe from Your cunning?"' If they had not known that His cunning is endless, as His decisions have no limits, they would not have said, 'But who is safe from Your cunning?', for he had told them, 'I have promised you safety.' His cunning would then surely have ended with His words, and they would have recognized the end of His

> cunning. But they feared the cunning beyond that, which was concealed from their view, and they knew that they could not grasp the heart of the hidden God. For He is the knower of hidden things, and for one who is all-knowing, no knowledge ever ends, and there is no attribute that brings the hidden things to an end. Hence they were not fully convinced that He was concerned for them and looked graciously upon them.[82]

For the early Sufis, it was Satan who suffered worst on account of God's cunning. He was in a hopeless situation: God commanded him to kneel before the newly created humans, while Satan had eyes only for God. When God cursed Satan for refusing out of love to follow His command and praise any being other than Him, Gabriel and Michael began to weep and continued for a long time.

'Why are you weeping so?' asked God.

'Lord, we do not feel safe from Your cunning.'

'And rightly so! You should not feel safe from my cunning!'[83]

Al-Qushayri (d. 1074), who tells this story, also quotes the following remarks by Hatim al-Asamm (d. 851):

> Do not be fooled by a good place! No place is better than paradise, and yet Adam experienced his famous misfortune there. Do not be fooled by an abundance of worshipful acts! For what happened to Satan happened after a long period of worshipful acts. Do not be fooled by great knowledge! For Bal'am [the biblical Balaam, who in Koran exegesis is the prototypical wise man who is led astray by pride and lust] had good knowledge of the greatest name of God; but look what became of him! Do not be fooled when you see pious men! For no one was greater before God than the Chosen One, but it was no use to his relatives and enemies that they met him.[84]

Not even the prophets can feel safe from God: Sahl at-Tustari (d. 896) sees thirty of them in a dream, and asks what they feared most in their lives. 'Doom!' they answered.[85]

In *The Book of Suffering*, Attar also describes God's cunning – for example, when Satan is asked why he did not kneel before Adam when God commanded it. Then Satan tells the story of a Sufi who sees a princess and finds her so beautiful that he falls in love with her immediately.

'Just wait until you see my sister', says the princess: 'Look, there she comes!'

When the Sufi then turns around to look, she has him beheaded (26/1, pp. 242ff.)

Elsewhere, an impoverished thorn-gatherer from the steppe who can scarcely feed his wife and children begs Moses to ask God if He can provide for his family. When the prophet conveys the request to God,

God answers that this is unfortunately impossible. But he is willing to grant the thorn-gatherer two wishes. Meanwhile a king has arrived in the area, and he steals the man's beautiful wife and puts her in a box. In his desperation, the thorn-gatherer wishes for his wife to turn into a bear. Then he goes into town to get bread for his hungry children. After arriving at his palace, the king has the box opened and finds a bear instead of the woman. Afraid that it might be an evil fairy, he has her returned to the thorn-gatherer's house. When the man returns home, he finds his children in complete terror of the bear. What else can he do but utter his second wish: for God to return his wife to her original state (26/3, pp. 245ff.).

One can certainly read the story as a warning to be content with one's lot. But one could also understand it to the effect that God amuses himself by stringing the poor thorn-gatherer along; after all, it would have been in His power to grant the pious man's request for a livelihood. Attar does not portray the thorn-gatherer as demanding anything unreasonable; his request was understandable, even justified – especially if one considers that he was not even concerned for himself, but for his starving family. In addition, it is hardly a coincidence that Attar treats the motif of livelihood (*rizq*) in this way: in the Koran, God expressly commits himself to providing for humans. He almost promotes himself with the fact that, unlike the old gods, He looks after his creatures:

> God is He that created you,
> Then he provided for you,
> Then He shall make you dead,
> Then He shall give you life;
> Is there any of your associates
> Does aught of that?
> Glory be to Him!
> High be He exalted above what they associate with Him! (Surah 30:40)

In Attar, however, as often in Islamic mysticism, God shirks the responsibility He has imposed on Himself. He has nothing better to do than to punish humans for their justified desires and sincere prayers; this was evidently understood by Ibn Adham, who put his hands in front of his face after every prayer for fear that God would slap him about the ears with it (36/3, p. 322). God torments humans purely as a pastime, for fun and out of vanity, presenting His reference to the treasure that wanted to be recognized and therefore created the world in a very different light: God created humans to have fun, to trick them and to revel in his own narcissism. In *The Book of Secrets*, Attar also portrays God as a potter who moulds his first pots very artfully in order to smash them for his amusement and relish the clattering of the death pangs.[86] 'But we are the poor musicians and our bodies the instruments', writes Georg Büchner, God's chief prosecutor among German writers, with a similar image. 'The ugly sounds scratched out on them: are they just there to rise up higher and higher and gently fade and die like some voluptuous breath in heavenly ears?'[87]

Perhaps Büchner's Valerio is right, and God was simply bored: Sultan Mahmoud of Ghazna, whom Attar often uses to exemplify the omnipotent ruler, is sitting alone in his palace. No one visits him, no one has a request, and not even beggars seek an audience. He roams alone through the expansive halls of his palace. He is bored and lonely. What is the matter, he asks his vizier, why does no one come to him any more? 'Because justice currently prevails', answers the vizier. Then Mahmoud sends out his soldiers to attack the villages, stirs people up against one another, and demands extortionate fees, taxes and toll charges. At once the king's hall fills with supplicants, people in search of advice, and those seeking mercy. Sultan Mahmoud leans back, satisfied (37/12, pp. 336f.).

The God presented by Attar in many stories is a cynic, someone who catches humans in a net and watches mercilessly as they become entangled in it. Caliph Umar ibn al-Khattab (d. 644) has to embark on a journey, even though his wife is pregnant. Before he leaves, he entrusts the unborn child to God. After a few weeks he returns, and learns that his wife has died. He goes to the cemetery and hears a voice from his wife's grave. He opens the grave and finds one half of her alive, with the infant at her breast, while the other half of her body is already rotting. Umar takes the infant in his arms and hears a voice call out to him: 'God has returned to you what you entrusted to Him. For you had not entrusted the mother to Him' (23/9, p. 225).

Only after reading such stories can one understand why Gabriel and the other angels, and in fact all the creatures passed by the 'wanderer of thought', are sick with fear. 'Those of His servants fear God who have knowledge', states Surah 35:28. It is 'the fear of a person caught in the current of a flood or close to a great fire', as Muhammad al-Ghazali describes the condition: 'That is exactly how the fear of God the Sublime feels, whether because one knows Him and His attributes, and knows that it would mean nothing to Him if He let all mankind perish, and that no one could prevent Him from doing so; or because man committed so many sins and is thus guilty of so many crimes; or because both of these apply.'[88] For the early Islamic ascetics and mystics whose spirit pervades *The Book of Suffering*, this fear is in no way metaphorical, neither a religious attitude nor a necessary phase on the way to spiritual annihilation, as believed by the later mystics. It is an everyday fear, insurmountable and utterly real, and indeed suffered physically as a 'burning of the heart', as al-Ghazali expounds:

> Afterwards the effect of the fire moves from the heart to the body, the limbs and the character. In the body the fear manifests itself as emaciation, yellowness, fainting, screaming and weeping, and sometimes it makes the gall bladder burst and causes death. Or it rises to the brain and destroys the mind. Or it takes it over completely, causing hopelessness and despair.[89]

Such descriptions relate to historical persons. Abu Muhammad Ata as-Salimi al-Abdi (d. after 757), for example – to name one of the early Sufi masters whose moroseness and fear took on extreme proportions – looked like 'a dried-up tube', as a contemporary reports.[90] 'Whenever I saw him, his eyes were overflowing', another recalls: 'When I looked at him, the only comparison I could think of was a woman who has lost her child. Ata did not seem of this world.' Fear paralyzed Ata – and by no means in a merely metaphorical sense. It is said that he lay in bed for forty years without the courage to get up, let alone leave the house. At night he touched his body all over, afraid that he had been transformed into a low creature. When he awoke, he said: 'Woe to you, Ata, woe to you!' After completing his ritual ablutions, he trembled and wept heavily. Asked why, he responded: 'I want to undertake something momentous: I want to stand (in prayer) before God.'[91] If someone happened to mention death, Ata usually fainted. His fear was so great that he even forgot the Koran. His wife convinced Ata's friends to scold him for all his weeping, but her reprimanded husband defended himself, saying: 'What is it like for someone when his hand is tied to the back of his neck and he is dragged into the fires of hell? Does he not scream and weep? And what is it like for someone who is being tormented? Does he not weep?' Ata's prayer was scarcely more than a cry for help: 'O God! Have mercy upon me as an outsider on this earth. Have mercy upon me when death strikes me down. Have mercy upon me when I lie alone in the grave. Have mercy upon me when I stand before You.'

Such is the piety of the holy men of whom Attar collected accounts his entire life. That is the world he brings back to life in his poetry. He finds the essential aspects of his own hardship in the Sufi accounts of the Prophet, his companions and the earliest ascetics: the ubiquity of death (supposedly the Prophet would already speak the prayer for the dead over a new-born child and ask God to preserve it from the torment of the grave and hellfire),[92] the longing for nothingness ('I wish I had never been created', Abu Zarr and Talha supposedly said),[93] for eternal rest ('I wish no one would awaken me after my death', Caliph Uthman is quoted as saying),[94] and for ultimate annihilation – Ibn Mas'ud sometimes wished that he would be turned to ash, sometimes to a pile of excrement.[95] 'If only my mother had never borne me!' the mystics also quote the second Caliph Umar, whose face supposedly had two black lines from the constant flow of tears. Both Umar and Aisha, the Prophet's wife, inverted the worst curse among Jews – 'may you not be remembered' – into an expression of longing when they identified with Mary's exclamation in Surah 19:23: 'Would I had died ere this, and become a thing forgotten!'[96]

While it is likely that the mystical tradition projected its ideas into the first generation of Muslims, there is little historical doubt that, one or two centuries after Mohammed, an entire religious movement was in fact characterized by the fear of the world described above. Al-Hasan al-Basri, the most famous exponent of early Islamic asceticism, already made the following impression on his contemporaries:

> When he turned his face towards one, he looked like a man returning from the funeral of a relative; and when he turned his back, like a man with the fire of hell hanging over his head; and when he sat, like a prisoner being led to his beheading; and in the morning, like a man returning from the hereafter; and in the evening, like a sick man marked by suffering.[97]

In the course of time, the ascetics and early mystics virtually categorized the cursing of life and opposed it with the fear of death. The aforementioned Ata, for example, yearned for a long time for death, until someone in a dream asked him if he was quite sure about that. Suddenly the disastrous nature of death was revealed to him, and he hastened to assure himself that he would rather stay alive. From then on his appearance became all the more desolate, and he spoke like a figure from *The Book of Suffering*: 'If you know the hardship and agony of death so well that the knowledge filled your heart, you would never sleep again in your whole life, and your mind would become so confused that you would walk distraught among men.'

Nonetheless, in spite of his fear of what awaited him in the grave, Ata did not stop craving for death: 'I long for death, even though I do not believe I will find peace through it', he explained his paradoxical yearning: 'But I know that a dead man can no longer act. Thus he is saved from committing a sin, and his soul is denied success. But a living man must fear his soul every day, and the end of all that is death.'[98]

Theology of fear

If, beyond descriptions of fear in the lives and experiences of the mystics, one searches for a specific theology of the divine terror poetically invoked in *The Book of Suffering*, one will not find it in Islam. One would have to go back to the late works of Augustine to bring to the surface what is special about Attar's understanding of God. Augustine's thought, shaped by the conditions of his time, also became increasingly dark. For Christians, the fall of Rome to the Visigoths in 410 seemed a catastrophe of apocalyptic proportions. Because of countless heresies and schisms, the Church in Augustine's later years was as depressing to witness as, seven centuries later, Islamic erudition for the aged Attar. In those years, Augustine repeatedly spoke of God's punishment, which strikes all humans indiscriminately, the inevitable decline of all material things, and the world's imminent entrance into old age. The Vandal invasion, after which his African home was no longer part of the Roman Empire, confirmed the church father's suspicions and visions of disaster. In old age, the intense, ever-present fear of disaster that had tormented Augustine since his youth took on proportions probably equalled only by the all-consuming fear of life experienced by the early Islamic ascetics. He quoted the preacher Solomon's words 'for with much wisdom comes much sorrow' (Ecclesiastes 1:18), adding: 'A heart that understands cuts like rust in the bones.'[99] Even after forty years of serving God, Augustine looked with dismay at the cracks that can suddenly open up in the life of even the most devoted person, and listed examples of righteous people who fell prey to sin in old age: 'For no one is known to another so intimately as he is known to himself, and yet no one is so well known even to himself that he can be sure as to his conduct on the morrow.'[100] He saw no possibility of an intrinsically good community in a world so beset by evil.

While, as a priest, Augustine had described despair as an unpardonable sin against the Holy Spirit, emphasizing free will and hence human responsibility for evil, the last decades of his life saw such an insistence on providence that his opponents soon accused him of regressing into heathen fatalism. The break with his earlier view is marked by the doctrine of grace he formulated in 397 in a letter to the Milanese theologian Simplician (d. 400), the same year in which Augustine penned his autobiographical *Confessions*. For the first time, he sees humans completely dependent on God, even in the original desire to believe in God. Augustine speaks of the dirt heap and the mass of sin from which God takes the clay to form what He wants: some become figures of ruin, others become heirs to heaven. Such images of mankind reject any humanistic dilution, as Kurt Flasch emphasizes: 'a lump of sin and wrath, hecatombs of executed prisoners, streams of blood: the panopticon of a Baroque-poetic pedagogy of horror. And above it all a God who – clearly – is merciful only to a few.'[101] In *The Book of God*, Attar likens humans to a polo ball which the player asks to make sure it does not roll into the ditch. As the course of the ball is determined by the mallet, however, the ball is not to blame if it deviates from its intended path.

> The sin is not yours.
> But you are stuck with it nonetheless.[102]

In *The Book of Suffering* people can also do what they please; it does not necessarily have any bearing on their salvation or damnation. The *pir* in the following episode explicitly refuses to attribute even a part of God's favour to human agency.

'The sadness of humans', says an old man to his friend, 'comes from the fact that God does what He wants, not what humans want and need. Even if He hears one prayer in a hundred, He only hears that one prayer because it has requested something he desired anyway' (23/7, pp. 244f.).

According to Augustine, God does not dispense His mercy in keeping with principles of human logic; His decisions are those of a being that says of the twins Jacob and Esau that it loves one and hates the other – before they have even been born, and regardless of their actions. Jacob and Esau, Isaac's sons and Abraham's grandsons, are the unequal twins who already fight in their mother's womb. Esau, the firstborn, is raw and boisterous, his face red and his skin as rough as an animal's. He loves hunting, and always provides his father with the game he loves to eat. The other, Jacob, has delicate skin and is his mother Rebekah's favourite. He is a good boy and stays at home. But the hot-tempered Esau is the man of the house, because he happens to be the firstborn. He is talked into selling his birthright to Jacob, however, who subsequently also manages to gain the necessary blessing from his father by trickery: instructed by his mother, Jacob wraps his hands and neck in goatskin and brings his blind, dying father a final dish of venison. The dying man mistakenly blesses Jacob, and the blessing thus remains with the deceiver and his descendants. By the time Isaac realizes he has been fooled it is too late; once bestowed, the blessing cannot be taken back. And so he is forced to tell his beloved son in dismay: 'I have made him lord over you and have made all his relatives his servants, and I have sustained him with grain and new wine. So what can I possibly do for you, my son?' (Genesis 27:37).

The biblical story taken up by Augustine is made of the same material from which Attar wove his poetry; the motifs Attar employs are far closer to the Hebrew Bible than the Koran. 'God calls whomever He calls without reason, and turns away whomever He turns away without reason', Attar writes (8/1, p. 119). Nothing we do makes us worthy of God's grace – that is the doctrine Augustine derives from the story of Jacob and Esau. There is no reason why God loved Jacob and hated Esau even before they were born. Whatever humans do, God is merciful to whomever He pleases.

'I don't know, I don't know, my God', speaks the mystic Shibli in *The Book of God*: 'Only You know, only You know what You want. You called the one man to You with a hundred favours, and chased away the other with a hundred blows. The one did not display any act of obedience, nor the other any sin.'[103]

Rejecting the Mu'tazilite emphasis on freedom, most Sufis maintained God's omnipotence without reservations. Attar too follows the Ash'arite theology in believing that misfortune is also caused by God. The following witty anecdote about Moses related by al-Ghazali is characteristic of this view:

'O Lord, where do medicine and healing come from?' asks Moses.

'From me', answers God.

'So what do doctors do?'

'They collect their pay and keep my servants in good spirits until I either heal them or choose not to.'[104]

From this perspective, the idea of human free will seems heretical. But religion is not a thought system free of all contradictions. Religion 'can certainly contain a *complexio oppositorum*', as the influential Swedish bishop and Middle East scholar Tor Andræ (d. 1947) noted, referring both to Islam and to the notion of strict predestination in Calvinism: 'A paradox, such as the doctrine of predestination, may well be the only possible way of expressing the truth that our salvation rests entirely in the hand of God.' If religion followed the matter to its conclusion and also extended the paradox to the question of human responsibility, for example, a disastrous situation could well ensue: the complete non-responsibility of humans. 'But the believer does not draw these conclusions. That which has to follow, in the opinion of the critics, does not happen at all.'[105] What Andræ expresses here is summarized concisely by the Prophet's well-worded saying, 'Trust in God, but tie up your camel.'[106] This surely applies to the faith of many Muslims, even today. Attar, however, in contrast to Ash'arite orthodoxy, follows the principle of predestination to its conclusion and makes God directly responsible for the injustice that befalls humans.

In this view, which, among the Sufi masters, Talib al-Makki came closest to expounding theoretically, humans are absolutely dependent on God. Their fate is preordained, their will only seemingly free. Not even actions or knowledge of the law matter, only that which has been engraved on the heavenly tablet at God's command (8/0, p. 117). The insights of the early mystic Abu Sulayman ad-Darani, whom Makki cites as a witness, are identical to Augustine's doctrine in parts:

> God is too sublime for the deeds of his creatures to arouse His wrath. Rather, He looked upon some men with the eyes of wrath before He created them, and therefore, after He had brought them forth, used them for those acts that bring down wrath and then let them live in the house of wrath. And He is too great for the acts of his creatures to cause His favour. Rather, He looked upon some men with the eye of favour before He created them, and therefore, after He had brought them forth, used them for those acts that find favour and then let them live in the house of favour.[107]

But Attar, and before him Augustine, goes even further than simply attributing the greatest possible free will to God and thus placing humans completely at His mercy. In their late works, both give God direct responsibility for evil. Evil is not a force that acts independently of God, but rather – for Augustine at least – a necessary part of good.

'Can one say that God is a tyrant?' a fool asks an old *pir* in *The Book of Suffering*.

'God is not a tyrant, but he always has a hundred thousand slaves who are tyrants' (4/6, p. 92).

If one reads history from Augustine's perspective, the tyranny of existence is just, as for him all humans are like a single 'mass of sin owing a debt of punishment to the divine and loftiest justice'.[108] Some of these godless beings are forgiven by God, while the rest are made by Him as 'vessels of wrath' in order to 'reproach' the others.[109] God's decision to refrain from giving some humans their just punishment cannot be interpreted as injustice; on the contrary, it is a further reason to be thankful. 'Let us also believe most firmly and tenaciously that God has mercy on whom he will and whom he wills he hardens, that is, he has or has not mercy on whom he will. Let us believe that this belongs to a certain hidden equity that cannot be searched out by any human standard of measurement'.[110] God is thus responsible for evil – but He is not evil. For God, terror is a means to the end of discipline and education, as Augustine also notes in his *Confessions*.[111] He still sees Jesus Christ as a similar taskmaster. When Augustine looks back on his works thirty years later, he scolds himself for writing in his book

Of True Religion that Jesus never used violence.[112] The people in *The Book of Suffering* also see violence and terror, but can no longer believe in their purpose. A number of people complain to al-Hajjaj (d. 714), the tyrannical governor of Iraq, who is infamous to this day for his shameful deeds. The governor gathers the entire population together and mocks those who suffer innocently: 'What bad people you are, that God has let me loose on you!' (38/8, pp. 343f.).

The difference between Attar's and Augustine's conceptions of God determines a diametrically opposed conception of humans. The question of suffering, which preoccupied Augustine until his death and cast him into despair, paradoxically changed into anger at the human race – even though he largely denied that they bore responsibility for their actions. Augustine repeatedly defends the collective punishment whereby God persecutes Adam's sin in the body of every single one of his descendants, even when Julian, the most vehement critic of the later Augustine, accuses him of thus declaring God the kind of criminal 'one can barely imagine among barbarians'. In a letter, Julian, later Bishop of Eclanum, asks Augustine, currently Bishop of Hippo: 'Tell me then, tell me: who is this person who inflicts punishment on innocent creatures? You answer: God. God, you say! God! He who commended His love to us, who has loved us [Rom 5:8], who has not spared His own son for us [Rom 8:32] . . . He it is, you say, who judges in this way; He is the persecutor of new-born children; He it is who sends tiny babies to eternal flames.'[113] Augustine opposes Julian's optimism with the Holy Scriptures, in which God sends tremors through the human sense of justice with the announcement that he 'punishes the children and their children for the sin of the fathers to the third and fourth generation' (Exodus 34:7). God, according to Augustine, sees further. In His omniscience, He will make no mistakes when He wages his blood feud against the descendants of Adam. God must have the right to be angry, and humans cannot deserve any better because they are already born guilty. If certain individuals happen to be chosen by God, there is no justification for it. For Augustine, this ruled out any further inquiry into God's reasons: even discussing God's decision is the epitome of indecency, namely pride and 'impudence'.[114]

For Attar, however, humans are by no means guilty by definition, and hence the pain of existence is not always just. For this reason, one does not have to be grateful to God for the mercy he shows at least a few sinners. On the contrary: in Attar's tales, that pain usually strikes innocents – holy men, fools, simple people, the population of a city – while their suffering is mocked by the godless who are permitted to enjoy their lives. Like Augustine, Attar interprets God's omnipotence in the strictest possible sense: as the absolute impotence of humans. For Attar, however, mere reference to God's unfathomable nature and human sinfulness is certainly not enough to shrug off the question of theodicy. His figures do not accept this God as He reveals himself to them. They rebel. While Augustine's God complains about sinners, Attar's humans complain about God. They cannot understand divine actions, but they certainly do see His wilfulness and the evil and injustice it holds. In this sense they also cling to the third attribute in the triad of goodness, omnipotence and cognizability, albeit in an unconventional manner: they recognize God, but that is precisely their problem. Instead of omnipotence and comprehensibility, Attar's figures dare to deny the divine attribute that would seem a constitutive part of monotheism, namely goodness, with all its aspects such as justice, love and compassion. God is responsible, and no one else. At the pinnacle of despair, man no longer turns away from his creator but towards him – as an enemy: 'You turn on me ruthlessly'. Job, who speaks these words (30:21), provides the archetype of this affect.

> He has blocked my way so that I cannot pass; he has shrouded my paths in darkness. He has stripped me of my honour and removed the crown from my head. He tears me down on every side till I am gone; he uproots my hope like a tree. His anger burns against me; he counts me among his enemies. His troops advance in force; they build a siege ramp against me and encamp around my tent. (Job 19:8–12)

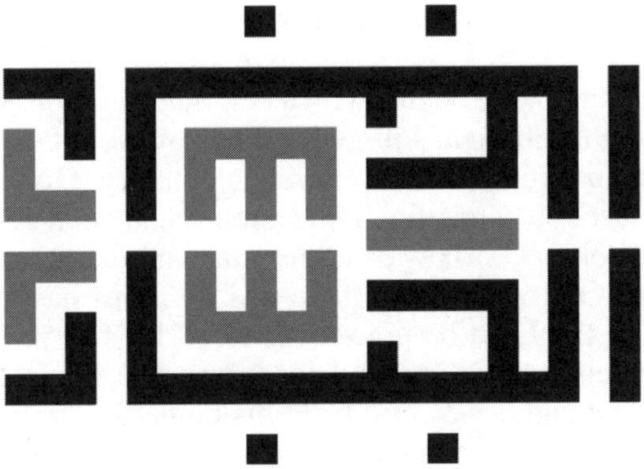

— 4 —

THE REBELLION AGAINST GOD

The Job motif

The Book of Job famously begins with a bet: Satan claims that even the most God-fearing of all men, Job, will turn away from God as soon as he finds himself in dire straits. To prove the contrary, God gives Satan permission to cast Job into ruin. Thereupon Satan robs Job of all his livestock and labourers, strikes dead his sons and daughters – yet Job remains loyal to God: 'The Lord gave and the Lord has taken away; may the name of the Lord be praised' (Job 1:21). The devil does not give up, and afflicts Job with painful sores from the soles of his feet to the top of his head and drives him from his home. Job, once honoured by all who knew him, as pious as he was happy, now lies naked on ashes, covered with open sores, his children murdered, his house stolen. In his hands he holds his only possession, a piece of broken pottery with which he scratches himself day in and day out, yet cannot stop the itch that torments him – this is one of the most disturbing images in world literature, for it reminds us that misfortune can strike anyone, and, unlike in tragedy, it does so without any necessity or logic, just arbitrarily and senselessly.

At this point Job still trusts in God, as much as his wife mocks him for it. When his three friends hear of the disaster that has befallen Job they come, each from his hometown – Eliphaz from Teman, Bildad from Shuha and Zophar from Naama – and sit on the ground with him for seven days and seven nights, unable to do anything but weep and tear their clothes in sorrow, 'for they saw how great his suffering was' (2:13). Only now does Job begin the lament whose opening we have already encountered in Attar's variation and various others: 'May the day of my birth perish, and the night it was said, "A boy is born!"' (3:3).

> Why is light given to those in misery, and life to the bitter of soul, to those who long for death that does not come, who search for it more than for hidden treasure, who are filled with gladness and rejoice when they reach the grave? Why is life given to a man whose way is hidden, whom God has hedged in? For sighing comes to me instead of food; my groans pour out like water. What I feared has come upon me; what I dreaded has happened to me. (3:20–24)

The decisive aspect of this lament is that there is no reason for Job's suffering. He cannot attribute his hardship to his actions. God allowed him, the most morally distinguished of all people, to be cast into misery. 'Then know that God has wronged me and drawn his net around me', Job calls out. 'Though I cry, "I've been wronged!" I get no response; thou I call for help, there is no justice' (19:6–7). If he had sinned, Job would understand his suffering as punishment; yet God is punishing him without any apparent reason. The causality of sin and punishment, righteousness and reward has been disabled: 'He destroys both the blameless and the wicked' (9:22). And Job rebels against God, because he knows full well that he has done nothing wrong. God has made an unjust world.

> Even if I were innocent, my mouth would condemn me; if I were blameless, it would pronounce me guilty. Although I am blameless, I have no concern for myself; I despise my own life. It is all the same; that is why I say, 'He destroys both the blameless and the wicked.' When a scourge brings sudden death, he mocks the despair of the innocent. When a land falls into the hands of the wicked, he blindfolds its judges. If it is not he, then who is it? (9:20–24)

Job's friends are dismayed by his words and try to convince him that all suffering comes from guilt – but Job rejects all their arguments. A fourth visitor appears, Elihu, who reprimands Job before God finally answers – if his words can even be called an answer. For God does not explain himself, he does not even respond to Job's questions; he only stubbornly points out his greatness and the impotence and ignorance of the questioner, who cannot 'bind the chains of the Pleiades' (38:31), an incompetent, helpless, clueless worm before the almighty Lord. He scoffs that Job does not even know 'when the mountain goats give birth' (39:1). Job does not know any answer to God's never-ending eulogy on Himself, whose grotesque elements Robert Gernhardt highlighted both aptly and humorously in a short adaptation.[1] He admits to having spoken rashly, and places his hand over his mouth to remain silent henceforth, before the story takes a second surprising turn: God justifies Job before his pious friends, even though he had rebelled against God and they had defended God. Job is rewarded with treasures, starts a new family and lives for another 140 years, accompanying his children and their children to the fourth generation, and dies 'full of years'. That is the story of Job, which Attar retells in many of his stories.

The biblical Book of Job follows two contrary lines: Job's unconditional submission is as pronounced as his vehement rebellion. Ernst Bloch held that the aspect of submission was added later to the original text 'as a cover for the heresy Job wanted so fearlessly to proclaim'.[2] Here he takes up Horace Meyer Kallen's argument that the book's final editors placed the orthodox framework of a prologue and reconciliation around the original heretical tale.[3] It seems to me that the combination of conflicting tendencies is what defines the Book of Job. Even if the editors smoothed out and augmented the text, it is surely unlikely for philological reasons that the changes were limited schematically to the beginning and the end, or to softening the book's provocation. Some researchers have claimed that the framing prose narrative was combined with the poem of Job only afterwards; it is more likely, however, that the Job poet already knew it as an oral or written folk tale and reworked it himself.[4] But, even without such text-historical arguments, a schematic division into a rebellious and a submissive Job is equally unconvincing in its content. This is precisely the concern in the Book of Job: to show the contrasting affective responses to suffering. It is not a piece of committed literature, but rather a complex composition of opposing motifs that do not cancel each other out. Bloch thus underestimates the speeches of Job's friends, at least three of which probably belonged to the original poem. The friends are not the gloomy moralizers as denounced by Bloch; they present a serious case, especially Eliphas, not least in the poet's view. Reading Attar helps to understand more precisely this ambivalence that characterizes the Book of Job and makes it so remarkable.

While Job is the central biblical book on the experience that God can be unjust, it does not stand alone in the Bible. To the children of Israel, it almost went without saying that God brings misfortune on humans, and they did not always accept it as their just punishment. If one pays attention to the subtext, there is a running thread of man's rebellion against God in the Hebrew Bible (assuming one does not read its books in their order of writing, as the motif appears mostly in the later, post-exilic texts). From Adam and Eve via the legend of Cain, the Tower of Babel and Jacob's fight at the Jabbok, to prophets such as Jonah or Hosea's unfaithful wife, humans distrust God's counsel, come into conflict with him or rebel openly. Even Moses asks: 'O Lord, why have You brought trouble upon this people?' (Exodus 5:22), and Elijah similarly cries out: 'O Lord my God, have You brought tragedy also upon this widow I am staying with, by causing her son to die?' (1 Kings 17:20). While Moses and Elijah at least receive answers, there is no consolation for those souls who cannot find justice in the success of the sinful King Manasseh (2 Kings 21:1–18) and the misfortune of his loyal successor Josiah (2 Kings 22:1–27). 'You are always righteous, O Lord, when I bring a case before You', Jeremiah begins; 'Yet I would speak with You about Your justice: why does the way of the wicked prosper? Why do all the faithless live at ease?' (Jeremiah 12:1). In his lamentations, this questioning of God is both intensified and stylized into a literary form of its own:

> Look, O Lord, and consider: whom have You ever treated like this? Should women eat their offspring, the children they have cared for? Should priest and prophet be killed in the sanctuary of the Lord? Young and old lie together in the dust of the streets; my young men and maidens have fallen by the sword. You have slain them in the day of Your anger; You have slaughtered them without pity. (Lamentations 2:20–22)

This text, which is considered the earliest of Jeremiah's five lamentations and was probably written shortly after the destruction of Jerusalem by Nebuchadnezzar II (d. 562 BC) in 587 BC, is harrowing in the realism with which it depicts the catastrophe: women driven to cannibalism, priests and prophets murdered in the temple, children and old men slaughtered. Admittedly, the lamentations consist largely of self-reproach; in passages such as this, however, they repeatedly point to God, whose actions are too cruel and wilful for His goodness not to be in doubt. Children, even unborn ones, being eaten by their mothers do not fit into any model of guilt and punishment (or a connection between action and consequence, to be more precise). The praying man of the Old Testament does not simply lament; again and again, he accuses. He who speaks directly *to* God dares say things that the teacher who speaks *about* God would not. The prophet Habakkuk, for example, is driven by a direct experience of injustice to turn to God without being addressed first, demanding an answer and thus inverting the conventional relationship between God and the prophets:

> How long, O Lord, must I call for help, but You do not listen? Or cry out to You, 'Violence!' but You do not save? Why do You make me look at injustice? Why do You tolerate wrong? Destruction and violence are before me; there is strife, and conflict abounds. Therefore the law is paralyzed, and justice never prevails. The wicked hem in the righteous, so that justice is perverted. (Habakkuk 2:2–4)

In the Hebrew Bible, the well-worn religious explanation that guilt leads to suffering, which at least offered some security and provided tools in the form of rites and prayers, is undermined almost as often as it is supported.[5] Half of the Book of Psalms alone consists of songs lamenting God's causing, or at least not preventing, senseless suffering. More theologically and poetically harrowing than atheist criticism could ever be, they bring up the subject of God-made misery. Psalm 74, for example, the people's lament upon the destruction of the temple, dispenses with the typical hymnal address for Yahweh, and already asks reproachfully in the very first verse, 'Why have You rejected us forever, O God? Why does Your anger smoulder against the sheep of Your pasture?' Like this song, Psalm 88 does not hint at any confession of a guilt that could justify God's anger as a punishment. The text is the hopeless protest of one who has been ill his entire life and monstrous as a prayer, not least because – unlike the Book of Job – it ends without any hope:

> O Lord, the God who saves me, day and night I cry out before You.
> May my prayer come before You; turn Your ear to my cry.
>
> For my soul is full of trouble and my life draws near the grave.
> I am counted among those who go down to the pit; I am like a man without strength.
> I am set apart with the dead, like the slain who lie in the grave, whom You remember no more, who are cut off from Your care.
>
> You have put me in the lowest pit, in the darkest depths.
> Your wrath lies heavily upon me; You have overwhelmed me with all Your waves.
> You have taken from me my closest friends and have made me repulsive to them. I am confined and cannot escape; my eyes are dim with grief.
>
> I call to You, O Lord, every day; I spread out my hands to You.
> Do You show Your wonders to the dead? Do those who are dead rise up and praise You?
> Is Your love declared in the grave, Your faithfulness in destruction?
> Are Your wonders known in the place of darkness, or Your righteous deeds in the land of oblivion?
>
> But I cry to You for help, O Lord; in the morning my prayer comes before You.
> Why, O Lord, do You reject me and hide Your face from me?
>
> From my youth I have been afflicted and close to death; I have suffered your terrors and am in despair.
> Your wrath has swept over me; Your terrors have destroyed me.

All day long they surround me like a flood; they have completely engulfed me.
You have taken my companions and loved ones from me; the darkness is my closest friend.

This God has consistently proved an enemy since the youth of the psalmist,[6] who sees no blame on his part and will not be persuaded otherwise. Like Job, like Attar's fools and saints, he suffers for no apparent reason. Man is God's victim: 'Your terrors have destroyed me.' This may also have been what Jesus Christ thought; his last words, as reported by the evangelists Mark (27:46) and Matthew (15:34), take up the lament tradition of the Hebrew Bible – Psalm 22:2, to be precise: 'My God, my God, why have You forsaken me?' Read against mainstream Church exegesis, these passages are every bit as implacable as Jean Paul's 'Speech of the Dead Christ from the Top of the Universe: That There Is No God'. While Jean Paul depicts the abandonment even of God's son as a dream, it appears as an incontrovertible reality in Gérard de Nerval's (d. 1855) poem 'Christ on the Mount of Olives'. In the twentieth century, Rainer Maria Rilke gave Jean Paul's and Nervals's image of Christ new expression in his poem 'The Olive Garden':

And still he climbed, and through the grey leaves thrust,
quite grey and lost in the grey olive lands,
and laid his burning forehead full of dust
deep in the dustiness of burning hands.

After all, this. And this, then, was the end.
Now I'm to go, while I am going blind;
and, oh, why wilt Thou have me still contend
Thou art, whom I myself no longer find.

No more I find Thee. In myself no tone
of Thee; nor in the rest; nor in this stone.
I can find Thee no more. I am alone.

I am alone with all that human fate
I undertook through Thee to mitigate,
Thou who art not. Oh, shame too consummate . . .[7]

The poem then speaks of an angel who came later; that is how the story goes. But it was only the night.

For angels never come to such men's prayers,
nor nights for them mix glory with their gloom.
Forsakenness is the self-loser's doom,

> and such are absent from their father's cares
> and disincluded from their mother's womb.

Angels do not come to those who utter such prayers; they are abandoned by their fathers. There is theological justification for the view that Jesus not only began his prayer with the words of Psalm 22 on the cross, but was genuinely forsaken by God. Jürgen Moltmann writes: 'What caused Jesus's death? Not only the legal understanding of his fellow Jews and the Roman politics of power, but ultimately his God and Father. This godforsakenness was the ultimate torment in his torment.'[8] Moltmann uses the fact that Jesus suffered through God as a conceptual bridge to God's own suffering. But when God himself suffers, He is no longer present as the recipient of the accusation. Read from the perspective of the Book of Job, the Psalms or Jeremiah, such a theodicy, in which God Himself becomes a supplicant, seems as curious or at least as one-sided as the image of God as a paternal but – God forbid! – not overly severe friend; a loving but certainly not despotic helper in all situations, emancipatory but by no means awe-inspiring or even destructive – in short, everything humans could desire. And yet the mere recollection of Isaac, bound as a sacrificial offering, goes against everything that human emotion and thought normally associate with a benevolent God. George Steiner has formulated strikingly what anyone reading their child the stories of the prophets has felt in response to incredulous questioning: 'How might we best define God, how do even partial justice to Him in our imagination? Precisely as a being that would never order a man to plunge a knife into his child's throat.'[9] This was precisely the focus of Gnostic criticism of Christianity: the sinister aspects of the Old Testament image of God. The incredible influence of the Gnostics would be inexplicable if they had not formulated, and thus freed from taboos, a very natural interpretation that even had witnesses in the Holy Scripture itself, namely Job and the psalmists. Using a number of biblical passages as evidence, Marcion taught that the Jewish God 'lies, makes experiments as in ignorance, deliberates and changes his purpose, envies, hardens hearts, makes blind and deaf, commits pilfering, mocks, is weak, unjust, makes evil things, does evil.' A God who is 'false', who 'loves wars, is not faithful to his promises, loves the wicked and adulterers and murderers, changes his mind, chooses evil men.'[10] His frequently unprovoked, apparently completely wilful wrath is such a prominent characteristic of the biblical God that it took centuries of looking away for it not to disturb the general consciousness.[11] It is always understood that His wrath is just, but the biblical texts describe it at such length that it seems out of all proportion to its cause.

Very often the God of the Hebrew Bible is a war hero, unyielding in His vengeance, which wipes out entire peoples.

Though the New Testament no longer describes the eruption of God's wrath in detail, His wrath becomes a subject of its own that, especially in the epistle to the Romans and the Book of Revelation, is directed mercilessly at all people outside of the Christian community in a manner unknown from the Hebrew Bible. The sugar-coated image of Jesus born of complacency, half-knowledge and good intentions also disappears upon closer reading, for he 'did not come to bring peace, but a sword' (Matthew 10:34). Even in the Sermon on the Mount, one can hear the full passion of the God who loves humans beyond measure, but is also disappointed and angry at their falseness. As is well known, Jesus does not use kind words to drive the traders from the temple. He hurls the words 'You snakes! You brood of vipers!' at the Pharisees, pouring out a sermon of punishment on them that still makes readers shudder today. In addition to their own misdeeds, they are to be collectively punished for all wrongdoing in the history of mankind: 'And so upon you will come all the righteous blood that has been shed on earth, from the blood of righteous Abel to the blood of Zechariah son of Berakiah, whom you murdered between the temple and the altar. I tell you the truth, all this will come upon this generation' (Matthew 23:35–6). Whoever speaks such words does not understand gentleness as some theological soft option. Entire communities are excluded from Jesus's brotherly love – the Nicolaitans, whom he hates (Revelation 2:6), or the Jews of Smyrna, whom he views as 'a synagogue of Satan' (Revelation 2:9). It is Jesus, the preacher on the Mount, who casts Jezebel on a bed of suffering, forbids John to tolerate her illegitimate children out of compassion and instead strikes them dead: 'Then all the churches will know that I am he who searches hearts and minds, and I will repay each of you according to your deeds' (Revelation 2:23).

Everyone is free to imagine Jesus as they wish, but the New Testament – especially those descriptions from the charismatic early Christian community[12] – does not suggest that he behaved like the Good Person of Szechuan or the vicar on national television after the Saturday night show.[13] His words were not for Sunday; they were for eternity. The Bible tells of one condemned to love, a man possessed, an extremist who also demanded unconditional devotion – 'Anyone who loves his father or mother more than me is not worthy of me' (Matthew 10:37) – and the readiness to die: 'whoever loses his life for my sake will find it' (Matthew 10:39). His absolutist claim is unprecedented in religious history: 'No one comes to the Father except through me' (John 14:6) – and yet he asked God to forgive his own murderers: 'Father, forgive them; for they know not what they do' (Luke 23:34). To imagine now what Jesus was like, one should perhaps look not so much to his clerical representatives as to certain figures on the margins that our society considers peculiar – crazy at best, and perhaps fanatical. Was Jesus not an extremist in his time, an extremist who threatened all things existing and established? If John fell to the ground 'like a dead man' at the sight of Jesus, one should take Jesus's exhortation 'Do not be afraid!' (Revelation 1:17) in a concrete sense, as a calmative for someone who is scared to death. 'Out of his mouth comes a sharp sword', says John, 'with which to strike down the nations. He will rule them with an iron sceptre. He treads the winepress of the fury of the wrath of God Almighty' (Revelation 19:15).[14] Such statements do not mitigate a single syllable of the Sermon on the Mount, but they form part of the multi-layered image the Bible presents of Jesus and God alike.

Another aspect of the Bible's multi-layered nature is the fact that protests against the Creator are not always caused by His mercilessness, but sometimes the opposite, namely by His goodness: the prophet Jonah complains to God about His patience and kindness, seeing these qualities as an expression of vacillation, indecision and general ambiguity. Time and again, thinkers and theologians in the Greek philosophical tradition attempted a theological reconciliation between the many sides of God. But these attempts stumble over the experience of a God who reveals Himself in ever new and different ways, a God who says of Himself: 'I will be what I will be' (Exodus 3:14).[15] It is precisely in his impenetrability, in the impossibility of unifying the elements, colours and contours into one bright, harmonious whole that this God (who, at least to my mind, is very different from the God of the Greek philosophers) repeatedly sends us back to His embodiments, externalizations and words – because we know that these old, cumbersome verses have something to tell us, that they concern, confuse or captivate us without ever completely revealing their meaning. If the holy texts simply said what people think anyway or understand immediately, there would be little reason to assume that they are holy, and hence come from a different world from our own.

Examples of a similarly disturbing stimulation of fear that cannot be twisted into anything emancipatory, something the Bible contains in more passages than the apocalyptic account alone, can be found in great numbers in the Koran. The unbelievers who are to be pursued, and whose necks are to be struck, are repeated so frequently on all channels in the discussion on Islamic fundamentalism, which has transformed European poets, publicists and politicians into Koran exegetes, that providing evidence is superfluous. What is more disconcerting is the highly double-edged picture that God paints of Himself in the Koran: as Michael Cook summarizes, 'God can be merciful and compassionate, responsive to those who turn to Him in repentance, generously providing guidance and help to His worshippers, not to mention rewards in this world and the next. But He can also be vengeful and hostile, not just punishing those who fail to respond to His guidance, but actively leading them astray, and thereafter consigning them to hellfire.'[16] In addition there are the sonorous and rhythmically oppressive warning sermons, the depictions of hell and apocalyptic visions, which do not exactly present God as a figure of hope, to say the least. Using the example of Moses, the Koran makes the fear of the God who reveals Himself tangible:

> And when Moses came to Our appointed time
> and his Lord spoke with him, he said,
> 'Oh my Lord, show me, that I may behold Thee!'
> Said He, 'Thou shalt not see Me; but behold
> the mountain – if it stays fast in its place, then thou shalt see Me.'
> And when his Lord revealed Him to the mountain
> He made it crumble to dust; and Moses fell down swooning. (Surah 7:143)

In Europe, there is no need to prove that the God of the Koran is not simply the God of love – nor is this untrue. Certainly the Koran portrays God in various facets of goodness, but these, as in the Bible, are inseparably tied to His force, and indeed His cunning and His terror. In the early Surahs in particular, the Koran seems like the outburst of a creator whose desperate rage at the ingratitude, injustice and blindness of His creatures turns into a final appeal to mend their ways, accompanied by thunderous threats and imploring promises. Because books like this express not desired and idealized, but rather real and hence catastrophic, human experience more perfectly than any man-made texts, they would be bland and euphemistic without their violent aspect. They are divine to the same extreme as they are human.

C. G. Jung had something else in mind – the divinity of Christ – but probably meant something similar when, in his late and possibly strongest, densest book, he formulated an *Answer to Job*. Jung named for himself the point at which Jesus Christ attained divinity: at the exact moment when, for the first and only time, he gave an indication of reflecting upon himself, wondering about himself and pitying himself, and when he discovered what God had subjected His faithful servant Job to – namely on the cross.[17] 'To believe that God is the Summum Bonum is impossible for a reflecting consciousness',[18] Jung declares apodictically, and indeed: exegetically speaking, one can only wonder how the Bible or the Koran could be taken as the basis for an unshakeable belief that God is the embodiment of what people now consider good. A more realistic alternative would seem to be the complete refusal, renewed by Kant, of the medieval – especially Arab – philosophers to conceive of God anthropomorphically, or the inversion of the faith in a good God: turning to God in lamentation, even rebuking him in such a state of injury – as one only rebukes someone who is dear to oneself and an important part of one's life.

The devaluation of lament in Christian theology

Christian theology has largely suppressed the fact that people rebel against God, and that even God's son quarrelled with his father – just as Psalm 88 was toned down by its later editors through its assignment to those psalms emphasizing the aspect of human forbearance. Lament in general has been theologically devalued in a variety of ways, assuming exegetes did not declare it in advance to be the opposite. This development is already visible in the New Testament: of the evangelists who had the Gospel of Mark at their disposal, with Christ's desperate cry of abandonment, only Matthew retained this drastic and true-to-life version of his death. Luke, on the other hand, has Jesus die after speaking the trusting words with which he places his spirit in his father's hands (23:46), and John finally makes Jesus as meek as a lamb in death: 'It is finished' (19:30). Although the early Christian community suffered persecution, and there must have been many moments and words of religious despair and godforsakenness, the New Testament features not one passage in which Christians turned to God in lament, or at least questioningly, because of the torment they had to endure innocently simply because of their Christian faith. Hence Paul, who suffered torture and imprisonment, prototypically overcomes his ordeal with no complaint, only affirmation and even gratitude:

> But he said to me: 'My grace is sufficient for you, for my power is made perfect in weakness.' Therefore I will boast all the more gladly about my weaknesses, so that Christ's power may rest on me. That is why, for Christ's sake, I delight in weaknesses, in insults, in hardships, in persecutions, in difficulties. For when I am weak, then I am strong. (2 Corinthians 12:9–10)

For many Christian theologians, the very word 'lament' already has an unseemly, impious undertone – for one should not lament.

Hence lament, which is a constant, indeed conspicuously prominent part of prayer in the Hebrew Bible, 'no longer has any place' in the Christian Church, as the great Protestant Old Testament specialist Claus Westermann notes.[19] In liturgical prayer the motif of lament and accusation hardly appears at all, and it is even kept out of the justifications of God in the light of suffering: throughout the entire history of Christian theodicies, from the Patrists to the twentieth century, the dimension of rebellion against God is virtually never considered.[20] Claus Westermann shows that, in almost all Christian commentaries and studies on Old Testament lamentations, lament is either 'devalued' or spoken of only 'with pejorative reservations'.[21] 'But where accusations against God are rejected as part of prayer, because it would be irreverent to accuse God of anything, the inevitable consequence is that this whole side of reality, the inexplicable and the terrible, is eliminated from the relationship with God', writes Westermann, and continues: 'It is kept quiet when speaking to God. And that means a grave loss of reality in speaking to God.'[22]

With the devaluation of lament, the main line of Western theology, which covers up the shimmering, raging, passionate God of the Bible with the philosopher's God of Marcion, also diluted or airbrushed away God's wrath, or examined it purely defensively, excusing it as the other side of love.[23] This applies also – and especially – to interpretations of Job. We already encounter Job in the New Testament as one who merely endures (James 5:11), then primarily in the early Church, for example in Tertullian (d. c.220), as well as in medieval literature.[24] In the Christian mysticism of the Middle Ages, the affirmation of suffering as the point where, as Mechthild of Magdeburg (d. c.1282) says, God's glory is fulfilled in humans removed all reason to lament: 'for now God is strangely with me, now His estrangement from me is more welcome than He is Himself.'[25] The comparatively sober, realistic Meister Eckhart (d. 1327) also preaches: 'Therefore lament thee not, or rather, lament thee that thou still lamentest.'[26] Hence Kierkegaard (d. 1855), who generally saw humans as being in the wrong before God, went against theological history and reminded readers of the biblical Job. 'Job! Job! O! Job! Did you really say no more than these beautiful words: the Lord gave, and the Lord has taken away; blessed be the name of the Lord?' asks Constantine Constantius in Kierkegaard's philosophico-literary text *Repetition*.

> Woe unto him who consumes widows and orphans, and defrauds them of their inheritance, but woe also unto those who cunningly defraud the grief-stricken of grief's temporary comfort, to vent itself and to 'quarrel

> with God'. Or is the fear of God so great in our age that the grieving person no longer needs what was customary in days of old? Does one no longer dare to complain to God? Has the fear of God, or merely fear and cowardice in general, become greater? Nowadays people believe that the genuine expression of grief, passion's despondent language, should be left to poets, who, like attorneys on behalf of a client, present the case of the sufferer before the tribunal of human sympathy. No one dares to do more than this. Speak, therefore, memorable Job![27]

Naturally Christians have formulated their protest against God, but this affect was significant neither in Christian theology nor in the liturgical practice of the Church. Immanuel Kant noted: 'Before any court of dogmatic theologians, before a synod, an inquisition, a venerable congregation, or any higher consistory in our times (one alone excepted), Job would have likely suffered a sad fate.'[28] The background and causes of this suppression have meanwhile been subjected to several examinations,[29] and in recent years there have been attempts, especially in Germany, to develop a Christian theology that acknowledges rebellion against God as an aspect of piety and attempts to bring lament back into the liturgy – for example by Dorothee Sölle, Walter Gross, Fridolin Stier, Karl-Josef Kuschel or Johann Baptist Metz:

> Could it be that there is too much singing and not enough crying out in our Christianity spirituality? Too much rejoicing and too little mourning, too much approval and too little sense for what is absent, too much comfort and too little hunger for consolation? Does not the church in its moral teaching stand here too much on the side of Job's friends and too little on the side of Job himself, who thought faith could include even insistently questioning God?[30]

The Job motif in Islam

In Islamic literature, the history of the Job motif goes partly in the opposite direction to the Christian version: instead of being increasingly suppressed, it comes to the surface only gradually. Though Job already laments in the Koran itself (Surah 12:86), he does not accuse. The dimension of theologically sanctioned protest and the believer's rebellion against God is ruled out. The Koran reduces the story of Job to the aspect of forbearance:

> And Job – when he called unto his Lord,
> 'Behold, affliction has visited me,
> and Thou art the most merciful of the merciful.' (Surah 21:83)

Job does not appear as a rebel. God praises him in the Koran: 'How excellent a servant he was! He was a penitent' (38:44). When it is not a punishment, suffering in both the Koran and the Sunna[31] serves as a test, just as in the dominant Jewish and Christian exegeses. That God gave Job back his original good fortune, as mentioned in the Koran, is interpreted in the classical commentaries as a reward for his silent patience and as an incentive to follow his example. The Koran does not permit any form of lamenting piety, let alone one that accuses God. In contrast to Christian theology, Muslim theology did not need to suppress Job's rebellion, the protest of humans against their God or even their questioning in the first place, as the Koran itself already rejected it in Surah 21:23. The Prophet is explicitly warned against following the example of Jonah, who was angry and rebelled instead of patiently awaiting his Lord's decision (Surah 68:48).

I should add by way of explanation that the Koran gives a more uniform account of the relationship than the Hebrew Bible, with less variation, less ambivalence and fewer contradictions. In its genesis and self-identity, the Koran is a completely different text from the Bible. However the Koran ultimately came into being, it did so – even for Western critics of the traditional textual history – in a narrower temporal and geographical space than the Bible. In addition, it is not an assortment of collective religious experiences accumulated over many centuries, passed on from generation to generation by word of mouth, it was also altered and edited in many phases. Above all, the Koran speaks neither of God nor to God; by its own claim, it is the direct word of God. The textual concept itself already precludes the possibility of humans complaining about God, as it is He who speaks in the first person in the Koran (in the Bible, strictly speaking, he speaks only in quotations), and God speaks to a single person at a moment in history that is sometimes even specified to the exact day. This God quotes as He chooses from the Koranic present or the biblical past, so it is hardly surprising if his self-image differs from how he is seen by Job, who can no longer control himself in circumstances of utmost, inexplicable distress. God presents himself in a light that, to his immediate addressees at that historical moment (1,400 years later the same deeds and words can certainly appear questionable), seemed especially favourable, urgent and effective in conveying the message – that is, in all His compassion, His justice, and indeed His sublimity, omnipotence and menace, ruthless towards his foes, but hardly with open wilfulness, brute force and a forbiddingly enigmatic nature. God punishes, He rages and fills humans with fear and dismay, but the punishment has a reason, and the raging a specific cause. In the Koran, the terror of God serves to purify.

In addition, the Koranic God, for all his anthropomorphic characterizations, does not have any such pronounced personal traits. He is less temperamental and fickle than the Old Testament God. The human qualities that make God imaginable are more clearly revealed as metaphors than in the Hebrew Bible. Through the more spiritualized concept of God, His relationship with the individual seems more uniform and less tension-laden, despite all creation- and religion-historical drama. Thus the sense of personal enmity felt by Job, Jeremiah or some psalmists does not even come about. That nothing is left of Job's revolt in the Koran is due not only to the submissive mentality of Islam, as Ernst Bloch implies,[32] but also to the specific textuality of the Koran. This is clear not least in the fact that the revolt against God returned early, and all the more sharply, once Muslims began speaking about God theologically: obviously they did not find his actions as convincing in their justice and reason as He had asserted, and the extremely lofty claim in Surah 67:3 that, wherever one looks, the creation is without a single flaw provoked objection in the face of real conditions.

Certainly it was not only Islamic orthodoxy but also large parts of Sufism that presented in Surah 6:84 the Job who is halved and elevated to prophetic status as an example, in order to hammer the maxim of submission into people: 'God taught Job the neediness of asking in order to bestow on him the grace of magnanimity and giving', says the mystic al-Junayd (d. 910).[33] Sahl at-Tustari removes Job's lament from the realm of criticism as a 'secret dialogue with God'. The Sufi Abu Ibrahim Isma'il al-Mustamli (d. 1042) claims that Job's words are not a lament at all, but rather a form of thanks; Job knew, after all, that the testing of the saints by God was an act of mercy.[34] Other Sufis, however, adopted the Job motif in its Old Testament breadth, and thus ignored its Koranic restriction. Educated Muslims and Koran commentators were certainly familiar with the story of Job only hinted at in the Koran, including his lament and his curses upon being, from the *Histories of the Prophets* (*qiṣaṣ al-anbiyā'*).[35] Just as earlier Muslim authors relied more on conversations with Jews, Christians and converts than reading the Bible themselves, which is why extended literal quotations are rare,[36] Job's lament in the Islamic tradition is entirely un-Koranic: 'And death would be better for me.'[37] The reception of the biblical subject matter (together with the rabbinical additions in the Talmud and midrash) may have mingled with the pre-biblical Job legend of Arab origin, which is considered one of the sources, if not the only one, used by the biblical poet, but seems to have been preserved in Arab folklore independently of the Bible.[38]

The chronicler Wahb ibn Munabbih (d. 728) already declares it a quotation from the Torah when he mentions humans reproaching God: 'Whoever complains of misfortune complains directly about his God.'[39] The mystic Ibn Adham later quotes the same statement, likewise 'from a book of God'.[40] Perhaps ancient scepticism, which was spreading in the religious thought of the time,[41] also contributed to a renewed posing of Job's question, albeit not initially using Job's example. One of the first Muslims to dispute God's goodness – precisely with reference to theodicy – was Jahm ibn Safwan (murdered 745), founder of the theological-rationalist Jahmiyya school. He reportedly took his comrades to see lepers and other afflicted people, telling them: 'Behold, this is what the Most Merciful of the merciful does.'[42] Other ascetics even went so far as to warn people of God. 'Nothing is more destructive for creatures than the Creator', the conservative Ibn Qayyim al-Jawziyya (d. 1350) disapprovingly quoted an anonymous heretic;[43] he probably meant none other than the great Sufi scholar Abu Talib al-Makki.[44] Despite the distrust in orthodox quarters, quarrelling with God (*taẓallum ʿalā r-rabb*) grew into a topos of its own within mystical literature. Ibn Qayyim gives an account of the quarrellers:

> And sometimes the ignorant feels especially clever, and then the devil incites him to dispute with the Lord. And some of you say about your God: 'How can He predetermine things and then punish people?' And some say: 'Why does He make the pious man's daily sustenance scarce and that of the sinner abundant?' [. . .] And some say: 'What's the wisdom in His tearing down these bodies? He torments them with destruction, after having previously built them up![45]

Quarrelling with God was especially widespread among the poets of the Turkish Bektashi order. The Anatolian mystic and poet Yunus Emre (d. c.1321), who is immensely popular to this day, criticized the Sirat bridge, which all the dead had to cross even though it is finer than a hair, and he also disapproved of the scales with which God weighs up the good and bad deeds of humans. A bridge, Yunus said, is built for people to cross it, not to fall down; scales are fit for a grocer, but not for a God.[46] A different Bektashi Dervish, Kaygusuz Abdal (d. 1397), said: 'You've built a bridge from hair, so that Your servant comes and walks across it. We want to stay where we are, and if You're a hero, God, then walk across it Yourself!'[47] Outside of mysticism, too, doubts about the justice of God's actions run through the entire poetry of Arab-Persian culture; one need only recall Daqiqi (tenth century), al-Maʿarri, or the quatrains of Omar Khayyam:

> When the creator embellished the forms of nature,
> Why did he condemn them to defeat and failure?

If they came out well, why break them?
If they didn't, who is at fault?[48]

The motif can also be found in modern literature: the God presented by Naguib Mahfouz in some of his novels, for example, is a ruler who keeps humans at a distance and does not care whether they consider him unmerciful. Mahfouz takes the traditional Islamic conception of God, in which the almighty God decides the fates of humans as He pleases, and reduces it to a hard, unpleasant core rid of all goodness. In *Children of the Alley* (1959), Mahfouz describes, with undisguised sympathy, the accusations of Idris, who stands for Satan (Iblis), against his father Gabalawi, who represents God. 'You were always a boss and a bully and that's all you'll ever be! We're your own sons and you treat us the same way you treat all your other victims!'[49] In a different, lesser-known novel, *The Search* (1964), Mahfouz openly mirrors God in the figure of the filthy rich playboy Sayyid Sayyid ar-Rahimi ('the compassionate'), who has mistresses and wives on all continents but shows no concern for the numerous resulting children. One of his sons, Sabir ('the patient', surely a reference to Job), born of a prostitute, goes in search of his father to demand financial support, but all he can find out is that, firstly, his father has departed for an unknown destination and, secondly, he does not feel under any obligation to Sayyid anyway. Mahfouz alludes to God's central quality in the Koran, which was always given a central role in traditional theology and popular devotion and was also the basis of some of the accusations related by Attar: ensuring a livelihood (*rizq*) for all people. With the worldwide affairs of Mr Compassionate, Mahfouz also takes up an idea from Islamic mysticism and presents it in a sarcastic light: God's omnipresence understood as a constant outpouring of love. Despite the playful, even frivolous use of traditional notions, Mahfouz is always deadly serious when he portrays God in ever new ways in his novels. Among the great contemporary Arab writers, he is one of the few who can be considered religious in the stricter sense, albeit anything but orthodox Islamic in his beliefs.[50]

It seems to me, however, that *The Book of Suffering* still constitutes the most violent outburst of heretical piety within the Islamic cultural realm. Some of the mystics probably spoke similarly presumptuously of God, for example al-Hallaj, Bayezid Bestami and above all Eyn ol-Qozat Seyyed Ali Hamedani (executed 1131), whose motifs Attar adopts directly in many places, such as the portrayal of Satan.[51] But none of them reprimanded God as passionately as Attar. He certainly used many stories and images from earlier writings, just as later authors continued to quarrel with God, but the sheer quantity and crudeness of his protagonists' invective against God and being are unparalleled.

Quarrelling with God in *The Book of Suffering*

The God-devouring accusations against God concentrated in *The Book of Suffering* are all the more conspicuous because the general tendencies in the culture to which Attar belongs made trust in God's justice a central part of its religious conception. In the context of Islam as a whole, the quoted statements by those Muslims who criticized the Creator are on the outermost fringe (and often preserved only through citation by their opponents); and, leaving aside orthodox Islam, they do not even represent the position of the Sufis, who generally submit consistently to God. One need only recall al-Ghazali's opinion-forming doctrine of the best of all worlds to imagine the religious environment in which Attar spat in the face of the creation. Not only, as the treatises of the great Sufi theorists such as al-Ghazali, as-Sarraj (d. 988) or al-Qushayri teach, should the believer cling to God without further deliberation, like the infant at the mother's breast, completely relinquishing his own will and allowing himself to be kneaded, formed, destroyed and created anew; he should also be especially grateful for every blow struck by God – indeed, welcome it joyfully – for what ultimately counts is to maintain, even in the greatest need, God's 'good opinion' (*ḥusn aẓ-ẓann*), as the Koranic example of Job teaches. True piety is not proved in times of good fortune, they write, but rather when ordinary people begin to doubt God's love.

'Patience' (*ṣabr*), 'contentment' (*riḍā'*) and above all 'trust' (*tawakkul*) have remained the fundamental attitudes of Islamic piety in suffering and need to this day. According to this view, which is far more characteristic of eleventh-century Islamic mysticism than Attar's curses, faith in God demands trust in the perfection of everything that exists, and often even more: the unadulterated, joyful acceptance of everything that comes from God.[52] Certainly poets such as Omar Khayyam or Daqiqi mocked such sermons, but their opinions were outside or at least on the outermost fringes of religion. In Attar's case, however, God is being attacked by someone who is devoted to Him. This is what gives the accusation its gravity and its specific character.

The fact that atheists are more harmless for God was already recognized by Ibn al-Jawzi (d. 1200), the conservative theologian and contemporary of Attar, when he said of the freethinker Ibn ar-Rawandi: 'Had he denied the Creator altogether, it would have been better for him than to admit His existence but polemicize against Him and defame Him.'[53] Only someone who believes in the Highest can throw stones up to heaven. Whoever denies Him cannot accuse Him of anything. But whoever has been abandoned, cast out or rejected – by their mother, their lover or God – feels their solitude the most cruelly. That was the attitude to life among the early Islamic ascetics whose world Attar captures in poetry, their 'faith like a guillotine, as heavy, as light', to use Kafka's words.[54] 'O human, you will die alone and enter the grave alone and be awakened alone, and you will be called to account alone', taught al-Hasan al-Basri. 'O human being, it is you who is meant, you are the target.'[55] Asked how he is faring, Hasan smiled and answered: 'What would you say about some people who set off on a ship, but were shipwrecked once they were far out at sea, so that each of them is now holding on to a single plank: what state are they in?'

'In a bad state.'

'My state is worse than theirs.'[56]

It is this impression of metaphysical forlornness that has remained in Attar's work, even though it was written at the dawn of Persian love mysticism, which views God not so much in His frightening inaccessibility as in His all-consuming beauty. In *The Book of God*, Attar tells of a child that loses sight of its mother at a bazaar. It weeps bitterly and throws earth in its own face in despair.

'What is your mother's name?' ask some good people, fearing that the child will die of sorrow.

'I don't know.'

'Have you lost your mind? Where is your house? Please tell us.'

'I really don't know. I can't remember the way there.'

'What quarter do you live in, what street?'

'I don't know.'

'What shall we do with you then?'

'I just don't know. I have lost my way, I don't know my mother's name or where we live, all I know is that I want my mother. All I know is that I want my mother to be here. That's all I know.'[57]

The impression of having been abandoned by God, which is accompanied by an agonizing yearning for Him, has spawned very similar metaphors in Western literature to al-Hasan al-Basri's shipwreck or Attar's lost child – especially in the work of Pascal, albeit with Christian connotations of guilt:

> Let us imagine a number of men in chains, and all condemned to death, where some are killed each day in the sight of the others, and those who

remain see their own fate in that of their fellows, and wait their turn, looking at each other sorrowfully and without hope. It is an image of the condition of men.[58]

In the twentieth century such images of humanity return most clearly in Kafka, supported by the Jewish tradition of the concealed God. 'Seen with the terrestrially sullied eye, we are in the situation of travellers in a train that has met with an accident in a long tunnel', Kafka writes in his third Octavo Notebook, 'and this at a place where the light of the beginning can no longer be seen, and the light of the end is so very small a glimmer that the gaze must continually search for it and is always losing it again, and, furthermore, both the beginning and the end are not even certainties.'[59]

There is no inner-worldly explanation for the burning fervour in *The Book of Suffering*. It is the radiance of heaven and the fire of hell. It is the glowing embers of God, in which humans burn without being burned up and thus released.

Every fool among the knowers of secrets
   Writhed in death hour after hour,
In turmoil, though without strength,
   His face a cloud, his blood the rain.
O God, he spoke, granter of souls, why did You
   Give us souls at all if You take them again?
It would be better for me if I were not,
   I would be safe from such mortal agony,
Would not have to give my life in exchange for death,
   And You would be spared having to grant and take souls. (4/4, p. 91)

One can see how far Attar pushed the Islamic tradition of quarrelling with God, which was established before his time, by comparing him to Muhammad al-Ghazali, who lived a century earlier and devoted a whole section of his central work, *The Revival of the Religious Sciences*, to this motif.[60] As is characteristic of al-Ghazali, who mediated between mysticism and orthodoxy, he discusses quarrelling in a well-meaning fashion, and thus simultaneously defuses it. Hence al-Ghazali refers only to a handful of individual fools and other laymen, focusing instead on stories about prophets such as Moses, Balaam or Jonah, as well as the early Islamic ascetics. Here he looks particularly at cases in which the pious, through their vehement reproaches, cause God to do or refrain from doing something. The pious demand mercy from God – and God grants it. A typical example of the way al-Ghazali treats the subject is the tale of two Sufis that he tells in a different passage. After one of them sins, he confides in his comrades and leaves it to his discretion to terminate his brotherhood with him. 'I shall never break that bond with you on account of your sin.' Thereupon he made a pact with God that he would neither eat nor drink until God had forgiven his brother's sins. Then God had to relent and forgive the sinner.[61]

More orthodox mystics also accepted the practice of quarrelling with God (*taẓallum 'alā r-rabb*), but limited it strictly to the 'friends of God' (*awliyā'*), who have a particularly intimate relationship with God. Just as lovers occasionally make accusations in mutual trust or have an affectionate dispute (*'itāb*), holy men were permitted an occasional presumptuous word. 'Those who know God are entitled to complain, because they complain to their Lord of their state during their trials', writes the mystic Sahl at-Tustari. 'The highest level among the patient is complaint. Those who know God are entitled to it, but for all others it is a sin.'[62] For Sufism as a whole is by no means defined only by God's frightening power, but equally by His beauty and compassion. 'Fear is male, hope is female', writes Attar in his *Lives of the Saints*, quoting a statement by at-Tustari; 'The child of the two is faith.'[63] Fear and hope thus constitute the scales of religious sentiment, which leaned towards fear among the early ascetics – that is, in the eighth and ninth centuries – but moved ever more clearly towards hope over the centuries. Attar too knows and invokes not only the *mysterium tremendum* but also the *mysterium fascinans*, especially in *The Conference of the Birds*. It is only *The Book of Suffering* – an exceptional case not only in Sufism but also in Attar's œuvre – that almost entirely eliminates the fascination of God. Attar does emphasize in *The Book of Suffering* that only those who are intimate with God may quarrel with Him, but the quarrelling itself often turns out to be so drastic that the term 'quarrel', if it expresses only struggle and doubt – rather than sheer desperation – hardly captures it: in Attar, the quarrelling repeatedly turns into an unreserved accusation that eliminates any notion of reconciliation. Unlike in al-Ghazali's account, the presumptuous prayer is almost never answered; and, when it is, the story has so sarcastic a tone that it can hardly be read as proof of God's goodness. He has the power to fulfil all human wishes – but He likes to fulfil the harmful ones most. A destitute fool enters the mosque and asks God for a hundred dinars. Nothing happens. The fool grows angry and calls out: 'If You don't want to give me the money, You might as well bring the mosque crashing down!'

The roof of the mosque begins to crumble away, and the tiles threaten to bury the fool.

'That's one request You've certainly fulfilled very quickly. If I know You, You'll probably even skimp on the blood money after You've killed me.'

The ceiling continues to crumble, and the fool makes a run for it (27/14, pp. 245f.).

The God in *The Book of Suffering* gives nothing – not voluntarily, at least. Whoever wants something from Him has to take it, fight for it, or steal it if need be. A starving, freezing fool is begging in vain at every door in the city for a piece of bread. 'May God give you bread', all the people say. Finally he steals a vase from the mosque, but is caught on his way out.

'Everyone says, may God give you bread', the fool apologizes, 'but He doesn't give anything of his own accord, so I wanted to take something myself' (22/4, p. 216).

Attar is familiar with Job. He mentions him in *The Book of God*, referring to him as the one who is tormented by God so that he might groan – unlike Zacharias, who is also tormented, but forbidden from complaining.[64] Anticipating Bloch, Attar asserts that God does not care about the suffering of humans; it matters no more to him whether Job laments his condition than it matters to Joseph that Suleika perishes because of him.[65] The aspect of positive forbearance and ultimate reconciliation, which is also found in the Hebrew Bible yet is the only aspect that remains in the Koran and its orthodox exegesis,[66] but also in much of Islamic mysticism in general – Attar does not mention this God-pleasing Job once. This is an interesting circumstance in reception-historical terms: Attar takes the biblical Job without the filter of the Koran and Islamic tradition, even accentuating Job's rebellious profile in his interpretation. Hence this Islamic author preserves a biblical motif that was largely suppressed by mainstream Judeo-Christian exegesis – an example of the way in which the religious traditions of the Near and Middle East did not develop alongside one another in abstract proximity, but actually refer to one another and can infuse and illuminate one another. Attar's insights into the vanity of all things earthly and the striving of humans for understanding and happiness, his meditations on the sequence of birth and death, as pointless as it is rapid, are influenced – even down to individual formulations – by Old Testament poems such as those of the preacher Solomon: 'The sun rises and the sun sets, and hurries back to where it rises' (Ecclesiastes 1:5).

> For the wise man, like the fool, will not be long remembered; in days to come both will be forgotten. Like the fool, the wise man too must die! So I hated life, because the work that is done under the sun was grievous to me. All of it is meaningless, a chasing after the wind. (Ecclesiastes 2:16–17)

A fool who lives in the steppe comes to the city and gazes speechlessly at the commotion: hundreds and thousands of people running eagerly this way and that for reasons only they can consider important. When he has seen enough, he moves on with the words: 'Woe to these sacks, woe to the sack-maker – there are already so many sacks, and yet He brings ever new ones' (38/6, 342f.).

> As a dream comes when there are many cares, so the speech of a fool when there are many words. (Ecclesiastes 5:3)

A second fool wishes to know why the pilgrims cut their hair before they leave for Mecca.

'That is religious custom (*sonnat*)', one of them answers.

'If that is religious custom, then it is surely a religious duty (*farīżeh*) to cut off one's beard; after all, every beard contains so much useless air that it is a plague for every door that stands open' (36/1, p. 321).[67]

> Who knows what great souls
> Have drowned in this deep, deep sea?
> Who knows those hearts, full of love
> That became blood, become blood, just like yours?
> Who could suspect what pure bodies
> Sank blood-soaked under the earth?
> Nothing but lamentation is the fruit of both worlds,
> Nothing but lamentation in the hearts of men.
> How could anyone sit still,
> When we are swept away again so quickly?
> Crooked and confused is this world,
> Rubble erected on ruins. (16/8, pp. 179f.)

The loving relationship with a personal God who is at once the saviour and destroyer of mankind – 'A robber You are, rob me' (E 16, p. 377) – is present more between the lines than explicitly in the Koran, but immediately evident in much of the Hebrew Bible, where people do not seek refuge with such a mixture of fear and love in anyone except God, of whom they are simultaneously scared to death: 'Do not be a terror to me' (Jeremiah 17:17). In the countless lamentations of the fools, the holy men and equally the poet himself, the never-ending heavenly sighs and hellish screams, Attar is likewise continuing biblical views not taken up in the Koran.

> From every pore, my beloved, I cry and bleed,
> As if I were the lute that pleases you. (0, p. 17)

A fool is asked by an understanding man what has made him so sad.

'God', answers the fool. 'I don't know whether I am coming or going for sorrow over him.'

> I fear Him, and if they could see,
>   All people would fear him.
> How could humanity not fear one
>   Who unleashes the wolf upon the flock
> So that he can mourn with the shepherd afterwards?
>   Little wonder that He causes us grief.
> He has made faith bitter for me today,
>   What will He do to me tomorrow? (38/4, p. 341)

Such words are not familiar from the Koran; if anything, one knows them from early Islamic asceticism, of whose suffering from God and pessimism, both religious and existential, Attar reminds us from time to time. Their literary roots, however, lie in the lament tradition in the Hebrew Bible, which often holds God responsible for the tribulations of humans:

> I am the man who has seen affliction by the rod of his wrath.
> He has driven me away and made me walk in darkness rather than light;
> indeed, he has turned his hand against me again and again, all day long.
>
> He has made my skin and my flesh grow old and has broken my bones.
> He has besieged me and surrounded me with bitterness and hardship.
> He has made me dwell in darkness like those long dead.
>
> He has walled me in so that I cannot escape; he has weighed me down with chains.
> Even when I call out or cry for help, he shuts out my prayer.
> He has barred my way with blocks of stone; he has made my paths crooked.
>
> Like a bear lying in wait, like a lion in hiding,
> he dragged me from the path and mangled me and left me without help.
> He drew his bow and made me the target for his arrows.
> He pierced my heart with arrows from his quiver. (Lamentations 3:1–13)

The cunning (*makr*) of God, which was so real a factor of life for Attar's Sufis and fools that some cannot get even a minute's sleep, because, like Malik ibn Dinar (d. c.748), they live in constant fear of a 'nocturnal ambush' (35/6, p. 317), is only hinted at in the Koran; in the Hebrew Bible, however, it is painfully familiar. There, God gave His people intoxicating wine to drink so that they would sin (Psalm 60:3).

> You have covered yourself with anger and pursued us; You have slain without pity.
> You have covered Yourself with a cloud so that no prayer can get through.
> You have made us scum and refuse among the nations.
>
> All our enemies have opened their mouths wide against us.
> We have suffered terror and pitfalls, ruin and destruction.
> Streams of tears flow from my eyes because my people are destroyed. (Lamentations 3:43–8)

Attar too knows that God deliberately makes the prayers of humans inaudible simply to avoid having to listen to them. When the drowning Pharaoh tries to utter the creed, the *Šahāda*, at the last moment, Gabriel stuffs his mouth with sludge from the water so that he is unable to finish and dies an unbeliever. If he had managed to speak the entire *Šahāda*, he would have been forgiven for unbelief and four hundred years of sinful life (0/2, pp. 15f.).

The idea that humans not only cannot hope for anything from God, but should actually beware of Him, often returns. A visitor to an asylum asks an inmate if he has a wish.

'I have not eaten for ten days', answers the madman, 'and I am as hungry as ten men.'

'Then cheer up!' exclaims the visitor. 'I'll go and get you some bread, meat and sweets!'

'Keep your voice down, you blabbermouth, or God will hear you; and then I'm sure He'll stop you from bringing me bread and tell you to let me starve' (2/6, p. 79).

As the Old Testament texts describe people's dealings with God far more concretely in the sense of a personal relationship, the question of theodicy in them is a question of trust, a question of God's integrity of character, which His people have to rely on. Abraham, who pleads for the fate of the inhabitants of Sodom and Gomorrah, demands that God display the justice He claims to have:

> Far be it from You to do such a thing – to kill the righteous with the wicked, treating the righteous and the wicked alike. Far be it from You! Will not the Judge of all the earth do right? (Genesis 18:25)

Certainly the prayers of lament in particular no longer presuppose God's fundamental justice; but they demand that God at least fulfil the covenant He has sealed with His people, including the promise to impose suffering only as a punishment. When people suffer through no fault of their own – or, worse still, when a righteous person must suffer *because* of his righteousness, not in spite of it – those who pray to God accuse Him, and would probably drag Him before a court if they could. No one says this more clearly than Job: 'I am blameless' (9:21). For Job, God's decision to punish him nonetheless is a breach of the covenant, that agreement between God and humans, that enabled the chosen people to constitute itself as such in the first place. 'I am with you and will watch over you wherever you go', God swears to Jacob (Genesis 28:15), and Jacob makes a vow of his own: 'If God will be with me and will watch over me on this journey I am taking and will give me food to eat and clothes to wear so that I return safely to my father's house, then the Lord will be my God' (Genesis 28:20–21). Almost from the outset, the relationship between Israel and God is formulated in the terminology of a contract, one of whose use God must first convince humans through numerous miracles. Job now accuses God of going against the covenant. He cannot bring God to justice, however:

> He is not a man like me that I might answer him, that we might confront each other in court. If only there were someone to arbitrate between us, to lay his hand upon us both, someone to remove God's rod from me, so that his terror would frighten me no more. Then I would speak up without fear of him, but as it now stands with me, I cannot. (Job 9:32–5)

In Attar, God's accuser, who is considered a madman by those around him in the biblical case of Job, has often completely lost his mind. In *The Book of Suffering* it is the fools, the crazy people, the idiots, who call out most loudly what most believers hardly dare to think: that God has evil intentions. A fool is asked if he knows God.

'How could I not know him! He is the one who cast me into misery' (27/9, pp. 251f.).

This is exactly Job's experience: one can no more deny God than one can fight Him. No one else would have the power to wreak such havoc.

> God does not restrain his anger; even the cohorts of Rahab cowered at his feet. How then can I dispute with him? Though I were innocent, I could not answer him; I could only plead with my judge for mercy. Even if I summoned him and he responded, I do not believe he would give me a hearing. He would crush me with a storm and multiply my wounds for no reason. He would not let me regain my breath but would overwhelm me with misery. If it is a matter of strength, he is mighty! And if it is a matter of justice, who will summon him? (Job 9:13–19)

It is no coincidence that Attar's tales usually deal with anonymous ascetics, and most of all madmen, in order to develop the Job motif: with historical figures of Islamic mysticism one has to show consideration for the sources and the traditional perception of their character. Many sheikhs may have moaned about God and protested against Him in certain statements, but none of them openly and lastingly declared God his enemy. None of them broke into loud mooing during prayer like the fool in Rey[68] – and if one of them did, he was branded not a heretic, but only mad, like Loqman as-Sarakhsi. It is said that, as an old and venerable Sufi sheikh in the eleventh century, he asked God to be released like a slave after long service. God granted him his request. The sign of freedom, however, was that Loqman lost his mind. Since then he has been one of the most famous of the many wise fools who are at once derided and revered in Sufi literature.[69] Islamic culture granted them the freedom to blaspheme, and Attar's provocation hence lies only partly in their words, and more in the fact that he always emphasizes their closeness to God and credits them with a higher understanding of His nature. It is precisely because they see the full extent of the life's misfortune that they know it can be ascribed only to an almighty God. 'If it is not he, then who is it?' as Job says (9:24). In *The Book of God* a poor fool who does not even have a garment left on his body asks God for a sheet to cover up his nakedness.

'I will give you a sheet', God's voice calls out: 'Your burial shroud.'

'Yes, I know You and I know how You treat Your slaves', the fool exclaims in outrage. 'A helpless man has to die before You will give him a sheet!'[70]

There is probably no other Islamic text in which Job's motifs are as central and as varied as in *The Book of Suffering*: the motif of cursing existence, suffering from death after a long life, but above all the turn against God in hardship and the appeal finally to keep the promise he has made to humans. The charge of breaching the law that underlies Job's lament returns in *The Book of Suffering* as, among other things, the accusation that God has violated his Koranic duty to ensure a livelihood (*rizq*) for all people. I have already cited the story of the thorn-gatherer who asks for a livelihood, only to be led a merry dance by God. That the people here genuinely see an almost legal responsibility that is not upheld by God becomes even clearer in an anecdote where, for a change, He actually does what is asked. One day a fool is asked why he is not cursing God for a change, and even praying. He answers: 'Yesterday God filled my belly for once, and if He behaves, so will I' (27/11, p. 252).

Just as Attar's fools ask themselves why God would so torment them other than out of sheer sadism, Job does not know why God has cast him into misery. Job asks and asks but receives no answer, until he too finally concludes that God must enjoy tormenting His servant.

> Do not condemn me, but tell me what charges You have against me. Does it please You to oppress me, to spurn the work of Your hands, while You smile on the schemes of the wicked? (Job 10:2–3)

The people in Attar's cosmos lose their patience; they refuse to be put off any longer. A hungry, desperate fool is weeping bitterly over his fate.

'Be patient, poor fellow', someone consoles him. 'God, who created the heavens without pillars, will help you.'

'Oh, He can use a hundred pillars to support the heavens for all I care – if He could only give me a single piece of bread' (22/10, pp. 219f.).

To the fools, God is such a mischief-maker that they try to keep others away from Him too, as is probably illustrated most curiously by the aforementioned fool in *The Book of God* who disrupts the Friday prayer with loud mooing. In *The Book of Suffering* it is a merchant from Attar's home town of Nishapur, once particularly devout, who actually warns people of God. Fifty years after he falls into poverty and loses his mind, he addresses a young person in front of the mosque: 'Yes, go on in, go quickly to prayer, then He'll get you in the same mess as me' (2/8, p. 80).

The only way to succeed with God, if at all, is through resistance. A hermit in a barren area who, without thinking of food, devotes himself exclusively to God and his worship is visited one day by hungry guests. He waits until evening, hoping to obtain food somewhere, but finds nothing and is ashamed before his guests. Then he looks up to heaven and cries out: 'If You have to send guests to me of all people, then at least see to it that I have something to serve up to them! I'll let the matter go if You send me some food now, otherwise I'll take this club and smash all the chandeliers in Your mosque to pieces!'

Sure enough, a servant with an opulent dish of food very soon appears. The two guests are horrified by their host's words. He grumbles: 'One has to bare one's teeth at God, that's the only thing that helps' (22/5, pp. 215f.).

The fools accuse God, they refuse to do His bidding or defend themselves; they are even at war with God like the mad saint Loqman Sarakhsi. He mounts a wooden horse and leaves the city with a stick in his hand to fight God. Out in the fields he is accosted by a huge Turk, who grabs him, beats him black and blue and takes away his stick. Blood-covered and dejected, Loqman returns to the city.

'Well, how did the fight turn out?' sneers one of the many onlookers.

'Can't you see my bloody shirt? God didn't dare tackle me himself, but he called a giant Turk to help him instead. I didn't have a chance against him, of course' (33/8, p. 300).

The fools

The fact that Attar uses fools (*diwāneh*, *mağnūn*, *bi-del*) far more often than biblical or Muslim saints to develop Job's motifs turns the rebellion against God into a grotesque, but only rarely takes away its existential urgency. There is probably no other writer in the history of world literature, not even Shakespeare, who took such fools as seriously as Attar. The fools are wise, hence their pain; they remember the secrets that all the other people have forgotten, as Estragon aptly puts it in Beckett's *Waiting for Godot*: 'We are all born mad. Some remain so.'[71] Attar's use of the term *diwāneh* is extremely broad, far broader than is the folk and mystical literature he draws upon. For Attar, almost anyone who expresses an opinion deviating from the norm is a saint, a fool, or both. The statements made by Attar's fools are incomparably more barefaced, drastic, heretical and inflammatory than in the Arabic sources.[72] What characterizes them is defined not pathologically, but socially and theologically: they are free because they stand outside of the community politically and religiously, like Jean-Paul Sartre's figure of the bastard. They dispute God's goodness and wisdom in the name of humanity as if it were a natural part of their class. The emancipatory impulse that can go against even the highest authority, namely that of God, also leads to social critique. It is the same impulse, and it is the same figure that embodies it: the fool. More than with all other Islamic authors, what sets Attar's fools apart from their fellow humans is that they can do and say all the things that normal people cannot.

'Be mad and let your reason go', says Leyla to Majnun, 'then no one will lay a finger on you when you come to my village' (27/1, p. 249).

The fools' relationship with God is characterized by the fact that the angelic scribes do not write down their words and deeds, and they therefore feel no obligation to follow the commandments of the Koran.

'As God wanted me to be mad, I will talk as I please', says a fool to an ascetic who rebukes him for his shameless talk. 'Those with reason are obliged to follow the law, and fools are obliged to honour love' (17/2, p. 249).

The word 'love' should be taken literally: the fools speak to God as if to a careless father, a wayward relative, a cruel lover. However numerous their accusations may be, God remains a father, a relative, a lover. As always in life, anger is most passionate where love is involved, where people are drawn in and disappointed in their trust. 'Mediation does not apply to these people, so they address God directly', Attar explains. 'As they view everything except Him as a parable, they hear everything about Him and speak directly about Him' (22/11, p. 220). Scenes from an unequal marriage:

On a public holiday, a fool sees people walking about dressed in new clothes, while he wears only rags. 'You knower of secrets', he calls to the heavens, 'kindly give me some shoes, a shirt and a turban, then I won't bother You until the next holiday!'

When nothing happens, the fool tries being more modest. 'At least give me a turban. Then I'll do without the shoes and shirt.'

A prankster hears the fool's prayer and throws a flea-ridden old turban from the roof. The fool flies into a rage and throws the turban onto the roof. 'I'm not putting on a rag like that, You can give that to Your Gabriel' (27/3, pp. 249f.).

For all the insight with which Attar credits them, the fools give Job's message a different thrust from the biblical book and the Islamic tradition of asceticism and mysticism. 'The world of tragedy and the world of grotesque have a similar structure',[73] writes the Polish theatre theorist Jan Kott in an essay on *King Lear*. Grotesque, Kott argues, adopts the dramatic schemata of tragedy and raises the same fundamental questions, but with different protagonists and accordingly different answers: 'Tragedy is the theatre of priests, grotesque is the theatre of clowns.'[74] In this sense, the Book of Job is a theatre of priests: the metaphysical order of the world is out of joint but not in ruins; otherwise Job would not seriously appeal to God, nature and history. *King Lear* and Beckett's *Endgame* both enact the same drama as Job in the Hebrew Bible – 'As flies to wanton boys are we to the gods, / They kill us for their sport'[75] – except that the drama is played by fools.

> O you mighty gods!
> This world I do renounce, and, in your sights,
> Shake patiently my great affliction off:
> If I could bear it longer, and not fall
> To quarrel with your great opposeless wills,
> My snuff and loathed part of nature should
> Burn itself out.[76]

Shakespeare's and Beckett's figures likewise call upon the gods, but the silence of the latter makes the people seem increasingly ridiculous. They know or sense it themselves, and accept their own degradation. King Lear calls himself 'the natural fool of fortune' (IV.6). His madness is no mere illness, but rather a philosophy, 'a conscious cross-over to the position of the Clown'.[77] Kott uses the example of Gloucester's pitifully failed suicide, which Beckett re-enacts in *Waiting for Godot*, to indicate the transition to a literary experience of the world in modernity. Gloucester wishes to kill himself in protest against undeserved suffering and the injustice of the world. His suicide is an appeal.

> But if the gods, and their moral order in the world, do not exist, Gloucester's suicide does not solve or alter anything. It is only a somersault on an empty stage. It is deceptive and unsuccessful on the factual as well as on the metaphysical plane. Not only the pantomime, but the whole situation is then grotesque. From the beginning to the end. It is waiting for a Godot who does not come.[78]

This is different in Attar. In *The Book of Suffering,* God is an absolute reality; although the futility of waiting frequently seems apparent, Attar's figures, unlike Lucky and Estragon, are certain that their Godot exists out there. Sometimes both comedy and terror ensue in Attar because no one answers the raging fool, or only the joker next door; at other times, however, it is God's active intervention that produces slapstick scenes. A madman in the desert, miserable and hungry, asks God: 'Is there anyone more hungry than I?'

'There is', says God, and sends a wolf that promptly attacks the fool.

The wolf throws the fool to the ground, tears the shirt from his body and bites him half to death until the fool finally screams: 'Lord! Be so kind not to kill me in such a pitiful way. Life is so precious. It's alright, I believe You: there are even hungrier beings than myself. I'll never ask for bread again. I'm completely full, I really am. At this moment there's no one who is as full as I am. I'll never ask You for anything again, I promise. But did You really have to set a wolf of all things on me, here in this wilderness, where I haven't seen a living thing in weeks?'

Then God hears the fool's pleading and sends the wolf away (2/7, pp. 79f.).

Time and again, Attar's poetry turns into grotesque, and this transition anticipates the destruction of the very order to which he appeals. The roots of this are already present in the tale of Job, which, even with a different, desolate ending, would by no means be absolutely tragic in Kott's sense. In the eyes of those around him, Job's behaviour resembles that of a fool. Joseph Roth (d. 1939) saw this, and accordingly underlined this very aspect in his adaptation of the story. When the neighbours discover that Mendel has set his house on fire, he calls out to them: 'I want to burn more than a house and more than a person. You will be astonished when I tell you what I really intended to burn. You will wonder and say: Mendel is crazy, too, like his daughter. But I assure you, I am not crazy. For more than sixty years I have been mad, but today I am not.'

'Then tell us what you wanted to burn.'

'I want to burn God.'[79]

As dear as Attar's fools are to him, the basic disposition of *The Book of Suffering* is nonetheless tragic. The terror of God depicted in it is a reality, not a fantasy. Attar's figures – just like Job, Jeremiah or some of the psalmists – experience God as an opponent, an enemy, a danger beyond all rationale against which one must protect oneself, even literally duck. Attar describes some of these experiences with grotesque elements, thus creating a transition from the world of the Bible to that of literary modernity; but the experience is by no means exposed as imagined. The mystic Shibli visits an asylum. There a young madman – one of those who are intimate with God, Attar emphasizes – asks the famous mystic a favour. He requests that, in his next prayer, Shibli ask God why He torments him, the madman, so terribly; why He keeps him in a strange place, bound and freezing, far from his parents, in hunger and cold, clothed only in rags; why He is so unmerciful, so devoid of generosity; why He has cast a fire into his heart, but offers no water to extinguish it; why God does not allow the madman to free himself from Him. Like many of Attar's descriptions, this refers to the life of an actual person (in this case the starving inmate of a lunatic asylum) and applies at once to the overall fate of humans: to be in a strange place, bound, uprooted, far from the security of childhood. Shibli promises the madman to pass on his message and turns away, weeping. After he has already left the room, the madman suddenly calls after him: 'No, no, please don't tell God any of the things I asked you to, you mustn't. If you tell Him, He'll only make it a hundred times worse. I won't ask Him for anything; nothing impresses Him anyway, he's content with Himself' (2/5, pp. 77f.).

The struggle with God in *The Book of Suffering* is not grotesque because God does not exist, but because He is overwhelmingly powerful. An impoverished fool sees Sultan Mahmoud of Ghazna riding out with a great army and almost five hundred elephants, looks up to the heavens and calls out: 'You can learn from him how to be a king!'

'You mustn't say that', says the shocked sultan.

'So what should I do?' the fool defends himself. 'If you ride out with your army and your elephants, are you going to fight a beggar? No! You're going to war against a king! A king fights a king, never a beggar. But God leaves you in peace to be a sultan, and wages war day and night against a beggar like me instead' (22/1, p. 215).

Man raises himself above God

That humans could surpass God in their morality is one of many possibilities that Attar did not find in the Koran. In the Hebrew Bible, however, the thought does appear: at many points, except for His superior power, Yahweh is behind the humans. This sentiment is voiced explicitly by Job, who insists on his own blamelessness and God's wrongdoing. In opposition to God's acts of violence, which run through the entire Bible to the Revelation of St John, where no more than 144,000 people escape His judgement – in opposition to this history of fury, Job unceasingly insists on obedience to the law, honesty and charity, as commanded by that same God: 'If I have seen anyone perishing for lack of clothing, or a needy man without a garment, and his heart did not bless me for warming him with the fleece from my sheep [. . .] then let my arm fall from the shoulder, let it be broken off at the joint' (31:19–22). By reacting to Job's appeal to His morality with a demonstration of His power, and humiliating him in the dust, he inadvertently elevates Job, as C. G. Jung noted: 'By so doing he pronounces judgement on himself and gives man the moral satisfaction whose absence we found so painful in the Book of Job.'[80] Ernst Bloch also observes: 'A man has overtaken, has enlightened his own God. That, despite the apparent submission at the end, is the abiding lesson of the Book of Job.'[81] Following the same logic, and completely inverting the Koranic view, Attar's fools call out to God that He should take humans as an example, behave Himself and learn from humans how to love. 'But me, if I were almighty, do you see, if I were omnipotent, I couldn't bear people suffering, I would save them, save them',[82] says Büchner's Lenz in very similar terms. And Schopenhauer shudders as he imagines what God might feel: 'If a God made this world, I would not be that God: for its misery would tear my heart to shreds.'[83] A merchant falls into poverty, and Attar describes it with his usual devotion: the man is hungry, his heart and mind lost, he is old, helpless, and bankrupt to boot, thrown into prison by his creditors, and so on.

> One night he spoke silently to God:
>   O leader, O guide on my path,
> If I were in Your place and You were I,
>   I would have peace from You forever,
> And not for a second would I send You such grief;
>   I would treat You better than You treat me. (22/2, pp. 215f.)

In *The Book of God*, Attar even uses the cruelty of God as a sarcastic proof of the truth of Islam, as if he had asked himself the same question as C. G. Jung, some centuries later: 'What kind of father is it who would rather his son be slaughtered than forgive his ill-advised creatures who have been corrupted by his precious Satan?'[84] A Christian merchant's handsome and loving son dies. His father, wasting away with grief, subsequently converts to Islam. 'Now I see that Muslims are right when they say that God cannot have a son; for if He had had a son, He would not have done this to me.'[85]

Elsewhere, another grieving father's capacity for sympathy raises him morally above God: 'You are forgiven for what You have done to me, for You have no son of Your own and do not understand a father's pain.'[86]

There is scarcely trace of forgiveness for God in *The Book of Suffering*. He is not only no better than humans; no, He is much worse. He has no manners, and disregards the most basic rules of politeness, decency and charity. That is why the fools no longer appeal to God's goodness, only to the possibility that He will grow bored of tormenting them sooner or later:

> That fool stood up, raised
> His face to the heavens, and called out:
> Maybe Your heart has not grown tired
> Of these pitiful goings-on,
> But mine did long ago! How long shall this continue?
> Do You never grow weary of such things? (27/6, p. 251)

Even God's bitterest enemies are more compassionate than He is: Pharaoh sees a box containing little Moses being carried away by the water. To save the child, he promises freedom to whichever one of his slave-girls retrieves it. All four hundred of them plunge into the water. When one swims back to land with the box in her hands, he sets all the others free too. Asked why he made this peculiar decision, he replies that he had placed hope in the hearts of all the slave-girls; and because hopes should not be dashed, he chose to give all four hundred of them their freedom.

> Even this accursed man showed mercy,
> Though his heart held only hatred for God.
> All creatures, secretly or openly,
> Yearn for the Truthful One.
> They all want Him, but He must not want them,
> And as long as he does not, their desire is in vain.
> The accursed Pharaoh, even his heart full of goodness,
> Wanted deep down to be close to his Lord.
> But it did him no good, for the Truthful One
> Would not grant the accursed man's wish. (6/5, pp. 108f.)

However great Pharaoh's sins may have been, whatever reasons one might cite to excuse God's implacability – such actions are immensely remote from the morals that Attar demands of humans in countless tales. A youth is dejected because he has missed the pilgrimage. Thereupon, the theologian Sufyan ibn Thawri (d. 778) gives him his own four pilgrimages (34/8, p. 308). The Seljuq Vizier Nezamolmolk eats the bitter cucumbers offered as a gift by a gardener out of kindness to avoid showing up the gardener in front of the court, and even thanks him with a sum of thirty dinars (6/3, p. 107). A financial advisor embezzles Sultan Mahmoud's money. The sultan confronts his official, who confesses his crime. He is poor and the sultan is rich, he had thought to himself, and had trusted in Mahmoud's goodness. Thereupon the sultan pardons him (6/4, pp. 107f.).

The New Testament virtue of repaying evil with good was familiar not only to Attar but to Islamic mystics in general. The corresponding words from the gospels, especially the Sermon on the Mount, 'became common property in Islam',[87] as Tor Andrae writes in his short but extremely substantial book on the early Sufis. 'Maintain your connection with those who break with you, give to those who deny you, forgive those who wrong you', the Prophet reportedly said.[88] Al-Ghazali, who cites this *hadith*, subsequently quotes Matthew 5:38–41 to reinforce his words:

> You have heard that it was said, 'Eye for eye, and tooth for tooth.' But I tell you, do not resist an evil person. If someone strikes you on the right cheek, turn to him the other also. And if someone wants to sue you and take your tunic, let him have your cloak as well. If someone forces you to go one mile, go with him two miles.

This is a constantly recurring pattern in Sufi logic, especially in Attar, and is often applied literally: showing leniency towards enemies, repaying hatred with love, rewarding attacks instead of avenging them, bringing thieves who have robbed a house the things they have left behind, and pardoning those who have done wrong. 'Among men, he who allows his creatures the greatest freedom is closest to God', says Bayezid Bestami.[89] Sahl at-Tustari practically defines Sufism as the renunciation of all retribution: 'The Sufi is one who believes that his blood may be spilled without punishment, and that his possessions are abandoned goods.'[90] The model for this ethos, which the Sufis seem to have mentioned more often than their own last prophet, is Jesus. Hence early Islamic asceticism was also simply described as 'following the way of Christ'. According to Shiite tradition, the first imam of the Shia, Imam Ali (murdered 661), stated that the exemplary believers were those who command the world to 'follow the way of Christ'.[91] For the Sufis it is Jesus who repays evil with good, and goes to the houses of prostitutes because a doctor must visit the sick, and asks the children of Israel: 'Where does the seed grow?'

'In the dust.'

'Truly, I tell you: wisdom can only grow in a heart that has become like dust.'[92]

Jesus's statement 'whoever exalts himself will be humbled, and whoever humbles himself will be exalted' (Matthew 23:12) is varied in the following story, recorded by Abu Nu'aym al-Isfahani (d. 1037):

> One time, Jesus and one of his disciples walked past a robber who was lying in wait in his hiding-place among the rocks. When the robber saw them, God made him feel the urge to repent. He thought, 'Here now is Jesus, son of Mary, God's spirit and His word, and here is this disciple of his. But what are you, wretch? You are a robber among the children of Israel. You have lain in wait by the roads, have taken people's possessions and spilled their blood.' So he came down from the mountain, full of regret about the life he had lived. When he had reached Jesus and the disciple, he spoke to himself: 'You want to walk together with them? You are not worthy. Go behind them – you must walk like a blasphemer and sinner.' When the disciple turned around and recognized the robber, he thought, 'Look at this wretched villain walking behind us!' But God saw the thoughts in their hearts – in the one regret and repentance, in the other arrogance and contempt – and sent down a revelation to Jesus. 'Tell the disciple and the robber that they must both begin their good works anew. For I have forgiven the robber all the crimes he committed in the past, because he regretted them and atoned, and all the disciple's previous acts of righteousness have lost their worth, because he was proud of himself and looked upon the penitent with contempt.'[93]

The ethos of the early Islamic image of Jesus, which the Sufis also attributed to the Islamic prophet himself (Mohammed 'does not repay evil with evil, but is conciliatory and forgiving'),[94] runs through all of Attar's epics. In *The Book of Suffering*, al-Junayd is robbed of his only possession: a shirt. The thief gives it to a merchant to sell. A customer wants to buy the shirt – provided he finds someone who knows it and can confirm the legitimacy of the product. Al-Junayd comes along, observes what is happening, and assures the customer that he knows the shirt and it can safely be bought (18/4, pp. 191f.). In *The Book of God*, Jesus is showered with insults by Jews, yet asks God to be good to them. Asked why he has done so, he answers: 'Each heart gives of what it has.'[95]

In *The Conference of the Birds*, the mortally wounded Imam Ali tells those who offer him a drink to give it to his murderer first.[96]

In *The Conference of the Birds*, as in *The Book of God*, Attar also often uses God as an example of his idea of compassion. Here he refers to the promise in Surah 39:54:

> Say: 'O my people who have been prodigal
> against yourselves, do not despair of
> God's mercy; surely God forgives sins
> Altogether; surely He is the All-forgiving, the All-compassionate.'

One of the recurring motifs in these two epics is that God practically goes in search of sinners merely so that he can forgive them, a variation on the *hadith*: 'If you didn't commit sins, God would do away with you and bring forth people who did sin, in order to forgive them.'[97] In *The Conference of the Birds*, Attar tells of a man selling honey in Baghdad: 'I have honey and I'm selling it cheaply!'

'Are you selling it for free too?' asks a Sufi.

'You must be crazy.'

Then God calls out to the Sufi: 'Come into our shop! Here you will receive everything for free, and if you want more, you will receive it too.'[98]

God repeatedly appears as a role model in *The Conference of the Birds*. A pious ascetic comes across the funeral procession of a sinner and turns off the path to avoid having to speak the prayer for the dead. That night he sees the deceased in a dream, walking through paradise.

'How did you make it there?' the ascetic asks the sinner.

'Because you were so unmerciful, God made His own mercy all the more visible.'[99]

In *The Book of Suffering*, on the other hand, God forgives only rarely – for example when he has Dhu n-Nun (d. 859) declare that all sin should disappear from heaven and earth on the edges of the divine carpet of honour (34/7, p. 308). God is not painted in dark colours throughout, but, unlike in the anecdote from *The Conference of the Birds* just mentioned, His goodness in *The Book of Suffering*, when it does manifest itself, hardly ever stands for itself and above all things human, but almost always with didactic intentions – so that humans become good. An unbeliever asks Abraham, known in the Muslim tradition as the 'friend of God', for a piece of bread.

'If you accept the true faith', the prophet answers, 'you can have anything you want.'

As soon as the beggar is gone, Gabriel appears and conveys a message for Abraham for God: 'Who has so far given bread to unbelievers?

God! As you are the "friend of god", you should be as generous as He is' (34/6, p. 317).

Attar likewise sees the gentleness of Jesus as the true ethical model. The *pir* instructs the wanderer that Jesus is the supreme example of magnanimity (*karam*), goodness (*lotf*) and purity (*pāki*): because he himself was pure, he saw everything purely. Jesus even directed his loving gaze at those creatures normally considered, along with pigs, the embodiment of impurity in Muslim societies: one day he passes a dead dog. Its mouth is standing open in the ugliest way, emitting such a terrible carrion stench that everyone around it is disgusted and unwilling to look at it. 'This dog belongs to Him', says Jesus to his companion. 'Look how white its teeth are!'

But in Attar's poetry the other prophets, the Muslim holy men and many fools have also internalized the commandment to love one's neighbour, and even – perhaps encouraged partly by Indian religious practice – extended it to animals. A dove flees from a falcon into one of Moses' sleeves. The falcon asks the prophet to hand over its prey. He does not want to deliver the dove, but does not want the falcon to starve either. So he cuts off a piece of his own flesh (34/3, pp. 304f.). One particularly touching story from *The Book of God* tells of Imam Ali, who accidentally injures an ant while walking. Terribly distressed, he bursts into tears and tries to help the ant to its feet. At night, to crown it all, Ali is reprimanded by the Prophet: he should look out while walking; the whole of heaven was in mourning for two days because of the ant, which was constantly busy praising God. Tormented by remorse, Ali starts trembling, until the Prophet finally consoles him with the news that the ant itself has interceded on his behalf.[100]

Such unconditional, attentive love is remote from the God of *The Book of Suffering*. Not all humans, but certainly the prophets, saints and fools repeatedly surpass the Creator in their compassion, as exemplified in Sufi literature by the oft-cited anecdote about Bayezid Bestami, who passes a Jewish cemetery and says to God: 'What are these people now that You torment them with punishment? A handful of bones that were subjected to predestination. You should forgive them!'[101]

Bayezid is even willing to sacrifice himself to save humanity from hell: 'My God, if, in Your infinite knowledge, You know that You will punish someone with hell, make my body so large in hell that there will be no room for anyone else beside me.'[102]

Just as Shibli declared that, unlike the Prophet, at the Final Judgement he would intercede not only for Muslims, but for all people, 'so that no one at all remains in hell',[103] this believer in *The Book of Suffering* also wants to deliver unbelievers from hell:

A great believer, in prayer one night,
  Spoke oh! and oh woe! before the Truthful One:
O God! On the day of judgement I will sit
  Patiently at the edge of hell
To gain possession of a dagger of light
  With which to drive all sinners out of hell,
So that they may finally be safe from its embers
  And forever enter the heavenly garden.
Then a voice called out to him:
  Sit down and be quiet,
Or I will broadcast your sins to the whole world,
  So that your companions will stone you.
The great believer heard these words, yet did not cease:
  Tell me, what have I said wrong?
If You continue thus, You will make me
  Open my mouth to all men
And tell of Your goodness,
  Until none on earth kneel before You any longer. (E 15, p. 376)

This believer at least has some hope. On the basis of his own compassion, he challenges God also to be compassionate. He struggles with God to make Him fulfil His own commandments, like Job or the prophet Habakkuk:

> Your eyes are too pure to look on evil; You cannot tolerate wrong. Why then do You tolerate the treacherous? Why are You silent while the wicked swallow up those more righteous than themselves? (Habakkuk 1:13)

Through their experiences, many of Attar's heroes have reached a more sober view of the matter. A deceased beggar is seen in a dream and asked how he fared in heaven with God.

'He asked me what I had brought with me', says the beggar. 'What possessions should I have? I answered. I went begging from door to door for almost fifty years; I roamed through the whole world like that. No one gave me a single morsel of bread, they all directed me to You. Now I come to You, and not only do You not give me anything – You even demand something from me, a beggar? A king does not beg' (E 13, p. 375).

This hardship caused by the supposedly charitable Creator is often cleansed of all pathos, and the anger pressed into a dark sarcasm, in this tale in a mere three verses:

An idiot asked for a piece of bread,
  Said all hope is lost, now only God can help.

You wretch, called a fool, you are wasting your time.
When hunger was rampant, I tried my luck with God,
For many years, it was war and dead people were everywhere.
What did it get me? Not even a breadcrumb. (27/8, p. 251)

The pleasure of suffering

Attar does not tell such stories as a warning; he and almost all other mystical poets show respect for the fools. 'Love speaks from their words', Attar repeatedly emphasizes, 'whether you believe it or not' (27/11, p. 252). Yes, they love God, the people in *The Book of Suffering*, the fools and wise men – but also the parents and children, the merchants, the beggars, and even many unbelievers, Zoroastrians, Christians and Jews, of whom Attar tells. And not only they: the entire cosmos yearns for the Creator. Together with the cosmology of pain, Attar at once produces a creation history of the longing for one's own origin, which lies in the Creator. In his introduction, the poet spends many pages talking to God simply to insist that every single element of nature and the cosmos is overflowing with love for the Creator – the firmament, for example, which twists with longing, or the earth, which stretches out to heaven in an invocation of the Creator. The sun is pale with shame – not out of shame before God; it would never dare show such naked emotion. No, it is 'out of shame before the dog in your alley' (0, p. 8). The rising moon is a horseshoe in the fire, but is happy because it is God who lit the fire. The dawn awakes all creatures to life each day with its coquettish smile, by which it seeks to charm God, while the night comes down each day like His revelation, revealing the stars like teeth in the mouth of the cosmos. Because the sky is without God, it flashes with jealousy and rains tears, and the fire makes itself a laughing stock because it is so consumed by desire for God. Suleika stands at the road's edge while Joseph strikes her with his whip to drive her away. She lets out just one cry of pain, with such fiery breath that the whip catches fire and Joseph is forced to let go. Then Suleika says: 'This fire has been burning in my soul for as long as I can remember, but you cannot even bear a breath of it on your hand. And yet you are the man and I am the woman' (32/4, pp. 291f.).

The circumstance that God's creatures cannot hate Him or be indifferent to Him, as they burn with love for Him, is what causes their immeasurably great and wretched pain. For the Creator rejects them; He turns away or does not even perceive them. 'He is at one and the same time fearfully noticeable and unperceivable',[104] as Martin Buber writes about Job's God, who is so near despite His great distance. 'If only I knew where to find him; if only I could go to his dwelling!' says Job (23:3), after speaking one verse earlier of God's hand that lies so heavy upon him. Like Job, Attar's figures also struggle with God, who not only rages, but is also – and no less terribly – silent.

The further the archer draws it back,
  The deeper the arrow pierces you. (0, p. 12)

'Is there any barrier that separates the knower of God from God?' someone asks Bayezid.

'You miserable wretch', the holy man replies: 'What could separate Him who is His own barrier!'[105]

In *The Conference of the Birds*, Attar describes how Bayezid finds God's royal hall completely empty: 'It is part of the majesty of this place that beggars keep away from our door.'[106]

In their hope that God will show interest in them, perhaps even return their love, humans are as laughable as the bug that lived on a plane tree. After a year it decides to move on, and apologizes to the plane tree for any trouble it may have caused. The tree laughs at the bug: 'You should save yourself the trouble of thanking me. It's all the same to me whether you're there or not; I don't even notice' (13/4, p. 161).

Any emotion or address from God to humans would be good, even a curse would be valuable (33/5, p. 298) – if only God would take notice of them. Majnun is asked his favourite word.

'My favourite word is "no".'

'But why, why not the affirmative?'

'Just once I was allowed to speak to Leyla. I asked her if she loved me. "No", she replied. Since then I have loved this word above all others' (39/4, p. 352).

Even insults constitute a longed-for act of communication, the worst treatment still creates a form of relationship, or, as Ahmad Ghazali says: if the archer wants to hit you, he must look at you. 'Are you looking for a target? Here is my heart!'[107]

To be noticed by God, humans are willing to be mocked, exposed or driven away or to become unbelievers like the venerable Sheikh San'an; in perhaps the most moving, and certainly the most famous, tale in *The Conference of the Birds*, he lives in complete asceticism and equally high regard in the holy district of Mecca, then one day falls in love with a Christian girl. He subsequently dismisses his disciples and blindly obeys her demeaning orders, which serve no other purpose than to humiliate him: he turns to wine, burns the Koran, kneels before the cross, follows the girl's family on their travels, and ends up as the

Christian family's swineherd in Rome, finding himself in self-denial.[108] Attar does not portray San'an as a saint who fell from faith. The sheikh is holy by virtue of falling from faith and going to the utmost limit in his love; he is revered in his disloyalty. In *The Conference of the Birds*, Attar says:

Whoever is firmly rooted in love
Will go beyond unbelief and Islam.[109]

Moving even beyond loss of faith and self-abandonment, annihilation becomes the ultimate encounter under such circumstances. A common man falls in love with an elegant prince. Without any hope of getting close to his beloved, he hides on the shooting range where the prince practises his archery every morning. The man lies down exactly where the prince's arrow has to land. The prince shoots, and the earth turns red from the injured man's blood. The prince rushes to him.

'Why did you do that?' he asks in dismay.

'So that you would ask me that question', the man answers. 'If only I had a hundred lives to give them to your arrow', he sighs, and is dead (32/1, pp. 286ff.).

Naturally there is also pleasure involved, and there is beauty and desire. Feelings of terror and attraction towards the beloved condition each other, and are often even identical. Beauty in such perfection exceeds human powers – which is why Baudelaire cannot imagine a beauty 'which has nothing to do with sorrow'.[110] When Moses returns from Mount Sinai, his face is so bright with the radiance of God that whoever looks at him goes blind (27/12, pp. 252f.).

The kind of experience related by Attar is often fatal and pleasurable at once. It is not only lamented; on many occasions it is even sought and enjoyed. People cannot tear themselves away from it – even if it kills them.

Drink up seven seas and die
Of yearning for another drop. (0, p. 14)

For sixty years, David sang the psalms so splendidly that listeners lost their minds, feet forgot how to walk, the leaves on the trees turned into ears, the water stopped flowing and the birds stopped flying. There was joy everywhere, not a trace of sorrow. But one day David was struck by fate, and henceforth sang only songs of mourning. Everyone who listened to him died, so that God Himself had to reproach him.

Since Adam we have sought the pain of faith
With which to adorn the world. (33/1, pp. 295f.)

Attar heightens not only Job's lament but also the passion of Jesus Christ, for he sings of martyrdom as a pleasure, a grace and a distinction. As Baudelaire says:

Je sais que la douleur est la noblesse unique	I know that sorrow is the one human strength
Où ne mordront jamais la terre et les enfers,	On which neither earth nor hell can impose,
Et qu'il faut pour tresser ma couronne mystique,	And that all the universe and all time's length
Imposer tous les temps et tous les univers.	Must be wound into the mystic crown for my brows.[111]

Even Georg Büchner, whose texts alternate between reproach and denial of God, seems to have reached a decidedly religious view of suffering in his last days, resolving the fundamental antinomy in his work: 'We do not have too much pain', he supposedly said on his deathbed, 'but too little, for it is through the pain that we reach God!'[112] The pleasure in pain referred to by Büchner in his statement about Jesus being the best of all Epicureans is expressed in a more concentrated form in Attar than in any other author in Persian literature. A lover is about to go on a pilgrimage and asks his beloved if she has any assignment for him. The beloved immediately takes a brick and throws it at the poor man with all her might. He kisses the brick, ties it around his neck and leaves joyfully for Mecca (33/6, p. 298).

More than a few of Attar's protagonists practically haggle with God or their beloved – who embodies Him – over the pain they want Him or her to inflict upon them; they are willing to give up everything else, but not this pain.

I have a pain as great as the world.
I want as much again, I'll take out a loan if I have to. (0, p. 15)

Pain becomes an end in itself: whoever is not wounded cannot be healed. The mad saint Loqman as-Sarakhsi holds a stone in one hand and a tinder fungus for cooling wounds in the other. With the stone he beats his head bloody, and with the fungus he soothes the pain.

How can you hope to have peace from your friend
If his blows do not stir you up first? (9/5, p. 130)

A novice constantly calls on God by a thousand different names. One day the sheikh has had enough and commands his student to be quiet at last, telling him that God has no name; whatever names the student calls God, they are simply names for himself, the student, and whatever the student thinks he knows about God reveals only something about himself. God can be neither named nor studied, only experienced through pain:

> An atom of pain from Him in your heart
> Is better than anything you will ever find in both worlds. (0, p. 14)

The affirmation of pain goes so far that some men even refuse to see their beloved when she surprisingly returns their desire – that the lovers turn away, for otherwise they would become happy and no longer able to suffer; and suffering through love is a thousand times sweeter than any caress, for it is more deeply felt. A wise man asks God to blind all other people at the resurrection so that he alone will see Him, no one else. Then he reflects for a moment and says: 'Make me blind on the Day of Judgement so that I crave Your beauty' (37/6, p. 333).

In the pain over the beloved, the pain itself becomes the beloved whose grace the lover seeks.

> O pain, you are my medicine,
> Soul of my soul, my belief and unbelief,
> Even if you lay a hundred mountains upon me,
> It is you, your soul, that carries them.
> Who am I to carry such pain,
> To draw my coat through such dust?
> It is only strange that you are no pain to me,
> I want you, that is all I know.
> Why do you cry? you ask when I cry.
> Cry now, you command when I laugh.
> When I am awake, you say: you can see better in your sleep.
> When I sleep, you say: wake up to dream.
> When I do something, you say: stop that.
> And when I stop, you say: do something at last.
> When I eat, you say: fast, ignorant one!
> And when I fast, you say: why do you not eat, fool?
> What could I eat when you are with me,
> What could I do when you do your deeds with me?
> What you will is neither good nor bad.
> You are no enemy to me, much less a friend. (0, p. 65)

In this ontology of pain, death at the hands of the beloved is the pinnacle of emotional experience. The lovesick Arab prince who asks the sister of Sultan Sanjar not to visit him because he cannot bear her beauty thanks his beloved with the only gift he still possesses: the half of his life that remains. He utters these words and dies (14/1, pp. 163ff.). The shoemaker's son falls in love with the handsome son of the emir, and therefore has to leave the school they both attend. To prove that his heart belongs to his beloved, he cuts his heart out of his chest and has it brought to him on a platter (20/3, pp. 202ff.). Such devotion can only be surpassed by a complete dissolution of oneself in the beloved. When King Mahmoud is about to go hunting, he sees his slave Ayaz weeping.

'Why are you crying?' asks the king.

'Out of jealousy.'

'Why are you jealous?'

'Because you are going after a different creature.'

'But I want to catch it and strike it down.'

'That multiplies my jealousy a thousand-fold.'

'But I mean to kill it afterwards.'

'Now my jealousy is a hundred thousand times greater.'

'But I intend to eat it.'

'Now my jealousy knows no bounds. If only you would consume me as a dish, I would vanish and become Mahmoud entirely. Now I am but a poor slave' (39/6, p. 415).

At times, Attar's depiction of the relationship between God and humans verges on sexually charged sadomasochism. This includes not only the aspect of pleasurable, desired suffering, but also that of subordination, a complete absence of will, which is considered freedom. Sultan Mahmoud visits Ayaz in his sleep. He uncovers his foot, washes it with rosewater and tears, and lays his cheek upon it, all night long. In the morning, Ayaz notices that his foot is lying on the face of the unconscious sultan, but does not remove it.

'What are you playing at, slave, how dare you treat me, the ruler of seven countries, like a slave?' fumes the sultan when he awakes.

'You came to me not as a king but as a slave, and served me. Your heart was tired of being a king, and so it drove you to slavery. Stand up, for slavery does not befit you. You must come to terms in your own heart with your longing for submission. Who am I that you should be ashamed before me? I am the slave, I obey your commands' (32/5, pp. 292ff.).

Attar occasionally hints that humans are not the only ones who long for submission, that God conversely needs the slave as a sadist needs his object of desire.

'Why does God not let justice prevail?' asks the mad sage Ma'shuq-e Tusi (eleventh century). Attar lets him give a bold response: To bring God's power to light.

All that was, is and will be
  Was His, and all was good.

All was intact, except that
  Slavery and degradation were missing.
Therefore he created man, so that
  Slavery would elevate God's existence.
He cast the world's bazaar into turmoil,
  Upset all the horizons.
A hundred bad worlds under His rule by force,
  So that despair would rise up from the world of slavery. (37/11, p. 336)

Yes, God enjoys tormenting humans. If he pays attention to them at all, it is only to derive some amusement from their love, to pass the time like Sultan Mahmoud, who has the villages raided so that his palace will be full of supplicants; or out of vanity like a cruel, heartless beloved. A young man looks into the eyes of a veiled woman on the street. Lovestruck, he follows her. After a while, the woman turns around and asks the man what he wants. When he reveals his feelings, she lifts the veil, shows him her sunlike face and rushes home. The man, who has now completely lost his self-control, runs after the woman. When he finds her door closed, he throws stones at it to make her open up. The woman comes out and rebukes him: 'Are you insane, you wretch? Do you want to get your head cut off?'

'If you didn't want to be mine, why did you lift your veil before me?'

'Because I really do like it when someone likes me' (37/9, pp. 334f.).

No sensible person would involve themselves with such a beloved. Humans, however, love; they are not sensible. That is the essence of monotheism: one cannot get away from God for the simple reason that there is no other. Dangerous liaisons: a hermit who has spent his life worshipping God begs Jesus to ask God if He will grant him an atom of His love. When Jesus returns after a while, he finds the hermit's house of prayer in ruins, his beautiful mihrab broken into a thousand pieces, and the spring from which he used to draw water dried up. God informs Jesus that the hermit is meanwhile living on a mountain. Jesus climbs the mountain and hardly recognizes the hermit: his face is yellow, his lips parched, and his eyes covered in dust. More dead than alive, he lies in his own blood and does not even have the strength to return the prophet's greeting. Then God reveals to Jesus: 'This man demanded a tiny particle of my friendship. When I fulfilled his request, he forgot himself, gave everything up and became the man you see before you. If I had given him another particle of love, he would have crumbled into dust' (31/1, p. 278).

The characters in *The Book of Suffering* certainly do not all ask God for more blows; the enjoyment of pain is only one stage of the despair which Attar depicts as the path inwards. In the same way, there is also sheer rage, black sarcasm, mockery and scorn. One fixed element of the piety described by Attar to which the poet repeatedly returns, however – not in every chapter, but often enough – is love. Although God and the world as He has arranged it give little cause for contentment – on the contrary, there is every reason for complaint – humans yearn for Him. This is the reason to suffer and yet believe, to praise God and curse Him, to renounce Him and thirst for Him. Al-Junayd formulates this quite beautifully:

> My God, my God, even if You
> Show me all Your coldness and turn away,
> I can never escape my longing,
> Not even if I depart from this life.[113]

In *The Book of Suffering* a miserable, starving fool cast into ruin by the love of God constantly sighs, his words choked by sobbing: 'Just wait until I am dead, O God, then I will answer You.'

When the fool is on his deathbed, he draws up a will in which he requests that, after his death, the following sentence be written on his shroud and gravestone in the blood from his heart: 'This heart-rended man (*bi-del*), now that he has died and become a pile of dust, finally gives You his answer: as You and he did not both fit into the world, he left the world to You and departed' (19/3, p. 196).

The people in *The Book of Suffering* – the fools, the wise men, the lovers – cannot help it: they are damned to God. 'The closer someone is, the more confused and restless; those who are far away have an easier life', writes Attar. 'How, then, can anyone strive for closeness?' (2/2, p. 76). Here, too, Job returns in Attar's poetry: Job turns against God, but not away from God; he screams, he is silent, but he does not renounce Him. The very thing that Satan expects of him and Job's wife explicitly demands (Job 2:9), namely to abandon God so that he can die in freedom and relief, is most impossible for him. The love for God felt by Attar's wise men and fools does not contradict their rebellion; it conditions it. Fanatically devoted to the Creator, they experience Him in all His terror, as Job says before condemning himself – in the face of God's power, not His goodness: 'My ears had heard of You, but now my eyes have seen You' (42:5). It is precisely because St John loved God above all else and followed His commandments more strictly that, as C. G. Jung observes, 'he saw the fierce and terrible side of Yahweh. For this reason he felt his gospel of love to be one-sided and supplemented it with the gospel of fear: *God can be loved but must be feared*.'[114] Only those who come close to God encounter Him as so cruel that it becomes excusable for them to defend themselves. Attar places a play on the word *balā* in the mouth of the great Sufi Bayezid. It means 'misfortune', but in classical Persian also 'yes'.

One day Sheikh Bayezid got worked up,
  Said of God: when the Glorious One
Reckons my seventy years,
  I will reckon many thousands of years,
For many thousands of years ago, the One asked
  His new creatures: 'Am I not your Lord?' (Surah 7:121)
And thus cast them into despair forever,
  For their *balā* has brought them nothing but *balā*.
The *balā* of all creatures, on earth as in heaven,
  Comes from the *balā* with which they declared their love. (10/1, pp. 132f.)

The heresy of the most devout

In her book on Arab freethinkers in the Middle Ages, Sarah Stroumsa writes that a Muslim can certainly examine the question of theodicy, but that it is historically and theologically impossible in Islam to accuse God, let alone to portray him as an enraged, murderous enemy in the way Ibn ar-Rawandi did. Whoever did so 'could not remain a Muslim in any meaningful way'.[115] *The Book of Suffering* teaches that the paths taken by those who quarrel with God can lead straight through the heart of Muslim piety. Bayezid, who has the audacity to call God to account, is one of the greatest holy men of Sufism; nor does Attar present the fools as heretics, but rather as those who know the secrets and are allowed to utter what the rest of society may not even think. They are the opposite of disloyal. If anything, it is God who is disloyal, as He makes a mockery of His own revelation and denies humans the relationship for which He created them in the first place. The pious, on the other hand, oppose God by remaining loyal to His words when they appeal to his compassion (the philosopher of religion Emmanuel Lévinas described this attitude in Judaism as 'loving the Torah more than God').[116] A fool calls out to the heavens: 'If what goes on down here does not move Your heart, You can take mine. Is Your heart really so stubborn?' (27/6, p. 251).

Such thoughts are not permitted for ordinary people, while in Attar's world unbelievers and indifferents have no idea anyway. Rebellion against God is reserved for saints, prophets and fools, and by no means recommended as a general course of action. Only lovers can expect lenience for their sins (37/4, p. 332), only fools are exempt from the law (27/1, p. 249), and only Moses himself is allowed – out of love, as Attar repeatedly emphasizes – to break the tablets of the law (27/4, p. 250). A mother has exposed herself in wild lament for her dead son and is uttering blasphemies.

> Her back was bent like a bow,
> And the arrow of her mourning shot into the heavens.

When someone reproaches her and tells her to put her veil back on, the woman replies:

> If you too had a fire blazing in your liver,
> You would deem such actions not only allowed, but required.
> Until my fire has ignited your heart,
> Do not presume to be my judge.
> You are not the mother of a dead child,
> Do you think you can tell me how to lament?
> I see you, you are one of the free,
> You know nothing of those who are bound to suffering. (30/4, p. 271)

Attar – and this is central in order to avoid misunderstanding the concern of his fools, and *The Book of Suffering* as a whole, as a negation of religion – does not incite to heresy. He describes a specific emotional state among those who are intimate with God: 'Whoever burns with love for Him is pure' (27/1, p. 196). Lament and rebellion are absorbed into faith itself; they become a theological, spiritual and – viewed against the concrete background of mystical rituals – almost liturgical motif of the kind familiar from the Hebrew Bible. They are psalmists who reproach God in prayer; it is Job, the most faithful among God's servants, who rebels against Him. And this Job is not punished for his protest – he is richly compensated even though he does not forgive God, but merely submits in recognition of His superior power. This is an aspect overlooked by Ernst Bloch when he dismisses the entire denouement as a cover-up. God himself sanctions the rebellion by rewarding Job, not his three friends, at the end – and neither answers nor refutes his accusation, which thus remains. In a comparable fashion, *The Book of Suffering* compiles unheard-of charges against God that seem to be resolved suddenly in a happy end through an abrupt turn; precisely this turn, however, is shifted to the utopian realm once more in the epilogue, just as the Book of Job ends without explanation or resolution with a pure miracle. Neither Job nor Attar's figures are reconciled, nor is their judgement revised. Just as Job is rewarded without receiving any response to his questions, Attar suggests that, if any people at all are to find salvation, it will most likely be the rebellious fools and blasphemous saints. Bayezid, who wants to take stock of God's seventy thousand years when his own seventy years have expired, hears a voice at the end of his threats to heaven: 'Wait for the day of reckoning, then I will turn your seven limbs into atoms and each atom into an eye, and grant each eye an audience. This will be your reckoning for many thousands of years, and you will see more than you can look at. Whoever wants to see this sun will find here what was promised to him' (10/1, p. 133).

And Attar himself says (albeit in the introduction, where there is still room for hope) that God torments humans, but at once teaches weeping as a means of alleviation (0, p.18).

> When You push me to the ground of Your wrath,
> You pour a hundred treasures of goodness over me.
> And when the sword of Your justice wounds me,
> The balm of Your grace will heal me. (0, p. 17)

God is the tormentor and the only healer, the sword and the balm. These verses are a human rendition of what Yahweh says in the Bible: 'I have wounded and I will heal, and no one can deliver out of my hand' (Deuteronomy 32:39). Neither the Bible nor Attar call upon humans to blaspheme; rather, they present rebellion against God as an intimate, perhaps the most intimate aspect of faith: 'How could a sensible man dare speak as the lover does?' (33/7, p. 300). Bloch overlooks this dialectical aspect when he sees only the original, 'authentic' Job as a rebel. On the way to Mount Sinai, Moses meets an enlightened ascetic. The man speaks: 'O Moses, tell the Creator from me: your commands have been carried out, so show compassion.'

As Moses continues, he meets a man whose love for God has thrown him off course. He speaks: 'Tell the Truthful One from me: this piece of skin and bone loves You. Do You love it too?'

Moses continues, and finally meets a bareheaded fool with naked feet. He speaks impudently to Moses: 'Tell the Creator from me: how much misery do You still have in store for me? I have no more strength to bear it. Sorrow has spooned out the entirety of my soul, and the joyful day has become night. I turn my back on You – but will You too finally leave me alone?'

Having reached Mount Sinai, Moses dares extend only the first two messages to God. God grants both the ascetic and the lover their requests. As the prophet is turning to leave, the Lord speaks: 'You have kept the fool's message from me.'

'O Lord, I thought it better not to mention his unseemly words.

Even if You heard them, it would be improper to utter them a second time.'

'Tell the fool from me: even if you turn your back on me, I will still not turn my back on you' (33/7, pp. 299f.).

Only the first half of Bloch's famous statement (in so far as one applies it more generally, and speaks of believers and unbelievers rather than Christians and atheists) is supported by *The Book of Suffering*, namely that *only an unbeliever can be a good believer*. To Attar and the author(s) of the Book of Job, however, the second half, which states that *only a believer can be a good unbeliever*, the telos of Bloch's message would be irrelevant at best; for they are concerned not with defining the preconditions for atheism, but with showing the dangers of piety.

'How can you know the taste of religion?' asks Umar, the third caliph of Islam, and answers himself: 'I know it because I have sampled the taste of unbelief' (40/2, p. 358).

Attar avoids suggesting that the fools and saints who question the justice of God's order could receive an answer. He praises them as being intimate with God, but leaves their accusations unexplained. Attar does not justify God any more than God justifies Himself in the Book of Job. Bayezid, who wishes to call God to account, is rewarded rather than refuted. This is the very paradox of that heretical piety with which Attar follows on from the Bible: clinging to God, but simultaneously denying Him the attribute of goodness, and finally the rewarding of this negative emotion towards God – these are all elements of the Job motif, which is precisely not constituted by mere accusation or mere forbearance. The motif can be found in all of Attar's verse epics, though in an extremely pessimistic variation in *The Book of Suffering*; for here the poet describes suffering and the consequent rebellion more drastically than in any other work of Islamic literature, while salvation and a possible merit to the rebellion are merely hinted at.

Ernst Bloch and other modern exegetes assumed that the motif of submission was added to the Book of Job later; I wrote above that, aside from text-critical aspects, certain considerations of content and dramaturgy also contradict this assumption. *The Book of Suffering* sensitizes one to the fact that rebellion against God actually presupposes intimacy with Him. It is in this figure of thought that rebellion within piety is located, as the story about a student of Dhu n-Nun illustrates. He completes forty forty-day retreats, prays without interruption for forty years, fasts, stays awake and keeps silent without experiencing illumination or even a tiny glimmer of hope. He does not want to complain, he tells his master, but he simply does not know what else he can do to receive a sign. Dhu n-Nun tells him that, if God does not look upon him in goodness, He will perhaps do so in anger, and recommends that the student stop his prayers and fasting and instead feast to his heart's content. The student stuffs himself and lies down to sleep, and straight away he is finally visited in a dream by the Prophet, who bears a message from God: 'How could someone who deals with us come to any harm?' (9/1, pp. 125ff.).

Job or the fools, saints and Dervishes in *The Book of Suffering* do not lose their faith in God when they rebel against Him; in their despair, they are more religious than the believers who praise God, but turn a blind eye to the real state of His creation. Those whose love exceeds the conventional degree dare to demand the kind of God He Himself revealed to them. After all, God did not lose his bet with Satan; the fact that Job rebelled against God does not mean that he denies Him. Disobedience here becomes an act of submission; humans become pleasing to God by emancipating themselves from Him.

> The eye of Your forgiveness searched for a rebel,
> So I went out onto the field of resistance. (0, p. 18)

Job in the Islamic Republic

Do Job's questions, which Attar posed anew and more sharply, still have a place in today's Iran? Not within religion, at any rate. If orthodox authors such as Ayatollah Morteza Motahhari examine the problem of evil at all, then it is only in terms of theological history and with the ultimate purpose of justifying God.[117] His justice is also defended by authors who attack the orthodox understanding of religion, however. God's attributes in the state-defining discourse – perhaps most conspicuously in the case of the most important theorist of conservative governance, Ayatollah Mohammad Taqi Mesbah-Yazdi – are often so aggressive that a religious opposition would not even need to paint a more pessimistic picture of God. Therefore, anyone who questions the Islamic Republic from an Islamic perspective does so precisely by emphasizing God's compassion and goodness in contrast to state Islam. It is the gentle, compassionate God of Persian love mysticism whom a philosopher of religion such as Abdolkarim Sorush, the best-known reform thinker in Iran today, sets apart from the severe, implacable God of 'legal Islam' (*eslām-e feqhāhati*).[118] This distinction has become evident in recent years even in the appearance of streets. When the municipal administrations of almost all cities fell into the hands of reformers after the first local elections in Iranian history in February 1999, billboards and neon panels everywhere bore the Prophet's words: 'God is beautiful and loves beauty.'[119] Evidently they felt that, after twenty years of the Islamic Republic, it was important to remind people of God's glory. Here one can sense an insistence on God and those of his qualities that attract rather than intimidate believers. This insistence manifests itself most wittily in the satire *The Lizard* (*Mārmulak*), about a petty criminal. He escapes from prison in a mullah's gown and, once free, suddenly finds himself standing at a pulpit. This Iranian Schweik[120] then spontaneously invents an Islam that calls people to love one another instead of tormenting them with regulations, an Islam of tolerance and individual religious experience, with a God who is as compassionate as promised at the start of every Surah. His listeners are thrilled.

In present-day Iran, it is not so much literature as advanced cinema that poses Job's and Attar's questions anew – just as it is primarily film directors who engage with the subject of God. God's justice is called into question most openly in Majid Majidi's film *The Colour of Paradise* (or, as the original title *rang-e ḫodā* more fittingly puts it, *The Colour of God*) and most profoundly in Abbas Kiarostami's *The Taste of Cherry* (*ta'm-e gilās*). Alongside these directors, who are either religious or at least take religion seriously, there is an increasing rediscovery of quarrelling with God in modern Iran among directors who are scarcely concerned with God. In texts circulating in Iran as CD-ROMs or exile prints, several authors formulate their criticism of the theocracy as criticism of God – whether God as such or the Islamic view of God. The Islamic tradition of accusing God is hardly a factor here, however; it returns to Iran as a European reimport. It is very revealing that the most notable example of this type refers not to Persian journeys of the soul, but to Dante. The first-person narrator in Hushang Mo'inzadeh's retelling of *The Divine Comedy* attacks God on the Day of Judgement as a model of injustice:

> God! You promised me that I would stand before a court of justice. Or didn't You? What about Your promise? Where is the justice? What kind of court is this that neither allows me to bring forth a charge nor asks me about my deeds? What distinguishes the methods of Your court from the courts of the rabbis, the church inquisition or the sharia courts of the mullahs? Those courts pronounced the same judgements: crucifixion, burning, stoning, execution, shooting – whether the accused were guilty or not. That's exactly how it is here![121]

Such accusations against God, however – in other cases too, as far as I can see – are almost always satirically intended: the state or Islam always remain visible as the true objects of criticism. The aim is not to reproach God; if anything, it is to expose Him as an absurd construct. This leaves the political dimension of the attacks intact, but not their metaphysical dimension. The protests against God and being, which were so loud, so numerous and so radical in the religious culture of Islam, and also played a part in stimulating previously inconceivable advances in European thought, have now become an almost exclusively extra-religious phenomenon, both in Iran and in the Arab world. It is criticism from without, as found in numerous and prominent contributions from Iranian intellectuals, formulated perhaps most sharply by, of all people, the country's most famous writer, Sadeq Hedayat. Whenever one speaks of the far-reaching crisis and loss of creativity, tolerance and liberalism in today's Arab world or the political dictatorship in Iran, it is important to bear one thing in mind: most poets and mystics who attacked the dominant worldview and traditional conventions of their time saw themselves as devout Muslims. And not only that: they were an integral part of their own culture.

A culture proves its strength when it does not leave radical criticism to outsiders, but practises it itself – that is, when self-criticism is possible, and even institutionally supported. Just as God richly rewarded the rebel Job, later kings held on to their scoffers and fools, and today states strengthen their critical potential while cities fund advanced theatre. And, as transparent as the motives of the respective authorities may be for subsidizing their own subversion, critics do not necessarily stay within the confines of their jester's licence, but constantly overstep boundaries and thus expand what can be said. How else could religious and political conditions develop if their truths were not attacked time and again, if criticism did not perpetually force them to find new answers? And the notion of self-criticism, after all, indicates that one is still part of this self, just as the greatest critics in the West were a brilliant, outstanding part of their own Western culture – and just as I occasionally wish that today's European intellectuals would devote themselves more to the wrongs in their own world than to those in Islam. Criticism of other cultures is always affirmative in relation to one's own culture, and thus the opposite of what provides literature with its motivation and its tasks. Literature, art and intellectuality as a whole are at heart a self-critical act. Attar is the best example of this: he is a classic of Persian literature, not a heretic, and demonstrates what Islamic culture was once able to be – a culture that also included the opposite of what the religious elites defined as Islamic.

A rationalist or mystical understanding of religion, radically liberal erotic descriptions, acceptance of both political and religious criticism, even open heresy, scarcely have any place in the public life of Attar's homeland today – let alone a piety that encompasses heresy. Aside from individual countries like Lebanon and individual authors like Naguib Mahfouz, they are also absent from the Islamic world. 'I am greater than God', exclaimed the mystic Bayezid Bestami. Bestami is one of the great holy men of Islamic mysticism. Today, anyone who sincerely renewed his pronouncements would be branded a heretic – as much of a heretic as, according to Kant, Job was in the Christian world. The mark of a great culture is not least that it permits sentiment against its greatest authorities, even sentiment against God.

— 5 —

HISTORY OF A COUNTER-THEOLOGY

God's successors

Why did God create humans? Because He wanted to be recognized, we are told not only by the non-Koranic words of God, but also by the Koran itself. There is scarcely a thought formulated more often in the Islamic revelation than the idea that the world exists so that humans can recognize God in it.

> Surely in the creation of the heavens and the earth
> and the alternation of night and day
> and the ship that runs in the sea with profit
> to men, and the water God sends down from heaven
> therewith reviving the earth after it is dead
> and His scattering abroad in it all manner of
> crawling thing, and the turning about of the winds
> and the clouds compelled between heaven and earth –
> surely there are signs for a people having understanding. (Surah 2:164)

The entire creation, nature no less than civilization, human history as much as the divine books, the joys of love and food – everything that exists, occurs, is felt, seen, heard, smelt and experienced in the cosmos, on earth and in the hereafter is a revelation of God for humans. 'God brings to life the dead, and He shows you His signs, that perhaps you may have understanding [*la'alla ta'qilūna*]' (Surah 2:73). That final phrase, one of the most common formulations in the entire Koran – or, more precisely, the mere *la'alla*, the 'perhaps' – expresses the eternal drama between God and humans in the Koran. The Koranic God is visible; it is for humans to recognize the signs, and perhaps they will do so, perhaps they will not – *la'alla ya'qilūna*. God courts humans, He promises, threatens, punishes and forgives His creatures, but the course of the world, according to the Koran, is a history of human refusal that provokes God's wrath, yet simultaneously induces him to keep sending new envoys nonetheless. Their purpose is to make the signs clear to people until God, with Mohammed, gives humanity the last and greatest opportunity to recognize Him. The Koran itself would then be God's final attempt – and for this reason it often seems desperate, foaming, wildly beckoning and movingly human – to make humans aware of himself as on the first day: 'Am I not your Lord?' (Surah 7:121). Since then, humans have been left alone with the freedom to believe in God. By renewing the primeval 'yes', humans re-establish their natural state as Muslims in the literal sense, as 'ones who submit to God', thus fulfilling the purpose of the creation, namely for God to be recognized – or, more precisely, acknowledged as that which is greater: *Allāhu akbar*.

That God is fundamentally cognizable separates the view of God in the Koran from the predominant one in the Hebrew Bible: 'Truly You are a God who hides himself, O God and Saviour of Israel' (Isaiah 45:15). The Hebrew God is not always concealed, but, from Isaiah's complaint that Yahweh 'is hiding his face from the house of Jacob' (Isaiah 8:17) to modern Jewish reflections on the Holocaust, the distance of God has been felt – even if only as a potential danger. Kafka found something resembling archetypal parables for this perception. 'The revealed God of our Judeo-Christian spirituality maintains all the infinity of his absence which is in the personal order itself', writes Lévinas. 'He shows himself only by his trace, as in Exodus 33. To go towards Him is not to follow this trace which is not a sign; it is to go towards the others who stand in the trace.'[1] Christianity reacts to the impression that God is absent with the human incarnation of Jesus Christ, but His concealment is also thematicized in the New Testament when Jesus asks his father why he has forsaken him. The Bible says of God that He can approach humans, but equally turn away from them. God shows Himself or does not; we can only hope for the Lord, as Isaiah writes: 'I will wait for the Lord' (8:17). There is a passive element here that Beckett took to the point of absurdity in *Waiting for Godot*.

In the Koran, the roles are reversed.[2] The possibility of God's concealment is not mentioned anywhere, whereas the disloyalty of humans, their refusal to recognize God's signs, their closed eyes, ears, hearts and mouths, is brought up time after time. God is categorically and permanently declared visible; humans cannot await Him passively, but must rather decide: they turn either towards God or away from Him. In either case it is they, the humans, who are expected to act. 'We have indeed made clear for you the signs, that haply you will understand' (Surah 57:17). Hence the hardships described by Attar often include a biblical distance and concealment of the Creator, but even more often the cruelty of his closeness, as consistently as he might question the Koranic view of the relationship between God and humans.

Whoever is close to Him is in great danger
  Who would seek such closeness? (2/3, p. 77)

Attar turns the conventional view on its head – but it remains the Koranic view. A fool is caught unawares by a storm while wandering through the desert. The lightning tries to burn him, the rain tries to drown him. Then a voice calls out to the fool from the storm-lashed heavens (and one can certainly read this with a smile as a caricature of Old Testament scenes): 'God is with you, be without fear.'

'But that's exactly what I'm afraid of', screams the fool. 'It's because He is with me that I'm afraid' (38/5, p. 342).

It is not because death can mean destruction or eternal damnation (if this means the rejection of humans by God) that death is so monstrous that even Jesus sweats entire pools of blood (4/11, p. 94) at the thought of it; no, death is to be feared precisely because it promises the encounter with God. A wanderer is trembling and crying pitifully for fear of his imminent death. Someone tells him to be quiet, asking why he is so excessively afraid and saying that such horror is unseemly for any reasonable person. Impossible, the dying man responds. For now he is about to go to someone for whom this world and the world beyond, being and non-being, belief and unbelief, and good and evil are all the same. As firm and strong as one might be, surely the thought of someone who is indifferent to all this is enough to curdle one's blood (E12, pp. 373f.).

Because the Koran interprets the entire world as one great address from God to humans, it radically elevates humans, which are no longer a part or even the crown of the creation, but rather its meaning and purpose, its origin and telos. Thus man in the Koran is not the 'image' of God, but rather His 'successor, representative' (*ḫalīfa*, caliph). This is a fundamental contrast to the Bible, though, as far as I can tell, it is hardly ever reflected upon: man is not simply created in God's image, but rather is given the responsibility to complete the creation. The burden thus laid on humans by God was pointed out by Hafiz in the famous verses:

For Heaven's self was all too weak to bear
The burden of His love God laid on it,

He turned to seek a messenger elsewhere,
And in the Book of Fate my name was writ.[3]

The Koran declares humans autonomous beings, yet simultaneously expects them to give up their autonomy voluntarily. The word *Muslim* ('devote oneself, submit, make peace') refers to a conscious action; even if one assumes, as many do in the West, that this devotion entails the abdication of one's own will, the act itself – provided one does not read any strict predestination into the Koran, such that even human will is declared an automatism – by necessity occurs through one's own initiative. At the same time, however, the spectrum of actions is restricted to a bare minimum: if humans devote themselves to God – with gratitude and through good deeds, as the Koran constantly underlines – the purpose of the creation will be fulfilled. The biblical Book of Job contains the seed of the idea that God wants to be honoured for his own sake, without justification or sufficient reason. Perhaps that is why God did not grant Job any answer except references to His sheer power. In the Koran, however, the world is arranged in such a way that there is not even cause for critical questioning. The creation is not only God's work, it is also good at all times and everywhere; all people need to do is look, then they will recognize this and thank God. If they turn away – unbelief, *kufr*, literally means 'ingratitude' – they blaspheme and bring God's damnation upon themselves. The possibility of devoting oneself to God without gratitude, of recognizing His power yet still insisting on one's own significance, of acknowledging God's being but not submitting to His will, is not envisaged in the Koran. A fool passes a gathering of scholars. They are speaking about the creation, saying that God created man from mud and spirit (*gel wa del*). The fool is angered by these pious words: 'If even the mud and our spirit are His, what belongs to us in this world? Are we to own nothing except our desire? If everything is His, then who am I?' (23/3, p. 223).

In a certain sense, only resistance can be the truly autonomous, Promethean act that elevates man to God's successor, the one who simultaneously follows and replaces Him: man would thus be doing what God's plan does not envisage. His individuation would take place in the act of rebellion, with the precondition that he raises himself to be the representative of God, worthy of the veneration he expects the angels to show. The abandonment of hope would be the reason to go on living. In the poem 'Hiob', Yvan Goll (d. 1950) writes:

Why I am still alive?
Uncertain God
To prove You to Yourself.[4]

In Attar's case, however, Prometheus, who hates the Gods, would be transformed into a fool unhappily in love re-enacting the tragedy – albeit on the backstage, namely the world. Unlike the rebel of antiquity, he never becomes a threat to his divine adversary. His revolt remains an inconsequential escapade – not, as in Kott's interpretation of *King Lear*, because God does not exist, but because, on the contrary, God is omnipresent and hopelessly superior. Hence no one takes Attar's Prometheus seriously. A poor, desperate fool comes to Nishapur, hungry and thirsty. On the way he sees a meadow full of cows. 'To whom do the cows belong?' he asks.

'The governor of our city', he is told.

The fool continues and sees the steppe, black with horses.

'To whom do the horses belong?'

'The governor.'

Shortly afterwards he sees an enormous herd of sheep.

'To whom do the sheep belong?'

'The governor.'

Next he encounters a crowd of young, handsome and magnificently clothed Turkish slaves.

'Whose slaves are these?'

'They are the governor's loan slaves.'

Finally he reaches the city and sees a splendid palace.

'To whom does this palace belong?'

'That is the governor's palace, my boy', a man answers. 'Who are you that you don't know that?'

At this, the poor fool flies into a rage. He hurls his tattered turban into the sky and cries out: 'Here, take this turban too and give it to your governor. If he is to have everything, he can have my turban too' (27/13, pp. 253f.).

If one reads Attar while keeping Job in mind, one is tempted to see this as being precisely God's plan: that humans do not keep to the plan. According to the Koran, God created humans although the angels had warned Him that His new creatures would not sing His praises and worship him. But He knew something they did not:

> And when thy Lord said to the angels,
> 'I am setting on earth a viceroy.'
> They said, 'What, wilt Thou set therein one
> who will do corruption there, and shed blood,
> while We proclaim Thy praise and call Thee Holy?'
> He said, 'Assuredly I know what you know not.' (Surah 2:30)

When God created man, his first word was 'yes'. The Islamic creed, by contrast, begins with a negation: *lā ilāha illā Allāh*, 'no god but God'. It is between the primeval 'yes' and the 'no' in time that the creation takes place, almost a form of romantic relationship – 'Only me!' 'Yes, no one but you!' To be, man had to affirm; to become human, he must negate. In the Koran this is the negation of other gods; in *The Book of Suffering* it is a 'no' that is extended even to God in order to win the rights of humans. This is not unbelief, for that would mean denying God, refusing to take part in the relationship, turning away. The people in *The Book of Suffering*, however, believe in God; they believe in Him no matter what. Because they love Him, they cannot be content with the way He shows Himself in the world. They call Him to account.

It seems to me that the Book of Job is not so much a book about God or the injustice of His world; it is a book about faith, and how faith also includes being true to oneself against God, opening one's eyes to the creation, and wrestling with the Creator if necessary, because it expresses the most precious thing God has given humanity: freedom. The Hebrew Bible in general – like the Koran – speaks less of the Creator and how He is than of the fact that Israel does not simply accept this God as He is. Israel challenges God and demands that He keep His promises. When the people in *The Book of Suffering* are rewarded like Job, or, like Israel, can hope that the promise will be fulfilled, one could imagine that God actually wanted them to protest. To be pleasing to God, they would have had to accuse Him and elevate themselves above Him. If one follows this thought through, one would conclude that God cast humans into misfortune in order to teach them to refuse.

This is not purely speculative; it is a theological argument. Admittedly, one has to believe in it for it to become clear – hence the conditional formulation. But one could certainly look to the Sufi tradition itself as a witness: 'The moaning of the afflicted is praise of God, his screaming a declaration of divine unity, his sigh a gift of alms, his sleep worship, and his tossing and turning is jihad.'[5] This has rung true for me since watching my Aunt Lobat die. If there is a heaven, and if I have ever known a person who gained admission, it was she, who must have done so, and seemed to have lost faith in His justice at the end – but not her faith in God. For it was not merely horror that had driven the warmth from her still-clear eyes, not only suffering, helplessness and shame at having been stripped so bare, down to her skeleton, before us; she was also baffled. I could see it quite clearly: she did not understand how what was happening could happen to her, the most God-fearing woman in my world, the most just, loving and tolerant. Aunt Lobat was angry, perhaps most of all because she could not even give voice to her anger, since her tongue could only hang limply, and she thus had to place her whole bitterness into the prayer fragments she uttered like lamentations. But they were prayers all the same; she remained so devout to the end that God could not exist if He did not bless her. Naturally that is a matter of faith; but Attar, after all, speaks of God. And to me it is completely clear.

Anger at the gods

The orthodoxies of all three monotheistic religions suppress misfortune, even when they confront it, in their search for explanations. As deep, painful and sincere as their formulations may be in subjective terms, their answers do not leave the realm of canonic beliefs and traditions. Their whole efforts are aimed precisely at being able to remain within this realm, despite the knowledge of a reality full of disaster. By ascribing whatever sense to the injustice or coming to terms with their inexplicability in earthly terms, they cling to the moral perfection of the Creator, as the alternative seems to be unbelief. Only rarely is there an awareness that, alongside the denial of God in atheism and the justification of God in the many variations of theodicy, another, probably even older human reaction is conceivable: God exists, but He neither loves us nor is just. There is a meaning to it all, but a disastrous one.

It is fair to say that certain individuals – poets, mystics, theologians – in all the major religions have verbalized the experience of suffering through God, in some cases even underpinned it dogmatically. Outside of monotheism this is almost a natural act. As early as the Sumerians, a forerunner of Job complained that 'the swindler conspires against me, and You, my God, do not prevent it'.[6] We know several authors and dramatic figures from antiquity who rebel against the gods – for example Mimnermus of Colophon, who concludes his lament about life with the remark: 'There's none whom Zeus does not give a multitude of ills',[7] or Prometheus in Aeschylus's drama: 'I hate all the gods who, when I helped them, wronged me.'[8] People frequently shouted at the heavens in rage in ancient China, and even in Buddhism, which does not have any theology in the strict sense, the motif of (Buddha's) force is not absent if one recalls the messianic aspects of the appearance of Maitreya, the future Buddha, which have also served to justify political revolts on several occasions.[9] The rebellious believer as a character type is perhaps given most weight in the Indian religions, which include many gods, but emphasize individual deities in cosmological and cultic contexts, sometimes precisely honouring or fearing their terrible aspects (Shiva as *Bhairava* – the terrible – Kali as *Durga* – the invincible – and various others).

Hindu folk literature, like classical Indian poetry in general, is full of stories in which people complain of the man-eating greed of the gods, rebel against them and ultimately prove themselves morally superior to them. The poet Palkuriki Somanatha, for example, who lived a few decades after Attar, tells of a man named Halayudha who is visited by two pious men. They report that the virtuous Siriyala has sacrificed his son to the man-eating Shiva. In fact the two visitors are Siriyala and Shiva themselves, who expect this act of unconditional submission to fill their host with joy and admiration. But Halayudha is anything but impressed.

'What are you trying to tell me?' asks Halayudha. 'Is Shiva a man-eating demon? And is his follower Siriyala so devoid of all piety that he slaughters his own son like an animal? You are great men, so your words cannot be false, but is such a thing possible?'

The disguised Shiva assures him that millions of believers have sacrificed their wives to God, and billions their children. And that far more believers have sacrificed themselves. Shiva wanted to test Siriyala, and therefore demanded of him what he found hardest to give. Nonetheless, Siriyala did not hesitate to offer his son to Shiva as a meal. Since, people in all the villages of the world have been telling stories in praise of Siriyala.

'Why did that have to happen?' exclaims Halayudha in anger, and concludes that Shiva must have turned into a demon: 'May the demon that ate a disciple and the butcher who killed a disciple, as well as the many ignorants who write stories about it, be cast out of the community – along with those who read these stories.'

What is notable about the tale is that it makes Halayudha the hero. For Shiva, who, like God, is held up to the standard of his own self-image, is so intimidated by Halayudha's accusations that he asks his wife Uma for help. She and Siriyala's wife ask Halayudha to revoke his curse. When Halayudha finally agrees, Shiva embraces him and praises him for his wisdom, courage and stubborn determination. So, for all the differences resulting from the fundamental starting point of polytheism, the story resembles the Book of Job in one decisive aspect: at the end, the god even rewards rebellion against His cruelty.[10]

Quarrelling with God in Judaism

Many religions, then, are familiar with the piety that is angry with the gods, but it leads to a comprehensive change of values and notions of faith only where one single god is left. In monotheism, rebellion against God is at the same time a rebellion against religion itself, which teaches an opposing, more just notion of God. In a sense it is a counter-theology that runs through all monotheistic cultures and, though it does not remove the boundary separating it from atheism, certainly shifts it. In Islam, religiously approved reproach of God is restricted largely to mysticism. The Jewish tradition seems to make it easier for the individual to rise up against God from the foundations of the religion: one finds numerous expressions of revolt throughout the centuries whose self-identity and perception remain within religious tradition, rather than belonging, as in Christian culture, primarily to the realms of secular poetry and philosophy. A comparison between early commentaries on biblical stories – as shown impressively by Yvonne Sherwood using the example of the prophet Jonah[11] – reveals how human resistance to God's decisions, which was almost entirely passed over or reinterpreted in the Christian exegesis of the Patrists, is acknowledged as a religious phenomenon in the Jewish exegesis of the same verses. Certainly the predominant impulse in Judaism was likewise to accept suffering as a punishment or test, even to welcome it as a means of self-improvement or as a guide. There are numerous traditional accounts in which the great rabbis celebrated their own hardship, in particular their martyrdom, in the manner familiar in Islam from such mystics as al-Hallaj, who asked someone what love is: 'You will see today, tomorrow and the day after tomorrow.' That day they chopped off his hands and feet, the next day they hanged him, and on the third day they scattered his ashes into the wind.[12] Even under torture, Rabbi Akiba ben Josef intoned the Shema: 'Hear, O Israel: the Lord, our God, is one God.' When his pupils asked him during his torture how he could still praise God and be joyful when he could hardly catch his breath for pain, he answered: 'For my whole life I have yearned to love God with all my heart and all my soul, and now I can finally do so.'[13] Many Jewish reactions to injustice and hardship are based on the understanding of suffering as a potential sign of grace not only for the individual, but for the entire community of believers – such as the persecution by the Romans, the suffering caused by the Crusaders, the pogroms following plague epidemics, the torture under the Spanish Inquisition, the massacre by the hordes of the Cossack hetman Chmelnitzky (d. 1657) and, in the twentieth century, the anti-Semitic riots in Russia. Even some interpretations of the Holocaust still cling to the formula *u'mnpei hata'einu* – 'for our sins have we been punished'.

As in Christianity and Islam, the relationship between God and humans in Judaism is based first of all on the acknowledgement of His power and glory; Jewish prayers likewise express praise and submission to God's will above all else. What one wishes to receive from God is formulated not as a demand, but as a request and a plea. God is perfect in all He does, and 'therefore no one may criticize or consider God',[14] as the midrash states. At the same time, however, legal speeches against God or quarrelling and bargaining with Him are familiar and largely accepted forms – almost genres – in which to address the subject of God's injustice in the Jewish tradition as compared with other religions. They go back to Abraham and continue to the present day, as Anson Laytner has documented.[15] 'Impudence, even against Heaven, is of avail', teaches the Talmud.[16]

The constant focus of the appeal, and later the accusation, is the same impression that also nags at Attar's figures, even though they did not carry any formally sealed covenant in their memory: that God is not as He claims and has promised to be. God does not abide by the contract – hence the imagined place of trial to which the pious bring God (and only they, for the sinners have broken the covenant themselves by disregarding divine law), and hence the appeals to God's own words, to His standing: 'Sovereign of the universe! If You have no pity on us, why have You no pity on the sanctity of Your name?'[17] The anthropomorphic image of God in the Bible, which Jewish philosophy contested so vehemently later on, in the engagement with Muslim philosophy and on the basis of the shared Greek sources, was emphasized and expanded by the rabbinical scholars. Thus the protest against God, which is present in many biblical passages, was intensified. Whoever has human qualities, whoever can be angered and moved, can be turned to in a prayer of supplication, appealed to, and revolted against.

Accusation was considered legitimate, however, only when uttered by holy men – as in Attar, who also adds fools to the select group. Starting with Rabbi Akiba, who demanded that one should love suffering, the prayer of protest was gradually forced out of the liturgy to concentrate on the aspects of repentance and obedience. In this interpretation, as Rabbi Akiba wrote, Job did wrong by complaining about his suffering. Like almost all teachers in Jewish orthodoxy, the only aspects of Job he praised were his submission and forbearance.[18] Rebellion has been preserved in exegetical literature, where it usually stands starkly beside the opposing impulse of submission and unconditional praise. Alongside midrashim in which Moses, Jeremiah or

David are criticized or punished for questioning God's will, we find the opposite: prophets being praised precisely for confronting God. In some cases God himself or a rabbi complains that this or that figure did not rebel, while in other cases rebels bitterly regret their deeds and thus affirm God's justice. One sometimes finds both impulses formulated in the same text (the Jonah story, for example)[19] or even in the same sentence (such as Lamentations 3:42: 'We have sinned and rebelled, and You have not forgiven'),[20] augmenting and contradicting each other and thus encompassing the human experience in all its breadth. Yvonne Sherwood has compared the disjunctive character of traditional Jewish exegesis to the situation in the yeshiva, the Talmud school, where students work in pairs and speak the words of the wise men back and forth to each other.[21] This is expressed very poignantly by Rabbi David:

> How do you love your neighbour as yourself? By allowing yourself to be silenced by your neighbour's pain, a silence of awe and of openness. And by *not* allowing yourself to be silenced by your neighbour's pain, by speech which is powerful and comforting. And how do you love the Lord, your God, with all your heart? By allowing yourself to be silenced by the presence of God, a silence of amazement and of receptivity. And by not allowing yourself to be silenced by God, by speech which is strong and just.[22]

Nor did the prayer of protest vanish entirely. Complementing the prayer-books and their attitude of forbearance, it even found new expression in the *piyyutim*, the religious poems of medieval European and Arab culture – and so extensively that in some cases it returned from there to the liturgy (*keva*), partly restoring the simultaneity of the two aspects, submission and protest. The origins of this poetry, which was more open to current impressions, concerns and hardships than the texts of the prayer-books, probably lie in second- to seventh-century Palestine – i.e., the rabbinical and Talmudic period. As a reaction to formalized prayer and the domestication of human experience it occasioned, the *piyyutim* became more and more widespread in subsequent centuries and, particularly in Europe, increasingly became a medium of metaphysical lament and accusation. It was the situation of never-ending exile and, primarily in the West, the political oppression and physical extermination that made it impossible for Jews to repress their doubts and despair any longer, and caused them to ask anew those questions to God that are well documented in the Hebrew Bible. One need only recall the massacres during the Black Death in 1350, which had already halved the number of Jews in Germany six centuries before the Holocaust. The *piyyutim* allowed people to discuss with God face to face once more, also to appeal to Him in anger and argue with Him. Alluding to the Crusaders, a southern Italian contemporary of Attar, Elijah ben Shemayaj (d. 1160), wrote:

> You have despised, abandoned and let fall those who hold on to You. You have broken Your covenant with the three beloved (the patriarchs). You have made us outcasts; we are persecuted, punished and wounded. We are devoured by locusts and consumed by worms.[23]

While lament over persecution and social ostracism was scarcely ever a liturgical or poetic topos in the Jewish literature of the Islamic Orient,[24] the motif of quarrelling with God spread further through Europe as a result of the Hasidic movement. And with the change of genre (from prayers to stories) and language (from Hebrew to Yiddish), the audience also changed. The language of the midrashim and *piyyutim* was comprehensible virtually only to educated people at the time. The tales of the Hasidim, on the other hand, were told in all social strata of Eastern European Jewry. It is not only through their anecdotal or aphoristic form that they sometimes recall a masnavi or Attar's *Lives of the Saints*; the Tzaddikim share the ascetic spirit of the Sufi holy men, but also their awareness of how much suffering there is in our earthly existence. They share an idealization of suffering, a dry, wayward humour, as well as the ecstatic outbursts, the rapture and eccentricities, and not least their ethos, which measures religious zeal by humanity of behaviour, not external forms: 'Whether a man really loves God – that can be determined by the love he bears his fellow-men',[25] said Levi Yitzhak of Berdichev (d. 1810), known as *Derbaremdiger*, 'the compassionate'. Above all, the Tzaddikim have such an intimate relationship with God that they can take greater liberties with Him than their religion otherwise allows. Their bold, even presumptuous expectations are based on the principle that they can declare God's commands invalid, while God will affirm what they command. As Rabbi Levi Yitzhak spoke:

> In our generation the Holy One, blessed be He, says to the Tzaddik, who now stands in the place of Moses: 'I, the Lord, am your God! [Exodus 20:2] You may' – dare one utter the words? – 'do with Me as You wish!'[26]

And some Hasidic masters did exactly that: they spoke of the Lord without fear of punishment. Rabbi Levi Yitzhak, for example, frequently reminded God that He too must ask His people to forgive Him for the suffering they endured for His sake. Hence his introduction of the plural 'Yom Kippurim' instead of Yom Kippur: for Levi Yitzhak, atonement was a reciprocal affair. The rabbi often interrupted his Hebrew prayers in front of the congregation to rail at God. 'Zol Ivan blozen shofar!' [Let Ivan blow the shofar] he shouted. 'If You prefer the enemy who suffers less than we do, then let the enemy praise Your glory!'[27] Not once has God been just towards a single Jew, declares Levi Yitzhak,[28] whose holiness, because of its completely unconventional humanity and his ecstatic behaviour, was not without a certain nimbus of folly. He threatened his Lord, cursed, haggled with Him, tried to coerce Him into showing compassion, and, like some of Attar's figures, reminded Him that not only does the sinner need God, but God also needs the sinner. Once, in the middle of a prayer, Levi Yitzhak spoke:

> Lord of all the world! A time there was when You went around with that Torah of Yours and were willing to sell it at a bargain, like apples that have gone bad, yet no one would buy it from You. No one would even look at You! And then we took it! Because of this I want to propose a deal. We have many sins and misdeeds, and You an abundance of forgiveness and atonement. Let us exchange! But perhaps You will say: 'Like for like!' My answer is: Had we no sins, what would You do with Your forgiveness? So You must balance the deal by giving us life, and children, and food besides![29]

Another time, the rabbi interrupted the prayer for Rosh Hashanah, the New Year, at the words 'And Your throne will be established and You shall sit upon it in truth.'

> O Lord, if You want the throne of Your glory to be established so that You may sit in that glory which alone is fitting for the King of kings, then deal mercifully with Your children and issue decrees for their salvation and consolation. But if You deal with us harshly and issue harsh decrees, Heaven forbid, then Your throne will not be established and You will not sit upon it in truth. For the Tzaddikim of the generation will not permit You to sit upon Your throne. You may decree, but they will annul.[30]

Like Attar's holy men, Levi Yitzhak suspected God of not keeping his end of the bargain, of deceiving humans: 'Know that if Your reign does not bring grace and mercy, Your throne will not be a throne of truth!'[31]

One day Levi Yitzhak, like the fool in *The Book of Suffering* who demands that God behave properly if He also expects him to behave properly towards God, stood still at his pulpit from morning until evening with his lips closed. For he had warned God: 'If You refuse to answer our prayers, I will not go on saying them!'[32]

Like the old, impoverished merchant in *The Book of Suffering*, Levi Yitzhak also encouraged other believers to speak out against God. A simple tailor prays: 'You wish me to repent my sins, but I have committed only minor offences: I may have kept some leftover cloth, or I may have eaten in a gentile house without washing my hands. But You, O Lord, have committed grave sins: You have taken babies from their mothers and mothers from their babies. Let's strike a deal: You forgive me, and then I will forgive You.'

'Why did you let God off so lightly?' Levi Yitzhak asked the tailor when he told him of his prayer the following day. 'You should have forced Him to redeem the whole of Israel.'[33]

Levi Yitzhak was notorious among the Tzaddikim for railing at God, condemning Him, and making himself the ambassador of humanity before Him. He was not the only one; Rabbi Jacob Isaac of Lublin (d. 1815) and Rabbi Mendele of Kotzk (d. 1859) veritably wanted to drag God to court for two crimes: firstly, for creating the spirit of evil and unleashing it on the Jews and, secondly, for not fulfilling His duty to provide Jewish women and children with sufficient sustenance.[34] Rabbi Moshe Leib (d. 1807), whose gentleness is the subject of the most curious tales, swore that after death he would hold out in hell long enough to take all its inhabitants away with him[35] – like the pious man in *The Book of Suffering* who promises to sit at the edge of hell until he obtains a dagger of light to drive the sinners out. For the psalm verse 'Blessed is the man You discipline, O Lord' (Psalm 94:12), the rabbi preferred a different interpretation: 'Blessed is the man who dares to discipline God.' When several children in a family died young, the mother turned to the rabbi's wife: 'What kind of God is the God of Israel? He is cruel, not compassionate. He takes what He has given.'

The rabbi's wife told her she must not talk like that; the Lord moves in mysterious ways, and people must learn to accept their fate. At that moment, Rabbi Leib appeared in the doorway and called out to the grieving visitor: 'And I tell you, woman: one does not have to accept it! One does not have to submit. My advice to you is to shout, to scream, to protest, to demand justice, do you understand me, woman? One must not accept it!'[36]

With the fading of the Hasidic tradition, quarrels with God also initially came to an end; the motif was continued only in Yiddish folk songs and the works of individual Eastern European poets of the late nineteenth and early twentieth centuries such as Hayyim Nahman Bialik (d. 1934), so outside of theology. A folk song from late nineteenth-century Russia calls out:

> Shout, Jews, shout loud and clear;
> Shout to the heavens.
> You can wake up the old man
> Who pretends to be asleep.[37]

Reform Judaism in the nineteenth century consciously excluded from worship the *piyyutim*, the religious poems that had been a constant part of the liturgy: an 'enlightened' religion did not require darkness in its view of God. Today, these poems are hardly to be found in any Reform Jewish prayer-books. Traditional prayer-books still contain *piyyutim*, but these too for the most part exclude protest and reproach, and the prayers of protest are not even known among most scholars, as Laytner notes critically. Cut off from the legacy of accusation, without knowledge of the concept and vocabulary or prayer as protest, today's Jews have no way to express their darker feelings towards God – at least, not within standard services in synagogues.[38] Another author who examined the theme of quarrelling with God in Judaism also found out that Jewish orthodoxy had evidently largely tabooed the motif: Shmuel Boteach tells of the charges, extending to those of dangerous innovation and open heresy, that were hurled at him after a series of lectures in the USA and England in which he took up the Jewish tradition of quarrelling and questioned God's justice.[39] It seems that the ignorance of one's own intellectual history displayed by strictly religious groups when accusing others in their faith of unbelief is a phenomenon not restricted to contemporary Islam.

It is not through the presence of the Bible in the Orient alone, but only with reference to the literature and liturgical practices of Judaism in the rabbinical and Islamic periods that one can sense how the biblical tradition of protest combined with Islamic mysticism, and how *The Book of Suffering* is connected to the Book of Job. With Levi Yitzhak's words to God in one's ear, the accounts of the Islamic mystics sound strangely familiar. A Sufi handbook from the thirteenth century tells of an occasion when the Prophet Mohammed met a Bedouin at the Kaaba. The man's simple piety impressed him. In the midst of their conversation Gabriel came down to the Prophet with a revelation from God: 'Say to the Bedouin: Your trust in my grace and mercy will not help you, for tomorrow I will call you to account for great things and small, even unto the raffia rope and the string of the wineskin.'

'Shall my Lord indeed call me to account?' the Bedouin asked the Prophet.

'Indeed He will call you to account, if it is His will to do so.'

'By his might and majesty! If He calls me to account for my sin, I will call Him to account for His forgiveness. If He calls me to account for my greed, I will call Him to account for His generosity.'

Then the Prophet wept until his beard became wet. But Gabriel descended with a greeting from God: 'Weep not, Mohammed! The angels who carry my throne forgot for a moment their songs of praise out of pure joy. Say to your brother the Bedouin that if he does not call me to account, neither will I call him to account.'[40]

The biblical figures were not taken up into Islamic culture in their biblical manifestations alone, but also with their Jewish and Christian reception. The portrayal of Moses by Ahmad Ghazali, for example, has only very distant precedents in the Hebrew Bible and none at all in the Koran; it is also the Moses of the midrashim, whose interpretative tales accentuate the aspect of quarrelling with God. Ghazali recounts:

> When Moses was told (by God): 'You will not see me' (Surah 7:143), Moses said: 'This is how You behave! First You choose Adam, then you make his face black and banish him from Paradise. As for me, You call me to Sinai and then cause my enemies to gloat over me! This is how You treat Your friends. Just imagine how You behave towards Your enemies!'[41]

Even more than in the Bible, Moses is characterized in Jewish exegesis as a man of fiery temperament. Here he often appears as an advocate who wrestles with God for his people, but also in his own interest, bargains with Him, threatens Him and even attempts to move God to mercy through cunning, flattery and persuasion. It is a Moses who involves God in exegetical duels and presents so many arguments that the Creator is sometimes forced to surrender out of sheer exhaustion. One of the locations in the Near and Middle East of the character type of the quarrelling saint, the grumbler and the fool portrayed in such varying ways by Attar is here, in the midrashim. It is hardly a coincidence that Muhammad al-Ghazali sets the following story in ancient Israel: after granting no rain for seven years and ignoring seventy thousand prayers for rain, God finally says to Moses: 'How can I answer their prayers when their hearts are darkened by sin and their souls are dirty? And then they think all they have to do is pray in order to escape my cunning. Send for my servant Burch.'

Moses and his followers go in search of a man named Burch and find a black slave. They ask him to pray for rain. Burch begins his prayer by reprimanding God harshly: 'Is this Your work? Is this supposed to be Your mercy? What's wrong with You? Have Your eyes grown weak, have the winds stopped obeying Your orders, or are Your supplies running out? Or are You perhaps angered by our transgressions? But are You not the forgiver? Did You not create compassion long before You created sin? Have You already forgotten how You told us to practise goodness? Don't You see that You are depriving us of food? Or are You afraid of missing something, that You are in such a hurry to punish us?'

Moses is shocked by the insolence with which Burch speaks to God, but God reassures him: 'That's just how Burch is. He makes me laugh three times a day.'

And it rains in torrents until the people are knee-deep in water and Israel blossoms.[42]

As later on with Attar's fools and holy men, it is precisely the closeness to God, the intimacy of their relationship with God, that allows the Israelites to defend themselves against God. When God decides that Moses must die, Moses tries everything to escape his fate: he whimpers of his fear and, now that he cannot conclude the mission with which God Himself entrusted him, laments ever having been born. To make God reverse His decision, he draws a magic circle and hurls prayers towards heaven. God immediately orders for the gates of heaven to be shut, but Moses' prayers strike the walls so loudly that all the angels tremble. God remains firm. Moses reminds Him of all the hardships and ordeals he endured so that the people of Israel would believe in God and follow His commandments. And now that the promise is being fulfilled and his people are finally allowed to cross the Jordan, he, Moses, is being recalled and deprived of the reward. By doing this, he charges, God is going against his own Torah, in which He promised Moses a reward (Deuteronomy 28:1–13).

'Is this the reward for the forty years of drudgery I took upon myself so that Israel would become a holy and pious people?'

God replies with other quotations from the Torah, and thus there ensues an exchange of blows between exegetes. God promises Moses a reward in the next life, but Moses is not satisfied.

'Lord of all the world! If you do not bring me to the land of Israel, then at least let me stay in this world so that I might live, not die.'

God replies that Moses must die for the next world to begin. Releasing Moses from death would mean proving the Torah untrue and God a liar. But Moses does not give up: 'If you do not bring me to the land of Israel, then at least make me an animal in the fields that eats grass, drinks water and enjoys the world. Make my soul like theirs.'

'Will you finally stop!' shouts God.

'Lord of the world! Make me a bird.'

'You have said enough, no more.'

But Moses is still not satisfied. He begins writing a Torah scroll so that the angel of death will be afraid to approach him. When God commands the angel to approach Moses a second time, the prophet chases him away with his staff. Finally God agrees to discuss the matter and reassures Moses: He Himself, God, will be present at the funeral, not simply an angel or a human. With sweet words He begs Moses for his soul, and weeps as He gives Moses the kiss of death. Once Moses is finally dead, he is placed on the wings of the Shechina and the angels mourn him with the words: 'He carried out the Lord's righteous will, and His judgements concerning Israel' (Deuteronomy 33:21). And God Himself laments: 'Who will rise up for me against the wicked? Who will take a stand for me, against evildoers?' (Psalm 94:16).[43]

Even heaven complains about God. In a famous midrash whose dramaturgy anticipates the *hadith* on intercession as well as the Persian-Arab topos of the heavenly journey, the patriarchs, matriarchs and prophets, the angels and even the Holy Ghost protest against the destruction of Israel and use their *zechuyot*, their 'merits', to intercede. They openly accuse God of being unjust and unmerciful, of breaking the covenant with Israel one-sidedly and without reason. God defends Himself, refers to the supposed sins of Israel, and summons the Torah, and – when that fails – even every single letter of the alphabet to confirm His counter-accusation. But Abraham persuades the witnesses, in the style of an experienced lawyer, not to testify against Israel. The choir of accusation becomes louder and louder, until Rachel finally softens God's heart and brings out His leniency by comparing herself with Him: God cannot, she says, allow a simple woman to appear more good than He.[44]

Attar and the Jewish tradition

The comparison with other Muslim authors has shown how pointedly Attar presents his subject in intra-Islamic terms. Only with reference to the Hebrew Bible, however, and above all the Jewish tradition, does it become truly clear how far Attar actually takes the motif of quarrelling with God. While the rabbis, the religious poets and later the Hasidic masters accuse God, they almost always do so with the intention of gaining his favour. Leaving aside rare exceptions, the prayers and stories generally begin with the speaker assuming God's fundamental justice, then accusing Him of acting unjustly. At the end, the speaker calls upon God finally to act in accordance with His own image, so that the precondition of faith mentioned at the start of the prayer is ultimately affirmed. The legal speech also serves the purpose of persuading God to intervene, as in the following tale: a famine breaks out in Ukraine, and the poor cannot buy any bread. Ten rabbis gather in the house of an old man to form a rabbinical court.

'I wish to bring a charge against God', speaks the old man. 'According to rabbinical law, a master who buys a Jewish slave must sustain not only the slave for a certain time, but also his family. Now, the Lord bought us as His slaves in Egypt, for He says: "The sons of Israel are slaves to me" [Talmud, Baba Metzia, 59], and the prophet Ezekiel declared that Israel is God's slave even in exile. Therefore, O Lord, I call upon You to abide by Your law and provide for Your slaves, together with their families.'

The ten judges decide that the old man is in the right. A few days later a large shipment of grain arrives from Siberia, enabling the poor to buy bread once more.[45]

The quarrellers in the Jewish tradition, then, still have hope in God. Their aim is generally didactic: to confront the questions raised by innocent suffering and, by the end, to have done away with the doubts that were spread most of all by Gnosticism in the rabbinical period. The expectation that God will answer is what drives the rabbis, and later the Hasidics, to protest. And God answers, showing His mercy in the end; when He does not, the prayers and stories end in the belief, or at least the strong hope, that He will do so later. This stands in contrast to some psalms – as well as the Book of Job, where God demonstrates His power and superiority at the end, but not exactly His justice – and to *The Book of Suffering*: most of Attar's fools accuse God without any hope. They find peace, if at all, only in resignation or insanity. God only rarely intervenes; generally the complaints remain unheard, and, worse still: most accusations are uttered in the knowledge that no God in heaven will be moved by them when heaven itself is full of lamenting souls, as the frame story describing one heavenly figure after another demonstrates. God in His justice is not simply hidden; if He were, one could call upon Him to appear. No – God is not just at all. That fact, or at least the fear that it is true, is what unsettles Attar's figures. Because God is terror for them, many of the fools are even afraid of being heard by Him, assuming that He will only torment them even more cruelly. It is better for such a God to remain distant. What good would it do for Him to appear? The fools do not need an unjust God. And Attar himself, the poet, ends the book on a completely disconsolate note with his epilogue. This brings him closer to the dark psalms than is the Jewish tradition of accusing God itself.

We cannot say how much Attar knew about the Judaism of his time. Until the invasion by the Ghuzz in his childhood, Nishapur, with a population of around one hundred thousand, was one of the largest multi-religious, multilingual cities at the time, with Muslims, Zoroastrians, Christians, Jews, and probably also Buddhists, with Persians, Arabs and Turks, long-standing citizens as well as constant influxes of nomads, who came to settle there. As one of the most important stops on the

Silk Road, Attar's hometown was a trade centre not only for goods but equally for stories and ideas, religions and worldviews.[46] One can assume that Attar would at least have dealt with Jews and followers of other religions in his pharmacy. It is less likely, however, that he would have had a Persian or Arabic translation of the Bible at hand, as he never quotes directly from it or mentions translations. Among numerous other Muslim authors one repeatedly finds, alongside quotations from the Torah or the psalms passed on by word of mouth, references to Arabic translations such as that of Sa'adiya Gaon. It is even said of some traditionists that they read the Torah every week, and that God's mercy came down upon them at the end of every reading.[47] Aside from Christian or Jewish converts to Islam, however, only a few early Islamic authors, for example Ibn Qutayba (d. 889) and Ibn Hazm (d. 1064), actually seem to have used Arabic translations of the Hebrew Bible or the New Testament, as precise and extensive biblical quotations in Muslim texts became common only in the fifteenth century with such authors as al-Baqa'i, who criticized al-Ghazali's doctrine of the best of all worlds.[48]

Although Attar does not seem to have first-hand knowledge of it, the Hebrew Bible, along with various attitudes, images and notions of God from the Jewish tradition, is so present in his work – and not only in parts where the prophets of Israel are directly mentioned – that coincidental analogies or a purely Koranic transmission of Judaism are not adequate explanations. The question inevitably arises: how did Attar's reception of Jewish religious literature take place? The biblical figures were known to any educated Muslim not only through the Koran[49] but also through oral tradition, religious upbringing and the genre of *qiṣaṣ al-anbiyā'* ('tales of the prophets'). There were also the *isrā'īlīyāt*, collections made by Islamic historians of biblical accounts and Jewish literary traditions considered necessary for an understanding of the Koran. Hence the biblical tale of Job, which is mentioned only briefly in the Koran, was first told in its Islamic version by later authors such as Muhammad ibn Abdillah al-Kisa'i (dates of birth and death unknown) or Abu Ishaq Ahmad ath-Tha'labi (d. 1036). A number of converts from Judaism, for example Abdullah ibn Salam (d. 663) or Ka'b al-Ahbar (d. 652), and in particular Wahb ibn Munabbih, who came from a Jewish family but was probably born a Muslim, provided their new communities with a wealth of canonical and apocryphal traditions in their writings from the outset. The traditionist Abdullah ibn Amr ibn al-As (d. 683) learned Hebrew in Medina, also spoke Syrian, and was widely known for his knowledge of the Bible, which he studied together with Christians and Jews. It is said that, as a young man, he dreamed that he was holding honey in one hand and butter in the other, eating of both. The prophet to whom he recounted the dream supposedly said: 'You will read two books: the Torah and the Koran.'[50]

Far beyond its Koranic reception, the Bible formed a part of classical Islamic erudition and culture.[51] In addition, with the discipline of *milal wa-niḥal* ('religions and sects'), Islam founded its first form of comparative religion and practised it extensively. This background explains how Attar and other mystics could quite naturally recount biblical tales not mentioned in the Koran, and even assume a familiarity with them among their readers, without necessarily having first-hand knowledge of their Jewish and Christian sources. But the Bible is present in a very different way in Attar's work: as a way of perceiving God and the world and writing about it. Such a presence can no longer be explained purely by the Muslim accounts of the prophets of Israel, whose purpose is to affirm, and possibly to augment, the Koranic view of God and the world. In Attar, however, the Job motif returns without its Koranic filter. This does not mean he has to mention or even think of Job specifically; it is not so much through quotations as through poetic patterns, attitudes, ideas, images and anecdotal structures that the Bible manifests itself in Attar's work. The poet does not have recourse to a foreign tradition that remains identifiable as such, but rather has internalized it; he has turned it into something of his own. And I think one can learn something fundamental from this about the culture to which Attar belonged: as long as one defines it via Islam, elements from Christianity, Judaism and other religions – if they are even noticed – are explicable only as influences from neighbouring traditions. That different cultures lived alongside one another peacefully or not so peacefully, and naturally had exchanges, does not strike me as sufficient to explain the numerous layerings, intertwinings and not infrequent symbioses of Islamic, Jewish and Christian motifs and discourses in the Middle East. It would be more appropriate to speak of osmotic processes.

Islam as a civilization developed within a geographical area that already housed various religions and highly developed cultures. It did not look for a vacant space within that area, nor did it attempt simply to force out the existing civilizations and create a vacuum. Rather, Islamic civilization came about through the fact that Islam – which had anyway professed to be following on from earlier religions – overlaid the other religious traditions of the Orient as a religious worldview, a language and a system of norms and traditions, and gradually permeated them. Early Islamic asceticism in particular, which was of such fascination to Attar, could hardly ever have developed purely from the Koran; instead, it followed – often explicitly – the living example of Syrian monks, as

Tor Andrae has shown. Hence Andrae was little surprised to find a form of piety among Sufis 'closer to the spirit and essence of the Gospel than any other non-Christian form of religion we know of'.[52] Subsequently, Islam not only absorbed Jewish and Christian culture but also infused Eastern Christianity, and Judaism even more strongly – one could almost say it 'Islamized' them. This, not the dialogue between peace-seeking religious representatives at Andalusian courts, is what the great Israeli Middle Eastern scholar Shlomo D. Goitein means when, instead of influences or cultural dialogues, he speaks constantly of a 'complete Jewish-Arab symbiosis' in the medieval Orient.[53] This does not mean that religious identities and traditions were unified, or that Muslims, Jews and Christians always lived together in peace and equality – if only because such superimpositions always lead also to their opposite, namely efforts to set oneself apart and remain distinct. It does, however, mean that Jewish, Muslim and Christian identities in the Near and Middle East should be thought of in much more processual, fluid terms than appears to be the case in retrospect. The political developments in the twentieth century have drawn boundaries through the shared Arab-influenced cultural realm that are both mirrored and deepened in the Western academic division into Islamic studies, Jewish studies and the study of the Christian Orient.

This makes it less surprising than is often believed, and only partly attributable to religious dialogues between Jews, Christians and Muslims, that the quotations, literary genres and attitudes of the Bible found so numerously in Muslim literature and theology are not based on any known body of text, as eagerly as scholars have kept on the lookout for one.[54] A poet like Attar does not need to have read the Bible himself for his thoughts and writings to be biblical, as biblical thought and writing had become part of Islam anyway. The boundaries between Jewish and Muslim mysticism are permeable – at least, more permeable than the intra-Muslim or intra-Jewish line drawn between mysticism and philosophy. The two motivic chains of God's theologically unjustifiable violence and its subjective experience run – like the whole discussion about suffering and injustice – counter to the monotheistic religions: the philosophical traditions of Islam and Judaism leave no room for a theodicy, let alone accusations against God, while criticism and mockery of God are equally common in the mystical and literary tendencies of both religions. The terror of God is likewise present in individual mystical experience, but also with political intentions, as a criticism of worldly conditions and the exercise of worldly power. Generally speaking, a counter-theology of this kind, which thematicizes God's violence and the subjective human experience thereof without looking to theodicy as a way out, is located not so much in dogmatic-scholastic texts as in mystical and literary documents, including those outside of monotheism.

As far as the specific Jewish and Muslim accusations of God are concerned, their connections would appear to go beyond the universality of the motif, being attributable also to concrete historical or literary encounters. Large parts of Jewish and Islamic tradition developed in parallel and in a shared cultural realm. They refer partly (despite being passed on through different traditions) to the same religious sources, especially the figures and stories of the Hebrew Bible. Quarrelling with God was an aspect of Jewish piety when Islamic culture developed – whatever oral and textual phases of transmission actually led to the absorption of biblical lamentation in Islamic mysticism and Attar's work. The Indian examples of talking back to God may have had a stimulating influence; after all, Indian religious attitudes were present in the mysticism of Khorasan, and Attar often introduces followers of Indian religions. I have not found any more concrete indications of this. One can, however, say with certainty that, without the far more extensive history of the motif in Judaism, without the shared geographical, intellectual and lingual realm, and without the erratic nature of cultural processes, it would be incomprehensible how the tradition of quarrelling with God found a place in Islam even though the Koran had not featured it, and even ruled it out.

The interlocking of motivic chains is also strikingly evident in the way the chutzpah of the holy men and Attar's mournful sarcasm sometimes have a Jewish character. The connotations of the Yiddish word *meshugge*, derived from the Hebrew *meshugah*, describe the eccentricity found in many tales in *The Book of Suffering* more exactly than any other word. Attar does not need to mention Job, nor even to think of him, in order to tell of Job. But the motif may also have travelled in the opposite direction. Initially, the early Jewish mysticism of the Middle Ages only developed at all through the direct reception of Sufi texts and rituals that were translated into a Jewish form.[55] Why should the topos of the quarrelling saint found in Islamic mysticism not conversely have entered the literature of Arab Jews, and from there European Judaism? One can hardly prove this in detail, admittedly, as it is not based on dialogues between clearly delineated social and religious collectives.

In the formative phases of Judaism and Islam (and indeed Christianity), identities were scarcely as clear and distinct as they seem today.[56] Often enough, for example, the 'we' in Arab philosophy or poetry does not mean 'we Muslims', 'we Jews' or 'we Christians'; it means 'we philosophers', in opposition to the 'you' of mysticism or legal scholarship, whether Islamic or Jewish. In the non-Arab part of Europe, Averroës and Maimonides were later identified as a Muslim and a Jew respectively; in the Arab cultural realm, the two were regarded more as exponents of Andalusian philosophy. Just as Maimonides referred to the works of Muslim authors, he in turn had Muslim readers, including teachers, who explained his philosophy to Jewish audiences. Though it is seldom considered worth mentioning, a Muslim philosopher such as al-Farabi (d. c.950) acquired much of his education from the Nestorian teacher Ibn Yunus (d. 940), who had had Christian and Muslim teachers. This and numerous other cases of interaction were possible, even everyday phenomena, because Jewish, Christian and Muslim intellectuals in the Arab-influenced cultural realm examined the same basic questions, without necessarily giving the same answers or negating the social and legal differences between the groups. To this day, there are many religious-philosophical texts of which we cannot even be certain whether they were written by Jews or Muslims.[57]

The permeable nature of the Arab-influenced cultural realm at that time is perhaps not so different to that of today's Western-influenced literature, in which authors such as Sadeq Hedayat, Wole Soyinka or Haruki Murakami participate without denying their individual origins and national ties, and without having to describe themselves as Western or even merely Westernized. Studying Arabic, Hebrew or Persian texts from the Middle Ages from an exclusively Jewish or Islamic perspective is probably as unfaithful to the reality of the time as dividing up protagonists from modern, Western-influenced civilization purely according to confessional allegiance, cultural background or geographical origin. It leads to a restriction of interpretative possibilities and a disproportionate emphasis on religious-confessional literary aspects. Thus authors who had long ceased to refer directly to a specific religious or cultural identity, instead dealing with general theological, poetic or philosophical themes, are read after the fact with a view to their confession.

Rather than explaining the connections between Attar and Judaism in the sense of influences, it would perhaps be more fitting to use the image of a river, a common river fed by many subterranean springs, starting from the eastern Mediterranean, joining other currents and flowing through regions that may be as distant as Khorasan. Many plants will be found only in one region, while others appear all along the river, even if their blossoms are not the same everywhere. The beech tree stands next to the oak, but is related to the beeches on the other riverbank. How remote the intimate tone in which Levi Yitzhak of Berdichev speaks to God is from the abstractions of Maimonides; but how close it is to the fools and holy men to whom Attar gives a voice. How distant Attar is from the rationalist faith in existence of Islamic theologians (*mutakillimūn*) or the hair-splitting of jurists; but how related he seems to some modern European authors. From this perspective, the analogous patterns within Jewish and Muslim piety require less explanation than the question of why they are absent from Christian mysticism, which otherwise has so much in common with the other two mystical traditions, both indirectly, through a common source and similar structures of religious experience, and directly, through the reception of Islamic texts, as became important for Meister Eckhart's work. Certainly the figure of the quarrelling saint, accused of heresy for his inflammatory or critical words, is no rarity within Christian piety; but the protest is consistently directed at the Church or earthly representatives of God's power as a whole. Christian mystics do experience a dark God, but this experience remains a necessary phase in order to reach divine radiance. Thus God is even to be thanked for the suffering He inflicts upon the mystic. St Bernard of Clairvaux (d. 1153), who also preached in favour of the Second Crusade, says: 'the most sublime philosophy which I have in this world is to know Jesus and Jesus crucified.' He wishes to carry Jesus's suffering with him at all times as the bride carries her bundle of myrrh:

> [. . .] this bundle of myrrh made up of all my saviour's bitter sufferings, of the privations He endured in His infancy, the toils He underwent in His ministry, the weariness He suffered in His journeyings, His watchings in prayer, His fasting and temptation, His tears of compassion, the snares laid to catch Him in His words, His perils among false brethren, the insults, the blows, the mockeries, the nails, in short the sorrows of all kinds which He endured for the salvation of men. And, among so many branches of that fragrant myrrh, I think that cannot be passed over, of which He tasted when upon the Cross, nor that wherewith He was anointed at his burial. In the first of these He applied to Himself the bitterness of my sins, in the second He pronounced the future incorruption of my body. As long as I live I shall proclaim the memory of the abounding goodness contained in these events; throughout eternity I shall not forget these mercies, for in them I have found life.[58]

God leads the believer's mind into the night in order to grant him a new, true insight there. Individual crises form the stations on the journey through which the believer is taken up into the life of Christ; feeling with the pain of the crucified saviour, German mystics such as Mechthild of Magdeburg, Meister Eckhart or Johannes Tauler (d. 1361) have placed their own suffering in a line with that of Jesus Christ, consciously causing and celebrating it. In the passion of the loving soul, Mechthild of Magdeburg writes:

> She carries her cross on every path,
> When she truly surrenders herself to God in all sufferings.[59]

Passion mysticism developed in the transition of salvation knowledge from Latin to German, setting itself apart particularly from Augustine's interpretation of suffering as a pedagogical tool of God. The more intensely the Christian empathizes with the suffering of Jesus Christ – the model being the stigmata of St Francis of Assisi (d. 1226) – the more bearable his own suffering appears. In Christian mysticism, God as the addressee of accusations had disappeared by the fourteenth century at the latest, with the emergence of the theology of *compassio*. If God Himself is suffering, there is no reason to protest against Him. Humanity alone is to blame for evil.

In the Modern Age

Unlike in Judaism and Islam, protest against God in Christian Europe was articulated rather later, and above all outside of religion. One could perhaps find a point in Meister Eckhart's doctrine *de malo*, which lies beyond the existential joy that focused on God, namely when Eckhart acknowledges that even evil is a divine tool.[60] The function of Jesus as scapegoat in medieval passion plays may indicate the preservation of an element of emotion against God, albeit in a highly coded form.[61] Likewise, baroque theology occasionally personified the metaphysical forlornness of humans in the image of a grim, cruel God; human rebellion against a transcendental authority become a literary theme in the true sense, however, only in the Enlightenment – or, more precisely, in the wake of the disappointment and unease of reason upon realizing that it could not rationally prove the wisdom and goodness of God. Susan Neiman locates the beginning of this revolt in the reign of the Castilian King Alfonso X (d. 1284), who had close connections to the Islamic-Jewish culture of Andalusia. He too came into contact with philosophical, literary or scientific views that God's wisdom should no longer simply be accepted. In a statement that was incriminated for centuries, he said: 'If I had been of God's counsel at the Creation, many things would have been ordered better.'[62] The circumstance that this first Christian accuser of God would thus be located precisely at the intersection of Eastern and Western culture would show a logic that today remains almost entirely overlooked in Western histories of philosophy

– including that of Susan Neiman. In those accounts, this turn against the Creator seems to have appeared from nowhere in cultural-historical terms.

The myth that Western culture came, practically by virgin birth, from the spirit of antiquity originates in the Renaissance; it was essentially formed in the nineteenth century, which assigned the Orient a fixed role as the absolute cultural other. In the specific case of literary scholarship, the still dominant paradigm of an exclusively Western literary history can be attributed to two German studies of great brilliance and no less influence, both published at the end of the 1940s: Erich Auerbach's *Mimesis* of 1946 and Ernst Robert Curtius's *Europäische Literatur und lateinisches Mittelalter* of 1948. In Curtius's view of European literature, which came to be canonical, non-European elements hardly appear at all. Yet a work such as *The Decameron* is so deeply shaped in its narrative strategies and many of its motifs and stories that one can hardly speak any more of influences; it would be more appropriate to call Boccaccio an Oriental author, just as one could speak of Japanese or Middle Eastern authors today as part of modern world literature. Even in his long chapter on Dante, Curtius names no Arab precursors, contacts or sources, despite the fact that corresponding studies had long been available at the time. The effects of Arabic poetry as a whole are treated in a few pages under the heading 'Western-Eastern Aspects'. There he is concerned primarily with calligraphy and writing metaphors. Even Arab references in medieval philosophy, whose quantity, consistent presence and prominence seem impossible to miss, are virtually passed over. Curtius ignores the seven-hundred-year presence of Arabs in Spain by beginning his history of the country's literature in the sixteenth century.

This standard work by Curtius is an especially vivid and significant example of the mechanism of exclusion by which Europe constructs its own history. Europe not only shares its two main cultural sources with the Middle East, namely Ancient Greece and biblical Israel; it was only able to develop an intellectually and historically distinct identity at all by setting itself apart from an other: not only from Islam, but from the entire Arab cultural realm, which, in the twelfth century, established paradigms for intellectual and academic life not only in southern France and southern Italy, but even in London, Paris or Bologna. It was a cultural realm of which the Muslim traditions formed a part, but equally Judaism and Eastern Christianity. But the demarcation, which is most clearly and symbolically evident in the texts of Christian scholasticism, was at once an appropriation of things originally considered Arab: dialectical theology and humanism. Hence, in their European versions, too, these two central intellectual movements of the Middle Ages 'clearly bear the handwriting of Islam in their essential and constitutive aspects',[63] as George Makdisi has pointed out. Europe absorbed the intellectual movements of Islam and Arab Judaism, made them its own, and subsequently transformed them. This dual process of demarcation and appropriation contributed decisively to the development of a secular modernity that did not abolish Christianity, but certainly abolished the dominant theological bent of the Middle Ages.

Since the German-language scholarship of Judaism, there has been no shortage of suggestions to view the Arab-influenced cultures of the Middle Ages, in particular that of Andalusia, not simply as passing on Greek sources, but as a genuine part of European intellectual history. The rejection of even the clearest philological or historical evidence (for example the etymology of the word 'troubadour'), however, is reminiscent – even in current debates on the future of Europe – of the reactions to Darwin's discoveries, as María Rosa Menocal observed: namely that humans cannot possibly be descended from apes.[64] Even a basic knowledge of Middle Eastern literature, philosophy and mysticism is sufficient to realize that this is 'one of the source regions of our Enlightenment', as Ernst Bloch wrote in his treatise on Avicenna.[65] Criticism of the Creator in particular had a long history in the Jewish and Islamic intellectual history of the Orient, as should by now be clear. It would therefore be symbolically significant, and by no means coincidental, that it was precisely the Castilian Alfonso X, the 'first Enlightenment hero', as Susan Neiman calls him,[66] who happened upon the inadequacy of the creation – and as an immediate reaction to studies in the Arab sciences, especially astronomy, for which he had summoned Jewish scholars especially from Toledo.

The rebellion of humans against God in Europe is thus very closely connected to the history of secularization – 'a testimony to its risks', as Karl S. Guthke remarks.[67] Further early witnesses are Shakespeare and Gryphius, whom we have already encountered. Leibniz's famous apologia for the Creator, hardly taken seriously today, was a response to the lesser-known but all the more current doubts about the purpose of the creation voiced by Pierre Bayle in his *Dictionnaire historique et critique*. Like Attar – if we recall tales such as those of Sultan Mahmoud, who sent out his soldiers and tax-collectors so that his palace would fill up with supplicants – Bayle compares God to a monarch who allows outrage and disorder to grow throughout his kingdom simply to be recognized in His power. Bayle is also reminded of a father 'who had his children's legs broken so that he could demonstrate to the whole town his skill in healing broken legs'.[68] Related images can be found in David Hume's *Dialogues Concerning Natural Religion*: God as an ostrich, an amateur ship-builder or a vain fool. Unlike in *The Book of Suffering*, such comparisons by Hume and Bayle do not lead to open accusation, but rather serve initially to dispense entirely with positive characterizations of God. Nonetheless, their scepticism did lasting damage to the notion of a good God.

The stream of criticism of God that runs through the Bible and, less directly, branches out through the Jewish tradition of the entire Middle East, before flowing into Islamic culture, also travelled straight through Christian Europe in the wake of the Enlightenment. And even if Büchner and Schopenhauer, Bayle and Hume do not follow on directly from the Hebrew Bible when they question God or condemn fate, others who reject theodicy explicitly refer to the same tradition that previously informed Attar's work. Its line in the West extends from Voltaire through Kant to Kierkegaard. What they share is a foregrounding of Job's doubting and agnostic aspects. Working against the theology of submission, they discover this and other biblical tales in their full provocation and significance for world literature, a document of humanity's self-assertion, as the Christian Kierkegaard writes in opposition to Christian reception history:

> I need you, a man who knows how to complain loudly, so that it echoes in heaven, where God consults with Satan concerning His plans for a person. The Lord has no fear of complaints. He can defend Himself. But how can He defend Himself when no one dares to complain as seems fitting to Him? Speak, lift up your voice, speak loudly, God can always speak more loudly – after all, He has thunder. This is also an answer, an explanation, dependable, faithful, original, an answer from God Himself, which, even if it crushed a person, is more glorious than gossip and rumours concerning the justice of providence, invented by human wisdom, spread by hags and half-men.[69]

Using the example of Prometheus, Hans Blumenberg has shown how the revolt against God developed in the eighteenth and nineteenth centuries and led into the emancipation of mankind.[70] A decisive stanza in Goethe's poem reads as follows:

> I honour thee! And why?
> Hast thou e'er lighten'd the sorrows
> Of the heavy laden?
> Hast thou e'er dried up the tears
> Of the anguish-stricken?
> Was I not fashion'd to be a man
> By omnipotent Time,

And by eternal Fate,
Masters of me and thee?[71]

The Marquis de Sade takes this challenge to the extreme, but also theologically defuses it through his proclamation of cynicism. It is not entirely clear which is the masquerade: his atheism or the despair at a creator who is responsible for evil. At any rate, de Sade displayed a passion, unparalleled before or after him, for demonstrating the power of evil and proving the futility of virtue, just as Job experienced it. His malevolent heroes who conduct their cruel experiment with the virtuous Justine share traits with the God who places the righteous Job in Satan's hands in the prologue to the biblical book. While Justine is tortured time and again without receiving any answer when she asks what the reason is, her depraved sister Juliette is richly rewarded with pleasures. Telling their stories means fighting against any belief in the positive purpose of divine providence. In de Sade's novel *Juliette*, the minister Saint-Fond expressly urges all to abandon the premise of a good God: 'there exists a God; some hand or other has necessarily created all that I see, but has not created it save for evil; evil is his essence.'[72]

I must confess that I did not take upon myself the torture of reading de Sade's writings in their entirety, but refer here also to Susan Neiman's expositions. The novels *Justine* and *Juliette* are interesting as thought experiments, but as literature – at least for me – they are too dry to follow every unbelievable form of torture and rape for, in the unabridged editions, well over a thousand pages. They lose their connection to reality, probably because they exclusively describe evil. Not even the shabbiest devil would identify himself so obviously – let alone an almighty God. For modern literature it is Fyodor Dostoyevsky, with his creation Ivan Karamazov, who captured the incomparably more far-reaching type of rebel against God, the one who opposes Christian attempts to forgive boundless injustice: 'I do not want harmony, out of a love for mankind I do not want it', the outraged Ivan says upon witnessing a mother forgive the general for having her son torn to pieces by his dogs. The highest harmony 'is not worth one single small tear of even one tortured little child that beat its breast with its little fist and prayed in its foul-smelling dog-hole with its unredeemed tears addressed to "dear Father God"!' Ivan Karamazov certainly does not deny God, but he rejects any truth that is responsible for these children's tears: 'It isn't God I don't accept, Alyosha, it's just his ticket that I most respectfully return to him.'[73]

Similarly, after witnessing the death throes of a child together with Father Paneloux in Albert Camus's novel *The Plague*, Dr Rieux refuses 'to love a scheme of things in which children are put to torture'.[74] The fact that Rieux, like Büchner's Danton before him, takes the next step and exits religion altogether – 'since the world is shaped by death, mightn't it be better for God if we refuse to believe in Him and struggle with all our might against death, without raising our eyes towards the heaven where he sits in silence?'[75] – does not change his religious disposition: without it, the question would not arise. It is precisely in the plague that Dr Rieux experiences the unconditionality of moral good will, which cannot be explained in inner-worldly terms. Such atheism takes the world as the object of a higher power. Camus therefore calls it a 'metaphysical rebellion'[76] that requires the personal God of the Hebrew Bible in so far as He 'sets the energy of rebellion in motion'.[77] It is precisely because Rieux envisages a just God that he begins to doubt Him. 'The thing that gives meaning to human protest is the idea of a personal god who has created, and is therefore responsible for, everything.'[78] Strictly speaking, no longer believing in God does not mean disputing God's existence, but rather His dominion – not negating Him, but turning one's back on Him. An unjust God is irrelevant, whether He exists or not. 'And so the history of metaphysical rebellion cannot be confused with that of atheism', Camus writes. 'The rebel defies more than he denies.'[79]

In the literature of the twentieth century, protest against God grew into a massive choir; at the end of André Gide's first novel *The Counterfeiters*, the grandfather of the young suicide Boris calls out: 'He plays with us like a cat, tormenting a mouse. And then afterwards he wants us to be grateful as well. [. . .] Cruelty! That's the principal attribute of God.'[80] Such voices are too numerous to continue listing them. If I restrict myself only to those works that make explicit reference to Job (and hence exclude Kafka, Beckett and their effects, even though they naturally form part of a broader counter-theology within modern literature), the following come to mind: George Bernard Shaw's short story 'The Black Girl in Search of God', Bertolt Brecht's *The Blind Man*, H. G. Wells's novel *The Undying Fire*, Joseph Roth's famous adaptation of Job, the drama *J. B.* by Archibald MacLeish, or *Mars*, Fritz Zorn's account of dying, which made waves in 1977.

Almost all of these, however, are atheistic, or at least not strictly religious interpretations of the biblical story. A special position is held by Christine Lavant, whose poetic treatment of a personal God is the exception in modern German literature that proves the rule. 'Why, if there are angels, does none of them have the task of preventing things on earth that should only occur in the outermost reaches of hell?' she asks in *Aufzeichnungen aus einem Irrenhaus* [Notes from an Asylum]:

'Here I am, writing this with ordinary words, writing them like something or other, when I should really be breaking stone after stone off the walls and throwing every one of them at heaven, to make it realize that it still has a duty to us below.'[81] Literature was a substantial factor in the return of the Job motif in Christian theology: in Dorothee Sölle and Fridolin Stier, as well as Karl Rahner or Johann Baptist Metz. Thus Karl-Josef Kuschel speaks of a 'theological-historical tragedy that these traditions of protest against God had to be intensified in an atheistic context before those within the Church paid attention to them.'[82]

The eternal 'why?'

Among all modern readings of Job, what moves me most is the way Heinrich Heine wove biblical elements into his long dying process. And it is with him that German literature took up most directly the tradition of lament that had spread from Judaism to Islamic mysticism, while the Christian reception of the Bible had largely excluded it. As I approach the end of my book, I would therefore like to return to Heine in order to understand the continued presence of Job's question and the timelessness of Attar's poetry. 'Scepticism's Song of Songs', he called the Book of Job from his Parisian mattress grave: 'In it, the ghastly snakes hiss and whistle their eternal "Why?"' He often asked himself, he writes, 'why the temple archive commission took that book up into the Holy Scriptures'.

> I have the feeling that those God-enlightened men did so not out of ignorance, but because they knew in their great wisdom that doubt has deep roots in human nature and is justified, and that one should therefore not crudely suppress it, but only cure it. The method of their cure was entirely homeopathic, using like against like, but they did not administer a homeopathic small dose; instead, they made it monstrously great, and this overpowering dose of doubt is what the Book of Job is. This poison could not be omitted from the Bible, from the great medicine chest of humanity. Yes, just as a man must pour out his tears when he suffers, so too must he pour out his doubt when he feels cruelly hurt in his expectations of a happy life; and, as with the most intense weeping, the highest degree of doubt, which Germans so aptly call despair,[83] brings about the crisis of moral healing.[84]

Heine's late turn towards God, to which my attention was drawn by two poignant books by the Catholic theologian Karl-Josef Kuschel and the atheist writer Istvan Eörsis, is a turn to the God of the Hebrew Bible, a God who can be the subject of wrath and an object of outrage: 'The heathen Gods would not have inflicted on a poet what I must endure; only our old Jehovah does something like that!'[85] In his first public statement concerning his illness, in April 1849, the poet, still half-ironically, already wrote of a 'great transformation':

> I am no longer a life-loving, somewhat portly Greek, smiling condescendingly at gloomy Nazarenes – I am now a mortally sick Jew, an emaciated image of misery, an unhappy human being![86]

In subsequent years, Heine occupied himself with the biblical genre of lament and accusation, referring to it in statements and poems. He named cycles of poems *Lamentations* or *Hebrew Melodies*. It is thus almost natural that he shared motifs, ways of thinking and even particular expressions not only with the Jewish tradition but also with a Muslim poet, presumably unknown to him, like Attar. Heine, Levi Yitzhak of Berditchev and Attar belong to different cultures and times, but they visit the same archive; it is inevitable that they occasionally meet there. 'Only you, O God! are the true author of my demise', Heine notes from his 'mattress grave'.[87] Like the accusers in the Bible or the mystic al-Fodayl ibn Iyad (d. 803) in *The Book of Suffering*, who envies neither the angels nor the prophets but only those 'who are never born into this world' (E11, p. 373), Heine likewise curses existence:

> I envy not the sons of fortune
> For their lives, only do I
> Envy them their deaths,
> How fast and painlessly they die.[88]

Like Job and Jeremiah, the preacher Solomon and the fool in Attar's story, who wants nothing but for God to take back his life, Heine too knows of something better than death:

> O grave, you are true bliss
> For the snobbish, delicate soul –
> Death is good, but better 'tis
> Never to be born at all.[89]

Like the others, Heine is not driven by his despair to deny God, but rather to accuse him:

> Forget your holy parables,
> Forget your pious hypotheses –

Try to answer those damnèd questions
Without delay, if you please.

Why does the righteous drag his flesh,
Bloody and wretched beneath the cross
While the evil on high horses trot
In triumph and rejoice?

What is to blame? Could it be
That our Lord is not all-powerful?
Or is this nonsense His own work?
Such baseness would make me sorrowful.

So let us question constantly,
Until at last they stop our mouths
With a handful of earth – but still I ask:
Is that, in truth, an answer?[90]

With death before his mind's eye, in his final years Heine often conducts 'very grave conversations with Yahwe at night.'[91] He still has all his mocking wit, but his humour, now that it is God to whom the dying man is showing his teeth, almost takes on a hint of folly, confirming Nietzsche's explanation 'why man alone laughs: he alone suffers so deeply that he had to invent laughter. The unhappiest and most melancholy animal is, as is fitting, the most cheerful.'[92] The tormented Heine no longer makes anyone laugh; he laughs himself: 'How amusing God is!'[93] As in Attar's tales, where the fools keep believers away from the mosque with mooing, throw a turban at the heavens or ride out against God on a wooden horse, the grotesque quality comes about not simply because we see the most miserable and helpless of people threatening the almighty; it is because these people are fully aware of their powerlessness, and hence the absurdity of their threats. What distinguishes the fool from other people is not that he is ridiculous, but that he is aware of it. He knows that his jokes are the last before his demise, but in this humour, this self-irony, he preserves a final hint of resistance, even superiority: as long as he laughs at his destroyer, he foils His work, and is not yet destroyed. The line between affirmation of God and accusation, pathos and irony, and despair and humour becomes blurred:

Indeed, I have been experiencing a religious reaction for some time. God only knows if it is the morphine, or the poultices. That is how it is. I believe in a personal God once more! That is what one comes to when one is ill, mortally ill and broken! Do not make a crime of it! If the German people accept the King of Prussia in their need, why should I not accept the personal God?[94]

Long doomed, Heine jests:

> O Lord! I think 'twould be for the best
> If you left me upon this earth.
> Only cure my ailments first
> And grant me a little wealth.[95]

This humour is not meant to console; it is the final means of self-assertion to which his resistance has been reduced. 'Yes, the brine of mockery the master pours over me is ghastly, and his amusement is horribly cruel', Heine notes in his *Confessions* of 1854, after conceding a sentence earlier that he is pitifully inferior to God 'in humour, in colossal foolery'. But even a line later, his humility transpires as the most cunning pose, or at least the last remaining one, to mock the greatest of all mockers:

> But even if I lack that highest creative force, my spirit flashes with eternal reason, and I can even drag God's jests before its forum and subject them to reverent critique. And there I shall now venture to express the most humble intimation: it seems to me that the cruel prank the master is playing on his pupil is dragging on a little; it has already lasted more than six years, and is beginning to grow tedious.[96]

This helps us to understand why the posthumous poems from his *Lamentations* contain the following lines:

> When I die, they will cut my tongue
> Clean out of my head;
> For they fear I might return to speak
> From the realm of the dead.[97]

Heine's sarcasm – weary, fading, but unmistakeable – reared its dying head at least as late as 3 February 1856, exactly two weeks before his death, in his last surviving note to God:

> I am very wretched. Coughed terribly for 24 hours; hence headache today, probably tomorrow too . . . What an unpleasant state of affairs! I am near out of my mind with anger, pain and impatience. I will see to it that God is sued by the animal rights society.[98]

The Holocaust

In the feeling of being personally tortured by God, Heine's prayers and statements adopt the same presumptuous tone of intimacy in which anything can be said to God: words of accusation, blasphemy, jokes, mockery, bargaining, threats and curses. It is the tone of one who wants to smash the chandeliers in His mosque to pieces, like the hermit in *The Book of Suffering* to whom God sends guests, but no food. It is the tone that begins with Job and Jeremiah, the same tone in which Attar's Sufis and fools or the rabbis and Tzaddikim speak of God while experiencing disaster. It is a tone that grew loudest in the history of Judaism and Islam in times of oppression, persecution and massacre, a way of speaking of and with God that would return in the twentieth century. In Angel Wagenstein's autobiographical novel *Pentateuch, or, The Five Books of Isaac*, which describes a Jewish life in two world wars, three concentration camps and five countries as a rogue's tale, Rabbi Shmuel says in a sermon:

> So I ask you, doesn't Jehovah see all this? Is He dozing away and picking His nose? Or has Jehovah, blessed be His name for all eternity, turned into a goofy uncle who finds it flattering that people are dying in His name? I don't know, brothers, I can't give you an answer. But I think to myself: if God had windows, people would have smashed them long ago![99]

It is important to remember: during the Second World War, as at all other times, rebellion against God was the reaction of certain individuals. Though it cannot be measured proportionally, the memories and literary documents seem to suggest that far more practising Jews in the death camps, even on their way to the gas chambers or before the rifles of the firing squads, entrusted themselves to divine providence, lamenting to God rather than accusing Him. Evidently this is particularly true of the Hasidic Jews, of whom only a few rose up against the God who allowed all this to happen.[100] Not even the Nazis could tear three and a half thousand years of religious conviction and liturgical practice, which taught that one must endure suffering and persecution, from the hearts and mouths of their victims. To avoid losing sight of the special status of quarrelling with God, I would like to quote two accounts that are probably more characteristic of most practising Jews' reactions to Nazi persecution than protest against God. At the Nuremberg Trials, Fritz Gräbe, an Oscar Schindler-like figure who has remained practically unknown in Germany, bore witness to what he had seen in the Ukrainian town of Dolmo:

> The people who had got off the trucks – men, women and children of all ages – had to undress on the order of an SS man, holding a riding whip or dog whip, sort their clothes into shoes, outer clothing and underwear, and put them down in particular places. I saw a pile of shoes, about eight hundred to a thousand pairs of shoes, and large piles of underwear and

> clothes. Without screaming or crying, these people took off their clothes, stood together in family groups, kissed one another and said farewell, then waited for the gesture of another SS man who stood by the ditch and was also holding a whip. In the quarter of an hour I spent next to the ditches, I didn't hear a single complaint or plea for mercy. I watched a family of about eight people, a man and a woman, both around fifty years old, with their children, around one, eight and ten years old, as well as two adult daughters between twenty and twenty-four years old. An old woman with snow-white hair was holding the one-year-old child in her arms, singing to it and tickling it. The child gurgled with delight. The couple watched with tears in their eyes. The father was holding the hand of a boy of around ten, speaking to him quietly. The boy was struggling to hold back his tears. The father pointed to the sky, stroked the boy's head and seemed to be explaining something to him. Then the SS man at the ditch shouted something to his comrade, who then counted off about twenty people and told them to go behind the mound of earth. The family I've described was among them.[101]

Decades later, Gräbe returned to that family in an interview:

> There was one thing that struck me about this Action. As I looked back it was true of every Action. Not one of the victims protested, not one really resisted. Four guards, six militia, but no resistance. Why? Why? Why? Then I realized what had happened. It had nothing to do with the numbers or weapons. At that moment I realized what the father had said to his son as he pointed to heaven.[102]

Submitting to God's will in Auschwitz is the opposite of that piety found in the barracks courtyard, which Judaism too has produced. Clinging to faith, even blindly, could be an act of resistance that gave countless people the strength to stand tall under the worst possible blows of fate, even in their final seconds. Elie Wiesel describes this, writing about the type of believer which I meant at the start of this book and Attar also means. He speaks of what he saw in the Nazi death camps. I cannot relate to that; the experience lies outside of the world I know. But if I imagine who, among all the people I have known, would probably keep their composure in the same way Wiesel describes among priests from the resistance and rabbis, it would be my Aunt Lobat, Mr Engineer Kermani and the former prime minister Mehdi Bazargan. It would be the saints I have met, whom anyone can meet, because they exist in the lives of all people. If any of the people in my world would have proved themselves in that catastrophe, it is those ones. Nothing is comparable to Auschwitz, yet I feel that Elie Wiesel's account says something universal about the attribute of humanity in its absolute priority.

> If you knew how many there were, and who, that almost stumbled and fell: it was not rare for fathers and sons to become bitter enemies over a piece of bread, friends and brothers came to blows over a spoonful of soup, a moment's reprieve, or a thicker coat. If you knew the number of free-spirited intellectuals and the number of sadists among the intellectuals! Yes, the number of people who chose evil was very great. They abandoned all the principles they were brought up with, they didn't pass the test they were confronted with. But the people of religious conviction, the priests from the resistance, kept their composure. None of them were prepared to collaborate so as to save their own skin. And that's also true, even more so, of the rabbis. None, I repeat, not one of them was prepared to seize the small possibility he was offered to live, or to live longer or better, at the expense of his comrades and companions. On the contrary: they showed a self-denial that embarrassed the murderers and, in a sense, distressed them. As far as the Hasidim are concerned, and I am thinking of two in particular, they rose above this as high as the heavens through the power of their faith and their community spirit. They prayed at New Year, they resolved with joy – yes, that's no mistake, with joy – to celebrate the Feast of the Torah. And all this happened under conditions that were meant to dehumanize the victims, while it was the murderers who divested themselves of all humanity.[103]

Belief in God, faith in the truth of one's own community, seems to have given many prisoners in Auschwitz and other death camps superhuman powers. For Jewish thought in the wake of the Holocaust, however, the question of how God could allow this was inescapable for Elie Wiesel too: 'Don't tell me that God has nothing to do with it. That goes against everything Judaism symbolizes. [. . .] Auschwitz can be understood neither with God nor without God.'[104] Most Jewish thinkers and theologians sought to justify God following the Old Testament doctrine that God, in his justice, also creates evil; some did so because they interpreted Auschwitz as a punishment, above all for the assimilation of European Jews (as stated by the long-standing spiritual leader of the Shas Party, Ovadia Yosef, and many other rabbis).[105] From a Zionist perspective, the suffering of European Jews could also be understood as a precondition for the founding of the state of Israel, and hence the end of exile: Jewish survival, according to Eliezer Berkovits, bears witness to the God of history.[106] Ignaz Maybaum disputed the uniqueness of the Holocaust, instead placing the persecution by the Nazis in the line of historical persecutions through which God has distinguished the Jews from other peoples and – this is what he seems to be saying – ennobled them; in this sense, even Hitler was a servant of God.[107] Other thinkers (most famously Hans Jonas) took God out of the equation; they pointed to human free will and declared the Creator a fellow sufferer. [108] For some Jews, God's actions had become fundamentally incomprehensible: because Auschwitz was the pinnacle of senselessness, any attempt to attribute religious sense was blasphemy. Hence one could respond to Auschwitz only politically, not theologically. The survivors were obliged not to let Hitler have the last laugh by despairing at God and letting Judaism die out. In this interpretation, the founding of the state of Israel, which followed National Socialism, can be elevated to a messianic event: God revealed Himself even through the Holocaust – Emil L. Fackenheim in particular has argued this.[109] Naturally the Holocaust made atheists of many Jews, or, like Richard L. Rubinstein, followers of a negative theology that declared God dead without discarding the cultural legacy of the Jewish tradition.[110] And then there were those who, like Job and Levi Yitzhak of Berditchev, despaired at God without doubting Him, His presence and His power. Paul Celan lent these people a voice:

> There was earth inside them, and
> they dug.
>
> They dug and dug, and so
> the day went past, their night. And they did not praise God,
> who, so they heard, wanted all this,
> who, so they heard, witnessed all this.
>
> They dug, and heard nothing more;
> they did not grow wise, invented no song,
> devised for themselves no sort of language.
> They dug.
>
> There came a stillness then, came also storm,
> all of the oceans came.
> I dig, you dig, and it digs too, the worm,
> and the singing there says: They dig.
>
> O one, o none, o no one, o you:
> Where did it go then, making for nowhere?
> O you dig and I dig, and I dig through to you,
> and the ring on our finger awakens.[111]

With the diggers who do not praise God, Celan is alluding to Psalm 115:17: 'It is not the dead who praise the Lord, those who go down to silence.' Just as the Jews in the camps and ghettos took up the biblical tradition of lament and legal speech in their Yiddish songs, the survivors also searched their collective memory to write about the world in which Auschwitz was possible. The very first author to interpret the Holocaust religiously already spoke of Job: his life mirrors the fate of the Jewish people, wrote Margarete Susman in 1946 in a book whose clarity, provocativeness and emphatic sadness was unparalleled in the mostly American Holocaust theology of the 1960s and 1970s. Israel suffered innocently, was cast out innocently, yet experiences through God that 'its guilt is utterly hopeless, that it cannot be atoned for and thus cannot be forgiven'. The web of guilt and fate is therefore 'Satanically entangled'. Like Job, God punished the people of Israel as His closest, His own people. Like Job, Israel would much rather 'know itself guilty than despair at God's justice'.[112]

Most Jewish philosophers and poets looked for biblical verses or figures of Jewish exegesis, images from the Kabbalah or the tales of the Hasidim, forms of behaviour, recurring patterns, familiar or almost forgotten motifs from Jewish tradition, to find echoes of their recent history. Because some of the shelves of this archive also contain Islamic culture, especially Sufism, connections and affinities emerge, as distant and distinct as the historical contexts may be. This also includes the motif of quarrelling with God, which in Judaism often takes on the form of legal speech.

> In one of the huts in Auschwitz, the remaining members of a rabbinical court, as witnesses of the terror being experienced there by Jews, decided to try God Himself for it. The verdict was declared at dawn: because of the monstrous negligence He has shown towards His children, the Holy Lord, praised be His name, is to be immediately cast out of the community! – It was as if the cosmos held its breath. 'Come', one of the rabbis finally sighed, 'let us go and pray now.'[113]

God is praised and condemned in the same breath. The rabbi banishes God, then says: 'let us go and pray now.' This is the essence of what Attar, the lamenting prophets and psalmists, Rabbi David and the dying Heinrich Heine mean. 'The tears of the insulted cry to God!' wrote Heine three months before his death, declaring in the next sentence that he will bear his misery 'with devoted faith in the unfathomable will of God'.[114] Heine condemns his destroyer and, without putting down his quill, honours his creator: 'O God! You wanted me to perish, and I perished. Praise the Lord!'[115] The same Jeremiah who argues with God about His justice also speaks of Him as the righteous judge (Jeremiah 11:20). Even the most desolate psalms address God as the beloved father. Levi Yitzhak interrupts his service on Yom Kippur to protest that God is not sufficiently protecting his people of Israel, while any king of flesh and blood looks after his people – and subsequently speaks the prayer of Kaddish, which begins with the words: 'May His great name be exalted and sanctified in the world'.[116] On another occasion he prays:

> Lord of all the world! I do not ask that You reveal the secrets of Your ways to me – I would not understand them. I do not want to know why I am suffering; only that I am suffering for You.[117]

In the twentieth century this is no longer enough. Hannah Arendt's mentor Rabbi Judah L. Magnes (d. 1948) varied Levi Yitzhak's prayer – 'I do not want to know why I am suffering' – instead saying: 'I only want You to know that I am suffering.'[118] Because of his insane love for Leyla, Majnun has fallen into misery and become an object of contempt. One day his father says to him: 'You fool! You have made yourself despicable. Now no one would so much as sell you a loaf of bread.'

'I am only enduring this torment because of my beloved. Does she know that I am suffering for her sake?'

'She knows.'

'That is enough for me to breathe until the end of days' (5/8, p. 101).

In the twentieth century, this is still what defines the motif of quarrelling with God, the Job motif, which runs – usually in the margins, often suppressed or even invisible for centuries – through all three Abrahamic religions: that it incorporates its apparent opposite. 'Though He slay me, yet I will hope in Him', says Job (13:15). At the end of Zvi Kolitz's oppressively beautiful tale about the fate of a Jewish father in occupied Warsaw, the first-person narrator speaks the prayer of a Sephardic Jew. It seems to be a variation on Shibli's exclamation – 'My God! If you made the whole of heaven a yoke and the earth a shackle, and if you made the whole world thirst for my blood, I would still not abandon you'[119] – and may even have come from there through a historically winding but not overly long journey, if one recalls the influence of Sufi literature on Jewish mysticism:

> God of Israel, I have fled here in order that I might serve You undisturbed, to follow Your commandments and sanctify Your name. You, however, do everything to make me stop believing in You. Now, lest it occur to You that by imposing these tribulations You will succeed in driving me from the right path, I notify You, my God and the God of my father, that it will not avail You in the least. You may insult me, You may strike me, You may take away all that I cherish and hold dear in the world, You may torture me to death – I will always love You! Yea, even in spite of You!
>
> And these are my last words to You, my wrathful God: Nothing will avail You in the least! You have done everything to make me renounce You, to make me lose faith in You, but I die exactly as I have lived, as an unshakable believer![120]

Satan's lament

Is it so different in our earthly loves? Those whom we love most worry us most deeply. No book could honour God more verbosely than *The Book of Suffering*, yet no other Islamic book curses Him as much. And no one in that book feels more anger and love towards God, remarkably enough, than Satan. The great Muslim religious historian Muhammad ibn Abdilkarim ash-Sharastani (d. c.1153) portrayed Satan as the first free spirit in creation history, as a tragically rebellious force comparable with his stylized form in European Romanticism, though in the latter case he is a purely literary figure intended to discredit Christianity.[121] In Islamic theology, Satan's apostasy is tied directly to the problem of theodicy. At times, Satan's position is taken so seriously that – as later in Lord Byron's poetic drama *Cain: A Mystery* – it even results in an inversion of good and evil, with the consesquence that Satan accuses God of injustice. Ash-Sharastani lists seven questions put to God by Satan, all of them revolving around the matter of why God deliberately made the world in such a way that evil exists: 'If God knew what would happen to me, then why did He create me?'[122]

The Sufi interpretation states that, when God commanded the angels to kneel before man, his newest creation, Satan, was forced to refuse, as his absolute love for God forbade him from devoting himself to any other being. So, against God's explicit command, he insisted on honouring God alone. That makes him, as Sufis often say, more monotheistic than God Himself. 'Whoever does not learn monotheism from Satan is a heretic (*zindīq*)', writes Ahmad Ghazali.[123] The millions of years of selfless devotion to God, which set Satan apart from all other angels, were no use to him. God cast away His most faithful servant. Since then, Satan has wandered through the cosmos, despised by all, the one who yearns most for God – an exile.[124] As in a classical drama, God placed the innocent Satan in an irresolvable conflict between two absolute necessities that inevitably led to the hero's downfall. This image of Satan is familiar in Europe only from modern literature, for example Baudelaire's 'Litany of Satan', and before him from Victor Hugo (d. 1885), who made Satan call out:

> A hundred hundred times I repeat my vow,
> I love! God tortures me, yet my only blasphemy,
> My only frenzy, my only cry, is that I love!
> I love enough to make the sky tremble! But in vain![125]

It would be a mistake to think that Hugo or Baudelaire are glorifying evil. In their reading Satan is not a perpetrator, but himself a victim.

This inversion, as provocative as it was for Christianity and as originary for French literature, was culturally prefigured in Sufism. For many Muslim mystics, Satan is a model and an omen as a martyr of love and a symbol of mankind's need. A famous metaphor for Satan's situation was coined by al-Hallaj, one of the first Sufis to rehabilitate him: God bound Satan and threw him into the sea, telling him: 'Be careful not to get wet.'[126] Al-Hallaj even placed Satan on the same level as Mohammed, who was revered precisely by the mystics as the 'perfect human' (*insān kāmil*): 'The only ones whose sermons will endure are Iblis (Satan) and Ahmad (Mohammed), God bless him and grant him salvation.'[127]

Even if the Sufis saw Satan's tragedy primarily as dealing with the theme of love, it is nonetheless connected to Job and the fools who rebel against God: Satan's fate is the most conspicuous example in Sufi literature of God's unjustified, wilful and devastating decisions. Satan's suffering is more than simply unjust; it takes justice ad absurdum, for his disobedience is the paradoxical but necessary consequence of his unconditional obedience. Satan does not stop loving God when he defies Him, just as Job loves God so much that he must stand up to Him. Both accuse God precisely because they are closest to Him. Unlike Job, however, Satan is not rewarded for his refusal. Satan's fate is hopeless, although some mystics, such as Eyn ol-Qozat, Ahmad Ghazali, Abdulkarim al-Jili (d. between 1408 and 1417) and in certain passages also Attar (26/2, p. 244), expressed the hope that Satan might return to God in the end – though that would also herald the end of days.[128] For Attar in particular, the utopia of reconciliation depended on the fate of Satan (see 26/1, pp. 242ff.).

In *The Book of Suffering* the wanderer also visits Satan. No creature has suffered as much as he, he says in his panegyric. For seventy thousand years Satan was closer to God than all the other angels, only to be banished for a single act of disobedience: he was enthroned in paradise and ended up in the depths of hell. Attar alludes to the Sufi interpretation that Satan had to defy God because he loved Him when he makes the wanderer ask in whom else the fire of unbelief was ignited precisely in belief. Now Satan is lord of this world, the wanderer knows, and asks him if he knows a secret path to the treasure.

This word drenched Iblis in blood,
  The fire burst glowing from his breast.
Many hundred thousand years, he said,
  I drank from the chalice of love,
And even turned it around in my thirst

To down the dregs of His curse.
There is no place in either of the worlds
Where I would not have kneeled to pray.
I myself cursed the devil so often,
And thanked God for His mercy.
How could I know that I was doing wrong,
And only cursing myself all day?
Misery seized me as suddenly as the tide,
The pain of His curse attacked me like a thief.
Many hundred thousand years of my good works,
All the flapping of my angelic wings,
Torn away by the tide of his damnation,
Left me someone else, a mockery of a creature,
Cursed, rejected, lost, robbed of all power,
An angel I was, the devil I am.
Once I shared a bed with Huris,
Now I lie as a demon in the dung.
From head to toe a weeping eye,
As a warning to the creatures of all horizons.
You will do well to learn from me,
But do not do the same as I have, never,
Go through a hundred worlds of compassion,
Only to end unwanted on the path of the cursed.
I bear the curse of the truthful, keep away,
You have not the power to bear it yourself. (26/0, pp. 241f.)

That is Satan's lament. Like all the other creatures, he too cannot help the wanderer, being helpless himself. Satan is more frank than the other creatures asked by the wanderer, however, declaring God responsible for his torment and that of all. He cannot believe what has happened to him, what God personally did to him. In this he resembles Job, who cries: 'Have pity on me, my friends, have pity, for the hand of God has struck me' (19:21). Job, however, is cursed *although* he loves God, whereas Satan is cursed *because* he loves God. Unlike Job, Satan goes so far as to call his own faith in God the reason for his misfortune. His judgement is harsher than any other about God; at the same time, he loves God more than any other creature. Satan in *The Book of Suffering* is Job taken to the extreme, a Job as sketched by Margarete Susman: guiltlessly guilty. Something peculiar happens: as at the end of every chapter in the frame story, the wanderer returns to his master, who puts him in the picture about the figure treated in the chapter. As already mentioned, these are usually pious, sometimes sanctimonious words presumably intended to stem the provocation of worldly laments. And so the *pir* likewise speaks a verse about Satan that matches the conventional image, telling of Satan's cunning, his egotism and falseness. But then, as if the master's own heart were breaking at the thought of the unwarranted misery of the cursed one, he has scarcely even started his habitual moralizing before he stops again abruptly. Instead, suddenly – for the first time – he tells a story himself, explaining with empathy why Satan keeps humans away from God: not out of wickedness, but out of a jealousy that comes from his love.

One called out to Satan: Accursed one,
  How can you bear the distance?
I stand in the distance, spoke Satan, the sword in my hand,
  And chase away all who approach His door
None shall come close to Him,
  This work is enough for me.
I stand in the distance, my eyes rainclouds,
  Because they do not see that face.
I stand in the distance, and cannot bear,
  That someone should see it while I cannot.
I stand in the distance, for on the way to Him,
  I was not worthy to enter His door.
I stand in the distance, distant from Him, with neither body nor reason,
  'twould be better for me to burn, than to be distant from Him.
I stand in the distance, cloaked in black since my fall,
  For I lack the strength of his nearness.
Even though I was chased from his doorstep,
  My gaze is still fixed on the path to Him,
Since I set foot in the street of my beloved,
  I have looked nowhere else but to Him.
Because I once knew the secret,
  I can look nowhere else but to Him. (26/0, p. 232)

Someone who loves so strongly cannot act any other way. Even when he brings guilt upon himself, he is guilty. Satan is a victim of God. Written by a religious Muslim despairing at God and the world, the twenty-sixth chapter of *The Book of Suffering* is one of the most harrowing artefacts of Iran's so frequently world-weary literature. God's terror is bad enough; but if humans even love this God and can neither leave Him nor hide from Him, if they even beg God to cause them more suffering, as every blow from their beloved is superior to a thousand acts of affection because it comes from the beloved, as Attar says – if this is the case, one will sometimes find such extreme expressions of a masochistic relationship with God that are closer to the age of extremes than one might like. It should be sufficiently clear that Attar describes a journey inwards, that his poetry is also a product of the real political experiences of his time, the years of massacres both remembered and experienced, and of imminent destruction. This author teaches us precisely that inner and outer experience coincide.

That people turn to God in times of need requires no explanation; and that despair drives many to accuse God is illustrated by numerous examples in the history of religion and literature. But Attar describes in many verses how the two can come together and culminate: how creatures can cling lovingly to God in the face of their destruction – not *despite* but, rather, *while* declaring Him guilty. 'Only in persecution, under an all-destroying threat, can Job still recognize some connection between God and his life',[129] wrote Margarete Susman, quoting in shuddering agreement from the midrash: 'When King Ahasuerus gave Haman his signet ring, thus enabling the latter's cruel persecution of the Jews, he did more for Israel than all the prophets.'[130] Conversely, Job and hence the Jewish people experience 'their full connection to God' in the fact that God 'persecutes them with all His cruelty'[131] and even excludes them from communality with other peoples, makes them pariahs, outcasts, eternal exiles like Satan in the Sufi tradition. Here a religion defines itself by the suffering that God inflicts on those who believe in Him: 'It is the scarcely utterable secret that the dark ring of fate in which God has imprisoned His people today is the ring of His love.'[132] Earlier on I recounted the story of Shibli's visit to the asylum, of the fool who called after him to refrain at all costs from passing on his complaints to God lest He make his suffering a hundred times worse; I also mentioned the other madman who begs his friendly visitor to speak quietly, so that God does not prevent him from obtaining bread. Elie Wiesel tells of a small group of Jews praying in a synagogue during the Nazi occupation. A Jew who is very pious but has gone mad appears at the door. He listens to the prayers for a while; then he says quietly, but urgently: 'Hush, Jews! Don't pray so loud. God will hear you, and then He'll know that there are still a few Jews left in Europe.'[133]

The counter-theology discussed above leads to the very heart of the twentieth century. Nor will it end in the twenty-first, which envisages man as his own creator. Whatever one might say about God, it is unlikely that humans will get up to anything better.

What remains

Perhaps theology ends only where not even protest finds its voice. My imagination is not sufficient to grasp the inner experiences of people whose corpses were thrown on top of one another in wars and conquests, pogroms and death camps. I can only imagine abandonment by God under conditions of everyday need, in experiences that any life can hold; that is why I must return to them. I have seen dead people who were not allowed to die, my Aunt Lobat and others in hospital. Heinrich Heine kept his humour even in the last weeks of his life. But he did not always succeed – 'I am now at rock bottom, poor and wretched, bent like a worm' – [134] and there probably followed a phase in which he could no longer manage even a second's mockery. He seems to have anticipated this in the poem about the dying Almansor, from his posthumous *Lamentations*:

Oh! Pain is born dumb,
No tongue inside its mouth;
With only tears, only blood,
From a deep, mortal wound.[135]

It is true that my aunt staved off her physical decline and her pain through laughter; that she did not stop making jokes; that she lost everything, but not her cheerfulness. It is true, and it always struck me as a genuinely lived myth of self-assertion, like a scene from *Happy Days*. But that was not the end, and the end was no *Endgame*. There was something after it, after the game. There was the black abyss, and I think I can say exactly when my aunt finally sank into it: when she could no longer laugh. Beckett does not speak about that, or at most he hints at it; he did not know it, at least not in his writing. But one finds it in Heine. Unlike my aunt, and with a precision only a German poet could display, he documented the feeling of being shattered by something so powerful that he called it God. And just as Heine clung desperately to God when all his means of resistance had literally been torn from his immovable, itching hand ('I have been wronged so much that I can no longer exact vengeance, so I have entrusted to the dear Lord the entire liquidation of my life'),[136] all that my Aunt Lobat had left when she was helplessly at the mercy of terror was God, who was Himself that terror. She must have surrendered herself to Him, for nothing else had remained in the reality of her final weeks. As with the forty-day retreat in his cell of the mystic, who steps out of his reality to be spiritually annihilated in God, my aunt had left behind our world, the world of her city Isfahan and her family, which had already shrunk to the courtyard room converted into a sickroom. She no longer had any access to it – at least none that would have enabled us to meet her. Attar says of the fools:

All they see is but a dream to them,
  People – a reflection of the air,

The world of turmoil and wailing,
  All that exists – but a sackful of air. (38/5, p. 342)

The only thing that was real for my aunt when she no longer seemed to recognize any of us was God, and all that we recognized was the horror in her eyes. No one was there for her any more, so she could speak only to Him. The way she moved her lips no longer betrayed anger – it was unfeigned panic that left her with only one choice: to beg for mercy. I cannot know whether God heard her, whether He wanted to hear her, or whether there is a God who could have heard her. But my aunt clung to something in her last weeks, and if it was an illusion, it was real as only a creator can be. Was she praying? Was she cursing? Was she wooing God or praising him? Sometimes we could hear it: *ḫodāyā*, 'my God'. Her God. The Koran is a very human book: it describes not only a God who speaks to humans so that they will desire Him, but also humans who desire a God who will speak to them. God existed for Aunt Lobat, so He exists. That is what Sartre meant, even if his own answer was a different one: the question is not whether God exists, but whether you need Him. Therefore He must exist. He was in the room overlooking the courtyard in which Aunt Lobat was dying for so long. Conversely, this could mean that God does not need humans.

And if I placed a world of obedience at Your feet,
  Why would You need it, being content with Yourself?
And if I bore witness to a world full of sins,
  What would you do with it, being so rich?
Because good comes from you without reason,
  No misfortune will befall those who speak ill of You. (E/16, p. 377)

Those are bold lines. One last time, and more clearly than anywhere else in his works, Attar states at the end of his great masnavi that it is all the same to God whether we pray or not, whether we believe in Him, deny Him or insult Him. In these final lines he seems to derive a freedom from this which, interestingly enough, is based not on conviction but on theological apathy: if God is indifferent, it makes no difference what people say about Him. If humans obey God, they do it for themselves. And yet here, in the negation of divine compassion, lies the only hope of mercy. If good and evil are the same to God, he can just as well do good. A few lines later Attar writes:

As all that You do is without reason,
  Have mercy without reason, O ruler of worlds.
Though unbelief and sin weigh heavily on me,
  A word of Your forgiveness, and I will be free.

If you can give me but an atom of joy,
Then do it, do you not always give without reason? (E/16, p. 377)

We find these lines, and those quoted previously on the last pages, in the sixteenth and thus third-last section of the epilogue. They are almost identical to the hope Attar permitted to entertain in the epilogue to *The Book of God*:

I had a heart that was full of His glory,
A witness to His oneness and uniqueness.
But He, despite all my efforts, without reason,
Cast me from His palace without warning.
None in the palace dared to ask,
'Why did you banish him so suddenly?'
If He took me back again without reason,
I would not be surprised, for nothing is surprising with Him.
If He sent me away without reason,
He needs no reason to take me back.[137]

In these lines it is Satan, in *The Book of Suffering* it is the words of a drunken Bedouin, but the context of the two epilogues, where the poet is speaking as himself, suggests that Attar is revealing his own beliefs. Hope in God has congealed into hope for His indifference. But such a God, who is indifferent to humans, can only become real through people who are not indifferent to God. It is immaterial whether He exists if people believe in Him. Two stories further, at the end of *The Book of Suffering*, Attar talks about the illusion of truth, but also the truth of illusion, which he argues is equally vital. Another love-drunk Bedouin: he lives in the salt desert and is scarcely able to survive on the undrinkable brackish water. After years of thirst, he finds drinking water for the first time and thinks it is the water of paradise. Overcome by joy, he fills a bowl with it and sets out to give it to Caliph Ma'mun (d. 786), expecting a reward. He meets the caliph just as he is returning from the hunt.

'I have brought a gift from highest heaven for the prince of the faithful.'

'What is it?'

'The water of paradise', exclaims the Bedouin and gives the caliph the bowl containing a warm, foul-smelling liquid. Ma'mun immediately recognizes the Bedouin's madness. But he drinks from the bowl offered to him without showing his disgust. Then he says to the Bedouin: 'You have done a wonderful thing: such splendid, clear water. It is truly the water of paradise. Now wish for whatever you want.'

The Bedouin speaks at length of his wretched existence in the salt desert and leaves it up to the caliph to decide on a reward. The caliph gives him a thousand dinars, but stipulates one condition: the Bedouin must turn back immediately and return home to the salt desert, as his life is in danger here. When asked later why he made that condition, Ma'mun answers: 'If he had travelled further, he would have reached the Euphrates and realized the worthlessness of his gift. I wanted to spare him that shame, for he came from afar to see me and gave all that he had' (E/18, pp. 378ff.).

After telling the story of the Bedouin, Attar returns to the great misery that enters his heart and grows every day, such that he could die of sorrow over himself: every night brings a thousand new gifts of blood. He comes from the saltlands of the earth, from the dust-wind of futile pleas, with a pipe on his shoulder filled with tears of longing. May God be as merciful as the caliph was to the Bedouin. And so the very last lines of *The Book of Suffering* formulate a hope, albeit the hope of the hopeless: that everything is but a nightmare.

> Pull me by the hand, if you can,
> From this confusion, as if nothing had happened. (E/18, p. 382)

Engāri ke hič – 'as if nothing had happened'. The miracle of her final weeks was that she, whose ability to articulate herself was restricted to groans, weeping, screams and the three-syllable invocation of God, would occasionally recite entire verses from a prayer or the Koran. She did so even long after her consciousness had been clouded. I could explain the utterances of *ey ḫodā* or *ḫodāyā*; they were hardly more than sighs, and slurred, so that we almost had to intuit the words ourselves. But the way her tongue, though no longer in her power, repeatedly managed to rise from its wordless dormancy and speak Arabic tongue-twisters could not be attributed to her own power, and thus only to a higher one. It did not happen often; I experienced it only a handful of times. But each time she uttered several complete sentences of Persian or Arabic. And each time, after completing the words, her features relaxed for a moment. She found relief. Some might say that is not much. And yet it was all that remained for her: to cling to God, and thus to the hope that the one who had created everything might also have the power to turn everything into nothing: e*ngāri ke hič*.

Mr Engineer Kermani had what we called a fine death. In the morning he went to the doctor, who said that he was in excellent health. Nonetheless, he spent the afternoon driving through Tehran to pay all the debts that were still outstanding here and there. He also cared for the poor who depended on him. In the evening my aunt wished him a good night's sleep. Who knows what the night will bring, replied Mr Engineer. God only knows. When my aunt awoke in the morning, she found him dead beside her. He died without any pain, said the doctor.

Innā li-l wa-innā ilayhī rāǧi'ūn.

NOTES

Chapter 1 Job's Question

1 Translator's note (henceforth, TN): The language of Iran is referred to throughout this book as 'Persian', rather than the comparatively recent term 'Farsi', which is simply the Persian word for 'Persian' (akin to *français*, *deutsch*, *italiano* etc.).
2 See Kermani, *Iran*, pp. 38ff.
3 TN: In Persian cuisine, these small, slightly sour berries are dried and used as spices (especially for rice).
4 Abū Nu'aym al-Iṣfahānī, *Ḥilyat al-awliya'*, quoted in Andrae, *In the Garden of Myrtles: Studies in Early Islamic Mysticism*, p. 78.
5 Al-Ġazālī, *Iḥyā'*, vol. 4, p. 397 (*Kitāb aṣ-ṣabr wa-š-šukr. Bayān wağh iğtimā' aṣ-ṣabr wa-š-šukr 'alā šay' wāḥid*).
6 Ibid., vol. 4, p. 324 (*Kitāb aṣ-ṣabr wa-š-šukr. Bayān maẓān al-ḥāğa ilā ṣ-ṣabr*).
7 TN: All citations from the Koran are taken from the translation by Arthur J. Arberry (Oxford University Press, 1964).
8 See Ritter, *The Ocean of the Soul*, pp. 241f., and Reinert, *Die Lehre vom tawakkul*, pp. 112ff.
9 Al-Ġazālī, *Iḥyā'*, vol. 4, p. 324 (*Kitāb aṣ-ṣabr wa-š-šukr. Bayān maẓān al-ḥāğa ilā ṣ-ṣabr*).
10 Ibid., vol. 4, p. 325.
11 Buber, *Tales of the Hasidim*, pp. 237f.
12 TN: All biblical citations are taken from the New International Version.
13 Lactantius, *The Wrath of God*, pp. 68, 70.
14 Concerning the approach to suffering of the Rabbis Kraemer, see Kraemer, *Responses to Suffering in Classical Rabbinical Literature*.
15 See Schäfer, 'Das Böse in der mittelalterlichen jüdischen Mystik', and Scholem, *Major Trends in Jewish Mysticism*.
16 See Schwarzbaum, 'The Jewish and Moslem Versions of Some Theodicy Legends', and Brown, *Apocalypse and/or Metamorphosis*, pp. 79ff.
17 Al-Ġazālī, *Iḥyā'*, vol. 5, p. 135 (*Kitāb at-tawḥīd wa-t-tawakkul. Bayān ḥaqīqat at-tawḥīd*).

18 Leibniz, *Theodicy*, p. 95.
19 Ibn Rušd, *The Philosophy and Theology of Averroës*, pp. 286f.
20 Thomas Aquinas, *Summa contra gentiles* III/1, chapter 71.
21 As-Suyūṭī, *Kašf aṣ-ṣalṣala 'an waṣf al-zalzala*, ed. A. as-Sa'dānī (Fez, 1971), p. 4; quoted in Ormsby, *Theodicy in Islamic Thought*, p. 262.
22 Quistorp, *Die letzten Dinge im Zeugnis Calvins*, pp. 159f.
23 I am aware of the problematics of Eurocentric classifications brought up by Edward Said, Maxime Rodinson and others, which goes beyond terms such as 'Middle Ages', 'Near East' or 'classical Islam' and also encompasses such ostensibly neutral words as 'human', 'religion', 'humanism' or 'state' (see Foucault, *The Order of Things*). I have not, however, found a solution that is both linguistically practicable and methodically convincing; see the reply by Joel L. Kraemer to accusations of using Eurocentric terminology unquestioningly in the paperback edition of his book *Humanism in the Renaissance of Islam*, pp. xiff.
24 Nietzsche, *Ecce homo*, p. 28; the aphorism was presumably a statement made in conversation which Nietzsche knew from a book by Paul Albert on French nineteenth-century literature; see D'Iori, 'Beiträge zur Quellenforschung', p. 400.
25 Nietzsche, *Thus Spoke Zarathustra*, p. 114.
26 Nietzsche, *Daybreak*, pp. 52f.
27 Büchner, *Werke und Briefe*, p. 107.
28 BT Kiddushin 39b; quoted in Brocke and Jochum, *Wolkensäule und Feuerschein*, p. 55; for more extensive information on the person, see Wiesel, *Wise Men and their Tales*.
29 Quoted from the Arabic text in Houtsma, 'Zum Kitāb al-Fihrist', p. 233.
30 Bloch, *Atheism in Christianity*, p. 250.
31 Ibid., p. 121.
32 Heine, *Säkularausgabe*, vol. 22, p. 298.
33 Werner, *Begegnungen mit Heine*, p. 155. My description of Heine's final years is based in substantial aspects on Karl-Josef Kuschel's book *Gottes grausamer Spass?*; I also found a wealth of insight and observations in István Eörsi's essay 'Hiob und Heine'. See also Kruse, 'Heinrich Heine – der Lazarus'.
34 Heine, *Säkularausgabe*, vol. 22, p. 298.
35 Ibid., p. 294.
36 Ibid.
37 Ibid., vol. 23, p. 225.
38 Ibid., p. 43.
39 Heine, *Sämtliche Schriften*, vol. 6 [1], p. 475.
40 Heine, *Säkularausgabe*, vol. 23, p. 134.
41 Heine, *Sämtliche Schriften*, vol. 6 [1], p. 476.
42 Marx, *Critique of Hegel's 'Philosophy of Right'*, p. 131.
43 Heine, *Sämtliche Schriften*, vol. 4, p. 111.
44 Büchner, *Werke und Briefe*, p. 107.
45 Heine, *Sämtliche Schriften*, vol. 5, p. 109.
46 Werner, *Begegnungen mit Heine*, vol. 2, p. 155.
47 Ibid.
48 Heine, *Säkularausgabe*, vol. 23, pp. 26f.
49 Ibid., XXIII, p. 56.

50 For biographical information about Attar, see first of all the articles by Reinert in *EIran* and by Ritter in *EI2*. Also Ritter, 'Philologika XIV'; Foruzānfar, *Šarḥ-e aḥwāl*; Nafisi, *Ǧostoǧū*; Šafi'i-Kadkani, *Zabur-e pārsi*; and Zarin-Kub, *Ṣedā-ye bāl-e simurġ*.

51 Many details about Attar's life were considered credible far into the twentieth century because they seemed to have come from Attar himself. Even Hellmut Ritter, in his first essay on Attar from 1938, painted a fairly precise picture of the poet's life that twenty years later he declared mostly invalid. Ritter's realization had come about through Sa'id Nafisi, whose groundbreaking 1942 study disputed the authenticity of most of the works previously attributed to Attar; they were in fact written by epigones or namesakes of Attar. Nafisi's proof was directed above all against *Maẓhar al-'aǧā'ib* ('Place of Miracles'), which contains most of the autobiographical information, such as the poet's alleged conversion to Shia. This also ruled out *Lisān al-ġayb* ('The Tongue of the Hidden'), which was undoubtedly penned by the same Shiite poet, as a valid source on Attar's life – which is nonetheless still merrily distributed in a Tehran reprint from 1997 as a work by Attar, and also referred to as such in works of Western scholarship, for example in the *EIran* or Peter Awn's *Satan's Tragedy and Redemption*. In fact, Western literature on Attar has generally not caught up with recent Iranian research, and is hence partly obsolete. *Lisān al-ġayb* describes a confrontation – colourfully milked by later Shiite propagandists – between the author and a Sunni cleric who pronounces a fatwa declaring him an infidel on account of his Shiite faith, whereupon a mob supposedly loots Attar's house and threatens his life.

52 Ritter, 'Philologika XIV', p. 5.

53 'Aṭṭār, *Tazkerat ol-ouliyā'*, p. 187.

54 Ibid., p. 31.

55 See Doulatšāh, *Tazkerat oš-šo'arā'*, p. 187.

56 See 'Aṭṭār, *Moṣibatnāmeh*, E0, p. 365, and E1, p. 367; *Elāhināmeh*, pp. 365f.; and *Manṭeq oṭ-ṭeyr*, p. 245.

57 TN: Owing to the lack of existing English translations, excerpts from Attar's works have been translated from the author's own German versions. *The Conference of the Birds* is the one work that is widely available in English; on account of the number of editions and the differences between them, however, this has not been used here.

58 See 'Aṭṭār, *Asrārnāmeh*, p. 183.

59 'Aṭṭār, *Tazkerat ol-ouliyā'*, pp. 30f.

60 See Zarin-Kub, *Ṣedā-ye bāl-e simurġ*, pp. 161ff.

61 See Solṭān Walad, *Entehānāmeh,* index entry 'Attar'. There appears to be no other source referring to Attar by name until *Golšan-e rāz* (*The Rose Garden of the Secret*), written by Maḥmūd Šabestari in the fourteenth century: 'In a hundred millennia there will be no other like him' (quoted in Qomše'i, *Maqālāt*, p. 272). Ḥamdollāh Mostoufi also mentioned Attar in 1330 in his history book *Tāriḫ-e gozideh* (see *EIran*, 'Aṭṭār'). At that time, Attar's collection of lives of the saints, *Tazkerat ol-ouliyā'*, was evidently widely read; his *Conference of the Birds* must also have been known, as Sheikh 'Ali Hamadāni (d. 1385, not to be confused with his better-known namesake 'Eyn ol-Qożāt) presented a selection of them (see Teufel, *Lebensbeschreibung des Scheichs 'Ali-i Hamadānī*, p. 50). Reinert's claim in the *EIran* that the earliest source to mention Attar after his death is Mostoufi's history book, and that Attar's

poems and verse epics remained undiscovered up until the fifteenth century, requires correction. Reinert overlooks several earlier pieces of evidence, such as the statements of Šabestari and the selection by ʻAli Hamadāni. On the latter, see Meier, ʻDie Welt der Urbilder bei ʻAli Hamadāniʼ.

62 Doulatšāh, *Tazkerat oš-šoʻarā'*, p. 193.

63 See Foruzānfar, *Šarḥ-e aḥwāl*, pp. 68ff., and Qomše'i, *Maqālāt*, pp. 268ff.

64 See Doulatšāh, *Tazkerat oš-šoʻarā'*, pp. 187f.

65 Ibid., p. 191.

66 For an extensive treatment of this, see Ritter, ʻPhilologika XIVʼ.

67 Concerning *Elāhīnāmeh*, see Meier, ʻDer Geistmensch bei dem persischen Dichter ʻAṭṭārʼ.

68 In order to explain the purely worldly character of the adventure novel, which is not congruent with the mysticism of his other works, scholars constructed a line of development according to which Attar began as a purely secular writer and turned to more spiritual themes only later, after a form of conversion. This theory, however, was always contradicted by the poet's own statements that he felt drawn to mysticism from an early age. Šafiʻi-Kadkani has listed a number of reasons why *Ḫosrounāmeh* is not simply an anomaly in Attar's output, but in fact the work of a completely different, later poet. Accordingly, the preface to *Ḫosrounāmeh* contains a widely overlooked statement that the book is the work of an aged poet – i.e. precisely not an early work. The book referred to by Attar as *Ḫosrounāmeh* in his list of works, Šafiʻi-Kadkani claims, is in fact *Elāhīnāmeh*, whose present title became established only later. Šafiʻi-Kadkani thus argues that Attar never mentions a book entitled *Elāhīnāmeh*, even though it was undoubtedly written by him. But because Attar refers to a certain *Ḫosrounāmeh*, and a king (*ḫosrou*) appears as a main character in *Elāhīnāmeh*, one can assume that *Elāhīnāmeh* was originally entitled *Ḫosrounāmeh* – especially as the earliest manuscripts of the work did not yet use the later title. The present title, according to Šafiʻi-Kadkani, probably came into use only in the fourteenth century, partly because in some manuscripts the work ends by addressing God: *Elāhi, Elāhi!*. If one follows Šafiʻi-Kadkani – like his colleague Zarin-Kub (*Ṣedā-ye bāl-e simurġ*, pp. 69ff.) – and assumes that Attar was not referring to what is known today as *Ḫosrounāmeh* when he listed his works in *Moḫtarnāmeh*, this eliminates the most important reason for considering this book, which seems to occupy such an isolated position in Attar's œuvre, to be his work nonetheless (Šafiʻi-Kadkani, *Zabur-e pārsi*, pp. 37ff.). An extensive overview of the content of *Ḫosrounāmeh*, which is an incredibly eventful and gripping account of the romance between Princess Gol and Khosrow, the illegitimate son of the Byzantine emperor, can be found in Ritter, ʻPhilologika Xʼ, pp. 160ff.

69 TN: The word refers here to the absence of needs, not to a lack of necessity.

70 See Šafiʻi-Kadkani, *Zabur-e pārsi*, p. 21.

71 Ḥamidi, *ʻAṭṭār dar masnawihā-ye gozide-ye u*, pp. 6f.

72 Ibid., p. 34.

73 Ḥamidi himself documented the debate in his book: ibid., pp. 87ff. In a letter to the journal *Yaġmā*, where Ḥamidi had first published his theses, a reader spoke of people who had wept after reading them, and of the suggestion among some Iranians in Europe that a paper effigy of the publisher should be publicly burnt.

74 It seems that Geoffrey Chaucer, born over a century after Attar, had already

heard (presumably through sources he encountered in 1372 on his trip to Italy) about the central motifs of *The Conference of the Birds*, as the parallels in his debate on love, *The Parliament of Fowls*, are very conspicuous. John Bunyan's (d. 1688) *Pilgrim's Progress* probably took certain cues from Attar's verse epic (or the Arabic source of the same name). After partial translations by Hammer and de Sacy, Garcin de Tassy produced the first complete translation into a European language in 1683. Meanwhile *The Conference of the Birds* also exists in a number of English translations, some published in popular paperback editions; extracts have also appeared in German, though only Annemarie Schimmel has made the effort to translate them directly from the Persian rather than from the English adaptation.

75 Buber, *Ecstatic Confessions*, p. xxxii.

76 Borges, *Die letzte Reise des Odysseus*, p. 241.

77 If one looks up *The Book of Suffering* in compendia and lexica of Persian literature, it is consistently listed as one of Attar's major works – yet, apart from the contents, a few hardly in-depth essays, many references and a glossary of its own, they contain almost nothing about it. As far as I can tell, the literary quality of the epic is undisputed, but larger-scale, independent studies on *The Book of Suffering*, comparable to the considerable number of essays on *The Conference of the Birds* and the few on *The Book of God*, the poems or *Lives of the Saints* are nowhere to be found.

78 Fritz Meier, himself hardly an insignificant figure in the study of Islamic mysticism, noted in his review: 'Furthermore, Ritter's work reaches so deep into general Islamic intellectual life that he has established new standards, or a sort of magnetic field that will now have to be filled with old knowledge and new finds' (Book review of Ritter, *Das Meer der Seele*, p. 320).

79 It is nothing short of baffling how little research on Attar has been carried out in the West since Ritter's *The Ocean of the Soul*, even though *The Conference of the Birds* has repeatedly managed to reach a wide audience – see Buber, Borges and Brook – like few other works of classical Persian literature. Various essays, Peter Awn's examination in his book on the Islamic figure of Satan, Annemarie Schimmel's description in her book *Mystical Dimensions of Islam*, brief commentaries in translations, a colloquium in Italy and the obligatory encyclopedia entries – nothing compared to the academic literature in the West dealing with other classics of Persian poetry. At least there have been international conferences on Attar in Nishapur and London in recent years; at the time of writing, I have not seen any of the resulting papers, some of which have not yet been published.

CHAPTER 2 *THE BOOK OF SUFFERING*

1 'Aṭṭār, *Tazkerat ol-ouliyā'*, pp. 199ff.

2 Concerning Attar's relationship with philosophy, see Purnāmdāriyān, *Didār bā Simorġ*, pp. 198ff.

3 Pascal, *Thoughts*, p. 72.

4 Nietzsche, *Daybreak*, p. 53.

5 Schopenhauer, *The World as Will and Representation*, vol. 2, p. 581.

6 Scholem, *On the Kabbalah and its Symbolism*, p. 7.

7 Ibid., p. 13.

8 Ibid., p. 18.
9 *The Tawasin of Mansur Al-Hallaj*, p, 139.
10 Quoted in Ritter, 'Die Aussprüche des Bāyezīd Bisṭāmī', p. 243.
11 Nietzsche, *The Gay Science*, p. 120.
12 See *EI2*, 'Shafā'a'. Zarin-Kub (*Ṣedā-ye bāl-e simurġ*, pp. 133f.) considers it unlikely, however, that Attar knew the *hadith* (as is generally supposed).
13 See Scholem, *Major Trends in Jewish Mysticism.*
14 See Bencheikh, *Le Voyage nocturne de Mahomet.*
15 For a comparison with Attar's works, see Purnāmdāriyān, *Didār bā Simorġ*, pp. 141ff.
16 Büchner, *Complete Plays, Lenz and Other Writings*, pp. 133f.
17 See Kremer, 'Islamische Einflüsse auf Dantes "Göttliche Komödie"', and Strohmaier, *Von Demokrit bis Dante*, pp. 449ff.
18 See Menocal, *The Arabic Role in Medieval Literary Theory*, pp. 115ff; also Meisami, 'Arabic Culture and Medieval European Literature'.
19 Borges, *Die letzte Reise des Odysseus*, p. 127.
20 Horkheimer, *Die Sehnsucht nach dem ganz Anderen*, p. 40.
21 Adorno, *Gesammelte Schriften*, vol. 11, p. 282.
22 Ibid., p. 425.
23 Hedāyat, *Payām-e Kāfkā*, p. 42; see Kermani, 'Der Auftrag des Dichters'.
24 Adorno, *Mahler: A Musical Physiognomy*, p. 137.
25 'Aṭṭār, *Asrārnāmeh* 12/12, p. 116.
26 See Holbein, *Ich bin grösser als Allah!*
27 'Aṭṭār, *Manṭeq oṭ-ṭeyr*, p. 255.
28 Ibid.
29 'Aṭṭār, *Elāhināmeh*, p. 380.
30 Ibid.
31 Adorno, 'The Sociology of Knowledge and its Consciousness', in *Prisms*, pp. 37–49, p. 39.
32 Schopenhauer, *The World as Will and Representation*, vol. 2, p. 577.
33 Nietzsche, *Writings from the Late Notebooks*, p. 97.
34 Hedāyat, *Payām-e Kāfkā*, pp. 66f.
35 See Lambton, *Continuity and Change in Medieval Persia*, pp. 16 and 20f.
36 Ibn Aṯīr, *Al-Kāmil fi t-tārīḫ*, ed. C. J. Tornberg, 4 vols. (Leiden: Brill, 1851–71); quoted in Lambton, *Continuity and Change in Medieval Persia*, pp. 14f.
37 Ritter, *The Ocean of the Soul*, p. 123.
38 See Zarin Kub, *Ṣedā-ye bāl-e simurġ*, p. 25. In his *Elāhināmeh* (p. 367), Attar had at least given Ferdowsi credit for handing on Maḫmūd's petty gift to a millet beer seller.
39 Neẓālmolmolk, *Siyāsatnāma*, pp. 101f.
40 For a long time, Attar was himself taken for a Shiite, or at least claimed by Shiite propagandists as one of their own; this was based on statements in his works, however, whose authenticity has meanwhile been disproved.
41 Wensinck, *Concordance*, VI, p. 249.
42 Zarin-Kub, *Ṣedā-ye bāl-e simurġ*, p. 171
43 'Aṭṭār, *Manṭeq oṭ-ṭeyr*, pp. 156f.
44 See (also regarding the justification of the term 'humanism') Kraemer, *Humanism in the Renaissance of Islam*, and Makdisi, *The Rise of Humanism.*
45 See Haskins, *The Renaissance of the Twelfth Century*; Nelson, *On the Roads to Modernity*; Stiefel, *The Intellectual Revolution in Twelfth-Century Europe*;

Haas, *Mystik im Kontext*, pp. 171ff.; and Makdisi, *The Rise of Humanism*, pp. 294ff.

46 See, concerning this and subsequent historical information, the corresponding entries in *EI2*, especially the article 'Nīshāpūr'; Zarin-Kub, *Ṣedā-ye bāl-e simurġ*, pp. 19ff.; Lambton, *Continuity and Change in Medieval Persia*; Morgan, *Medieval Persia*, pp. 41ff.; Bulliet, *The Patricians of Nishapur*; Boyle, *The Cambridge History of Iran*, vol. 5; and Barthold, *Turkestan*.
47 Zarin-Kub, *Ṣedā-ye bāl-e simurġ*, p. 29.
48 See Bulliet, *The Patricians of Nishapur*, pp. 76ff.
49 Melville, 'Earthquakes in the History of Nishapur', pp. 105f.
50 Zarin-Kub, *Ṣedā-ye bāl-e simurġ*, pp. 19f.
51 Gryphius, *Gedichte*, p. 8 ('Thränen in schwerer Krankheit').
52 Ibid., p. 7 ('Thränen des Vaterlandes').
53 Gryphius, *Lyrische Gedichte*, p. 477 ('Thränen- und Danck-Lied').
54 Ibid., pp. 476f.
55 Gryphius, *Gedichte*, p. 9 ('Thränen in schwerer Krankheit').
56 Ibid., p. 6 ('Menschliches Elend').
57 Foruzānfar, *Aḥādis-e masnawi*, p. 61 (no. 157).
58 Schopenhauer, *The World as Will and Representation*, vol. 2, p. 161.
59 Nietzsche, *Human, All Too Human*, p. 36.
60 Quoted in Röllecke, *'O wär' ich nie geboren!'*, p. 12.
61 Quoted ibid., p. 16.
62 Atabay, *Die schönsten Gedichte aus dem klassischen Persien*, p. 14.
63 Quoted in Ritter, *The Ocean of the Soul*, p. 136.
64 Quoted ibid., p. 132.
65 Gryphius, *Gedichte*, p. 96 ('Verleugnung der Welt').
66 See Röllecke, *'O wär' ich nie geboren!'* and Lütkehaus, *Nichts*, as well as the variety of quotations from world literature listed by Schopenhauer in *The World as Will and Representation.*
67 Freud, *Gesammelte Briefe* (Frankfurt: Fischer, 1960), p. 429, quoted in Lütkehaus, *Nichts*, p. 128.
68 Schopenhauer, *The World as Will and Representation*, vol. 2, p. 465.
69 Büchner, *Complete Plays, Lenz and Other Writings*, p. 58.
70 'Aṭṭār, *Manṭeq oṭ-ṭeyr*, p. 219.
71 Schopenhauer, *The World as Will and Representation*, vol. 2, p. 578.
72 Jean Paul, 'Speech of the Dead Christ from the Top of the Universe: That There Is No God', trans. Thomas Carlyle, in *Poems for the Millennium: The University of California Book of Romantic and Postromantic Poetry*, ed. Jerome Rothenberg and Jeffrey C. Robinson, vol. 3, pp. 133–37, here p. 136.
73 TN: The word *verleiden*, meaning 'to spoil, to put someone off something', is based on *leiden*, meaning 'to suffer'; the literal meaning is thus to cause something to create suffering. Payne's translation, where life becomes something 'which ought to disgust us', does not quite capture this.
74 Schopenhauer, *The World as Will and Representation*, vol. 2, p. 574.

Chapter 3 The Justification and Terror of God

1 See Birnbaum, *God and Evil*, pp. 16ff.
2 See Leibniz, *Theodicy*, p. 113.

3 Az-Zabīdī, *Itḥāf as-sādat al-muttaqīn*, 10 vols. (Cairo, [1311] 1894), vol. 9, p. 440, quoted in Ormsby, *Theodicy in Islamic Thought*, p. 2.
4 Leaman, *Evil and Suffering in Jewish Philosophy*, p. 235.
5 Jonas, 'The Concept of God after Auschwitz', pp. 8f.
6 Epicurus, quoted in Lactantius, *The Wrath of God*, pp. 92f.
7 Bayle, *Historical and Critical Dictionary*, p. 169 (article 'Paulitians').
8 Hume, *Dialogues Concerning Natural Religion*, p. 63.
9 See Neiman, *Evil in Modern Thought*, p. 189.
10 Al-Ġazālī, *Iḥyā'*, vol. 5, p. 135 (*Kitāb at-tawḥīd wa-t-tawakkul. Bayān ḥaqīqat at-tawḥīd*).
11 Yāqūt, *Mu'ǧam al-udabā'*, vol. 3, pp. 184f.
12 See, concerning this question and the various theological schools, the following standard works: Ess, *Theologie und Gesellschaft*; Watt and Marmura, *Islam*; and Nagel, *Geschichte der islamischen Theologie*.
13 See Ormsby, *Theodicy in Islamic Thought*, p. 23, and Nagel, *Geschichte der islamischen Theologie*, p. 145.
14 Moṭahhari, *'Adl-e Elāhi*, p. 54.
15 al-Aš'arī, *Al-Ibāna*, p. 25.
16 *The Philosophy and Theology of Averroës*, p. 281.
17 Ibid., p. 288.
18 aš-Šahrastānī, *Tawḍīḥ al-milal*, vol. 1, p. 71.
19 Calvin, *Institutes of the Christian Religion*, p. 270.
20 Luther, *Weimarer Ausgabe*, vol. 18, p. 755, quoted in Russell, *Mephistopheles: The Devil in the Modern World*, p. 35.
21 Ibn Sīnā, *Risāla fī sirr al-qadar* (Hyderabad: Osmania University, [1354] 1935), p. 2, quoted in Goodman, *Avicenna*, p. 88.
22 Ibn Sīnā, *Risāla fī l-arzāq*.
23 *The Philosophy and Theology of Averroës*, p. 288.
24 Maimonides, *The Guide for the Perplexed*, p. 285. A similar point is made by Saadia Gaon, who likewise discusses evil as a consequence of human freedom; see *The Book of Beliefs and Opinions*, pp. 109–36 and 186–91. For a comparison between the two philosophers on this question, see Goodman, 'Maimonides' Responses to Sa'adya Gaon's Theodicy and their Islamic Background'.
25 See Leaman, 'Job and Suffering in Talmudic and Kabbalistic Judaism' and *Evil and Suffering in Jewish Philosophy*, pp. 64ff.
26 Hermann Cohen, *Religion of Reason out of the Sources of Judaism*, p. 138.
27 Ibid., p. 17. Concerning Cohen's rejection of theodicy and the way in which it follows on from Maimonides, see Bruckstein, *Die Maske des Moses*, pp. 159ff.
28 *The Works of Saint Augustine: A Translation for the 21st Century*, part 1, vol. 12, p. 198.
29 Kant, 'On the Miscarriage of All Philosophical Trials in Theodicy', in *Religion and Rational Theology*, p. 24.
30 See Ormsby, *Theodicy in Islamic Thought*, pp. 98ff.
31 Blumenberg, *Matthäuspassion*, p. 93.
32 *Tahdīm al-arkān min laysa fi-l-imkān abda' mimmā kān*, Arabic manuscript, Princeton University, Garrett Collection, no. 464, quoted in Ormsby, *Theodicy in Islamic Thought*, pp. 135f.
33 Ibn Atā'illāh, *Šarḥ al-ḥikam* (Cairo, 1288), quoted in Ritter, *The Ocean of the*

Soul, p. 58; English edn: *The Book of Wisdom*, trans. Victor Danner (Mahwah, NJ: Paulist Press, 1978), here p. 52.

34 See Moṭahhari, *'Adl-e elāhi*, pp. 76f.
35 Al-Ġazālī, *Al-Maqṣad al-asnā*, p. 69.
36 Voltaire, *Mélanges*, p. 306 (original); *The Works of Voltaire: The Lisbon Earthquake, and Other Poems*, p. 12 (trans.).
37 See Weinrich, *Literatur für Leser*, p. 76.
38 Heine, *Sämtliche Schriften*, vol. 3, p. 594.
39 Kant, *Religion and Rational Theology*, p. 319.
40 Ibid., pp. 27f.
41 Schopenhauer, *The World as Will and Representation*, vol. 1, p. 326.
42 Ibid., vol. 2, p. 583.
43 Ibid.
44 Ibid., vol. 1, p. 325.
45 See Schelling, *Philosophical Investigations into the Essence of Human Freedom*.
46 Baudelaire, *Paris Spleen 1869*, p. 61.
47 Plotinus, *The Enneads*, p. 164.
48 See Harnack, *Marcion*; concerning the history and problematics of this book, see Kinzig, *Harnack, Marcion und das Judentum.*
49 See *The Works of Saint Augustine: A Translation for the 21st Century*, part 1, vol. 25, pp. 552ff.
50 Marquard, 'Schwierigkeiten beim Ja-Sagen', p. 93.
51 Concerning the question of God's omnipotence in the Bible from a Christian perspective, see Berger, 'Das Böse im Neuen Testament'; Bauke-Ruegg, *Die Allmacht Gottes*; Geyer, 'Das Übel und die Allmacht Gottes'; and Dietrich and Link, *Die dunklen Seiten Gottes*, pp. 24ff.
52 Arabic text in Ritter, 'Studien zur Geschichte der islamischen Frömmigkeit I', p. 79; see Schwarz, 'The Letter of al-Ḥasan al-Baṣrī', p. 22.
53 Arabic text in Ritter, 'Studien zur Geschichte der islamischen Frömmigkeit I', p. 74.
54 See Kuschel, 'Ist Gott verantwortlich für das Übel?', pp. 236ff.
55 Nietzsche, *Untimely Meditations*, p. 76.
56 Foruzānfar, *Aḥādis-e masnawi*, p. 29 (no. 70).
57 Ibid., p. 181 (no. 575).
58 Sölle, *Leiden*, pp. 147f.
59 See the numerous original texts in Kuhn, *Gottes Trauer und Klage in der rabbinischen Überlieferung*.
60 See Marquard, *Schwierigkeiten mit der Geschichtsphilosophie*, pp. 52ff.
61 Kasper, *Der Gott Jesu Christi*, p. 244.
62 Ibid., p. 242.
63 Ibid., p. 245.
64 Moltmann, *Der gekreuzigte Gott*, p. 266.
65 Jonas, 'The Concept of God after Auschwitz', p. 12.
66 Concerning the *tsimtsum* doctrine and the suffering of God in the Kabbalah, see Scholem, *Major Trends in Jewish Mysticism*, and *On the Kabbalah and its Symbolism*, pp. 110ff.; and Wolfson, 'Divine Suffering and the Hermeneutics of Reading'.
67 Jonas, *Philosophische Untersuchungen und metaphysische Vermutungen*, p. 247.

68 Rahner, *Im Gespräch*, vol. 1, p. 246.
69 'Aṭṭār, *Manṭeq oṭ-ṭeyr*, pp. 99f.
70 Al-Ma'arrī, *Risālat al-Ġufrān*, p. 343.
71 Ḥamidi, *'Aṭṭār dar masnawihā-ye gozide-ye u*, p. 26; see the debate on pp. 87ff.
72 Quoted in Schimmel, *Mystical Dimensions of Islam*.
73 See ibid.
74 Abū l-Mawāḥib 'Abdulwaḥḥāb aš-Ša'rānī, *Lawāqiḥ al-anwār al-Qudṣīya fi bayān qawā'id aṣ-Ṣufiya*; quoted in Andrae, *In the Garden of Myrtles*, p. 79.
75 Qurašī, *Kitāb makr Allāh*.
76 Ritter, 'Die Aussprüche des Bāyezīd Bisṭāmī', p. 237.
77 Al-Qušayrī, *Das Sendschreiben*, p. 42.
78 Ibid., p. 485.
79 'Aṭṭār, *Taẕkerat ol-ouliyā'*, p. 563.
80 Ibn Abbād, *Šarḥ al-ḥikam*, quoted in Gramlich, *Der eine Gott*, p. 213.
81 Sulamī, *Ṭabaqāt aṣ-ṣūfīya*, quoted in Gramlich, *Der eine Gott*, p. 214; for a longer version, see 'Aṭṭār, *Taẕkerat ol-ouliyā'*, p. 437.
82 Al-Makkī, *Die Nahrung des Herzens*, vol. 2, p. 166.
83 Al-Qušayrī, *Das Sendschreiben*, p. 195.
84 Ibid.
85 Al-Makkī, *Die Nahrung des herzens*, vol. 2, p. 166.
86 'Aṭṭār, *Asrārnāmeh*, p. 140.
87 Büchner, *Complete Plays, Lenz and Other Writings*, p. 69.
88 Al-Ġazālī, *Iḥyā'*, vol. 5, pp. 3f. (*Kitāb al-ḫawf wa-r-rağā'. Bayān ḥaqīqat al-ḫawf*).
89 Ibid., vol. 5, p. 4.
90 All quoted statements by or about Aṭā' and the description of him are taken from Gramlich, *Alte Vorbilder*, vol. 1, pp. 123ff.
91 The Shiite imam 'Alī Zayn al-'Âbidīn is quoted with almost exactly the same words; see as-Suhrawardī, *Die Gaben der Erkenntnisse*, p. 384.
92 Al-Makkī, *Die Nahrung des herzens*, vol. 2, p. 164.
93 Ibid., vol. 2, p. 163.
94 Ibid.
95 Ibid.
96 Ibid.
97 Quoted in Ritter, 'Studien zur Geschichte der islamischen Frömmigkeit I', pp. 18f.
98 Quoted statements by or about Aṭā' are taken from Gramlich, *Alte Vorbilder*, vol. 1, pp. 123ff.
99 Quoted in Brown, *Augustine of Hippo: A Biography*, p. 430.
100 Quoted ibid., p. 407.
101 In the introduction to Augustine, *Logik des Schreckens*, ed. Kurt Flasch (Mainz: Dieterich, 1995), p. 42.
102 'Aṭṭār, *Elāhināmeh*, p. 117.
103 Ibid., p. 377.
104 Al-Ġazālī, *Iḥyā'*, vol. 5, p. 169 (*Kitāb at-tawḥīd wa-t-tawakkul. Bayān ādāb al-mutawakkilīn*).
105 Andrae, *In the Garden of Myrtles*, p. 108.
106 Al-Ġazālī, *Iḥyā'*, vol. 5, p. 161 (*Kitāb at-tawḥīd wa-t-tawakkul. Bayān āḥwāl al-mutawakkilīn*).

107 Al-Makkī, *Die Nahrung des herzens*, vol. 3, p. 20.
108 *The Works of Saint Augustine: A Translation for the 21st Century*, part 1, vol. 12, p. 198.
109 Ibid., p. 202.
110 Ibid., p. 197.
111 Augustine, *Confessions*, p. 25.
112 *Retractationes* I, 13, 6.
113 Quoted in Brown, *Augustine of Hippo: A Biography*, p. 394.
114 *The Works of Saint Augustine: A Translation for the 21st Century*, part 1, vol. 12, p. 198.

Chapter 4 The Rebellion against God

1 Gernhardt, 'Das Buch Ewald'.
2 Bloch, *Atheism in Christianity*, p. 99.
3 See Meyer Kallen, *The Book of Job as a Greek Tragedy*; Lang, 'Ernst Bloch als Leser des Alten Testaments'; and Gradl, *Ein Atheist lies die Bibel*, pp. 199ff.
4 See Müller, *Das Hiobproblem*, pp. 23ff., and Ebach, 'Hiob/Hiobbuch', pp. 363f.
5 Concerning the tradition of lament in the Bible from the Christian theological perspective, see Brueggemann, *The Message of the Psalms*; Westermann, *Die Klagelieder*; and Lindström, *Suffering and Sin*.
6 This is more pronounced in other German translations of verse 16 (Zurich Bible, Unified Translation, Buber). Concerning the psalm, see also the commentary by Walter Gross, 'Ein Schwerkranker betet'.
7 Rilke, *Possibility of Being: A Selection of Poems*, pp. 28f.
8 Moltmann, *Der gekreuzigte Gott*, p. 142.
9 Steiner, 'Aschensage', p. 935.
10 Quoted in Marmorstein, *Studies in Jewish Theology*, p. 12. Concerning Marcion's assessment of the Hebrew Bible, see Kinzig, *Harnack, Marcion und das Judentum*. In a very similar fashion, and with the same arguments, the English theologian and mysticism scholar Robert Zaehner (in *Concordant Discord: Interdependence of Faiths*) rejected the God of the Hebrew Bible, accepting only the God of the New Testament as valid.
11 See Gross, 'Zorn Gottes, ein biblisches Theologumenon'; Ricœur, *The Symbolism of Evil*, pp. 63ff.; Kuschel, 'Ist Gott verantwortlich für das Übel?', pp. 227ff.; and Westermann, *Die Klagelieder*, pp. 78ff.
12 Concerning the distinction between the charismatic early Christian community's image of Jesus and that of the early church, see Theissen, *Das Neue Testament*.
13 TN: This refers to the weekly programme *Das Wort zum Sonntag* [The Word on Sunday], screened on channel 1 (ARD) of German national television before the late-night film, consisting of a five-minute (formerly ten-minute) speech by a clergyman or theologian.
14 See Jung, *Answer to Job*, pp. 139f.
15 See Heinrich, *Parmenides und Jona*, pp. 106ff.
16 Michael Cook, *The Koran: A Very Short Introduction*, p. 19.
17 Jung, *Answer to Job*, pp. 74ff.

18 Ibid., p. 93.
19 Westermann, *Die Klagelieder*, p. 78.
20 See Kuschel, 'Ist Gott verantwortlich für das Übel?', pp. 227f.
21 Westermann, *Die Klagelieder*, p. 6.
22 Ibid., p. 87.
23 An exemplary case can be found in Dietrich and Link, *Die dunklen Seiten Gottes*, vol. 1, p. 152; concerning the harmonization of the conception of God, see Gross, 'Zorn Gottes – ein biblisches Theologumenon', pp. 47ff.
24 See Ebach, 'Hiob/Hiobbuch', p. 371.
25 Mechthild of Magdeburg, *The Flowing Light of the Godhead*, p. 155.
26 *The Works of Meister Eckhart*, p. 41.
27 Kierkegaard, *Repetition; and, Philosophical Crumbs*, pp. 58f.
28 Kant, 'On the Miscarriage of All Philosophical Trials in Theodicy', in *Religion and Rational Theology*, p. 33.
29 See, for example, Westermann, *Die Klagelieder*, pp. 78ff., 354ff.; Fuchs, *Die Klage als Gebet*; Limbeck, 'Die Klage – eine verschwundene Gebetsgattung'; Kuschel, *Im Spiegel der Dichter*, pp. 175ff.; Kuschel, 'Ist Gott verantwortlich für das Übel?'; Oelmüller, *Worüber man nicht schweigen kann*, p. 152; and Hedinger, *Wider die Versöhnung Gottes mit dem Elend*.
30 Johann Baptist Metz, 'The Church after Auschwitz', pp. 125f.
31 See the numerous *hadiths* on this subject collected by Al-Ġazālī: *Iḥyā'*, vol. 4, pp. 398ff. (*Kitāb aṣ-ṣabr wa-š-šukr. Mawāḍi' aš-šukr fī l-balā'*).
32 Bloch, *Atheism in Christianity*, p. 102.
33 Quoted in Reinert, *Die Lehre vom tawakkul*, p. 116. See the folk tales about Job in Grünbaum, *Neue Beiträge zur semitischen Sagenkunde*, pp. 262ff.
34 See Reinert, *Die Lehre vom tawakkul*, pp. 117f.
35 See Nagel, *Die Qiṣaṣ al-anbiyā'*.
36 See Lazarus-Yafeh, *Intertwined Worlds*, p. 112.
37 Aṯ-Ṯa'labī, *Qiṣaṣ al-anbiyā'*, p. 139.
38 See Müller, *Das Hiobproblem*, pp. 27ff., and *EI2*, 'Ayyūb'.
39 Quoted in Reinert, *Die Lehre vom tawakkul*, p. 116.
40 See ibid.
41 See Ess, 'Skepticism in Islamic Religious Thought'.
42 Ibn Qayyim al-Ǧawzīya, *Iġāṯat al-lahfān fi maqāyid aš-šayṭān* (Cairo, [1320] 1903), p. 318, quoted in Ritter, *The Ocean of the Soul*, p. 165.
43 Ibn Qayyim al-Ǧawzīya, *Iġāṯat al-lahfān fi maqāyid aš-šayṭān* (Cairo, [1320] 1903), pp. 319f., quoted in Ritter, *The Ocean of the Soul*, p. 169.
44 See Al-Makkī, *Die Nahrung des Herzens*, vol. 1, p. 12.
45 Ibn Qayyim al-Ǧawzīya, *Talbis Iblīs*, p. 374; excerpts trans. in *Islamic Culture*, 12 (1938), p. 363; quoted in Ritter, *The Ocean of the Soul*, p. 168.
46 See Ritter, *The Ocean of the Soul*, p. 186.
47 Quoted ibid.
48 Omar Khayyam, *The Rubaiyat: A Selection*, p. 48.
49 Naguib Mahfouz, *Children of the Alley*, p. 12.
50 See Wielandt, 'Naǧīb Maḥfūẓ und seine Religion'.
51 See Awn, *Satan's Tragedy and Redemption*, pp. 134ff., pp. 167ff.; concerning 'Eyn ol-Qoẓāt, see also the two essays in Izutsu, *Creation and the Timeless Order of Things*, pp. 98ff.; Dabashi, *Truth and Narrative*.
52 See Reinert, *Die Lehre vom tawakkul*, pp. 112ff.; and Ormsby, *Theodicy in Islamic Thought*, pp. 41ff.

53 Quoted in Stroumsa, *Freethinkers of Medieval Islam*, p. 125.
54 Kafka, *The Great Wall of China and Other Pieces*, p. 155.
55 Quoted in Ritter, 'Studien zur Geschichte der islamischen Frömmigkeit I', p. 16.
56 Al-Ġazālī, *Iḥyā'*, vol. 5, p. 43 (*Kitāb al-ḫawf wa-r-rağā'. Bayān aḥwāl aṣ-ṣaḥāba*); see Gramlich, *Der eine Gott*, p. 217.
57 'Aṭṭār, *Elāhināmeh*, pp. 356f. (22/4).
58 Pascal, *Thoughts*, p. 77.
59 Kafka, *The Blue Octavo Notebooks*, p. 15.
60 Al-Ġazālī, *Iḥyā'*, vol. 5, pp. 236ff. (*Kitāb al-maḥabba wa-š-šawq wa-r-riḍā wa-l-uns. Bayān ma'nā al-inbisāṭ*).
61 Quoted in Andrae, *In the Garden of Myrtles*, p. 60.
62 *Kalām Sahl* (manuscript), quoted in Reinert, *Die Lehre vom tawakkul*, p. 116.
63 'Aṭṭār, *Tazkerat ol-ouliyā'*, p. 296.
64 'Aṭṭār, *Elāhināmeh*, p. 374.
65 Ibid., 116f.
66 See, for example, Reinert, *Die Lehre vom tawakkul*, pp. 117f.; al-Makkī, *Die Nahrung des Herzens*, index entry 'Hiob' [Job]; al-Qušayrī, *Das Sendschreiben*, pp. 269f.; al-Ġazālī, *Lehre von den Stufen zur Gottesliebe*, index entry 'Hiob'; Gramlich, *Alte Vorbilder*, vol. 2, p. 336.
67 Nurāni Weṣāl offers this variant of the verse in a footnote, but decides on the reading *del* instead of *dar* in his edition, which changes the meaning to 'hearts that stand open'; because this completely skews Attar's beautiful image, I consider this reading unlikely.
68 'Aṭṭār, *Elāhināmeh*, p. 99.
69 See Ritter, *The Ocean of the Soul*, p. 173.
70 'Aṭṭār, *Elāhināmeh*, p. 146.
71 Beckett, *Waiting for Godot*, p. 91.
72 See, for example, the tales of al-Ḥasan an-Nayšabūrī (d. 1015), which Attar probably used as models or at least knew in their content: Loosen, 'Die Weisen Narren des Naisabūrī'; concerning the most famous fool in Islamic intellectual history, see Marzolph, *Der weise Narr Buhlul*.
73 Kott, *Shakespeare our Contemporary*, p. 111.
74 Ibid., p. 112. TN: The German edition from which the author quotes uses the same word for 'clowns' that he uses in this book for 'fools', namely *Narren*.
75 Shakespeare, *King Lear*, IV.1, 36–7.
76 Ibid., IV.6, 42–8.
77 Kott, *Shakespeare our Contemporary*, p. 119.
78 Ibid.
79 Roth, *Job: The Story of a Simple Man*, p. 180.
80 Jung, *Answer to Job*, p. 36.
81 Bloch, *Atheism in Christianity*, p. 96.
82 Büchner, *Complete Plays, Lenz and Other Writings*, p. 162.
83 Schopenhauer, *Der Handschriftlicher Nachlass*, vol. 3, p. 57.
84 Jung, *Answer to Job*, pp. 91f.
85 'Aṭṭār, *Elāhināmeh*, 3/3, pp. 62f.
86 Ibid., 3/4, p. 63.
87 Andrae, *In the Garden of Myrtles*, p. 27.

88 Al-Ġazālī, *Iḥyā'*, vol. 4, p. 323 (*Kitāb aṣ-ṣabr wa-š-šukr. Bayān maẓān al-ḥāǧa ilā ṣ-ṣabr*).
89 Quoted in Ritter, 'Die Aussprüche des Bāyezīd Bisṭāmī', p. 238.
90 As-Suhrawardī, *Die Gaben der Erkenntnise*, p. 228.
91 See Andrae, *In the Garden of Myrtles*, p. 17.
92 Ibid.
93 Ibid., p. 18.
94 Ibid., p. 21.
95 'Aṭṭār, *Elāhināmeh*, pp. 235f.
96 'Aṭṭār, *Manṭeq oṭ-ṭeyr*, p. 30.
97 Al-Munāwī, *Faiḍ al-qadīr. Šarh alǦāmi' aṣ-ṣaġīr* (Cairo, 1938), no. 7487, quoted in Ritter, *The Ocean of the Soul*, p. 265. The same Ayyūb al-Quarašī who wrote a text on the 'Cunning of God' also devoted an entire treatise to this *hadith*, and thus to divine forgiveness; see Brockelmann, *Geschichte der arabischen Literatur*, vol. 2, pp. 449f.
98 'Aṭṭār, *Manṭeq oṭ-ṭeyr*, p. 103.
99 Ibid., p. 104.
100 'Aṭṭār, *Elāhināmeh*, pp. 53f.
101 Ibn Qayyim al-Ǧawzīya, *Talbīs Iblīs*, p. 359, trans. quoted in Ritter, *The Ocean of the Soul*, p. 335; also Ritter, 'Die Aussprüche des Bāyezīd Bisṭāmī', p. 238.
102 Ritter, 'Die Aussprüche des Bāyezīd Bisṭāmī', p. 238.
103 Quoted in Ritter, *The Ocean of the Soul*, p. 335.
104 Martin Buber, *The Prophetic Faith*, p. 191.
105 Quoted in Ritter, 'Die Aussprüche des Bāyezīd Bisṭāmī', p. 241.
106 'Aṭṭār, *Manṭeq oṭ-ṭeyr*, p. 90.
107 Ġazālī, *Gedanken über die Liebe*, p. 44 (faṣl 20); trans. quoted in Ritter, *The Ocean of the Soul*, p. 409.
108 'Aṭṭār, *Manṭeq oṭ-ṭeyr*, pp. 68ff.
109 Ibid., p. 67.
110 Baudelaire, *Intimate Journals*, p. 34.
111 Baudelaire, *The Flowers of Evil*, p. 9.
112 Büchner, *Werke und Briefe*, p. 391.
113 Abū Nu'aym al-Isfahānī, *Ḥilyat al-awliyā'*, quoted in Andrae, *In the Garden of Myrtles*, p. 117.
114 Jung, *Answer to Job*, p. 145.
115 Stroumsa, *Freethinkers of Medieval Islam*, p. 74.
116 Lévinas, *Difficult Freedom: Essays on Judaism*, pp. 142ff. Lévinas takes the formulation from Zvi Kolitz's story 'Yossel Rakover Speaks to God'.
117 See Moṭahhari, *'Adl-e elāhi*.
118 Soruš, 'Farbehtar az idi'oloği'.
119 Foruzānfar, *Aḥādis-e masnawi*, p. 42 (no. 106).
120 TN: A reference to the unfinished novel *The Good Soldier Švejk* by the Czech satirist Jaroslav Hašek.
121 Mo'inzādeh, *Komedi-ye ḫodāyān*, p. 113; see also by the same author *Ânsu-ye sar'āb*. Siyāwuš Ustā describes a conversation with a God who is very different from the God of Islam in *Ḫodā-rā dar ḫāb didam!* An author by the name of Dr Roušangar presents a theoretical disquisition on God's justice in Islam: *Allāhu akbar*, pp. 161ff.

CHAPTER 5 HISTORY OF A COUNTER-THEOLOGY

1 Lévinas, 'The Trace of the Other', p. 359.
2 See Rippin, '"Desiring the Face of God": the Qu'ranic Symbolism of Personal Responsibility', pp. 122f.
3 *The Garden of Heaven: Poems of Hafiz*, trans. Gertrude Lowthian Bell (Mineola, NY: Dover, 2003), p. 62.
4 Goll, *100 Gedichte*, p. 123.
5 Quoted in Andrae, *In the Garden of Myrtles*, p. 82.
6 Schwarzbaum, 'The Jewish and Moslem Versions of Some Theodicy Legends', p. 119.
7 West, *Greek Lyric Poetry*, p. 28.
8 Aeschylus, *Prometheus Bound*, p. 77.
9 See Kermani and Friedrich, 'Der Schrecken Gottes in Religion und Dichtung', and Shim, 'Evil and the Overcoming of Suffering in Buddhism'.
10 Somanātha, *Śiva's Warriors*, pp. 151ff.; see also Shulman, *The Hungry God*; Herman, *The Problem of Evil and Indian Thought*; and Anantharaman, 'The Hindu View on Suffering, Rebirth and the Overcoming of Evil'.
11 See Sherwood, *A Biblical Text and its Afterlives.*
12 Schimmel, *Gärten der Erkenntnis*, p. 42.
13 Berakhot 61b, quoted in Pöhlmann and Stern, *Die zehn Gebote im jüdisch-christlichen Dialog*, p. 190.
14 Sifre Deuteronomy Ha'azinu, piska 307, quoted in Laytner, *Arguing with God*, p. 66.
15 Laytner, *Arguing with God*, p. 244.
16 Sanhedrin 105a, quoted ibid., p. 184.
17 Gittin 58a, quoted ibid., p. 75.
18 See ibid., p. 115.
19 See Levine, 'Jonah as a Philosophical Book'.
20 In contrast to Buber's Jewish translation and the Unified Translation, Luther and the Zurich Bible add a causality to this verse that the Hebrew text deliberately avoids.
21 See Sherwood, *A Biblical Text and its Afterlives*, pp. 121ff., and Boyarin, *Intertextuality and the Reading of the Midrash*, pp. 22ff. and 39ff.
22 Quoted in David Blumenthal, *Facing the Abusing God: A Theology of Protest*, p. v.
23 Quoted in Laytner, *Arguing with God*, p. 158.
24 See Mark Cohen, *Under Crescent and Cross: The Jews in the Middle Ages*, pp. 180ff.
25 Buber, *Tales of the Hasidim*, p. 228.
26 Quoted in Dresner, *The World of a Hasidic Master*, p. 77. See also the portrait of Levi Yitzhak in Wiesel, *Souls on Fire: Portraits and Legends of Hasidic Masters*, pp. 89ff.
27 Quoted ibid., p. 7.
28 See Dresner, *The World of a Hasidic Master*, p. 81.
29 Quoted in Buber, *Tales of the Hasidim*, p. 209f.; also in Dresner, *The World of a Hasidic Master*, p. 82.
30 Quoted in Dresner, *The World of a Hasidic Master*, p. 81.
31 Wiesel, *Souls on Fire*, p. 10.
32 Ibid., p. 8.

33 Newman, *The Hasidic Anthology: Tales and Teachings of the Hasidim*, p. 57.
34 See Schwarzbaum, 'The Jewish and Moslem Versions of Some Theodicy Legends', p. 120.
35 See Wiesel, *Somewhere a Master: Further Hasidic Portraits and Legends*, p. 107.
36 Quoted ibid., p. 112.
37 Quoted in Laytner, *Arguing with God*, p. 191.
38 Ibid.
39 Boteach, *Wrestling with the Divine*, pp. 234ff.
40 'Afīfuddīn al-Yāfi'ī, *Rauḍat ar-rayāḥīn fī ḥikāyat aṣ-ṣāliḥīn*, quoted in Andrae, *In the Garden of Myrtles*, p. 4. The tale is a variation on a story by Abū Sulaymān ad-Dārānī; see ibid., p. 148.
41 Ibn al-Ǧawzī, *Al-Quṣṣāṣ wa-l-mudakkarīn*, MS Leiden Or. 998 III, quoted in Ritter, *The Ocean of the Soul*, p. 168.
42 Al-Ġazālī, *Iḥyā'*, vol. 5, pp. 232ff. (*Kitāb al-maḥabba wa-š-šawq wa-r-riḍā wa-l-uns. Bayān ma'nā al-inbisāṭ*).
43 *Sotah* 13b, quoted in Laytner, *Arguing with God*, pp. 64ff.
44 Lamentations Rabbah, introduction, 24, quoted ibid., pp. 76ff.
45 Newman, *The Hasidic Anthology*, p. 56.
46 See Bulliet, *The Patricians of Nishapur*, pp. 3ff.
47 See *EI2*, 'Tawrāt'.
48 See Lazarus-Yafeh, *Intertwined Worlds*, pp. 111f.
49 See Speyer, *Die biblischen Erzählungen im Qoran*.
50 Ibn Hağar, *Iṣāba*, vol. 6, p. 178, quoted in Sachedina, 'Early Muslim Traditionists and their Familiarity with Jewish Sources', p. 51.
51 See Kister, 'Ḥaddithū 'an banī isrā'īla wa-lā ḥaraja'; Adang, *Muslim Writers on Judaism and the Hebrew Bible*; Andrae, *In the Garden of Myrtles*, pp. 20ff.; Wasserstrom, *Between Muslim and Jew*, pp. 172ff.; Grünbaum, *Neue Beiträge zur semitischen Sagenkunde*; and Nagel, *Die Qiṣaṣ al-anbiyā'*.
52 Andrae, *In the Garden of Myrtles*, p. 124.
53 Goitein, *Jews and Arabs*, p. 95 and elsewhere; see also Wasserstrom, *Between Muslim and Jew*, pp. 3ff. and 216ff.
54 See *EI2*, 'Tawrāt'.
55 See Fenton, 'Judaeo-Arabic Mystical Writings of the XIIIth–XIVth Century', and Wasserstrom, *Between Muslim and Jew*, pp. 166ff.
56 How far this interlocking can extend, namely to the dissolution of supposedly self-evident religious identities, is shown by Daniel Boyarin in his book *Border Lines* using the example of Judaism and the Patrists. A comparable study on the relationship of Judaism to early and classical Islam has yet to be written.
57 The classic example in the Jewish tradition is the philosopher Salomo ibn Gabirol (Arabic: Abū Ayyūb Sulaymān ibn Yaḥyā'; in Latin sources Avicebrol, Avicebron or Avencebrol), who was taken for a Muslim or a Christian until the nineteenth century; see Hyman and Walsh, *Philosophy in the Middle Ages*, p. 358; Guttmann, *Die Philosophie des Judentums*, p. 130; and Steinschneider, *Die arabische Literatur der Juden*, p. 125. The case of the (presumably Jewish, or more precisely Kairitic) religious thinker Yūsuf al-Basir was presented by Sabine Schmidtke (Berlin) during a workshop as part of the project 'Jüdische und islamische Hermeneutik als Kulturkritik'. She provides an overview of her sources in an article published

in *Arabica*, 53/1 (2006): 'The Kairites' Encounter with the Thought of Abu l-Ḥusayn al-Baṣrī (d. 436/1044): A Survey of the Relevant Materials in the Firkovitch Collection, St Petersburg'. Together with Wilfred Madelung, Sabine Schmidtke has produced further studies and editions concerning the encounter between Kairites and Mu'tazilites. On the interaction between Jewish and Muslim theology in general, or the permeability of their boundaries, see Wasserstrom, *Between Muslim and Jew*, pp. 136ff., and Goitein, *Jews and Arabs*, pp. 140ff.

58 *Life and Works of Saint Bernard, Abbot of Clairvaux*, vol. 4, p. 268. See on this subject also Haas, *Gottleiden – Gottlieben*, pp. 127ff.; Fuchs, '"Wir sind sein Kreuz"'; and Schneider, 'Der dunkle Gott in der Mystik'.
59 Mechthild of Magdeburg, *The Flowing Light of the Godhead*, p. 118.
60 See Haas, *Mystik als Aussage*, pp. 291ff.
61 See Warning, *Funktion und Struktur*, pp. 184ff.
62 Neiman, *Evil in Modern Thought*, p. 15.
63 Makdisi, *The Rise of Humanism in Classical Islam and the Christian West, with Special Reference to Scholasticism*, p. 348.
64 Menocal, *The Arabic Role in Medieval Literary Theory*, p. 3.
65 Bloch, *Avicenna und die aristotelische Linke*.
66 Neiman, *Evil in Modern Thought*, p. 14.
67 Guthke, *Die Mythologie der entgötterten Welt*, p. 39.
68 Bayle, *An Historical and Critical Dictionary*, p. 169 (article 'Paulitians').
69 Kierkegaard, *Repetition; and, Philosophical Crumbs*, p. 59.
70 Blumenberg, *Arbeit am Mythos*, pp. 477ff.
71 *The Poems of Goethe*, p. 347.
72 Quoted in Neiman, *Evil in Modern Thought*, p. 189.
73 Dostoyevsky, *The Brothers Karamazov*, p. 320.
74 Camus, *The Plague*, p. 218.
75 Ibid., p. 128.
76 Camus, *The Rebel*, p. 23.
77 Ibid., p. 25.
78 Ibid., p. 28.
79 Ibid., p. 25.
80 Gide, *The Counterfeiters*, p. 365.
81 Lavant, *Aufzeichnungen aus einem Irrenhaus*, pp. 46f.
82 Kuschel, 'Ist Gott verantwortlich für das Übel?', p. 250.
83 TN: The word for 'despair', *Verzweiflung*, is derived from *Zweifel*, meaning 'doubt'. Taken literally, it thus suggests being overcome by doubt.
84 Heine, *Sämtliche Schriften*, vol. 5, pp. 190f.
85 Werner, *Begegnungen mit Heine*, vol. 2, p. 112.
86 Heine, *Sämtliche Schriften*, vol. 5, p. 109.
87 Ibid., vol. 6 [1], p. 549.
88 Ibid., p. 332.
89 Ibid., p. 189.
90 Ibid., p. 201.
91 Werner, *Begegnungen mit Heine*, vol. 2, p. 112.
92 Nietzsche, *The Gay Science*, p. 172.
93 Heine, *Säkularausgabe*, vol. 23, p. 20.
94 Werner, *Begegnungen mit Heine*, vol. 2, p. 123.
95 Heine, *Sämtliche Schriften*, vol. 6 [1], p. 208.

96 Ibid., p. 499.
97 Ibid., p. 325.
98 Heine, *Säkularausgabe*, vol. 23, p. 477.
99 Wagenstein, *Pentateuch*, p. 53. The formulation also appears in an old Yiddish saying: 'If the Lord God lived down there on earth, someone would long since have smashed his window' (Schwarzbaum, 'The Jewish and Moslem Versions of Some Theodicy Legends', p. 121).
100 Schindler, *Hasidic Responses to the Holocaust in the Light of Hasidic Thought*, p. 116.
101 Quoted in Huneke, *The Moses of Rovno*, p. 190.
102 Quoted ibid., p. 76.
103 Wiesel, *Was die Tore des Himmels öffnet*, p. 55. Concerning the Hasidic attitude in the death camps, see also Schindler, *Hasidic Responses to the Holocaust in the Light of Hasidic Thought*, pp. 120f. For general descriptions of Jewish devotion in the camps, see Rahe, *'Höre Israel'*, pp. 79ff.; Davidovic, 'Als Rabbiner in Auschwitz'; and Berkovits, *With God in Hell.*
104 Wiesel, *Macht Gebete aus meinen Geschichten*, p. 39.
105 See Brocke and Jochum, *Wolkensäule und Feuerschein*, pp. 20ff. and 261ff.; Schindler, *Hasidic Responses to the Holocaust in the Light of Hasidic Thought*; Boteach, *Wrestling with the Divine*, pp. 121f.; and Bowker, *Problems of Suffering*, pp. 37ff.
106 See Berkovits, *With God in Hell* and *Faith after the Holocaust.*
107 See Maybaum, *The Face of God after Auschwitz.*
108 Jonas, 'The Concept of God after Auschwitz'.
109 Fackenheim, *To Mend the World* and *God's Presence in History*. For a critical overview of Jewish-American Holocaust theology, see Katz, *Post-Holocaust Dialogues*; Münz, *Der Welt ein Gedächtnis geben*; and Leaman, *Evil and Suffering in Jewish Philosophy*, pp. 185ff.
110 Rubinstein, *After Auschwitz.*
111 Paul Celan, *Selected Poems and Prose*, p. 135.
112 Susman, *Das Buch Hiob und das Schicksal des jüdischen Volkes*, p. 43.
113 H. A. Gornik (ed.), *Tag- und Nachtgedanken: Ein Brevier durch das Jahr* (Freiburg: Christophorus, 1987), p. 210, here quoted in Dietrich and Link, *Die dunklen Seiten Gottes*, vol. 2, p. 93. Elie Wiesel told of a similar incident at a conference in Loccum; see Kuschel, *Im Spiegel der Dichter*, p. 244.
114 Heine, *Säkularausgabe*, vol. 23, p. 470.
115 Heine, *Sämtliche Schriften*, vol. 6 [1], p. 549.
116 See Fackenheim, *God's Presence in History*, p. 76.
117 Quoted in Laytner, *Arguing with God*, pp. 228f.
118 Quoted ibid., p. 229.
119 'Aṭṭār, *Tazkerat ol-ouliyā'*, p. 565.
120 Zvi Kolitz, *Yossel Rakover Speaks to God*, pp. 25f.
121 See Russell, *Mephistopheles*; and Stanford, *The Devil: A Biography.*
122 Aš-Šahrastānī, *Tawḍīḥ al-milal*, pp. 29f.
123 Ibn al-Ǧawzī, *Kitāb al-quṣṣāṣ wa-l-mudakkarīn*, ed. Merlin S. Swartz (Beirut, 1971), quoted in Schimmel, *Mystical Dimensions of Islam*; see Ritter, *The Ocean of the Soul*, p. 558.
124 See Awn, *Satan's Tragedy and Redemption.*
125 Victor Hugo, 'The End of Satan', quoted in Russell, *Mephistopheles*, p. 200.
126 Al-Ḥallāǧ, *'O Leute, rettet mich vor Gott'*, p. 25.

127 Al-Ḥallāğ, *Kitāb aṭ-ṭawāsīn*, p. 41.
128 See Awn, *Satan's Tragedy and Redemption*, pp. 176ff., and Scarcia, 'Iblīs in 'Aṭṭār'.
129 Susman, *Das Buch Hiob und das Schicksal des jüdischen Volkes*, p. 42.
130 Ibid., p. 119.
131 Ibid., p. 47.
132 Ibid., p. 131.
133 Quoted without attribution in Boteach, *Wrestling with the Divine*, pp. 111f.
134 Heine, *Sämtliche Schriften*, vol. 6 [1], p. 569.
135 Ibid., p. 311.
136 Heine, *Säkularausgabe*, vol. 23, pp. 19f.
137 'Aṭṭār, *Elāhināmeh*, pp. 376f.

REFERENCES AND BIBLIOGRAPHY

Adang, Camilla: *Muslim Writers on Judaism and the Hebrew Bible: From Ibn Rabban to Ibn Hazm* (Leiden: Brill, 1996).

Adorno, Theodor W.: *Gesammelte Schriften*, 20 vols, ed. Rolf Tiedemann (Frankfurt: Suhrkamp, 1997).

—: *Mahler: A Musical Physiognomy*, trans. Edmund Jephcott (Chicago: University of Chicago Press, 1996).

—: *Prisms*, trans. Samuel and Shierry Weber (Cambridge, MA: MIT Press, 1983).

Aeschylus: *Prometheus Bound*, trans. James Scully and C. J. Herington (Oxford: Oxford University Press, 1990).

Aflāki, Šamsoddīn Aḥmad: *The Feats of the Knowers of God (Manāqib al-ʻarifīn)*, trans. K. John O'Kane (Leiden: Brill, 2002).

Alcalay, Ammiel: *After Jews and Arabs: Remaking Levantine Culture* (Minneapolis: University of Minnesota Press, 1993).

Ammicht-Quinn, Regina: *Von Lissabon bis Auschwitz: Zum Paradigmawechsel in der Theodizeefrage* (Freiburg: Universitätsverlag, 1992).

Anantharaman, Tanjore J.: 'The Hindu View on Suffering, Rebirth and the Overcoming of Evil', in Peter Koslowski (ed.), *The Origin and the Overcoming of Evil and Suffering in the World Religions* (Dordrecht: Kluwer Academic, 2001), pp. 100–12.

Andrae, Tor: *In the Garden of Myrtles: Studies in Early Islamic Mysticism*, trans. Birgitta Sharpe (Albany: State University of New York Press, 1987).

Anijar, Gil: *The Jew, the Arab: A History of the Enemy* (Palo Alto, CA: Stanford University Press, 2003).

Anonymous: *Die Lebensweise der Könige: Adab al-Mulīk: Ein Handbuch zur islamischen Mystik*, ed. and trans. Richard Gramlich (Stuttgart: Deutsche Morgenländische Gesellschaft, 1993).

Aquinas, Thomas: *Summa contra gentiles*, 5 vols, trans. Anton C. Pegis et al. (Notre Dame, IN: University of Notre Dame Press, 1975).

Arberry, Arthur John: *Sufism: An Account of the Mystics of Islam* (Mineola, NY: Dover, 2001).

al-Ašʻarī, Abu l-Ḥasan: *Al-Ibānah ʻan uṣūl ad-diyāna*, ed. Fawqīya Ḥusayn Maḥmūd (Cairo, [1397] 1977).

Assmann, Jan: *Die mosaische Unterscheidung oder Der Preis des Monotheismus* (Munich, Carl Hanser, 2003).
'Aṭṭār, Faridoddin: *Elāhināmeh*, ed. Hellmut Ritter (Tehran, [1359] 1980).
—: *Asrārnāmeh*, ed. Ṣādeq Gouhareyn (Tehran, [1361] 1982).
—: *Moṣibatnāmeh*, ed. Nurāni Weṣāl (Tehran, [1973] 1994).
—: *Manṭeq oṭ-ṭeyr*, ed. Ṣādeq Gouhareyn (Tehran, [1374] 1995).
—: *Tazkerat ol-ouliyā'*, ed. Parvin Qā'emi (Tehran, [1381] 2002).
Auerbach, Erich: *Mimesis: Dargestellte Wirklichkeit in der abendländischen Literatur* (Tübingen and Basel: Saur, 1994).
Augustine: *The Works of Saint Augustine: A Translation for the 21st Century* (Hyde Park, NY: New City Press, 2001)
Averroës: see Ibn Rušd.
Avicenna: see Ibn Sīna.
Awn, Peter J.: *Satan's Tragedy and Redemption: Iblis in Sufi Psychology* (Leiden: Brill, 1983).
Banani, Amin, Hovannisian, Richard, and Sabagh, Georges (eds): *Poetry and Mysticism in Islam: The Heritage of Rumi* (Cambridge: Cambridge University Press, 1994).
Barthold, W.: *Turkestan: Down to the Mongol Invasion* (London: Luzac, 1977).
Baudelaire, Charles: *Paris Spleen, 1869*, trans. Louise Varèse (New York: New Directions, 1970).
—: *Intimate Journals*, trans. Christopher Isherwood (San Francisco: City Lights, 1983).
—: *The Flowers of Evil*, trans. Jackson Mathews (New York: New Directions, 1989).
Baudrillard, Jean: *The Transparency of Evil: Essays on Extreme Phenomena*, trans. James Benedict (London: Verso, 1993).
Bauke-Ruegg, Jan: *Die Allmacht Gottes: Systematisch-theologische Erwägungen zwischen Metaphysik, Postmoderne und Poesie* (Berlin: de Gruyter, 1998).
Bayle, Pierre: *An Historical and Critical Dictionary*, 4 vols. (London: Hunt & Clarke, 1826).
Beckett, Samuel: *Waiting for Godot* (New York: Grove, 1982).
Beinert, Wolfgang (ed.): *Gott – ratlos vor dem Bösen?* (Freiburg: Herder, 1999).
Bencheikh, Jamal Eddine (ed. and trans.): *Le Voyage nocturne de Mahomet* (Paris: La Documentation Française, 1988).
Berger, Klaus: 'Das Böse im Neuen Testament', in Friedrich Hermanni and Peter Koslowski (eds), *Die Wirklichkeit des Bösen: Systematisch-theologische und philosophische Annäherungen* (Munich: Fink, 1998), pp. 133–48.
Berkovits, Eliezer: *Faith after the Holocaust* (Hoboken, NJ: KTAV, 1973).
—: *With God in Hell: Judaism in the Ghettos and Death Camps* (New York and London: Sanhedrin Press, 1979).
Bernard of Clairvaux: *Life and Works of Saint Bernard, Abbot of Clairvaux*, 4 vols. (London: John Hodges, 1896).
Birnbaum, David: *God and Evil: A Unified Theodicy, Theology, Philosophy* (Hoboken, NJ: KTAV, 1989).
Bloch, Ernst: *Avicenna und die aristotelische Linke* (Frankfurt: Suhrkamp, 1963).
—: *Atheism in Christianity: The Religion of the Exodus and the Kingdom*, trans. J. T. Swann (New York: Herder & Herder, 1972).
Blumenberg, Hans: *Matthäuspassion* (Frankfurt: Suhrkamp, 1988).

—: *Arbeit am Mythos* (Frankfurt: Suhrkamp, 2001).
Blumenthal, David R.: *Facing the Abusing God: A Theology of Protest* (Louisville, KY: Westminster/John Knox Press, 1993).
Boccaccio, Giovanni: *The Decameron*, trans. Guido Waldman (Oxford: Oxford University Press, 1998).
Borges, Jorge Luis: *Die letzte Reise des Odysseus* (Munich: Hanser, 1987).
Boteach, Samuel: *Wrestling with the Divine: A Jewish Response to Suffering* (Northvale, NJ: J. Aronson, 1995).
Bowker, John: *Problems of Suffering in Religions of the World* (Cambridge: Cambridge University Press, 1975).
Boyarin, Daniel (ed.): *Intertextuality and the Reading of the Midrash* (Bloomington and Indianapolis: Indiana University Press, 1994).
—: *Border Lines: The Partition of Judaeo-Christianity* (Philadelphia: University of Pennsylvania Press, 2004).
Boyle, J. A. (ed.): *The Cambridge History of Iran*, Vol. 5: *The Saljuq and Mongol Periods* (Cambridge: Cambridge University Press, 1968).
Brocke, Michael, and Jochum, Herbert (eds): *Wolkensäule und Feuerschein: Jüdische Theologie des Holocaust* (Munich: Kaiser, 1982).
Brockelmann, Carl: *Geschichte der arabischen Literatur*, 2 vols. (Leiden: Brill, 1943, 1949); supplementary vols. 1–3 (Leiden: Brill, 1937–42).
Brown, Norman: *Apocalypse and/or Metamorphosis* (Berkeley: University of California Press, 1991).
Brown, Peter: *Augustine of Hippo: A Biography* (Berkeley: University of California Press, 2000).
Bruckstein, Almut S.: *Die Maske des Moses: Studien zur jüdischen Hermeneutik* (Berlin and Vienna: Philo, 2001).
Brueggemann, Walter: *The Message of the Psalms: A Theological Commentary* (Minneapolis: Ausgburg Fortress, 1984).
Bruijn, J. T. P.: 'Comparative Notes on Sana'i and 'Attar', *Sufi*, 16 (winter 1992–3), pp. 13–19.
Buber, Martin: *Ecstatic Confessions*, trans. Esther Cameron (Syracuse, NY: Syracuse University Press, 1996).
—: *The Prophetic Faith*, trans. Carlyle Witton-Davies (New York: Harper & Row, 1960).
—: *Tales of the Hasidim*, trans. Olga Marx (New York: Schocken, 1991).
Büchner, Georg: *Complete Plays, Lenz and Other Writings*, trans. John Reddick (London: Penguin, 1993).
Büchner, Georg: *Werke und Briefe*, ed. Karl Pörnbacher (Munich: Hanser, 1988).
Bulliet, Richard W.: *The Patricians of Nishapur: A Study in Medieval Islamic Social History* (Cambridge, MA: Harvard University Press, 1972).
Calvin, John: *Institutes of the Christian Religion*, 3 vols. (Edinburgh: Calvin Translation Society, 1845–6).
Camus, Albert: *The Plague*, trans. Stuart Gilbert (New York: Vintage Books, 1991).
—: *The Myth of Sisyphus and Other Essays*, trans. Justin O'Brien (New York: Vintage Books, 1991).
—: *The Rebel*, trans. Anthony Bower (New York: Vintage Books, 1992).
Cardini, Franco: *Europa und der Islam: Geschichte eines Missverständnisses*, trans. Rita Suess (Munich: Beck, 2000).

Celan, Paul: *Selected Poems and Prose of Paul Celan*, ed. and trans. John Felstiner (New York and London: Norton, 2001).
Chaucer, Geoffrey: *Complete Works of Geoffrey Chaucer*, ed. W. W. Skeat (Oxford: Oxford University Press, 1900).
Cioran, E. M.: *The Trouble with Being Born* (New York: Arcade, 1998).
Cohen, Hermann: *Religion of Reason out of the Sources of Judaism*, trans. Simon Kaplan (New York: F. Ungar, 1972).
Cohen, Mark R.: *Under Crescent and Cross: The Jews in the Middle Ages* (Princeton, NJ: Princeton University Press, 1994).
Colpe, Carsten, and Schmidt-Biggemann, Wilhelm (eds): *Das Böse: Eine historische Phänomenologie des Unerklärlichen* (Frankfurt: Suhrkamp, 1993).
Cook, Michael: *The Koran: A Very Short Introduction* (Oxford: Oxford University Press, 2000).
Curtius, Ernst Robert: *Europäische Literatur und lateinisches Mittelalter* (Berne and Munich: Francke, 1984).
Dabashi, Hamid: *Truth and Narrative: The Untimely Thoughts of 'Ayn al-Qudat al-Hamadhani* (Richmond, Surrey: Curzon, 1999).
Dante Alighieri: *The Divine Comedy*, trans. Mark Musa (London: Penguin, 2002).
Davidovic, Emil: 'Als Rabbiner in Auschwitz', in Günther Bernd Ginzel, *Auschwitz als Herausforderung für Juden und Christen* (Heidelberg: L. Schneider, 1980), pp. 431–8.
Dietrich, Walter, and Link, Christian: *Die dunklen Seiten Gottes*, 2 vols. (Neukirchen-Vluyn: Neukirchener, 2002).
D'Iori, Paolo, 'Beiträge zur Quellenforschung', *Nietzsche-Studien*, 21 (1992), pp. 398–400.
Dostoyevsky, Fyodor: *The Brothers Karamazov*, trans. David McDuff (London: Penguin, 2003).
Doulatšah ebn-e 'Alā'oddoulat: *Tazkerat oš-šo'arā'*, ed. Edward G. Browne (London and Leiden, 1901).
Dresner, Samuel H.: *The World of a Hasidic Master: Levi Yitzhak of Berditchev* (New York, 1986).
Ebach, Jürgen: 'Hiob/Hiobbuch', in *Theologische Realenzyklopädie*, vol. 15 (1986), pp. 360–80.
Eckhart, Meister: *The Works of Meister Eckhart*, ed. and trans. Franz Pfeiffer (Whitefish, MT: Kessinger, 1992).
Eliade, Mircea: *The Sacred and the Profane: The Nature of Religion*, trans. Willard R. Trask (Orlando, FL: Harcourt, 1987).
Encyclopaedia Iranica (London: Routledge, 1985–) [*EIran*].
The Encyclopaedia of Islam (Leiden: Brill, 1954–2008) [*EI2*].
Eörsi, István: *Hiob und Heine: Passagiere im Niemandsland* (Klagenfurt: Wieser, 1999).
Ess, Josef van: 'Skepticism in Islamic Religious Thought', *al-Abhath*, 21 (1968), pp. 1–18.
—: *Theologie und Gesellschaft im 2. und 3. Jahrhundert Hidschra: Eine Geschichte des religiösen Denkens* (Berlin: de Gruyter, 1997).
Faber du Faur, Curt von: 'Andreas Gryphius, der Rebell', *Publications of the Modern Language Association of America*, 74 (1959), pp. 14–27.
Fackenheim, Emil L.: *God's Presence in History: Jewish Affirmations and Philosophical Reflections* (New York: New York University Press, 1970).

—: *To Mend the World: Foundations of Future Jewish Thought* (New York: Schocken, 1982).
Fāżeli, Qāder: *Farhang-e mouż'i-ye adab-e pārsi: Moṣibatnāmeh wa Maẓhar ol-'ağāyeb* (Tehran, [1374] 1995).
Feiz, Reza: 'Le merveilleux et paradoxal voyage de 'Aṭṭār à travers le *Livre de l'Épreuve*', *Luqman: Annales des Presses Universitaires d'Iran*, 14/1 (1997–8), pp. 7–21.
Felstiner, John: *Paul Celan: Poet, Survivor, Jew* (New Haven, CT: Yale University Press, 2001).
Fenton, Paul B.: 'Judaeo-Arabic Mystical Writings of the XIIIth–XIVth Century', in Norman Golb, *Judaeo-Arabic Studies* (London and New York: Routledge, 1997), pp. 87–101.
Fielding, Henry: *Journey from This World to the Next* (Oxford: Oxford University Press, 1997).
Foruzānfar, Badi' oz-zamān, *Aḥadis-e masnawi* (Tehran, [1361] 1982).
—: *Šarḥe aḥwāl wa naqd wa taḥli-e āsār-e Šeyḫ Faridoddin-e Moḥammad-e 'Aṭṭār-e Neyšāburi* (Tehran, [1374] 1995).
Foucault, Michel: *The Order of Things: An Archaeology of the Human Sciences* (London and New York: Routledge, 2002).
Frye, Richard N.: *The Golden Age of Persia: The Arabs in the East* (London: Weidenfeld & Nicolson, 1988).
Fuchs, Gotthard (ed.): *Angesichts des Leids an Gott glauben? Zur Theologie der Klage* (Frankfurt: Knecht, 1996).
—: ' "Wir sind sein Kreuz": Mystik und Theodizee', in Fuchs (ed.), *Angesichts des Leids an Gott glauben?* (Frankfurt: Knecht, 1996), pp. 148–83.
Fuchs, Ottmar: *Die Klage als Gebet: Eine theologische Bestimmung am Beispiel des Psalms 22* (Munich: Kösel, 1982).
al-Ġazālī, Abū Ḥāmid Muḥammad: *Al-Maqṣad al-asnā fi šarḥ ma'ānī asmā' Allāh al-ḥusnā*, ed. Fadlou A. Shehadi (Beirut, 1971).
—: *Iḥyā' 'ulūm ad-dīn*, 6 vols. (Beirut, n.d.); partial trans.: *Al-Ghazali's Book of Fear and Hope*, trans. William McKane (Leiden, Brill: 1965).
Ġazālī (Ghazzali), Aḥmad ebn-e Moḥammad: *Gedanken über die Liebe*, trans. Gisela Wendt (Amsterdam and Bonn: Castrum Peregrini, 1989).
Gernhardt, Robert: 'Das Buch Ewald', in Gernhardt, *Kippfigur* (Munich: Heyne, 1995).
Geyer, Carl-Friederich: 'Das Übel und die Allmacht Gottes: Die Theodizeefrage in der Philosophie', in Michael Nüchtern (ed.), *Warum lässt Gott das zu? Kritik der Allmacht Gottes in Religion und Philosophie* (Frankfurt: Lembeck, 1995), pp. 36–61.
Gibbs, Robert, and Wolfson, Elliot R. (eds): *Suffering Religion* (London and New York: Routledge, 2002).
Gide, André: *The Counterfeiters* (New York: Knopf, 1951).
Ginzel, Günther Bernd: *Auschwitz als Herausforderung für Juden und Christen* (Heidelberg: L. Schneider, 1980).
Goethe, Johann Wolfgang von: *The Poems of Goethe* (Whitefish, MT: Kessinger, 2004).
Goitein, Shlomo D.: *Jews and Arabs: A Concise History of their Social and Cultural Relations*, intr. Mark R. Cohen (Mineola, NY: Dover, 2005).
Golb, Norman (ed.): *Judaeo-Arabic Studies: Proceedings of the Founding*

Conference of the Society for Judaeo-Arabic Studies (London and New York: Routledge, 1997).

Goll, Yvan: *100 Gedichte*, ed. Barbara Glauert-Hesse (Göttingen: Wallstein, 2003).

Goodman, Lenn E.: 'Maimonides' Responses to Sa'adya Gaon's Theodicy and their Islamic Background', in William M. Brinner and Stephen D. Ricks (eds), *Studies in Islamic and Judaic Traditions II: Papers Presented at the Institute for Islamic-Judaic Studies, Center for Judaic Studies, University of Denver* (Atlanta: American Scholars Press, 1986), pp. 3–22.

—: *Avicenna* (London and New York: Routledge, 1992).

Gradl, Felix W.: *Ein Atheist Liest die Bibel: Ernst Bloch und das Alte Testament* (Frankfurt: Lang, 1979).

Gramlich, Richard: *Alte Vorbilder des Sufitums*, 2 vols. (Wiesbaden: Harrassowitz, 1995–6).

—: *Der eine Gott: Grundzüge der Mystik des islamischem Monotheismus* (Wiesbaden: Harrassowitz, 1998).

Gross, Walter: *'Ich schaffe Finsternis und Unheil!': Ist Gott verantwortlich für das Übel?* (Mainz: M. Grünewald, 1992).

—: 'Ein schwerkranker betet: Psalm 88 als Paradigma', in Gotthard Fuchs (ed.), *Angesichts des Leids an Gott glauben?* (Frankfurt: Knecht, 1996), pp. 83–118.

—: 'Zorn Gottes – ein biblisches Theologoumenon', in Wolfgang Beinert (ed.), *Gott – ratlos vor dem Bösen?* (Freiburg: Herder, 1999), pp. 47–85.

Grünbaum, M.: *Neue Beiträge zur semitischen Sagenkunde* (Leiden: Brill, 1893).

Grunebaum, Gustav Edmund von: 'Observations on the Muslim Concept of Evil', *Studia Islamica*, 31 (1969), pp. 117–34.

Gryphius, Andreas: *Lyrische Gedichte*, ed. Hermann Palm (Hildesheim: G. Olms, 1961).

—: *Gedichte: Eine Auswahl*, ed. Adalbert Elschenbroich (Stuttgart: Reclam, 1996).

Guthke, Karl S.: *Die Mythologie der entgötterten Welt: Ein literarisches Thema von der Aufklärung bis zur Gegenwart* (Göttingen: Vandenhoeck & Ruprecht, 1971).

Guttman, Julius: *Die Philosophie des Judentums*, intr. Fritz Bamberger (Berlin: Jüdische Verlagsanstalt, 2000).

Haas, Alois Maria: *Gottleiden – Gottlieben: Zur volkssprachlichen Mystik im Mittelalter* (Frankfurt: Insel, 1989).

—: *Mystik als Aussage: Erfahrungs-, Denk- und Religionsformen christlicher Mystik* (Frankfurt: Suhrkamp, 1996).

—: *Mystik im Kontext* (Munich: Fink, 2004).

Al-Ḥallāǧ (al-Hallaj), Al-Ḥusayn ibn Manṣūr: *Kitāb aṭ-ṭawāsīn*, ed. Louis Massignon (Paris, 1913).

—: *The Tawasin of Mansur Al-Hallaj* (London: Diwan Press, 1974).

—: *'O Leute, rettet mich vor Gott': Worte verzehrender Gottessehnsucht*, trans. and intr. Annemarie Schimmel, ed. Gertrude Sartory and Thomas Sartory (Freiburg: Herder, 1985).

Ḥamidi, Mehdi: *'Aṭṭār dar masnawihā-ye gozide-ye u wa gozide-ye masnawihā-ye u* (Tehran, [1347] 1968).

Harnack, Adolf von: *Marcion: Das Evangelium vom fremden Gott: Eine Monographie zur Geschichte der Grundlegung der katholischen Kirche* (Leipzig: Hinrichs, 1924).

Hary, Benjamin, Hayes, John L., and Astren, Fred (eds): *Judaism and Islam: Boundaries, Communication and Interaction: Essays in Honor of William M. Brinner* (Leiden: Brill, 2000).
Haskins, Charles Homer: *The Renaissance of the Twelfth Century* (Cambridge, MA: Harvard University Press, 1973).
Hedāyat, Ṣādeq: *Payām-e Kāfkā* (Tehran, [1342] 1963).
—: *Zendeh be-gur* (Tehran, [1342] 1963).
—: *The Blind Owl*, trans. D. P. Costello (London: Weidenfeld & Nicolson, 1989)
Hedinger, Ulrich: *Wider die Versöhnung Gottes mit dem Elend: Eine Kritik des christlichen Theismus und A-Theismus* (Zurich: Theologischer Verlag, 1972).
Heine, Heinrich: *Säkularausgabe der Werke – Briefwechsel – Lebenszeugnisse*, ed. Fritz H. Eisner (Berlin and Paris: Akademie-Verlag, 1972).
—: *Sämtliche Schriften*, 6 vols., ed. Klaus Briegleb (Munich: dtv, 1997).
Heinrich, Klaus: *Parmenides und Jona: Vier Studien über das Verhältnis von Philosophie und Mythologie* (Frankfurt: Stroemfeld, 1982).
Herman, Arthur L.: *The Problem of Evil and Indian Thought* (Delhi: Motilal Banarsidass, 1976).
Hermanni, Friedrich, and Koslowski, Peter (eds): *Die Wirklichkeit des Bösen: Systematisch-theologische und philosophische Annäherungen* (Munich: Fink, 1998).
Höhn, Gerhard (ed.): *Heinrich Heine: Ästhetisch-politische Profile* (Frankfurt: Suhrkamp, 1991).
Holbein, Ulrich: *Ich bin grösser als Allah! Lebensbilder komischer Derwische* (forthcoming).
Horkheimer, Max: *Die Sehnsucht nach dem ganz Anderen: Ein Interview mit Kommentar von Hellmut Gumnior* (Hamburg: Furche, 1970).
—: *Critique of Instrumental Reason* (London and New York: Continuum, 1983).
Houtsma, M. T.: 'Zum Kitāb al-Fihrist', *Wiener Zeitschrift für die Kunde des Morgenlandes*, 4 (1890), pp. 216–35.
Hume, David: *Dialogues Concerning Natural Religion* (Cambridge: Cambridge University Press, 2007).
Huneke, Douglas K.: *The Moses of Rovno* (New York: Dodd, Mead, 1985).
Hyman, Arthur, and Walsh, James J. (eds): *Philosophy in the Middle Ages: The Christian, Islamic and Jewish Traditions* (Indianapolis: Hackett, 1983).
Ibn 'Abbād: *Letters on the Ṣūfī Path*, trans. and intr. John Renard (New York: Paulist Press, 1986).
Ibn al-Ǧawzī, Abdurraḥmān ibn 'Alī: *Talbīs Iblīs* (Cairo, [c.1347] 1968); excerpt trans. D. S. Margoliouth: 'The Devil's Delusion', *Islamic Culture*, 12 (1938), pp. 352–64.
Ibn Maymūn (Maimonides): *The Guide for the Perplexed* (Charleston, SC: Forgotten Books, [1925]).
Ibn Rušd (Averroës), Abu l-Walid Muḥammad ibn Aḥmad: *The Philosophy and Theology of Averroës*, trans. Mohammad Jamil-ur-Rehman (Baroda: A. G. Widgery, 1921).
Ibn Sīnā (Avicenna), Abū 'Alī al-Ḥusayn: 'Risāla fī l-azrāq', *Maǧallat al Maǧma' al-'ilmī al-'arabī*, 25 (1950), pp. 199–209.
Izutsu, Toshihiko: *Creation and the Timeless Order of Things: Essays in Islamic Mystical Philosophy* (Ashland, OR: White Cloud Press, 1994).
Jonas, Hans: 'The Concept of God after Auschwitz: A Jewish Voice', in

Alan Rosenberg and Gerald E. Myers (eds), *Echoes from the Holocaust: Philosophical Reflections on a Dark Time* (Philadelphia: Temple University Press, 1990), pp. 292–305.
—: *Philosophische Untersuchungen und metaphysische Vermutungen* (Frankfurt: Suhrkamp, 1994).
Jung, C. G.: *Answer to Job*, trans. R. F. C. Hull (London and New York: Routledge, 1984).
Jung, Leo: *Fallen Angels in Jewish, Christian and Mohammedan Literature* (Eugene, OR: Wipf & Stock, 2007).
Kafka, Franz: *The Great Wall of China and Other Pieces*, trans. Edwin Muir and Willa Muir (London: Secker & Warburg, 1933).
—: *The Blue Octavo Notebooks*, ed. Max Brod, trans. Ernst Kaiser and Eithne Wilkins (Cambridge, MA: Exact Change, 1991).
Kant, Immanuel: *Religion and Rational Theology*, trans. Allen W. Wood and George Di Giovanni (Cambridge: Cambridge University Press, 2001).
Kasper, Walter: *Der Gott Jesu Christi* (Mainz: M. Grünewald, 1982).
Katz, Steven T.: *Post-Holocaust Dialogues: Critical Studies in Modern Jewish Thought* (New York: New York University Press, 1983).
Kermani, Navid: 'Der Aufrag des Dichters: Ṣādeq Hedāyat über Kafka und über sich selbst', in Stephan Guth, Priska Furrer and Johann Christoph Bürgel (eds), *Conscious Voices: Concepts of Writing in the Middle East: Proceedings of the Berne Symposium, July 1997* (Beirut and Stuttgart: Steiner, 1999), pp. 121–42.
—: *Gott ist schön: Das ästhetische Erleben des Koran* (Munich: Beck, 1999).
—: *Iran: Die Revolution der Kinder* (Munich: Beck, 2001).
Kermani, Navid, and Friedrich, Michael: 'Der Schrecken Gottes in Religion und Dichtung', in Dieter Grimm (ed.), *Wissenschaftskolleg zu Berlin: Jahrbuch 2001/2002* (Berlin, 2003), pp. 366–9.
Khayyam, Omar: *The Rubaiyat: A Selection,* trans. Parvine Mahmoud (New York: Carlton Press, 1996).
Kierkegaard, Søren: *Repetition; and, Philosophical Crumbs*, trans. M. G. Piety (Oxford: Oxford University Press, 2009).
Kinzig, Wolfgang: *Harnack, Marcion und das Judentum: Nebst einer kommentierten Edition des Briefwechsels Adolf von Harnacks mit Houston Stewart Chamberlain* (Leipzig: Evangelische Verlagsanstalt, 2004).
Kister, Kurt: 'Ḥaddithū 'an banī isrā'īla wa-lā ḥaraja: A Study of an Early Tradition', *Israel Oriental Studies*, 2 (1972), pp. 215–39.
Kolitz, Zvi: *Yossel Rakover Speaks to God: Holocaust Challenges to Religious Faith* (Hoboken: KTAV, 1995).
Koslowski, Peter (ed.): *The Origin and the Overcoming of Evil and Suffering in the World Religions* (Dordrecht: Kluwer Academic, 2001).
Koslowski, Peter, and Hermanni, Friedrich (eds): *Der leidende Gott: Eine philosophische und theologische Kritik* (Munich: Fink, 2001).
Kott, Jan: *Shakespeare our Contemporary*, trans. Bolesław Taborski (London: Methuen, 1967).
Kraemer, David Charles: *Responses to Suffering in Classical Rabbinic Literature* (Oxford: Oxford University Press, 1995).
Kraemer, Joel L.: *Humanism in the Renaissance of Islam: The Cultural Revival during the Buyid Age* (Leiden: Brill, 1992).
Kremer, Dieter: 'Islamische Einflüsse auf Dantes "Göttliche Komödie"', in

Wolfhart Heinrichs (ed.), *Neues Handbuch der Literaturwissenschaft: Orientalisches Mittelalter* (Wiesbaden: Aula-Verlag, 1990), pp. 202–15.

Kruse, Joseph A.: 'Heinrich Heine – der Lazarus', in Gerhard Höhn (ed.), *Heinrich Heine: Ästhetisch-politische Profile* (Frankfurt: Suhrkamp, 1991), pp. 258–75.

Kuhn, Peter: *Gottes Trauer und Klage in der rabbinischen Überlieferung (Talmud und Midrasch)* (Leiden: Brill, 1978).

Künkel, Hans: *Das Labyrinth der Welt: Der Roman des Comenius* (Stuttgart: Reclam, 1956).

Kuschel, Karl-Josef: *'Vielleicht hält sich Gott einige Dichter': Literarisch-theologische Porträts* (Mainz: W. Grünewald, 1991).

—: 'Ist Gott verantwortlich für das Übel? Überlegungen zu einer Theologie der Anklage', in Gotthard Fuchs (ed.), *Angesichts des Leids an Gott glauben? Zur Theologie der Klage* (Frankfurt: Knecht, 1996), pp. 227–61.

—: *Im Spiegel der Dichter: Mensch, Gott und Jesus in der Literatur des 20. Jahrhunderts* (Düsseldorf: Patmos, 2000).

—: *Gottes grausamer Spass? Heinrich Heines Leben mit der Katastrophe* (Düsseldorf: Patmos, 2002).

Lactantius: *The Wrath of God*, in *Minor Works*, trans. Sister Mary Francis McDonald (Washington, DC: Catholic University of America Press, 1965).

Lambton, Ann K. S.: *Continuity and Change in Medieval Persia: Aspects of Administrative, Economic and Social History, 11th–14th Century* (New York: State University of New York Press, 1988).

Lang, Bernhard: 'Ernst Bloch als Leser des Alten Testaments', *Theologische Quartalsschrift*, 158 (1978), pp. 110–20.

Langenhorst, Georg (ed.): *Hiobs Schrei in die Gegenwart: Ein literarisches Lesebuch zur Frage nach Gott im Leid* (Mainz: M. Grünewald, 1995).

Lavant, Christine: *Aufzeichnungen aus einem Irrenhaus*, ed. Annette Steinsiek and Ursula A. Schneider (Salzburg and Vienna: Otto Müller, 2002).

Laytner, Anson: *Arguing with God: A Jewish Tradition* (Northvale, NJ: Jason Aronson, 1990).

Lazarus-Yafeh, Hava: *Intertwined Worlds: Medieval Islam and Bible Criticism* (Princeton, NJ: Princeton University Press, 1992).

Leaman, Oliver: *Evil and Suffering in Jewish Philosophy* (Cambridge: Cambridge University Press, 1997).

—: 'Job and Suffering in Talmudic and Kabbalistic Judaism', in Peter Koslowski (ed.), *The Origin and the Overcoming of Evil and Suffering in the World Religions* (Dordrecht: Kluwer Academic, 2001), pp. 80–99.

Leibniz, Gottfried Wilhelm: *Theodicy: Essays on the Goodness of God, the Freedom of Man, and the Origin of Evil* (La Salle, IL: Open Court, 1990).

Leibowitz, Yeshayahu: *Judaism, Human Values, and the Jewish State*, ed. and trans. Eliezer Goldman et al. (Cambridge, MA: Harvard University Press, 1992).

Lentz, Wolfgang: 'Attar als Allegoriker: Bemerkungen zu Ritters *Meer der Seele*', *Der Islam*, 35 (1960), pp. 52–96.

Lévinas, Emmanuel: *Difficult Freedom: Essays on Judaism* (London: Athlone Press, 1990).

—: 'The Trace of the Other', trans. A. Lingis, in M. C. Taylor (ed.), *Deconstruction in Context* (Chicago: University of Chicago Press, 1986), pp. 345–59.

Levine, Etan: 'Jonah as a Philosophical Book', *Zeitschrift für die alttestamentliche Wissenschaft*, 96 (1984), pp. 235–45.

Limbeck, Meinrad: 'Die Klage – eine verschwundene Gebetsgattung', *Theologische Quartalsschrift*, 157 (1977), pp. 3–16.
Lindström, Frederik: *Suffering and Sin: Interpretations of Illness in the Individual Complaint Psalms* (Stockholm: Almqvist & Wiksell International, 1984).
Loosen, P.: 'Die weisen Narren des Naisabūrī', *Zeitschrift für Assyriologie und verwandte Gebiete*, 27 (1912), pp. 184–229.
Lütkehaus, Ludger: *Nichts: Abschied vom Sein: Ende der Angst* (Zurich: Haffmans, 1999).
al-Ma'arrī, Abu l-'Alā': *Risālat al-Ġufrān* (Beirut, 1964); partial trans: 'The *Risālatu'l-Ghufrān* by Abu l-'Alā' Ma'arrī: Summarized and Partially Translated by Reynold A. Nicholson', *Journal of the Royal Asiatic Society* (1900), pp. 637–720; (1902), pp. 75–101, 337–62, 813–47.
Maḥfūẓ, Naǧīb (Mahfouz, Naguib): *Aṭ-Ṭarīq* (Cairo, 1967).
—: *Children of the Alley*, trans. Peter Theroux (New York: Doubleday, 1996).
Maimonides, Moses (Mose ben Maimon): see Ibn Maymūn.
Makdisi, George: *The Rise of Humanism in Classical Islam and the Christian West: With Special Reference to Scholasticism* (Edinburgh: Edinburgh University Press, 1990).
al-Makkī, Muḥammad ibn 'Alī Abū Ṭālib: *Die Nahrung des Herzens*, 4 vols., trans. and intr. Richard Gramlich (Stuttgart: F. Steiner, 1992–5).
Marmorstein, Arthur: *Studies in Jewish Theology*, ed. J. Rabbinowitz and M. S. Lew (Oxford: Oxford University Press, 1950).
Marquard, Odo: *Schwierigkeiten mit der Geschichtsphilosophie* (Frankfurt: Suhrkamp, 1982).
—: 'Schwierigkeiten beim Ja-Sagen', in Willi Oelmüller (ed.), *Theodizee – Gott vor Gericht?* (Munich: Fink, 1990), pp. 87–102.
Marx, Karl: *Critique of Hegel's 'Philosophy of Right'*, trans. Annette Jolin and Joseph O'Malley (Cambridge: Cambridge University Press, 1977).
Marzolph, Ulrich: *Der weise Narr Buhlul* (Wiesbaden: F. Steiner, 1983).
Maybaum, Ignaz: *The Face of God after Auschwitz* (Amsterdam, 1965).
Mechthild of Magdeburg: *The Flowing Light of the Godhead*, trans. Frank J. Tobin (New York: Paulist Press, 1998).
Meier, Fritz: 'Die Welt der Urbilder bei 'Ali Hamadāni', *Eranos-Jahrbuch*, 18 (1950), pp. 115–72.
—: Book review of Hellmut Ritter, *Das Meer der Seele*, *Oriens*, 9 (1956), pp. 319–31.
—: 'Der Geistmensch bei dem persischen Dichter 'Aṭṭār', *Eranos-Jahrbuch*, 13 (1945), pp. 282–353.
Meisami, Julie Scott: 'Arabic Culture and Medieval European Literature', *Journal of the American Oriental Society*, 111 (1991), pp. 343–51.
Melville, Charles: 'Earthquakes in the History of Nishabur', *Journal of Persian Studies*, 18 (1980), pp. 103–20.
Menocal, María Rosa: *The Arabic Role in Medieval Literary Theory: A Forgotten Heritage* (Philadelphia: University of Pennsylvania Press, 2003).
Metz, Johann Baptist: 'The Church after Auschwitz', in Metz, *A Passion for God: The Mystical-Political Dimension of Christianity*, trans. James Matthew Ashley (New York: Paulist Press, 1998).
Meyer Kallen, Horace: *The Book of Job as a Greek Tragedy, Restored with an Introductory Essay on the Original Form and Philosophic Meaning of Job* (Whitefish, MT: Kessinger, 2008).

Milton, John: *Paradise Lost*, ed. Gordon Teskey (New York and London: Norton, 2005).
Mo'inzadeh, Hušang: *Ânsu-ye sar'āb* (Essen: Âẕaraḫš-Verlag, [1377] 1998).
—: *Komedi-ye ḫodāyān* (Essen: Âẕaraḫš-Verlag, [1382] 2003).
Moltmann, Jürgen: *Der gekreuzigte Gott: Das Kreuz Christi als Grund und Kritik christlicher Theologie* (Munich: Kaiser, 1972).
—: *Gott im Projekt der modernen Welt: Beiträge zur öffentlichen Relevanz der Theologie* (Gütersloh: Gütersloher Verlagshaus, 1997).
Morgan, David O.: *Medieval Persia 1040–1797* (London and New York: Longman, 1988).
Moṭahhari, Morteżā: *'Adl-e elāhi* (Tehran, [1361] 1982).
Müller, Hans-Peter: *Das Hiobproblem: Seine Entstehung im Alten Orient und im Alten Testament* (Darmstadt: Wissenschaftliche Buchgesellschaft, 1978).
Münz, Christoph: *Der Welt ein Gedächtnis geben: Geschichtsphilosophisches Denken im Judentum nach Auschwitz* (Gütersloh: Gütersloher Verlagshaus, 1995).
Nafisi, Sa'id: *Ǧostoğū dar aḥwāl o āsār-e Faridoddin-e 'Aṭṭār-e Nišāburi* (Tehran, [1320] 1941).
Nagel, Tilman: *Die Qiṣaṣ al-anbiyā': Ein Beitrag zur arabischen Literaturgeschichte* (Bonn: Nagel, 1967).
—: *Geschichte der islamischen Theologie: Von Mohammed bis zur Gegenwart* (Munich: Beck, 1994).
Neiman, Susan: *Evil in Modern Thought: An Alternative History of Philosophy* (Princeton, NJ: Princeton University Press, 2004).
Nelson, Benjamin: *On the Roads to Modernity: Conscience, Science and Civilizations* (Lanham, MD: Rowman & Littlefield, 1981).
Neuhaus, Gerd: *Theodizee – Abbruch oder Anstoss des Glaubens* (Freiburg: Herder, 1994).
Newman, Louis I. (ed. and trans.): *The Hasidic Anthology: Tales and Teaching of the Hasidim* (New York: Schocken, 1963).
Neẕālmolmolk (Nizalmulmulk), Abū 'Alī al-Ḥasan: *Siyāsatnāma: Gedanken und Geschichten*, trans. and intr. Karl Emil Schabinger, Freiherr von Schowingen (Freiburg and Munich: Alber, 1960).
Nicholson, Reynold A.: *The Mystics of Islam* (London: Bell & Sons, 1914).
Nietzsche, Friedrich: *Daybreak: Thoughts on the Prejudices of Morality*, trans. R. J. Hollingdale (Cambridge: Cambridge University Press, 1997).
—: *Ecce homo: How One Becomes What One Is*, trans. R. J. Hollingdale (London: Penguin, 1992).
—: *Human, All Too Human*, trans. R. J. Hollingdale (Cambridge: Cambridge University Press, 1996).
—: *The Gay Science*, trans. Josefine Nauckhoff and Adrian Del Caro (Cambridge: Cambridge University Press, 2001).
—: *Thus Spoke Zarathustra: A Book for Everyone and No One*, trans. R. J. Hollingdale (London: Penguin, 1961).
—: *Untimely Meditations*, trans. R. J. Hollingdale (Cambridge: Cambridge University Press, 1997).
—: *Writings from the Late Notebooks*, trans. Kate Sturge (Cambridge: Cambridge University Press, 2003).
Nüchtern, Michael (ed.): *Warum lässt Gott das zu? Kritik der Allmacht Gottes in Religion und Philosophie* (Frankfurt: Lembeck, 1995).

Oelmüller, Willi (ed.): *Theodizee – Gott vor Gericht?* (Munich: Fink, 1990).
—: *Worüber man nicht schweigen kann: Neue Diskussionen zur Theodizeefrage* (Munich: Fink, 1994).
Ormsby, Eric L.: *Theodicy in Islamic Thought: The Dispute over Al-Ghazālī's 'Best of All Possible Worlds'* (Princeton, NJ: Princeton University Press, 1984).
Pascal, Blaise: *Thoughts* (New York: Cosimo, 2007).
Plotinus, *The Enneads*, trans. Stephen MacKenna (London: Penguin, 1991).
Pöhlmann, Horst Georg, and Stern, Marc: *Die zehn Gebote im jüdisch-christlichen Dialog* (Frankfurt: Lembeck, 2002).
Praz, Mario: *The Romantic Agony*, trans. Angus Davidson (Oxford: Oxford University Press, 1970).
Purğawādi, Naṣrollāh: *Bu-ye ğān: Maqālehā-i darbāre-ye še'r-e 'erfāni-ye fārsi* (Tehran, [1372] 1993).
Purnāmdāriyān, Taqi: *Didār bā Simorġ: Haft maqāleh dar 'erfan, še'r wa andiše-ye 'Aṭṭār* (Tehran, [1375] 1996).
Qomše'i, Ḥoseyn Elāhi: *Maqālāt* (Tehran, [1376] 1997).
Quistorp, H.: *Die letzten Dinge im Zeugnis Calvins: Calvins Eschatologie* (Gütersloh: Bertelsmann, 1941).
Qurašī, Ayyūb: *Kitāb makr Allāh*, MS no. 3237, in Wolfgang Ahlwardt (ed.), *Verzeichnis der arabischen Handschriften der Königlichen Bibliothek zu Berlin* (Berlin, 1887–).
al-Qušayrī, Abu l-Qāsim 'Abdulkarim: *Das Sendschreiben al-Qušayrī's über das Sufitum*, trans. and intr. Richard Gramlich (Stuttgart: F. Steiner, 1989).
Rahe, Thomas: *'Höre Israel': Jüdische Religiosität in nationalsozialistischen Konzentrationslagern* (Göttingen: Vandenhoeck & Ruprecht, 1999).
Rahner, Karl: *Im Gespräch*, ed. P. Imhoff and U. H. Bialowons (Munich: Kösel, 1982), vol. 1.
Reinert, Benedikt: *Die Lehre vom tawakkul in der klassischen Sufik* (Berlin: de Gruyter, 1968).
Ricœur, Paul: *The Symbolism of Evil*, trans. Emerson Buchanan (New York: Harper & Row, 1967).
Rilke, Rainer Maria: *Possibility of Being: A Selection of Poems*, trans. James Blair Leishman (New York: New Directions, 1977).
Rippin, Andrew: ' "Desiring the face of God": The Qu'ranic Symbolism of Personal Responsibility', in Issa J. Boullata (ed.), *Literary Structures of Religious Meaning in the Qu'ran* (Richmond, Surrey: Curzon, 2000), pp. 117–24.
Ritter, Hellmut: 'Studien zur Geschichte der islamischen Frömmigkeit I', *Der Islam*, 21 (1933), pp. 1–83.
—: 'Philologika X', *Der Islam*, 25 (1938), p. 134–239.
—: 'Die Aussprüche des Bāyezīd Bisṭāmī: Eine vorläufige Skizze', in Fritz Meier (ed.), *Westöstliche Abhandlungen: Rudolf Tschudi zum siebzigsten Geburtstag überreicht von Freunden und Schülern* (Wiesbaden: Harrassowitz, 1954), pp. 213–43.
—: *The Ocean of the Soul: Men, the World and God in the Tales of Farīd al-Dīn 'Aṭṭār*, trans. John O'Kane (Leiden: Brill, 2003).
—: 'Philologika XIV', *Oriens*, 11 (1958), pp. 1–70.
—: 'Philologika XV', *Oriens*, 12 (1959), pp. 1–88.
—: 'Philologika XVI', *Oriens*, 13–14 (1960–61), pp. 195–239.
Röllecke, Heinz: *'O wär ich nie geboren!' Zum Topos der Existenzverwünschung in der europäischen Literatur* (Mönchengladbach: Kühlen, 1979).

Roth, Joseph: *Job: The Story of a Simple Man*, trans. Dorothy Thompson (New York: Overlook Press, 1982).

Rothenberg, Jerome, and Robinson, Jeffrey C. (eds): *Poems for the Millennium: The University of California Book of Romantic and Postromantic Poetry* (Berkeley: University of California Press, 2009).

Roušangar, Dr: *Allāhu akbar* (San Francisco, [1375] 1996).

Rubinstein, Richard L.: *After Auschwitz: History, Theology and Contemporary Judaism* (Baltimore and London: Johns Hopkins University Press, 1992).

Russell, Jeffrey Burton: *Mephistopheles: The Devil in the Modern World* (Ithaca, NY: Cornell University Press, 1990).

Saadia Gaon: see Sa'īd al-Fayyūmī.

Sachedina, Abdulaziz: 'Early Muslim Traditionists and their Familiarity with Jewish Sources', in William M. Brinner and Stephen D. Ricks (eds), *Studies in Islamic and Judaic Traditions II: Papers Presented at the Institute for Islamic-Judaic Studies, Center for Judaic Studies, University of Denver* (Atlanta: American Scholars Press, 1986), pp. 49–59.

de Sade, Donatien Alphonse François, Marquis: *Juliette*, trans. Austryn Wainhouse (New York: Grove, 1988).

—: *Justine, Philosophy in the Bedroom, and Other Writings*, trans. Richard Seaver and Austryn Wainhouse (New York: Grove, 1990).

Šafi'i-Kadkani, Moḥammad Reżā: *Zabur-e pārsi: Negāhī be zendegi wa ġazalhā-ye 'Aṭṭār* (Tehran, [1378] 1999).

Safranski, Rüdiger: *Das Böse oder Das Drama der Freiheit* (Frankfurt: Fischer, 2000).

Šaġi'i, Purān: *Mosāfer-e sargašteh* (Tehran, [1363] 1984).

aš-Šahrastānī, Muḥammad ibn 'Abdilkarīm ibn Aḥmad: *Tawḍīh al-milal* (Persian edition of *al-Milal wa-n-niḥal*), ed. and trans. Moṣṭafā Ḫāleqdād 'Abbāsi, 2 vols. (Tehran, [1373] 1994).

Sa'īd al-Fayyūmī (Saadia Gaon): *The Book of Beliefs and Opinions*, trans. Samuel Rosenblatt (New Haven, CT: Yale University Press, 1948).

Sanā'i Ġaznawi, Abo l-Mağd Mağdud: *Diwān*, ed. Moḥammad Taqi Modarres Rażawi (Tehran, [1380] 2001).

Ṣāremi, Soheylā: *Moṣṭalaḥāt-e 'erfāni wa mafāhim-e barğaste dar zabān-e 'Aṭṭār* (Tehran, [1373] 1994).

as-Sarrāğ, Abū Naṣr: *Schlaglichter über das Sufitum*, trans. Richard Gramlich (Stuttgart: F. Steiner, 1990).

Scarcia, Gianroberto: 'Iblīs in 'Aṭṭār: il demiurgo come spia', in *Colloquio italo-iraniano sul poeta mistico Fariduddin 'Aṭṭār* (Rome, 1978), pp. 21–36.

Schäfer, Peter: 'Das Böse in der mittelalterlichen jüdischen Mystik', in Carsten Colpe and Wilhelm Schmidt-Biggemann (eds), *Das Böse: Eine historische Phänomenologie des Unerklärlichen* (Frankfurt: Suhrkamp, 1993), pp. 90–108.

Schelling, Friedrich Wilhelm Joseph: *Philosophical Investigations into the Essence of Human Freedom*, trans. Jeff Love and Johannes Schmidt (Albany: State University of New York Press, 2006).

Schimmel, Annemarie (ed. and trans.): *Gärten der Erkenntnis: Texte aus der islamischen Mystik* (Düsseldorf and Cologne: Diederichs, 1982).

—: *Mystical Dimensions of Islam* (Chapel Hill: University of North Carolina Press, 1978).

Schindler, Pesach: *Hasidic Responses to the Holocaust in the Light of Hasidic Thought* (Hoboken: KTAV, 1990).

Schmidt-Biggemann, Wilhelm: *Theodizee und Tatsachen: Das philosophische Profil der deutschen Aufklärung* (Frankfurt: Suhrkamp, 1988).
Schneider, Michael: 'Der dunkle Gott in der Mystik', in Wolfgang Beinert (ed.), *Gott – ratlos vor dem Bösen?* (Freiburg: Herder, 1999), pp. 173–216.
Scholem, Gershom: *On the Kabbalah and its Symbolism*, trans. Ralph Manheim (New York: Schocken, 1965).
—: *Major Trends in Jewish Mysticism*, trans. George Lichtheim (New York: Schocken, 1961).
Schopenhauer, Arthur: *Der handschriftliche Nachlass*, 5 vols, ed. Arthur Hübscher (Frankfurt: Kramer, 1966–75).
—: *The World as Will and Representation*, 2 vols, trans. E. F. J. Payne (Mineola, NY: Dover, 1958).
Schuller, Alexander, and Rahden, Wolfert von (eds): *Die andere Kraft: Zur Renaissance des Bösen* (Berlin: Akademie, 1993).
Schultz, Wolfgang (ed.): *Dokumente der Gnosis* (Munich: Matthes & Seitz, 1986).
Schwarz, Michael: 'The Letter of al-Ḥasan al-Baṣrī', *Oriens*, 20 (1967), pp. 15–30.
Schwarzbaum, Haim: 'The Jewish and Moslem Versions of Some Theodicy Legends', *Fabula*, 3 (1960), pp. 119–69.
Semprun, Jorge, and Wiesel, Elie: *Schweigen ist unmöglich*, trans. Wolfram Bayer (Frankfurt: Suhrkamp, 1997).
Shakespeare, William: *King Lear*, ed. Grace Ioppolo (New York and London: Norton, 2008).
Shaw, George Bernard: *The Black Girl in Search of God and Some Lesser Tales* (Read Books, 2006).
Shari'at-Kāshāni: 'Les Images symboliques et leur signification psychologique chez 'Aṭṭār Neyshāpuri', *Luqman: Annales des Presses Universitaires d'Iran*, 13/1 (1996–7), pp. 71–81.
Sherwood, Yvonne: *A Biblical Text and its Afterlives: The Survival of Jonah in Western Culture* (Cambridge: Cambridge University Press, 2000).
Shim, Jae-Ryong: 'Evil and the Overcoming of Suffering in Buddhism', in Peter Koslowski (ed.), *The Origin and the Overcoming of Evil and Suffering in the World Religions* (Dordrecht: Kluwer Academic), pp. 8–23.
Shulman, David: *The Hungry God: Hindu Tales of Filicide and Devotion* (Chicago: University of Chicago Press, 1993).
Sölle, Dorothee: *Leiden*, ed. Hans Jürgen Schultz (Stuttgart: Kreuz-Verlag, 1976).
Solṭān Walad, Bahā'oddin Moḥammad: *Entehānāmeh*, ed. Moḥammad 'Ali Ḫazāneh-Darlū (Tehran, [1376] 1997).
Somanatha, Palkuriki: *Śiva's Warriors: The Basava Purāna of Pālkuriki Somanātha*, trans. Velcheru Narayana Rao (Princeton, NJ: Princeton University Press, 1990).
Soruš, 'Abdolkarim: 'Farbehtar az idi'oloği', *Kiyān*, 3/14 (August/September 1993), pp. 2–20.
Speyer, Heinrich: *Die biblischen Erzählungen im Qoran* (Hildesheim: G. Olms, 1961).
Stanford, Peter: *The Devil: A Biography* (New York: Henry Holt, 1996).
Steiner, George: 'Aschensage', *Merkur*, 41 (1987), pp. 931–40.
Steinschneider, Moritz: *Die arabische Literatur der Juden: Ein Beitrag zur Literaturgeschichte der Araber, grösstenteils aus handschriftlichen Quellen* (Hildesheim: G. Olms, 1964).

Stemberger, Günter: *Geschichte der jüdischen Literatur: Eine Einführung* (Munich: Beck, 1977).

Stiefel, Tina: *The Intellectual Revolution in Twelfth-Century Europe* (London and Sydney: Croom Helm, 1985).

Stier, Fridolin: *Vielleicht ist irgendwo Tag: Die Aufzeichnungen und Erfahrungen eines grossen Denkers* (Freiburg: Herder, 1993).

Streminger, Gerhard: *Gottes Güte und die Übel der Welt: Das Theodizeeproblem* (Tübingen: Mohr Siebeck, 1992).

Strohmaier, Gottfried: *Von Demokrit bis Dante: Die Bewahrung antiken Erbes in der arabischen Kultur* (Hildesheim: G. Olms, 1996).

Stroumsa, Sarah: *Freethinkers of Medieval Islam: Ibn al-Rawāndī, Abū Bakr al-Rāzī, and their Impact on Islamic Thought* (Leiden: Brill, 1999).

Stump, Eleonore: *Die göttliche Vorsehung und das Böse: Überlegungen zur Theodizee im Anschluss an Thomas von Aquin* (Frankfurt: Knecht, 1989).

as-Suhrawardī, Abū Ḥafs ʻUmar ibn Muḥammad: *Die Gaben der Erkenntnisse*, trans. and intr. Richard Gramlich (Wiesbaden: F. Steiner, 1978).

Susman, Margarete: *Das Buch Hiob und das Schicksal des jüdischen Volkes* (Frankfurt: Jüdischer Verlag, 1996).

aṯ-Ṯaʻlabī, Abu l-Isḥāq Aḥmad an-Nīšābūrī: *Qiṣaṣ al-anbiyā' ('Arā'is al-mağālis)* (Cairo, n.d.) (*Dār iḥyā' all-kutub al-'arabīya*).

Teufel, J. K.: *Eine Lebensbeschreibung des Scheichs 'Ali-i Hamadānī: Die Xulaṣāt ul-Manāqib des Maulānā Nūr ud-Dīn Ca'far-I Badaxšī* (Leiden: Brill, 1962).

Theissen, Gerd: *Das Neue Testament* (Munich: Beck, 2004).

Tillich, Paul: *Der Mut zum Sein* (Berlin: de Gruyter, 1991).

Ustā, Siyāwuš (Ḥasan 'Abbāsi): *Ḫodā-rā dar ḫāb didam! Rāz-rāz geriye mikard* (Paris, [1378] 1999).

Voltaire, François Marie Arouet de: *Mélanges*, ed. Jacques van den Heuvel, intr. Emmanuel Berl (Paris: Bibliothèque de la Pléiade, 1961).

—: *The Works of Voltaire: The Lisbon Earthquake, and Other Poems*, trans. William F. Fleming (Akron, OH: Werner, 1906).

Wagenstein, Angel: *Pentateuch oder Die fünf Bücher Isaaks*, trans. Barbara Müller (Berlin: Das Neue Berlin, 2001).

Wagner, Harald (ed.), *Mit Gott streiten: Neue Zugänge zum Theodizee-Problem* (Freiburg: Herder, 1998).

Walter, Dietrich, and Link, Christian: *Die dunklen Seiten Gottes*, 2 vols. (Neukirchen-Vluyn: Neukrichener, 1995, 2000).

Warning, Rainer: *Funktion und Struktur: Die Ambivalenzen des geistlichen Spiels* (Munich: Fink, 1974).

Wasserstrom, Steven: *Between Muslim and Jew: The Problem of Symbiosis under Early Islam* (Princeton, NJ: Princeton University Press, 1995).

Watt, M. Montgomery, and Marmura, Michael: *Der Islam II: Politische Entwicklungen und theologische Konzepte*, trans. Sylvia Hofer (Stuttgart: Kohlhammer, 1985).

Weinrich, Harald: *Literatur für Leser: Essays und Aufsätze zur Literaturwissenschaft* (Munich: dtv, 1986).

Wensinck, A. J.: *Concordance et indices de la tradition Musulman*, 7 vols. (Leiden: Brill, 1936–69).

—: *The Muslim Creed: Its Genesis and Historical Development* (London: Frank Cass, 1965).

Werner, Michael (ed.): *Begegnungen mit Heine: Berichte der Zeitgenossen*, 2 vols. (Hamburg: Hoffmann & Campe, 1973).

West, M. L. (ed. and trans.): *Greek Lyric Poetry* (Oxford: Oxford University Press, 1999).

Westermann, Claus: *Die Klagelieder: Forschungsgeschichte und Auslegung* (Neukirchen-Vluyn: Neukirchener, 1990).

Wielandt, Rotraud: 'Nağīb Maḥfūẓ und seine Religion', *Forschungsforum: Berichte aus der Otto-Friedrich-Universität Bamberg*, 2 (1990), pp. 29–37.

Wiesel, Elie: *Macht Gebete aus meinen Geschichten: Essays eines Betroffenen*, trans. Hanns Bücker and Ursula Schottelius (Freiburg: Herder, 1986).

—: *Souls on Fire: Portraits and Legends of Hasidic Masters* (New York: Random House, 1972).

—: *Somewhere a Master: Further Hasidic Portraits and Legends* (New York: Simon & Schuster, 1984).

—: *Was die Tore des Himmels öffnet: Geschichten chassidischer Meister*, intr. Salcia Landmann (Freiburg: Herder, 1981).

—: *Wise Men and their Tales: Portraits of Biblical, Talmudic and Hasidic Masters* (New York: Schocken, 2005).

Wolfson, Eliot: 'Divine Suffering and the Hermeneutics of Reading: Philosophical Reflections on Lurianic Mythology', in Robert Gibbs and Elliot R. Wolfson (eds), *Suffering Religion* (London and New York: Routledge, 2002), pp. 101–62.

Yāqut ibn 'Abdillāh ar-Rūmī al-Ḥamawī: *Mu'ğam al-udabā'*, 20 vols. (Cairo, n.d.) (Maktabat al-qirā'a wa-ṯ-ṯaqāfa); Persian translation: 2 vols., ed. and trans. 'Abdolmoḥammad Âyāti (Tehran, [1381] 2002).

Zaehner, Robert C.: *Concordant Discord: Interdependence of Faiths* (Oxford: Clarendon Press, 1970).

Zarin-Kub, Abdolḥasan: *Ṣedā-ye bāl-e simurġ: Darbāre-ye zendegi wa andiše-ye 'Aṭṭār* (Tehran, [1378] 1999).

Zirker, Hans: '"Er wird nicht befragt . . ." (Sure 21:23): Theodizee und Theodizeeabwehr in Koran und Umgebung', in Udi Tworuschka (ed.), *Gottes ist der Orient – Gottes ist der Okzident: Festschrift für Abdoldjavad Falaturi zum 65. Geburtstag* (Cologne: Böhlau, 1991), pp. 408–24.

INDEX